D1483661

Peasants, Primitives, and Proletariats

World Anthropology

General Editor

SOL TAX

Patrons

CLAUDE LÉVI-STRAUSS
MARGARET MEAD†
LAILA SHUKRY EL HAMAMSY
M. N. SRINIVAS

MOUTON PUBLISHERS · THE HAGUE · PARIS · NEW YORK

Peasants, Primitives, and Proletariats

The Struggle for Identity in South America

Edited by

DAVID L. BROWMAN
RONALD A. SCHWARZ

MOUTON PUBLISHERS · THE HAGUE · PARIS · NEW YORK

ISBN 90-279-7880-8
Jacket photo by permission of De Spaarnestad, Haarlem, The Netherlands
Cover and jacket design by Jurriaan Schrofer
Indexes by Society of Indexers, Great Britain
Phototypeset in V.I.P. Times by
Western Printing Services Ltd, Bristol
Printed in Great Britain

General Editor's Preface

This is one of two complementary volumes describing aspects of the populations and cultures of South America. The present volume describes mainly the interrelations of the people and their social institutions. The companion volume (*Spirits, shamans, and stars*) treats their thought and the symbolic and expressive aspects of their cultures. Unlike many of the volumes in this series, which tend to deal with topics rather than with regions, these volumes contain papers which concern a continental area — South America — over a substantial historical period. It thus honors the tradition in anthropology of deriving theory from data located in particular time–space frameworks. It is especially appreciated when specialists on different geographical areas meet to discuss problems of their own continents and to display to other specialists their conclusions. In the present case there were many scholars native to the continents being studied.

Like most contemporary sciences, anthropology is a product of the European tradition. Some argue that it is a product of colonialism, with one small and self-interested part of the species dominating the study of the whole. If we are to understand the species, our science needs substantial input from scholars who represent a variety of the world's cultures. It was a deliberate purpose of the IXth International Congress of Anthropological and Ethnological Sciences to provide impetus in this direction. The *World Anthropology* volumes, therefore, offer a first glimpse of a human science in which members from all societies have played an active role. Each of the books is designed to be self-contained; each is an attempt to update its particular sector of scientific knowledge and is written by specialists from all parts of the world. Each volume should be read and reviewed individually as a separate volume on its own given subject. The set as a whole will indicate what changes are in store for anthropology as scholars from the developing countries join in studying the species of which we are all a part.

The IXth Congress was planned from the beginning not only to include as many of the scholars from every part of the world as possible, but also with a view toward the eventual publication of the papers in high-quality volumes. At previous Congresses scholars were invited to bring papers which were then read out loud. They were necessarily limited in length; many were only summarized; there was little time for discussion; and the sparse discussion could only be in one language. The IXth Congress was an experiment aimed at changing this. Papers were written with the intention of exchanging them before the Congress, particularly in extensive pre-Congress sessions; they were not intended to be read aloud at the Congress, that time being devoted to discussions — discussions which were simultaneously and professionally translated into five languages. The method for eliciting the papers was structured to make as representative a sample as was allowable when scholarly creativity — hence self-selection — was critically important. Scholars were asked both to propose papers of their own and to suggest topics for sessions of the Congress which they might edit into volumes. All were then informed of the suggestions and encouraged to re-think their own papers and the topics. The process, therefore, was a continuous one of feedback and exchange and it has continued to be so even after the Congress. The some two thousand papers comprising *World Anthropology* certainly then offer a substantial sample of world anthropology. It has been said that anthropology is at a turning point; if this is so, these volumes will be the historical direction markers.

As might have been foreseen in the first post-colonial generation, the large majority of the Congress papers (82 percent) are the work of scholars identified with the industrialized world which fathered our traditional discipline and the institution of the Congress itself: Eastern Europe (15 percent); Western Europe (16 percent); North America (47 percent); Japan, South Africa, Australia, and New Zealand (4 percent). Only 18 percent of the papers are from developing areas: Africa (4 percent); Asia-Oceania (9 percent); Latin America (5 percent). Aside from the substantial representation from the U.S.S.R. and the nations of Eastern Europe, a significant difference between this corpus of written material and that of other Congresses is the addition of the large proportion of contributions from Africa, Asia, and Latin America. "Only 18 percent" is two to four times as great a proportion as that of other Congresses; moreover, 18 percent of 2,000 papers is 360 papers, 10 times the number of "Third World" papers presented at previous Congresses. In fact, these 360 papers are more than the total of *all* papers published after the last International Congress of Anthropological and Ethnological Sciences which was held in the United States (Philadelphia, 1956).

The significance of the increase is not simply quantitative. The input of scholars from areas which have until recently been no more than subject matter for anthropology represents both feedback and also long-awaited theoretical contributions from the perspectives of very different cultural, social, and historical traditions. Many who attended the IXth Congress were convinced that anthropology would not be the same in the future. The fact that the Xth Congress (India, 1978) was our first in the "Third World" may be symbolic of the change. Meanwhile, sober consideration of the present set of books will show how much, and just where and how, our discipline is being revolutionized.

Readers of this volume will be interested in others in the series that are particularly on South America. These include not only the companion volume and two others edited by the senior editor, but also at least a score which include substantial material on the anthropological and social problems of Latin America. David Browman has also edited a fifth volume in the series, on American archaeology, while Ronald Schwarz has collaborated with Justine Cordwell, on a volume on costume, cosmetics, and ornamentation.

Chicago, Illinois   SOL TAX
September 21, 1979

Preface

The papers in this volume are an extension of the session Sociocultural Development and Economic Patterns in the Andes, held during the IXth International Congress of Anthropological and Ethnological Sciences, September 1973. Most of the sessions at the Congress were organized around themes and topical areas. Geographical or regional considerations were involved in less than twenty percent of the symposia and normally were used to set the context for a research problem (for example, Changing Ethnic Identities in Modern Southeast Asia). For several of us with research and professional interests in South America, the scattering of information concerning the region throughout many sessions was viewed as inefficient and frustrating. It was obvious that, unless the scope of the original symposium could be expanded and the disparate articles brought together within a single geographic framework, only a small percentage of the material on South America would be readily available to scholars and students. It would be an even greater handicap for individuals residing outside North America, for whom libraries, books, and journals are very scarce resources. Moreover, we believed that the potential cross-fertilization of ideas, the very essence of such congresses, would bloom in such a mix of diverse approaches and would make these volumes exceptionally powerful.

These concerns were expressed to Dr. Sol Tax, president of the Congress, and Ms. Karen Tkach, Mouton editor. With their encouragement and permission, we reviewed all the Congress papers which dealt with South America and added a number of them to the core material presented in Browman's session. This has resulted in two volumes: *Peasants, primitives, and proletariats: The struggle for identity in South America*, and *Spirits, shamans, and stars: Perspectives from South America*. This preface, and the first portion of our general introduction, have been correspondingly generated in tandem to cover both volumes.

We wish to express our appreciation to Sol and Karen for the encouragement they gave us. We hope that this effort will make the results of the Congress more accessible to students and professionals who share with us an interest in the anthropology of South America. We would also like to thank Alejandro Camino, who served as cochairman with Browman of the original session in Chicago, through whose aid the sessions came to fruition.

DAVID L. BROWMAN
RONALD A. SCHWARZ

Table of Contents

General Introduction: "A Little Glass of Rum"

DAVID L. BROWMAN and RONALD A. SCHWARZ

> In Martinique I went over certain rusticated, half-abandoned rum distilleries where neither methods nor apparatus had been changed since the eighteenth century. In Puerto Rico, by contrast, the factories of the company which enjoys a quasi-monopoly of cane-sugar were agleam with white-enamelled tanks and chromium-plated faucets. And yet in Martinique, where the ancient wooden barrels are silted up with sediment, the rum was like velvet on the palate and had a delicious scent; in Puerto Rico, it was brutal and vulgar.
>
> CLAUDE LÉVI-STRAUSS, *Tristes tropiques* (1961: 381)

The continent of South America is as illusive and perplexing to its inhabitants as it is to the outsider. Few generalizations can be satisfactorily made about a single republic, and characterizations of the continent as a whole are as misleading as they are informative. In the present world situation, caricature and ignorance of the complexity of South America, which contains three hundred million people and a major portion of the world's yet unexploited resources, is unfortunate and dangerous. The rate of population growth in several of the nations is among the world's highest, yet the region has vast expanses of fertile land which could be exploited to reduce world food problems; and South America contains some of the largest reserves of unexploited mineral wealth so necessary for modern industrial economies. These factors — the high rate of population growth, and the large reserves of unexploited resources — suggest that events on the continent will increasingly have worldwide importance.

The pressures for modernization and change are today felt by millions of South Americans who are culturally and politically isolated from the decision-making processes. This powerlessness is not restricted to marginal aboriginal populations, but also characterizes the vast majority of rural and urban dwellers who share a common cultural framework with the political elite. For those who formulate policy, demographic and economic problems receive the most attention and, in this context, socio-cultural diversity is often transformed into an obstacle for development.

While the theme of both this volume, and its companion, *Spirits, shamans, and stars*, is the anthropology of South America, not its politics or economics, it is not always possible or desirable to separate them. Though more than three decades have passed since Lévi-Strauss first visited the Antilles, the undercurrent of social and cultural conflict persists. While today there are more white-enameled tanks, some still prefer their rum from silted wooden barrels.

PARAMETERS OF DIVERSITY

The native societies of South America had their beginnings at least twenty-five thousand, and possibly more than forty thousand, years ago. Descendants of the immigrants who crossed the Bering land bridge from Siberia drifted south, crossed the Darien region of Panama, and entered Colombia. Archaeologists are beginning to pick up their trail as far south as Peru some twenty to twenty-five thousand years ago. These early inhabitants moved into zones whose ecological resources were unfamiliar, and the early prehistory of the continent is basically one of people slowly discovering the riches of the new lands and experimenting with techniques to exploit available resources (Browman 1978).

Approximately eight to ten thousand years ago, man in South America reached a new level of achievement, a level which his fellows in Mesoamerica, Mesopotamia, China, and other areas of the world, were also just reaching — a stage characterized by the first tentative experiments in the domestication of plants and animals. The next half dozen millennia of man's prehistory in South America are characterized by the development of such major modern crops as potatoes, beans, sweet potatoes, and manioc, and by an increasingly sophisticated agricultural technology in those areas where it was appropriate for exploiting natural resources. Llama pastoralism also developed during the period and spread over the high central Andes. Only in later times as population pressure increased do archaeologists see a shift from the pastoral life-styles to the more efficient and intensive exploitative techniques of plant agriculture. These epochs also see the stabilization of the sea level following the postglacial variations due to climatic warming. With this stabilization, new fishing cultures sprang up, exploiting an incredibly rich marine resource base and giving rise on the Pacific coast to the first settlements to achieve the level of cultural complexity referred to as "civilization."

With shifts from nomadic life-styles to more sedentary ones, ethnic groups began accumulating material possessions in greater abundance and constructed more permanent dwellings. The material remains of these groups provide the basis for archaeological investigation and analysis, and have enabled scholars to reconstruct many patterns of cultural-ecological adaptation. More recently, some archaeologists have turned to more complex questions regarding boundary maintenance, economic organization, and the cosmology of prehistoric peoples. For example, it can now be argued that the dual structures which fascinated Lévi-Strauss (1961), in his analysis of South American societies, are a widespread trait with a time depth of at least five thousand years. Similarly, *mita*-type tax duties, still used and abused by modern political elites to coerce the rural populations into public labors, may be shown to have been practiced for more than two thousand years. Finally, the basic grist of archaeology, the self-statements of ethnic identity, are preserved for the prehistorians in terms of ceramic vocabularies, settlement patterns, and motif inventories. In short, thousands of years of sociocultural and technological evolution, trade, migration, and conflict have resulted in an indigenous cultural kaleidoscope the dimensions of which we are just beginning to explore.

When the Spanish arrived, peoples such as the gold-working Quimbayas, the San Agustin sculptors, the Tiwanaku merchant-missionaries, and the Mojos mound builders — societies that had once flourished and achieved great cultural wonders — had already perished. Along the western slopes of the Andes, many previously autonomous tribal groups had recently been conquered and incorporated into the Inca empire. Spread over the rest of the continent were hundreds of societies at various levels of technological and sociocultural development.

The impact of the conquest and subsequent colonization by the Spanish and Portuguese, coupled with epidemic diseases and social dislocation, had a devastating effect on the native cultures. Immediate mortality in areas of first contact ran as high as seventy to ninety percent of the local groups with depressing regularity, and the ripple effect of the diseases were felt deep into Amazonia in areas not penetrated by colonists until decades or centuries later. Severe cultural loss and social disorganization occurred among the indigenous societies, no matter whether they collaborated with or violently opposed the conquistadores. Subsequent domination, followed by widespread epidemics, frequently led to the collapse of the substance and autonomy of the native groups, and the incorporation of their impoverished relics into the colonial empire.

The patterns of conquest and control varied with ecological conditions, and more frequently, according to the local gold and silver supply. The willingness or capability of the indigenous groups to adapt to foreign rule also played a part in determining the postconquest settlement pattern.

Thus in the highlands of Bolivia, Peru, and parts of Ecuador and Colombia, where the cultural levels of the native peoples was roughly comparable to that of the Hispanic conquistadores, the shift from imperial Inca or Chibcha rule to imperial Spanish rule was relatively swift. In other areas, such as the upper Cauca valley in Colombia, the Napo in Ecuador, or the upper reaches of the Rio de la Plata, resistance to the conquistadores was fierce, and effective control was established only after decades of skirmishing, usually after the resisting population was largely destroyed or pushed back into a more remote region.

For Indians in isolated territories not directly affected by the initial military conquest, church missions and later economic interests were the vehicles of exploitation and control. Within fifty years of the landing of the first conquistadores, the majority of Indian leaders and their resources were subordinate to colonial European governments. As the politically dominant culture, Iberian cultural forms were relatively rapidly implanted in the Americas. Interaction between the two groups was in part reciprocal; Iberian ways were modified by indigenous customs, and Iberian technology and cultural forms were in turn woven into the native social fabric. The cultural unity found from northern Mexico to southern Chile is clear testimony to the effectiveness of Iberian tradition in bringing a measure of constancy and stability to a continent divided by geography, language, culture, and warfare.

The independence of the South American colonies, framed in the rhetoric of the French and American revolutions, did little to change the hierarchical structure inherited from colonial society. A native-born aristocracy replaced the Iberian administrators. The feudal structure of society remained but quickly fragmented into the independent republics of the continent. There was little desire and even less action on the part of the new ruling elite to share power with their fellow citizens. For much of the indigenous population, the situation remained unchanged; and for some, whose rights and territory had been partially protected under the empire, a bad situation became worse. Liberal ideas embodied in new constitutions and laws sought to remove the Indians from their third-class status, but these were mainly declarations on paper since it remained economically advantageous for the ruling elite to retain their subordination. In the independence and postindependence periods, the exploitation of Indian labor, expropriation of Indian lands, and deculturation of their societies continued and slowly expanded into the more isolated regions.

In the twentieth century, technological, social, and ideological changes have had a profound effect on the culture and organization of South American societies. Hispanic tradition, still strong throughout the continent, now competes with Marxist doctrine and a range of more moderate social philosophies. Industrialization, population growth, and technological developments, especially those in communication and transportation, have contributed to dramatic changes from the Brazilian interior to the Bolivian highlands to the Colombian coast. They have accelerated, almost simultaneously, processes of integration and separation at a number of social levels. On the one hand, there is a growing sense of cultural nationalism, in contrast to a previous European orientation, while on the other hand, there is a growing pattern of "internal colonialism" with respect to the indigenous groups whose members still struggle to maintain a measure of social and cultural autonomy. Ironically, both cultural nationalism and internal colonialism are related to a reevaluation and reaffirmation of the indigenous heritage. This has been accompanied by a wave of programs and agencies designed to "integrate" the Indian groups into national political and economic structures on a more egalitarian basis. While the motives of many involved in such programs may be liberal or revolutionary, their ability to achieve political and economic goals while allowing for and maintaining individual cultural integrity is open to serious doubt.

The extent to which acceleration of the integration process is generating strategies designed to maintain or reinforce cultural and social boundaries is difficult to estimate. While information presented by some of the papers reveals the difficulty or inability of traditional peoples to maintain their way of life, others suggest that indigenous groups have made some successful compromises to defend their ethnic identity.

Anthropological fieldwork by both national and foreign scholars has dramatically increased in South America in the last fifteen years. The earlier emphasis on research projects in Peru and Brazil is being balanced by investigations in other regions. The current pace and scope of research does not easily lend itself to classification and summary. In fact, it is the diversity of problems, methods, and theories, and the range of cultural-ecological settings, that distinguishes the present fieldwork from that of previous decades. Research on the continent as reflected in this and the companion volume (Browman and Schwarz 1979), is a microcosm of that being carried out throughout the world.

PEASANTS, PRIMITIVES AND PROLETARIATS

The analytical problems involved in the relationship between culture and social organization dominate the works of social theorists from Marxists to capitalists. The difficulties with terminology reflect corresponding uncertainties for the various ethnic groups themselves, who seek to obtain selective advantages and benefits from modernization while simultaneously struggling to maintain social identity and to retain control of their economic destiny. Half a century ago the operative term applied to many of these groups was "primitives," a quarter of a century ago "peasants," and today, in some sectors, "proletariats."

Anthropologists have unique analytical tools to offer in the examination of these problems. The theory associated with the basis of culture change is one such example. Anthropological contributions to theory have not yet been widely utilized outside of the discipline, primarily we guess, because of the previous narrow focus of application, in terms of time and space parameters.

Ethnohistoric studies (such as those in Part One) are increasingly frequent, and provide expanded temporal perspectives of indigenous politics. Such studies give us much greater facility in predicting both what cultural aspects are most susceptible to change, and the most likely direction of change.

Focus upon the social relations and the modes of production and distribution (such as papers in Parts Two and Three, Sections A and B) has advanced our capabilities for elucidating actual economic and political interrelationships between components of the cultural system. The unequal distribution of power has been approached through discussion of patron–client relationships, dependency theory, internal colonialism, and various arguments regarding "class." Several researchers, attempting to escape the limiting aspects of the microcosm of the local community while simultaneously avoiding the vacuous generalities which have been the pitfall of our colleagues who use the nation as the unit of study, have suggested definition of the "region" as a new level of analysis. Regional analysis is a rapidly developing area, and because of its developmental state, there are experiments with the utilization of divergent techniques.

Finally we see more frequent contributions to, and integration with, the applied specialists (see, for example, the contributions in Part Four). Anthropology increasingly has the utility for the solution of present-day problems in planning for economic development of Third World countries.

REFERENCES

BROWMAN, DAVID L., *editor*
  1978   *Advances in Andean archaeology.* World Anthropology. The Hague: Mouton.
BROWMAN, DAVID L., RONALD L. SCHWARZ, *editors*
  1979   *Spirits, shamans, and stars: perspectives from South America.* World Anthropology. The Hague: Mouton
LÉVI-STRAUSS, CLAUDE
  1961   *Tristes tropiques.* Translated by John Russell. London: Hutchinson. (Originally published 1962. Paris: Plon.)

PART ONE

Ethnohistory

Introduction

Early colonial interest in taxation, inheritance, and native customs has provided us with abundant source material contained in documents written by soldiers, clergymen, administrators, travelers, and businessmen. The documents include chronicles, letters, court proceedings, tribute and census lists, legislative and administrative codes, and investigative reports for both the crown and the church. Some of the material is published (such as de Andagoya 1865; de Cieza de León 1553, 1877, 1883, 1918, 1923, 1946–1958; Ortiz de Zúñiga 1967–1972; and Polo de Ondegardo 1916–1917), but most remains in unpublished archives in the American republics and Europe.

While there is a wealth of source materials available for ethnohistorical research, relatively few anthropologists or historians have been trained in this field. There are many fine local and national historians, but unfortunately their accounts of indigenous societies and customs often suffer from the lack of an anthropological perspective. Factual errors and generalizations cloud the diversity and complexity of Indian cultures, making it necessary to evaluate carefully the veracity of historical accounts in relation to local groups. Thus, while the broad outlines of historical events are well known, there is an urgent need for systematic studies at the regional and local levels.

In contrast to ethnographic fieldwork, the logistical problems involved in ethnohistorical research are often more complex. Regardless of the geographical scope of the effort, the ethnohistorian must deal with the fact that relevant documents are spread over several continents and more than half a dozen countries. Within each republic they may again be scattered throughout various cities and further fragmented among university, municipal and church archives, as well as private collections. The research task is also complicated by the absence of indexes to documents.

In spite of these handicaps, anthropologists are becoming increasingly aware of the value of historical perspectives and are beginning to undertake ethnohistorical research. Such investigation contributes to our understanding of shifting cultural orientations and categorizations. Studies of past struggles to maintain ethnic identity should also lead to reevaluation of models and explanations of cultural evolution in South America. In this section we have included three papers which make extensive use of ethnohistorical documents. They provide a sample of the kinds of information used by scholars in this field and some ways in which anthropological theory can be applied in an analysis of the data.

Porras's paper consists primarily of a document written at the turn of the century by the owner-administrator of a rubber plantation in Ecuador. Particularly valuable is the documentation of many indigenous beliefs and practices which have been lost or extensively modified by Western influences over the past two-thirds of a century. Additionally, it provides an insight into the minds of the early colonizers and to the interethnic relationships between early non-Indian immigrants and the indigenous inhabitants. The area is currently subject to intensive petroleum exploitation; the consequences of this development are discussed in Whitten's article in Part Three.

The papers of Hermitte and Williams utilize different approaches. Hermitte deals with the growth and structuring of a weaving community, and traces the role of women in the gradual development of a town into an important industrial center for textiles. Hermitte's basic approach consists of a description of demographic patterns during the two-century period from 1678 to 1864, and an analysis of changing ethnic and social classifications. Williams's approach is to apply recent theoretical developments in the cultural ecology of hunter-gatherer societies to data from a wide range of historical sources. His "reinvestigation" of the nomadic Tehuelche of Patagonia documents changes which have occurred over the centuries seen in the light of this model.

REFERENCES

DE ANDAGOYA PASCUAL
  1865   *Narrative of the proceedings of Pedrarias Davila in the provinces of Tierra Firme or Castilla del Oro, . . .* Translated and edited by C. R. Markham. London: Hakluyt Society.
DE CIEZA DE LEÓN, PEDRO
  1553   *Parte primera de la chronica del Peru . . .* Seville: M. de Montesdoca. (Translated and edited 1864 by C. R. Markham as *The travels of P. de Cieza de León . . .*, part one. London: Hakluyt Society.)
  1877   *Tercero libro de las guerras civiles del Perú, . . .* Madrid: Márcos Jiménez de la Espada. (Originally published 1554. Translated and

edited 1913 by C. R. Markham as *The war of Quito*. London: Hakluyt Society.)

1883   *The travels of P. de Cieza de León* . . . , part two. Translated and edited by C. R. Markham. London: Hakluyt Society. (Originally published 1554.)

1918   *The war of Chupas*. Civil Wars of Peru 4(2). Translated by C. R. Markham. London: Hakluyt Society.

1923   *Civil wars of Peru: the war of Las Salinas*. Translated by C. R. Markham. London: Hakluyt Society.

1946–1958   Tercera parte de la crónica del Perú . . . *Mercurio Peruano* 27–39.

ÓRTIZ DE ZÚÑIGA, ÍÑIGO

1967–1972   *Visita de la provincia de León de Huánuco en 1562*, two volumes. Huánuco, Peru: Universidad Nacional Hermilio Valdizán.

POLO DE ONDEGARDO, JUAN

1916–1917   *Informaciones acerca de la religion y gobierno de los Incas* . . . , two parts. Edited by H. H. Urteaga and C. A. Romero. Coleccion de libros y documentos referentes a la historia del Peru 3–4. Lima: Sanmanti.

The Discovery in Rome of an Anonymous Document on the Quijo Indians of the Upper Napo, Eastern Ecuador

PEDRO I. PORRAS

A manuscript which for some time has lain in the archives of the Josephine community in Rome has fallen into our hands by a remarkable coincidence. It must have been taken there by one of the first missionaries to go into the Napo region.[1]

It is in two parts, one of 71 pages and the other of 109, handwritten in an elegant script, in a fairly careful style but with uncertain spelling. The first is entitled "Los Indios civilizados" and the second, "El Oriente: la población blanca." The name of the author is unknown, although certain details given in the manuscript as reference suggest that he was a rubber producer who lived in the east of Ecuador from the last decade of the last century until the second decade of this one. His "factory", called Mascota, was situated at the confluence of the Villano and the Curaray and he forcibly recruited Indians from the pueblo settlements to work in it, that is to say, from places like Archidona, Puerto Napo, Tena, Aguano, San Javier de Pucaurco,[2] and Santa Rosa.[3] These people belong mostly to the Quijo tribe, improperly known as *yumbos*.[4] It seems that the manuscripts in question were written in the year 1913. We do not know if the author remained in Oriente for a few years longer, as seems likely, or if he had to leave at the end of the second decade of this century because of the fall in the price of cocoa and rubber on the world market.

---

[1] The first missionaries of the Order of St. Joseph arrived in the Napo in 1922, 26 years after the expulsion of the Jesuits from the territory.
[2] San Javier de Pucaurco is a settlement which has disappeared from the map. It was situated approximately 12 kilometers down river from Aguano.
[3] Santa Rosa disappeared like the above. It was approximately half way between Puerto Napo and the present-day city of Francisco de Orellana at the mouth of the Coca.
[4] The true *yumbos* of the chroniclers were the people who lived in the mountains west of the Andes. It was only in the middle of the last century that the name began to be applied to the Quijo Indians, creating much confusion among scholars.

When we consulted an old easterner, Gustavo Cornejo, he suggested that the manuscript must have been produced by a rubber merchant called Manuel Alomía Llory. The position of the plantation, he said, as well as information given, and even the type of script, pointed to Llory as the author. Mention is even made in the manuscript that the writer arrived in Oriente when he was only seven years old. In any event the author of the manuscript, although he draws a very exaggerated picture of the state of moral and physical degradation of the Quijos who, at the end of the last century, had experienced nearly 400 years of servitude, is extremely perspicacious and a magnificent observer of the customs and beliefs of the Indians with whom he lived for some years.

Old missionaries who served in the Napo for thirty or more years, on reading the manuscript, could only exclaim: "It's hard. It's cruel! But it's true." The missionaries, however, could not agree with the author's picture of the moral degradation of the Quijos. Their general line of argument is that the Indian is a model of conjugal fidelity, and, without fully realizing it, possesses many moral qualities which distinguish him from his white employer, who is himself a monster of iniquity and dissolute living.

Two divergent philosophies. Two exaggerations. The feature of our manuscript which makes it valuable is the ethnological information it contains. At times the author exaggerates, and frequently repeats himself, but he throws much light on the life and customs of a people who still lack a definitive and trustworthy ethnography.

The Quijos, according to Rivet (1924), were a Chibcha-speaking people, although nowadays they speak only Quechua. They live in the area between the valleys Quijos, Mishagualí, Anzupi, Yatunyacu and Suno, all tributaries of the Napo, in the montaña of the Ecuador Oriente (0° 5' to 1° 15' south latitude and 78° 10' to 78° 50' west longitude). At the present time, according to official census figures, this tribe comprises more than 20,000 individuals. De Cieza de León (1554) observed that the Quijos were not much different from the Panzaleos of the central provinces of the Ecuador sierra who, according to Jacinto Jijón y Caamaño (1941–1947), were also a Chibcha-speaking people with whom the Quijos had close links, the cacique of the Quijos being married to the sister of the Cacique of Latacunga, Don Sacho Hacho (or Jacho).[5]

Gonzalo Días de Pineda was the first white man to visit the Quijos in 1536. He encountered a great deal of opposition. Later, both Gonzalo Pizarro and Francisco de Orellana passed through Quijo territory as members of an expedition which finally reached the Amazon. The Quijos

---

[5]   Information about this cacique, who must have been very influential, if we are to believe the high regard in which he was held by the early conquistadores, is to be found in the record of personal services carried out by Gil Ramírez Dávalos at the time of the conquest of the Quijos and the foundation of Baeza (Ramírez de Avalos n.d.).

attacked Orellana and those of his party who had fallen behind, killing a number of them. The colonization of the Quijos began with the founding of the city of Baeza in 1559, followed by Archidona, Avila, Tena, and Alcalá del Río.

The Quijos, subjected to veritable slavery by the land trustees (*encomenderos*), found their ill-treatment very difficult to bear and rebelled on several occasions, destroying the cities of Archidona, Avila, and Alcalá, and besieging Baeza from time to time. The Spaniards made punitive expeditions in their anxiety to put the rebellion down with an iron hand. These finally resulted in the capture of Jumandi and other *pendes* or shamans. The chief among these were taken to Quito and executed with all the solemn savagery of the time; others were banished to the coast. As a consequence of this ill-treatment, of epidemic sicknesses, and the flight of many Quijos to other regions, the population of the tribe, which was about 30,000 persons in 1559, was reduced in the space of 50 years to less than 3,000.

The few Indians who remained were subsequently subjected to a more severe form of slavery then before, a state from which they have not totally emerged even to this day. They were attacked and forcibly put to work at the extraction of rubber, cocoa, and balata[6] by unscrupulous merchants who, from the high sierra of Ecuador, and even from neighboring countries, poured into the Oriente when the Jesuits were expelled in 1895. There were cases where ninety percent of the population of small towns (like Loreto and Avila) in the valley of the Suno disappeared, many of them being sold as slaves in the markets of Iquitos and Manaos. We owe this information to, among others, Diego de Ortegón, judge of the Audiencia of Quito and visitor of the province of Quijos (de Ortegón 1577); also to Jijón y Caamaño (1941–1947) and Steward and Métraux (1948:653), who published many of the details given by the Count of Lemus and Andrade (Lemus y de Andrade 1881). De Ortegón's account seems to us to be the most detailed, authentic of all those which have been written, superior in many respects to that of the Count of Lemus and Andrade, which was written in 1608, and which is frequently both forced and superficial. Gonzalez Suárez's study (cited by Jijón y Caamaño 1941–1947: vol. 1, 291–294) on the Quijos was based on the "Relación" of Diego de Ortegón. Jijon y Caamaño added nothing new. The Quijos are also mentioned in passing by the Jesuits Cáceres (1892) and S. (1894), and by Father Magalli (1896).

In 1870 Simson visited the Quijos and published interesting information (Simson 1882), as did Osculati (1850). Tessmann (1930) has been hitherto considered the bible of Quijo ethnography, especially in the English-speaking world. Unfortunately, Tessmann's accounts were based

---

[6] Latex extracted from a tree, like rubber, from which chewing gum is obtained.

on information supplied by acculturated Quijo Indians living in Iquitos, three of them altogether. It is therefore not surprising that his work is very incomplete and not worth serious attention. More recently, the German Udo Oberem (1967) has dealt with the Quijos in some detail. His work includes a stupendous bibliography, based both on his personal experience and also on information obtained in Oriente, almost all of it second-hand.

Neither Protestant nor Catholic missionaries are much concerned with probing into the sociology of the Indians, their customs, or their way of life. There are, however, some noted exceptions. Their main pre-occupation seems always to have been, and still is, to westernize them and encourage them to abandon the age-old traditions of which they were the heirs. The sparse contributions of the missionaries to books or reviews on the Quijos are nearly always in the form of an apology for their own proselytizing work.

In this state of affairs this new source fills an immense gap and supplies abundant information to scholars. The source gives, for example, very interesting details on the Quijos' clothing, including the use, by the adult men, of the *curu-balón*, short trousers made from a single piece of cloth on the Indian loom. The author of these lines has seen this garment in one other Quijo settlement, but unfortunately it is fast disappearing.

It is also very true that the Quijo is only superficially Christian and deep down continues to believe all the old superstitions. It is necessary to draw attention to the following lines from the manuscript:

. . . generally speaking, one can say to the Indian that there is no god, that he does not exist, that the sun does not shine, that day is night, and suchlike, and he will believe it. But if you tell him that sorcery is a farce, he becomes uncomfortable and does not accept this, even if you offer tangible proof. For his faith in this outlandish nonsense has been sucked in with his mother's milk, inculcated by his ancestors, handed down by ancient traditions, and imposed by the suggestions of the sorcerers themselves, and is so ingrained in the mind of the Indian that he would rather be burnt alive than abandon his beliefs . . . .

The account of the legend on the origin of the moon is truly poetic, a masterpiece of good narrative: "I have heard many more legends," he tells us, "for the most part improper and lewd, and for this reason I shall not bother to repeat them. They also seem to me to be devoid of meaning." It is a real pity that he did not do so.

The author describes with a great wealth of details the sessions when the witch doctors are called to attend the sick, and especially to sup-posedly sick women who in fact are deceiving their credulous husbands: "I have deduced that the women and the sorcerers are the only ones who do not sincerely believe in sorcery," writes our anonymous ethnologist. He devotes a great deal of space to the Indian's moral degradation resulting from drunkenness and belief in *curanderos*. It is a shame that more than fifty years after these lines were written, the same excesses so vividly described by our author are no rarer among the Quijos.

Only the first part of this manuscript is reproduced here, that is, the section entitled "Los Indios civilizados." The second part is about the exploitation of rubber and the difficulties which the producer has with the Indians who did not take kindly to being snatched from their villages and their homes and sent into the deepest part of the forest for months and even years.

The manuscript is generally in a fair state of preservation, although the topmost pages in particular show evidence of damage caused by damp and insects, as might be expected in the humid, tropical climate of Curaray.

We have sought, wherever possible, to preserve the integrity of the manuscript which is being reproduced here. The presentation has not been altered. We have only omitted two paragraphs which comprised a boring description, a digression from the argument, of the diet and conduct of the author. We hope that the publication of these lines will be a real contribution to our knowledge of a people as interesting as they have been unfortunate.

*   *   *

THE CIVILIZED INDIANS

Introduction

Before passing on to a description of the villages, I shall give a general picture of the race of Indians who inhabit them and describe some of their most important customs.

The race of Indians in Archidona is the same as that which inhabits the settlements of Tena, Napo, Pucaurco, Aguano, and Santa Rosa, differing from each other only in dialect, there being a separate one for each of the areas named. The men are generally tall, handsome, and muscular, fairly strong and well-equipped for journeying on foot. If I am not mistaken, they are the same tribe who, in Quito, are known as *yumbos* or Quijos.

Character

The character of these Indians is not totally savage: they are astute, fawning, and sly. Some of them are also daring and abusive, since I have often seen one of them press close against a white man on a path, pushing the latter off the path forcibly or making a point of outstriding him.

Food

The Indian, especially in the villages of Archidona and Tena, where fish is very scarce, eats mainly vegetables: plantains, yucca, sweet potatoes, and hearts of palm. He very rarely eats meat, not because he does not like it, but because hunting (the only thing the Indian cares about) is not very good and since his obstinate laziness ensures that there is never a substantial increase in chickens or other domestic animals. He constantly lacks meat except the flesh of snakes, frogs, insects, and grubs of various kinds. But the staple item in the Indian's diet is chicha . . . the chicha of Oriente, the food and drink of dirty people.

It must be made clear that the chicha of Oriente is not very similar to the yellow maize-water of which Montalvo speaks so ill. The chicha from hereabouts is made from cooked yucca or chonta fruit, beaten to powder in a large trough around which all the women gather for the purpose of chewing. They pick up a handful of beaten yucca or chonta, place it in their mouths and chew it until it becomes a watery paste. When this is in an almost liquid state they spit it back into the trough, and so they continue until the whole quantity has been chewed. It is in this way that they make the chicha which the *yumbos* take into Quito to sell, under the name of *chantaruro*. Chicha can therefore be said to consist of 30 parts saliva to 65 parts yucca or chonta and 5 parts germs from all the chewing mouths, sometimes more than 20. Is it possible that anyone drinks this filthy mixture? Yes, there are even civilized white men whose refreshing drink is Indian chicha which they buy greedily. With my own ears I have heard men of good appearance and, apparently, civilized tastes say that they prefer a glass of this filthy drink to one of beer! (There are some people who deserve to be beaten for their taste!) The aficionados of chicha prove that instead of civilizing the Indians by their company, they are making savages of themselves by learning the Indian's customs.

Household Goods

In their houses, the Indian has no objects of value save a blowpipe, an ax, and a machete. These are his weapons and his tools. In their houses or huts, they also have six or seven huge earthen vessels full of chicha and a bed of *guadúa* planks.

Clothing

The men's dress consists of short trousers some 25 cm. wide (the *curubalón*) which leave their legs completely bare, and a strip of material with a hole in the middle (*cushma*) which, worn like a poncho, covers their chests and shoulders. The only article of clothing which the women use consists of five strips of material sewn together in the manner of a sheet (*pacha*). They wrap themselves in this, from the chest to the knees, securing the ends with rough needles or with pins of sharpened chonta. Add to this a sash worn round the waist and there you have the complete dress of the females.

This is certainly how the majority of the Indians dress, women and men. It cannot be denied that there are some among the men who have shotguns, wear long trousers and shirts, but, among the women, there is little variation since they replace the five strips of linen with two hoops of material with the width of two of the strips. These they fasten at the waist with a sash, and then wear a small sack or jacket to cover their chests, shoulders, and arms. This feminine wardrobe is used when good fortune, or civilization, has forced a woman to abandon the *pacha*. She will continue to wear the latter, however, at home as a dress during the day and as a blanket at night. Indians, both men and women, are invariably laden with a greater or lesser weight of shells or colored beads worn round their necks and of which they are very proud. I once saw an Indian woman, in Aguano, so laden with beads that she could scarcely move. Out of curiosity I weighed them and they came to 30 pounds.

Vices

Among the vices prevalent in the race of Indians with whom I am concerned, the principal ones are laziness, drunkenness, and theft. The little that the Indian earns from his travels, or from his work in pita or rubber, he spends almost entirely on aguardiente, and when he has no more money to buy this, they extract it, in earthen pots, from the ripe plantain. On the other hand, those enormous pitchers, always bubbling with that drink as strong as it is dirty, mean that these shameless people are never free from intoxication.

The Indian grows no crops apart from bananas and yucca: the first for aguardiente and the second for chicha.

They also sow rice, maize, beans, sugarcane, and other vegetables, but in such small quantities that it is not worth mentioning them. The Indian is absolutely dominated by laziness. He never lends himself voluntarily to the task of earning a single real save for the purpose of getting drunk if he has not the wherewithal to become so. There will assuredly be those who will ask: "How is it that the white inhabitants of these towns secure the services of the Indians?" The answer is very simple: the Indian serves the white man because he believes that he is obliged to do so. The Indian's ignorance is such that he does not even suspect that individual freedom can exist and therefore they believe that they are all the slaves of our race. But even so, if a traveler needs bearers, the authorities have to intervene and force the Indians to do it with threats and even with blows. As for the white inhabitants of these places, they achieve everything by means of alcohol and this never runs out. Indeed, how could it, since in Archidona in particular, there are more stills than there are white inhabitants? Without doubt, the day that the Indian obtains the certain knowledge that he is free he will cease to serve the whites and they will be forced to do the work themselves or abandon their estates.

Disease

Most of the Indians of Oriente suffer from a disease which they call *siso* and the whites *carate*. It is a disease of the blood and is highly contagious. The skin becomes covered with red, black, and white spots which cause itching and stinging and exude an unbearable odor. It is a disease for which neither the native pharmacopoeia, nor medicine, perhaps, has discovered a remedy.

This disease spreads through lack of hygiene, can be hereditary, spreads by contact and also intentionally, since the women have a method of inoculating the germ and allowing the disease to take its course in a few days. This method consists in giving to the individual a mixture of ground snail-shell and the dust from a grinding stone, together with the germs and scabs which fall from the skin of an infected person. This disease is, without doubt, a kind of leprosy.

Egoism

The Indian's nature is egoistic in the extreme. If an Indian owns something in his own right and sees that this thing may be useful to someone else, he destroys it although this may mean having to work harder on another occasion. Many times I have seen one or more Indians come to a swollen river where it has been necessary to construct a bridge, but the moment they have crossed they destroy the bridge.

Beliefs

They profess the Catholic religion, the beliefs inculcated by the Jesuit missionaries, but these are so imperfectly developed in the dull imagination of the Indian that they have become a series of absurdities, interpreted by each one for his own convenience, and used to excuse even the most disgraceful acts. And they profess this religion on the surface only, without observing even the least important of its precepts, perhaps because the Indian's limited imagination is given over completely to witchcraft, metempsychosis, and other mean beliefs which I have been able to observe. These beliefs have great similarity to those of the Zaparos and those of savage tribes, so that I do not doubt in the slightest that they proceed from the same source. The Indians bury their dead because the missionaries have introduced them to this custom, but after burial they place chicha, food, ripe plantains, and other things in clay pots on the graves. In the solitary place which serves as a cemetery, there are different species of animals such as rabbits and rats which come, especially at night, to eat the provisions placed there for the dead. Seeing this, the Indians believe, in all sincerity, that the dead person has eaten and drunk. This charge continues for a year "until the dead man has a garden in the next world."

The affinity in the beliefs of the Indians and those of the Zaparos binds the two groups closely together. I have been able to observe the same superstitions, the same beliefs, with slight variations. The Indians believe that when witchdoctors die they are transformed into jaguars which roam around causing as much damage as possible. To effect this transformation, it is necessary to drink, while one is still alive, a concoction made from a herb called *puma-yuyu* ["puma plant" or "puma grass"], whose leaves carry the shape of the female jaguar. Anyone who has done this while alive, can, as soon as he is buried, transform himself from the very first day into a diminutive jaguar, no bigger than a flea. This grows rapidly to become the awesome cat, ruler of the forest. If this jaguar is killed and burnt, and its ashes scattered over water or dispersed by the wind, it will rise up again and grow from among the ashes, out of the water, or in any spot where the wind has deposited the smallest fragment of it, for it is indestructible.

I suppose that this is a belief derived from metempsychosis, modified by certain inventions of the old people to ensure that their families do not abandon them, as was customary when they became old, for fear of the vengeance of the elderly after death in their manifestation as jaguars. But all of this is to no avail, for when an Indian becomes useless through old age or sickness, he is regarded with scorn by his family and is completely abandoned even by his children who frequently address him with these words: "Die quickly, you useless old man, you are good for nothing!" In this way, death, which for our kind carries a certain consolation when the dying man has a family and relations, must be, for the Indians, a bitter and horrible end, because they die, hated and despised even by their own children, with no one to care for them in any way. Most of them die tormented by hunger and thirst with no one to give them food or drink. Yet I have seen Indians die and do so peacefully. Perhaps they are insensitive to deeper feelings and moral considerations. Perhaps they have only a material being.

In Aguano (I could cite many more similar cases), there was an enormous jaguar which fed itself on the Indians' dogs and domestic animals. It captured the dogs within sight of their owners who, instead of killing it, shouted insults at it, telling it that there was no lack of animals in the mountains on which it could feed without prejudice to human beings. A white man, an inhabitant of the town, stalked the jaguar and shot it. It turned out to be a beautiful female jaguar. When the Indians heard of this, they all came to see the carcass of the beast. The brave hunter expected to hear some word of gratitude or even some expression of pleasure that he had freed them from the terrible beast. But after looking at it, and touching it, they said coldly: "You have not killed the jaguar, because it is not really a jaguar and it will come back to life even if you burn it. It is Casita Dagua [an Indian woman who died a year before] who drank *puma-yuyu* — even down to her bracelets." And they pointed out some black stripes on the jaguar's paws!

Among their many absurd beliefs, I shall mention only a few. Every Indian believes that the rainbow is an *amarón* [boa] which the lightning kills in order to eat it. They believe that lightning is a fearsome man whose power is limited by the evening star (*cuillor*), younger sister of the morning star (*ducero*), who on one occasion, when the lightning had killed an Indian family, killed it with a stone fired from a catapult and sent it rolling down a ravine, not far from Archidona. But because the lightning was immortal, it left its original body and nowadays it is its soul which wanders letting off shots. In this ravine there is, in effect, a precipice of yellowish clay which looks a bit like old bones. Fragments which fall off this cliff are collected by the Indians and sold for a good price among themselves under the name of *rayo-rumi* [lightning stones] or *rayo-tulli* [lightning bones]. These are grated and the powder, mixed with tobacco, is taken as a panacea for all types of illness.

THE LEGEND OF THE MOON. The moon (*quilla*) is, for them, a supernatural being whose story is perhaps the only tradition which they preserve. I shall tell it as it was told to me:

There was an Indian girl, unmarried, an orphan and very beautiful, who lived in a large house with many other Indians including her only brother. With no hope of marriage, her life was sad, dedicated to her various tasks during the day, and sleeping alone at night in her bunk (*cahuito*). A certain night a young Indian came to her bed and told her such things that he made a deep impression on her, opening her heart in a blind love for the unknown man. Finally, she gave way to passion. The nocturnal visitor imposed on her the condition that he would never divulge his origin to her nor who he was, nor would he try to meet her during the day. This life continued for some months and the nocturnal lover never failed to turn up in his mistress's bed even for one night, until, after some time, she knew that she was pregnant. Seeing that she was soon going to be a mother without even knowing who was the father of her child, the woman, overcome by curiosity, resolved to break her promise, without arousing her lover's suspicions, because although she believed that he lived in the same house she did not know which of the young men it was. She therefore took a *hurítuc* seed [a fruit whose juice stains the skin shiny black and does not come off until some time has elapsed], grated the fruit onto a leaf and placed it in her bed within reach of her hand. The nocturnal visitor arrived as usual and spent the night. In the middle of their caresses, the girl moistened her hand in the juice of the *hurítuc* and passed it over her lover's face. On the following day, she arose early and set herself to serve chicha to all the young men, one by one, examining the face of each one very carefully, to see whose face showed the *hurítuc* marks. What was her surprise when she saw the marks on the face of her own brother! She collected her wits and managed to keep her composure so that no one was aware of her emotion. That night, her lover came again and she received him passionately as before but informed him that she had discovered who he was, and how she had done so, assuming that their love would continue.

The brother-lover got up saying that after what had happened he could no longer stay and that if she wished their love to continue she would have to follow him without a moment's delay. The girl got up at once, hurriedly wrapped herself in her *pacha* and looked around for the sash to tie round her waist. But while she was doing this, she saw that her brother was beginning to assume a luminous form and that he was rising from the Earth and ascending to heaven. Now that she had secured her sash, she sought to follow her lover, but he had already gone on ahead and she could not raise herself from the ground by her own strength.

She began to cry bitterly while the incestuous brother ascended indifferently into space and was completely transformed into the moon. The woman gave birth and was then transformed into a *geloco*, a nocturnal sparrowhawk which sings plaintively on moonlit nights, from the moment the moon appears over the horizon. The child, being smaller, was transformed into a nightingale (*tuayo*) which also sings in melancholy fashion on moonlit nights.

In the songs of these two birds the Indians believe that they can hear the sad lament of the abandoned woman crying "Oh! My husband!" (*ñuca carilla*), and that of the child calling his father: "Yayá." In the moon's luminous disk they see the *hurítuc* marks made by the hand of the Indian woman to discover who her lover was.

Many Indians, referring to this legend, have said to me with real feeling: "That sash! All because of a sash! Were it not for that sash our nights would be better lit, since, if she had not lingered to look for it, we should have two moons".

I have heard many more legends, for the most part improper and lewd, and for this reason I shall not bother to repeat them. They also seem to me to be devoid of meaning.

SUPERSTITIONS. The Indian is generally superstitious. He believes in dreams which are grounded in his own fantastic imagination. If they dream of drinking, it will rain on the second day; if they dream of sensual pleasures, they will be wounded with some weapon; if they dream of marriage, they will die soon. In short, nothing passes, nothing happens that has not been dreamed of previously. There are so many omens that every incident is announced by a dream or an actual happening. Thus, if an Indian slips on a path, it is because something bad will happen to him on his journey, and generally, he will call off the journey.

If a pregnant woman walks on top of a new canoe, it will split. If a pregnant woman enters a pool, river, or arroyo set with traps, not a single fish will die. There are innumerable others which it is useless to quote. There are rare birds, animals, and reptiles whose presence announces disaster, like the *tapia-chicuán* [a bird], the *tapia-machacui* [a snake], the *tapia-pellán* [a small quadruped], and many others. These superstitions link the Indian very closely to the Zaparo savage and the roots from which he is directly descended.

I have said that the Indians profess the Catholic religion in appearance only, and perhaps this is incorrect. There are Indians who can say a few prayers taught by the missionaries or other whites, but they do not know who God is or who Jesus was, nor indeed anything else, since the Indian's religious beliefs are cemented in the most total and absolute ignorance.

They possess no tradition which could be described as rational. They retain only the vaguest memories of their ancestors and are as ignorant of the past as they are of the future.

COSMOLOGY.Their ideas on our planetary system are: that it is a flat surface; that the sun is a live coal of fire which comes out of a hole in the east, and after traversing the heaven, enters another hole in the west. It passes through a subterranean passage during the night and reappears the following day, out of the original hole! Various beliefs surround the stars. Thus, some believe that they are tiny mirrors; others that they are little luminous creatures like fireflies; and the majority that they are sparks which fall from the sun in its daily course and which are scattered by the wind. They have not the least idea of the distances between us and the planets, nor even of the size of these, diminished as they are by the distance from which we see them. They believe that the sun, the moon, and the stars are seen in their actual dimensions and that with a long ladder, a man would be able to reach them and touch them with his hand. Their notions of arithmetic are so limited that they are unable to count correctly beyond the number ten, this being the number of fingers they have. One hundred is an imaginary number whose value is unknown (some rubber workers understand it). Although in Quechua it is possible to count up to one hundred thousand (*pátsac-guaranga*), these figures are fabulous, unknown, ten (*chunga*) representing the measure of their arithmetical knowledge. The commonest practice among the Indians is to count on their hands (five on each). The sum or the remainder of any problem are both totally unknown.

They measure time only by days and months (*puncha* and *quilla*). They know when a year has passed by the harvest of fruit trees; days by the sun; and months by the phases of the moon.

They divide the day into three phases or hours: morning (*tutamanta*), midday (*chaupi-puncha*), and afternoon (*chishi*). Night is known as *tuta*. An Aguano Indian, some 80 years old, was asked by me how many years he had lived. He thought about it for a long time and finally said "Five years" (*Pichica guata*), and when I told him that he was probably 80, he became annoyed and thought that I was making fun of him.

Healers

Each Indian village has its Indian sorcerers called *ságrag* or *mirico*. It is believed that they are in league with the devil (*supai*), and they take what they please. Woe to those who do not give them what they ask for, since they can kill them by means of sorcery. The Indian sorcerer is generally strong, and more astute than the rest, since only in this way can he acquire his magnetic and unlimited powers.

The methods by which the sorcerers trick the others are to play upon their extreme slowness of intellect. Only the Indian's consummate stupidity and his belief in tradition keep this miserable practice in vogue. In itself, it is the cause of many crimes.

An Indian beginning his studies in sorcery is completely isolated from the others; he takes tobacco (cut and diluted with water) every night over a long period. Tobacco is generally taken through the nose, a full *dumbique*'s bill being applied. He abstains from eating certain types of meat, does not drink alcohol, sleeps separately from his wife, and persists with this régime (*sasig*) for a month, at the end of which, he begins to possess his powers. The first death of an Indian in the village or its environs or even in some distant place (for sorcery reaches further than the imagination) serves to give fame to the novice, since the latter will assert that he has killed the deceased by such and such a method and has eaten his soul. Nothing else is needed to establish his reputation as a sorcerer. I have known Indians whose attempts to become sorcerers were not favored by chance employ barbasco or some other poison to dispose of an enemy.

They perform their cures with the seriousness of an accomplished doctor. When they are called to a sick person's side, they make many excuses to begin with, and finally promise to cure him if they are paid. They never cure for nothing since if they do, the sick person will not get well.

The sorcerer's treatment is as follows: he takes *ayahuasca*, a powerful narcotic, and gives it to the patient as well. He takes off most of the patient's clothing, especially when the patient is a woman. Then, the affected parts, wherever they may be are sucked, after a few mouthfuls of tobacco smoke have been expelled. On taking his mouth away from the patient's skin he spits out a piece of sharpened chonta, saying that this has been extracted from the patient's body. The reader will understand that these bits of chonta which the Indian says are taken from the patient's body are kept in readiness by the sorcerer. He can, as the bits are small, keep up to 15 or 20 of them in his mouth, expelling them at the end of every bout of sucking. In the same way, he can remove from a patient's flesh iron keys, munitions, bullets, needles, matchsticks, buttons, grains of maize, beans, and so on, often replacing those in his mouth from a stock held in his hand. The sucking can go on for about two hours, and when it is finished the sorcerer fans the patient with special leaves from a mountain plant which, when shaken, produce a jingling noise known as *zurupaniga*. More tobacco smoke is expelled and, to the sound of a funeral chant which contains confused and unintelligible words mingled with the devil's name (*supai*), the trance produced by the *ayahuasca* is completed in total darkness.

The women are more often ill and more easily cured. They inform their fathers, husbands, or whichever persons under whose guardianship they live that they are ill and the sorcerer is brought to them. The latter carries out his cure out of the sight of witnesses, *freely*, in the middle of the night. When the women are not ill it is their young children whom they have cured whether they are ill or not, thus providing themselves with a pretext for their *relationships* with the sorcerer, since the latter, apart from the payment which he exacts in clothing, money, or whatever he fancies, also "recoups" from the wife, sister, or kinswoman of the patient, or from the patient herself, should this be the case. This is accepted as the most natural thing in the world, since it is legitimate for the sorcerer to exact these extra "payments," outside the scenes of their drunken sprees. From all that I have seen, I have deduced that the women and the sorcerers are the only ones who do not sincerely believe in sorcery, but they maintain the illusion of "science" for their personal convenience, the women because they are corrupt and the sorcerers because they want to maintain their absolute power. There are women who sacrifice the material substance of their cuckolded husbands, obliging them, by this system, to surrender all their earnings to the sorcerer with whom they openly live under the pretext of paying for treatment, thus converting the pious husband into the slave of them both.

I have observed this closely among my own laborers as well as in the villages, but I have not been able to remedy it because, generally speaking, one can say to the Indian that there is no god, that he does not exist, that the sun does not shine, that day is night, and suchlike, and he will believe it. But if you tell him that sorcery is a farce he becomes uncomfortable and does not accept this, even if you offer tangible proof. For his faith in this outlandish nonsense has been sucked in with his mother's milk, inculcated by his ancestors, handed down by ancient traditions, and imposed by the suggestions of the sorcerers themselves, and is so ingrained in the mind of the Indian that he would rather be burnt alive than abandon his beliefs.

There is no doubt that the will of a sick man can be the cause of cure in some not very serious illnesses, and faith feeds the will. Consequently, some of those who undergo this system of treatment, which I shall not scruple to call "magnetic," are cured, though not by the actions of the sorcerer, but by the arousal of new hope through the blind faith of the *subjects*, or, to put it more clearly, by therapeutic suggestion. These contribute, in good faith, to the sorcerer's prestige. Some patients die, but when this happens, the sorcerer says that he is annoyed because he has not been properly paid and has himself killed the victim.

It is not only sorcerers who have the power to bring rain or shine, but they have generously delegated this power to all Indians. Every Indian has in his garden a plant similar to the *yerba luisa*, except that its leaves are tubular like those of the onion and darker in color. They call this plant *dondoma*, and it can be used to bring rain by anyone who knows the correct formula.

They crush *dondoma* leaves to a pulp. Then, an Indian gets undressed, goes into the water, dives, and comes up with his mouth full of water which he squirts vertically up in the air. He wets the crushed *dondoma* and sprinkles the juice in the air in all directions, so that it falls like light rain. This operation is repeated four or five times and then the remains of the *dondoma* are thrown away (always behind). When rain and wind are required quickly, they puff vigorously, and should they want lightning they mix a small portion of *rayo-rumi* with the *dondoma*.

The other formula consists in taking a tortoise shell of any size and species, wetting chili and placing it inside the shell. They burn the shell and chili in the fire and then throw it, still hot, into the water. Then the naked Indian enters, and does the same as with the *dondoma*. The point of this second formula is that its effects are immediate and violent, and a terrible storm can be expected within moments. For the Indian, it never rains without some good reason, and when there is no one to blame, there are always the *saginos* which roam in great bands and who are also capable of making rain, as are steamboats! Such is the faith which they have in these superstitions that no one is ever at a loss to make rain should he want to swell a river, or drench some traveler, and when the *paje* fails (for so the system is called) they say that the *dondoma* was badly cultivated, or that the chili was not ripe. If, days later, rain does come, they say that it is the rain which they have invoked which has arrived late.

Stopping rain is easier. It is enough to raise one's face to the sky and blow several times, in different directions. They also blow out tobacco smoke believing that this will have a more rapid effect. During the rainy season, Indians can be seen everywhere, blowing. The shower may not stop but the Indian continues to blow. Finally, after some time, it stops raining and the Indian proudly attributes this to the effectiveness of his blowing. These things bring fame to the Indians, and confirm them in their brutish superstitions.

The *ságrag* [sorcerer] is the absolute king over the others. He is a god in the village and has power to bring rain or stop it as he chooses. He kills his enemies however far away they may be and sometimes he kills people who have merely displeased him in some way. All illness is attributed to sorcery. In the case of dysentery, it is because the patient has bits of chonta in his intestines. In the case of neuralgia, there are many bits of chonta in the painful area. Even birth pains are attributed to sorcery, since there is no Indian woman who, before the critical moment, does not pass some pieces of chonta which, in her judgement, might impede the free passage of the child and kill the mother. This religious belief causes a disproportionate mortality in the villages since illnesses are never combated by any means other than sorcery and the sick persons and their relations are fantastically convinced that "what the *ságrag* has not been able to do not even God could have achieved." They die in the firm belief that everything possible has been done to save their lives. Intermittent dysenteric fevers and other diseases, easily treated by simple, known remedies, have frequently destroyed villages, for it is undeniable that although therapeutic suggestion can be effective for some illnesses, and for some acute conditions by the direct influence of massage and even by the sheer force of will, for others it is totally useless since they need to be combated by mechanical means, working in a proven physical way, by emptying the stomach, eliminating parasites, correcting the digestion or the circulation, stimulating or controlling the functions of certain organs, and so on, according to the type of disease.

Among the various occasions when smallpox has destroyed the villages of the Alto Napo, I shall cite only the most recent, that of 1896. The Indians, struck down by the terrible *muruy* [smallpox] had recourse to sorcery and only spread the disease more quickly. Indians already infected with the disease fled from their houses and their villages, taking the disease with them, wherever they went. Many families, already affected, emigrated to hide themselves from the disease and left their route littered with many sick and dying who were left unburied after suffering cruel agonies. There was one family of 28 individuals of whom only one escaped (the father), and he had been vaccinated. Indians who had been vaccinated or who had seen vaccination performed, believing that the fluid of the vaccine had been extracted from the smallpox pustules, inoculated healthy persons with the disease and spread it forthwith even more widely. The villages were left abandoned. When they were reorganized, 65 percent of the population, including sorcerers, had perished.

As the fees which sorcerers charge for their treatment are exorbitant and constant, they do not need to work to clothe themselves. They have more than enough clothes and money for their needs, and tools and weapons of the highest quality. They do not have gardens since those of the other Indians are more than enough to sustain them. The first piece of game an Indian bags while hunting is for the sorcerer, since if the hunter does not offer it to him the sorcerer will damage his rifle, his dog, or the blowpipe with which he has caught it. In this way, they live their shameless lives, wallowing in greatness at the expense of others.

I have often met Indians who have been gravely ill from some disease. Moved by compassion, I have cured them with remedies which have never failed. I have listened to them talking when they have been well again and they have never attributed their cures to the medicines of the hated white man, but to the *ságrag*. I have noticed that even when they see and are convinced of the effectiveness of the white man's remedies they show the same strong repugnance that one of us might have to confess that he had been cured of an illness by Indian sorcery.

The sorcerers sell their craft and they teach it to anyone who will pay them well. Certainly, during the month of *study,* the *teacher* teaches his disciple all the tricks of which this clumsy hoax is composed. It is shameful that among these tricks the most important part is played by one of the most powerful forces of nature, that of animal magnetism. Here it is grossly and disgracefully exploited.

Prostitution and Infanticide

Apart from barefaced prostitution and scandalous scenes of adultery, Indian women have other pretexts for prostitution, one of which is the *supai* [devil]. When an unmarried woman becomes pregnant, her offspring is the son, not of a man, but of the *supai*. In Aguano, there was an Indian known as Mucu whose daughter became pregnant. When the father asked her who was the father of her unborn child, she answered that the *supai* had surprised her alone in the mountains and that the child in her womb had been fathered by the *supai*. The day of the birth arrived, and, as soon as the child was born, they burnt a quantity of chonta sticks which Mucu had prepared for the occasion, and put the child into a new earthenware dish which they placed in the middle of the hearth. The innocent creature was thus burnt alive while his heartless mother watched the barbaric act with great satisfaction knowing that her lie had now been seen through to its desired conclusion.

This incident was related to me by Don Antonio Llori who had property in Aguano. He was told what was happening and he ran to the scene of the crime to see whether he could save the child but, when he arrived, all that remained was a small mound of ash inside the dish which was itself reddened by the fire and almost consumed. Corruption and crime go together among this degraded people. They are corrupted even before they are seemingly ready for it and, among the women, I believe that, with the exception of those who are barren, there is not a single one who has not been guilty of infanticide. This frequently occurs when an unmarried woman becomes pregnant. When the time comes for her to give birth, she kills the poor creature at that very moment by drowning it or breaking its vertebral column. During the short time that I lived in Aguano, I had knowledge of at least 25 infanticides. These were all perpetrated by the mothers themselves. And this in a village consisting of only 50 families.

Alcoholism and Debauchery

Corruption in the Indian race passes the limits of the imaginable. They lose no occasion, including their almost daily drunken states, to indulge in the most disgraceful and scandalous adulteries. These bacchanalias (which are now better regulated among the rubber workers) last for a whole week, except for the one day when they leave their villages. They are shared by the families who comprise a certain group, each family being obliged to supply chicha on a given day and to invite all their neighbors, who come flocking, even women with babes at the breast, their faces painted with achiote, indigo, and other such muck. Installed in the drinking house, the Indian women who have provided the chicha begin to serve the filthy brew in large clay pans (*pilches*) or bowls. After each one has had two or three drinks of chicha, which the Indian women continue to stir with their hands plunged inside the vessels up to their dirty wrists, the men stand up with their drums (*cajas*) and whistles (*pingullos*). Asking for the company's permission, they begin to beat their drums, all following the same tempo with a range of about a third of that heard in our theaters during the *entr'acte*. They place themselves one behind the other and then form a complete circle which then begins to turn round and round uninterruptedly on its center until the party ends in an infernal uproar. They call this the *cajeada* and they exchange positions with each other interminably. The *cajeada* is, as it were, the period of preparation or conquest. The women seated all around the house do not remove their eyes for a second from the men turning all about them, and the men, in their turn, look over the women dwelling longest on those whom they desire. There is no need to speak since the looks and the signals say it all. Soon one Indian detaches himself from the human eddy, gives his drum to another who takes his place, and leaves the house, making his way to a yucca or banana plantation. Immediately, and with no show of pretence, the woman he has singled out follows him, in the sight and presence of her husband, father, or kinsman (who all know where she is going) and — there is no need to say more. After a few minutes this pair returns and another leaves and so on. Sometimes four or more leave at the same time and go off in different directions, to be followed by other men's wives or unmarried women as the case may be. Some husbands, already drunk, become jealous when they see their wives with other men, but cease to be so by indulging in a game of tit-for-tat (*randi*), getting their own back by going off with their rivals' wives or by beating their own. There is no drinking session which does not end with some women being badly beaten, but nevertheless it is they who initiate these sessions since they control the supply of filthy chicha.

The infernal noise of the drums, within which the ear sometimes catches and then loses the sharp, tuneless whining of the *pingullos*, much as a fragile bark plunges and rises up again on a stormy sea, has a remarkable power to arouse desire in the women. I have seen them sitting silent, sanctimonious and prim with their eyes fixed on the ground, at the beginning of a feast, only to raise their heads all at the same time, at the first sound of the drums. When they see the human whirlpool which, following the drum, begins to turn with a slow, measured step, their eyes become lively and send out flashing looks. Their nostrils become distended as though they were not big enough to expel all the air contained in their lungs. With moistened, half-opened lips, they begin to entice the men with obscene signs and gestures, and finally expose, with little pretence, those parts of the body which every woman considers sacred. Drunk in fact and in appearance, they begin to laugh deeply and provocatively and then to shout loudly and hysterically and to throw themselves on the shoulder of the first Indian who falls down drunk, or drag him out into the bushes.

I have seen all this, dear reader, and having seen it, recount it. I have attended these execrable occasions in order to study the Indians' most secret customs and I have witnessed even more disgraceful and shameless acts which I shall not relate for fear of giving offense against modesty.

My observations have convinced me that the Indians' drinking bouts do not appeal because of love of drink alone but more as an excuse for adultery and boundless corruption, for the opportunity which they offer to exchange women and the freedom to take whichever one pleases. They satiate themselves with chicha until, as they put it, "they are full from the stomach to the roots of the tongue," and when they are no longer capable of holding another drop, they leave the house and regurgitate all that they have drunk. After this they go inside again and recommence their drinking of this poison, until they have to leave to regurgitate once more. In a word, the Indian may be compared to a distilling machine which is filled, absorbs all the alcohol it can, while the chicha is in the stomach, and then expels the must by the same route by which it entered. The alcohol is collected in the brain at each stage until it is completely utilized. As yucca chicha contains seven to twelve percent alcohol, if we calculate that only half is absorbed by the human system, this means that in order to get drunk the Indian needs to go through at least ten phases and ten discharges of the still. This is why, dear reader, the drinking feast of the Oriente Indians is the filthiest thing imaginable, not only because of the horribly immoral behavior but also because of the method by which drunkenness occurs, leaving as it does the whole area surrounding the house littered with disgusting vomit.

When intoxication is general, modesty completely disappears. I have already drawn attention to this. No longer is it a question of occasional comings and goings with debauchery in mind, but the scene is one of horrific and indescribable disorder. When they are exhausted by all this and when the chicha is finished, they return to their homes, only to attend the same bacchanalia on the following night, in another place.

These orgies are hidden from nothing and no one. Young children see it all and strive, in their games, to imitate the behavior of their parents, relations, and elders. This means that the Indian, male and female, is generally corrupted in body and soul from an age which, in our race, would seem impossible. I myself have more than once surprised children less than five years old in unsavory practices. I have reported this to their parents, pointing out that the children should be corrected, and the parents, instead of reproving the children, have laughed with criminal satisfaction as you or I would laugh to see a child of this age read or write. If a child, by some rare instinct of repulsion, is not corrupted by the age of six or seven the parents intentionally corrupt him, with practices the very thought of which make me burn with shame.

At first I believed that these "disorders" were caused by drunkenness, but I soon revised my opinion when I saw that, generally speaking, the Indian does not need to be drunk in order to indulge in adultery. The drinking party is only a well-known and accepted pretext for getting together, since, even when the quantity of chicha is small, the Indians pretend and act the part of being drunk so that they can indulge in debauchery with freedom. With freedom? No! With scandalous abandon!

In order to get to know these habits and customs I had to be a very careful observer, since, as I have said, after some years in Oriente, when I believed that I already understood the Indian's character and customs and had already written on the subject, I realized that I was only beginning to understand them when I took under my command a group of laborers from one of the villages. With them, I set up my first estate, La

Mascotta, at the mouth of the Villano river. The first thing the Indians said to me was that they wanted to live a life similar to that which they led in the villages, so that they would not become estranged from their kinsfolk, and I allowed them to do so freely. Once their yucca gardens were ready, I began to notice disorderly behavior and shameless adultery. The Indians had divided the seven days of the week so that every couple had a day on which they were obliged to provide chicha for a feast. This meant that they did not have a single day free for work. Convinced through my observations of the horrors which took place at these orgies, I thought I had an obligation to make the Indians live a better life, demanding that they respect the matrimonial bond, that women should be faithful to their husbands. To achieve this, I took advantage of a system to disparage their behavior and to explain to them some of the advantages of monogamy. The women were the loudest protestors; they had had these customs since the time of their ancestors (*aula manta pácha*) and no white man, that most despised of creatures, was going to discontinue them. They plotted to kill me. Five armed Indians, straight from a feast, were sent to my house with this in mind, and I only managed to save myself by my prudence (1909). In spite of this I managed, by more prudent and covert means, to regulate the feasts which took place on the estate. I allowed them their excesses on Thursdays and Sundays, leaving the rest of the days free for real work. Three years later (1912), believing them to be in a sufficiently rational state, I once more introduced my project of reform and sought to introduce some morality into the habits of my laborers, obliging each woman to live only with her husband thus eliminating scandalous adultery. But the women organized another plot against me with the object of killing me and my family, sacking and burning the house and then fleeing. Then, at the risk of almost losing my life, I succeeded in regulating their drinking parties even more, by restricting them to Sundays only. Thus, little by little, and without force or violence but with cunning, I have reached the stage where my plan has almost been realized so that they now ask me for permission to hold their orgies, knowing that it will only be granted when there is a really good reason for them to celebrate and make merry, such as a wedding or the return from a long journey or the outcome of a productive enterprise. I have uprooted them from my immediate vicinity and made them build their houses 1,500 meters away from mine on the other side of the river, so that they cannot annoy me with their confounded drums, which, even when they are not being beaten continuously, I hate more passionately than a saintly woman hates the devil. Even so they still come from over there to ask my permission to hold a feast when there is a good reason to do so. I usually grant it although I still have reservations about the animal acts of adultery in which they indulge in these shameless orgies. I also know that over there, in their homes, they also drink secretly, without the accompaniment of the drums, but I tolerate this, seeing that it is materially impossible to effect a more rapid transformation in their savage ways, given that after living for nine years under the guardianship of a generous employer who has inculcated in them moral values, both by word and example, what has been achieved is simply some modification of vice and the pretexts to indulge in it, rather than a complete elimination of adultery and prostitution. They now proceed more covertly, but they have not renounced their customs nor changed their instincts which remain as they were when they lived in their villages. They have simply acquired a bit more modesty, and pretend a bit more as far as I am concerned, but what happens among themselves they know and understand perfectly well.

Nearly all the rubber extractors have succeeded in regulating the drinking sessions. Apropos of this, I recall an incident used by one of my colleagues to stop Sunday drinking. This man had given much thought to the problem of prohibiting Sunday drinking when it happened that the mail from Quito arrived at a time when three of his laborers were about. Three letters were handed to him and he read them softly himself. The laborers, with that curiosity which all Indians possess, asked him what news he had received in these *quilcas* [letters]. He, profiting from this conjecture to further his project, suddenly had a bright idea, and said to them with a composed and serious countenance:

The worst news imaginable, yet I cannot hide it from you, for you, yourselves, are to blame. Because of the intemperate way in which the Indians, since time immemorial, have desecrated Sundays, spending them thoughtlessly in drunkenness and disorder, Sundays have been abolished and henceforth all days are weekdays! This punishment is at once sensible and advantageous, since this fatal day deprives them of their health.

The Indians counted the days of the week. When Sunday came, they went and asked their employer what day it was, and he replied, in all seriousness: "Yesterday was Saturday, and today is Monday!" He was able to keep up his deception for three months and this gave him enough time to regulate their drinking habits.

Since it is most vulgar, I do not want to refer here to the widespread belief which the Indians have on the foetus's intrauterine period of gestation. The women slyly and enthusiastically nourish this belief in order to justify their animal behavior during pregnancy. During this time, driven wild by this belief which some accept in good faith, they exhibit an arousal of passion which borders on madness and surpasses the limits of nymphomania. They indulge in prostitution with a total lack of self-control, believing, or apparently believing, that this contributes to the swift development and robustness of the child. If you say to an Indian that the child his wife is carrying is not his, he denies it roundly and says: "Impossible, even if it had only feet, they would have to be mine."

One rubber extractor brought his laborers from the Napo region and founded his estate on this river to do his work there. One of the Indians did not want to bring his wife and left her behind in the village, where the woman led the sort of life to which she was accustomed. After two years, the Indian sent for his wife who came, accompanied by her mother. On meeting her, the husband noticed with disgust that she was pregnant and said as much to her and her mother, who sealed his mouth with the following words: "Whose child might it be if not yours? Your wife was pregnant when you went away, and it is natural that the child has not grown while his mother was without her husband" — an example this of the growth of a child being dependent of the mother's willing this to happen. The old woman continued: "The time which has passed before the birth has taken place is the best proof of your wife's fidelity and now that she is once more with you, she will not be long." In effect, she gave birth two months later and the husband recognized as his own a child born after 26 months of separation.

I have noticed that incest is very common among the Indians and can even affirm that the first steps on the road to corruption are taken in the company of siblings and kinsfolk who live in the same house. I have seen repeated cases of incest between parents and children. One in particular, among many, refers to the Indian known as Osha and his daughter Carmen. Neither the whites not the authorities in Aguano succeeded in making him desist. Nevertheless, marriage is never contracted between blood relations, however distant. It is also not uncommon, when Indians of the same sex meet in groups of two or more, to observe tendencies toward sodomy and other repugnant acts against nature. It is repugnant to me even to record them.

Among the Indians, to be a compadre or a friend is virtually to enter into a pact of concubinage, recognized even outside the set scenes of orgy. Indian women have an aversion to white men and I suppose that this aversion comes from race hatred and also from beliefs inculcated by the men, for I have heard many anecdotes about ourselves so false and filthy that I would shrink from relating any one of them. I have observed not only hate and aversion among Indian women for us but also horror based on superstition, and *tales* which they have been told. In this way, the Indian hopes to prevent miscegenation and keep his race pure. For them the white man is the most degraded being. He is ignorant (*upa*) because he does not believe in witchcraft, does not profess its beliefs and abuses, and because his customs are imposed on them; this hatred reaches such a pitch that an Indian woman who has had relations with a white man or has even served in his house is forever excommunicated from the rest of her people.

Among the Indians, theft is an aspect of religion which they all observe. No Indian is ever called "thief" by another, however often he has stolen. Only whites are thus designated. In the 16 years that I have lived here, I have never heard an Indian call another *shugua* [thief]. To denote this crime among themselves, they use the word *llángac* [toucher], from *llangar* ["to touch" or "to feel"], and anything outside the limit of this is known as *maqui purichic* [he who has allowed his hand to wander]. Entire bundles of merchandise are always disappearing from along the Quito road and it can also be seen where others have been broken into. If an Indian enters a white man's house he never leaves with empty hands, since he always takes with him some object stolen with great skill, thwarting the owner's vigilance. They do not steal out of necessity but merely out of habit, for I have myself seen in Indians' hands objects whose use is unknown to them.

Laziness

The Indian is a debtor from the moment he begins to reason. Business with the Indians becomes a matter of pure credit, and the creditor can only recover his money through heroic efforts. The white residents of Oriente make many sacrifices to recover their debts, and more often than not these sacrifices are useless and the debtors have to be made to work off what they owe. The Indian works when he is forced to but so badly and for so little that it is worth no more than if he did not work at all. He works from seven in the morning until eleven or twelve, when he stops working. A coastal laborer can achieve in a day the work that it would take ten Indians to do in the same space of time. The women work more than the men. The men do not work at home, except for making *birotes* [arrows for use with blowpipes] and wandering around in the mountains a bit. It is the women who clear the ground for planting yucca and bananas; they sow, look after the seedlings, make the chicha, cook, chop wood — in a word, provide the daily sustenance for their children and idle husbands.

When an Indian comes across a rubber tree, he goes on a two-week expedition to extract the precious sap and at the end of this time, he returns proudly with two or three pounds of rubber, which he uses not to pay off his debts but to buy what he wants from someone else to whom he owes nothing, or anyone else whom he can trick into letting him have what he wants on credit.

Killing for Pleasure

Hunting is one occupation by which the Indian can be judged since they all participate in it equally. The Indian does not hunt only to fill his stomach, but also for the pleasure of killing. He takes pleasure in killing birds and animals when he has more than enough for sustenance; he leaves them abandoned along his route. But his pleasure does not only consist in robbing innocent creatures of life but when he captures an animal alive he torments it and prolongs its agony, This is his principal delight. If he succeeds in catching an animal alive he will start to divert himself by setting fire to it. Each contortion of pain, each attempt to free itself from the flames produces happiness and satisfaction, giving rise to deep laughter. He prolongs the victim's life as long as possible. The death which he metes out to birds and animals with the blowpipe is the most merciful. The poisoned arrow penetrates almost without the prey feeling it; the poison circulates rapidly and, half a minute later, the creature falls, completely dead, without providing the Indian with the satisfaction of torturing it. It is perhaps for this reason that the Indian prefers the shotgun to the blowpipe, because, with the former, he can catch wounded or maimed animals which he can then torment with his savage and barbarous cruelty. I shall never forget a scene which I witnessed with my laborers. We were going through the mountains and met a troupe of monkeys (*Simia ursina*). The Indians began to shoot and I also killed one with my rifle since they were very fat and are excellent to eat. We had four, each one about the size of a child of six, that is to say, more than enough for everyone to eat and I therefore ordered them not to kill any more. The last shot was at a female with a young one. She fell, wounded in the stomach, still carrying the little one. The Indians all surrounded the unfortunate animal and laughed unrestrainedly at the futile movements which she made. They threw sticks and clods of earth at her, and pulled at her bared intestines to increase her misery. Blind with rage, I shouted at them from where I was standing that they should not make the animal suffer any more, and when I saw that they had not heard me or did not want to hear, I fired repeatedly with my rifle. What a scene! The Indians laughing with criminal pleasure, and the poor monkey desperately clutched her young one to her chest, as if they were going to take it away from her. With her free hand she wiped the tears from her open eyes so that she could see and then looked first at her tormentors and then at her offspring, as if she was imploring them to have pity on the young one. The tears ran down her face, giving her an expression which made my heart almost burst with grief. The Indians were preparing to roast her alive to continue their sport, and I could no longer resist. I took aim, fired, and put an end to the poor creature, shattering her brain with a single shot. Late in the day the Indians were still annoyed with me for having spoilt their favorite pastime. By the following day, they had already forgotten the incident. Nine years have passed since this incident took place and the memory of it is still fresh in my mind.

In cases where whites have been murdered by Indians, the victims have been horribly tortured owing to the murderers' instinctive and brutal cruelty.

And where this type of instinct (I shall not use the word *feeling*) is to be found, where reason is thus perverted, how can goodness and compassion flourish? It would therefore be useless to look for these qualities in the Indians of Oriente, who lack any sensibility of soul. For an essentially material being like the Indian of Oriente, moral pain and sensation do not exist, perhaps because their hearts are so dominated by deceit and so they do not experience feeling or pain. The Indian does not love his parents since he beats them cruelly every time there is a drinking session. He does not love his wife, hence adultery. He does not love his sons and therefore corrupts them, and a man who does not love someone with whom he lives and who forms the other half of his household, a man who does not love the defenceless beings who need his protection and whom he should cherish as "flesh of his flesh," what love can he have for his fellow men?

In December 1908, a number of Indians from the villages of Tena and Archidona, resident in the village of Atahualpa, came from the Napo, from Señor Secundino Urbina, down the Curaray. On the return journey some of them fell sick and one died in San Antonio. His body was thrown into the water by his companions and they continued their journey up the Curaray. Above Napo, another died and his body was abandoned on a river bank unburied. When they reached my property, La Mascotta, I sent for them, since I knew what state they were in, offering to treat them, and to allow them to recover their strength and to give them provisions for their journey. But that same night they went on, having told my laborers that there was no treatment for sorcery. Three of them were quite ill with tertian fever, to the extent that they could not row in the canoe while the fever lasted. One day, above the mouth of the Nushino, two of the sick men were abandoned on a beach where they died, doubtless of hunger. Another sick man was abandoned on another beach near Yahuate-yacu, and he also died. The three inhuman Indians who returned to their village were close relations of those whom they had deserted on the beaches of the Nushino. A few days later I had the opportunity of seeing the remains of these three unfortunate men when I attended the investigation of the supposed crime deemed to have been committed by the savages of the Nushino.

Ingratitude

Do not speak of thanks to any Indian since he does not know what it means. If he receives a present of clothes, food, or money he responds with a grunt which says something like *ari* [yes], but if he is given a little aguardiente or chicha, he mumbles indistinctly *"Dios pagarachu"* [May God reward you].

Conversations between Indians are on the subject of news, grievances against the whites, success at hunting or fishing, self-praise, sorcery, and, above all, "dirty jokes."

Indians laugh most heartily at obscene language, the more obscene the better. In these conversations, no one is exempt, not even themselves, and matters which we would consider "conjugal secrets" are related by them in the minutest detail.

Family Life

The Indian never caresses his wife, never lets fall an affectionate phrase in her direction, and his conversation with her tends to take the form of laconic orders and severe mandates. He never calls his wife by her proper name, but addresses her as *can* [you], refers to her as *pai* [she], or *uyarijuc* [the sleeping one], or other appellations which obviate the necessity for saying "my wife," or for calling her by her name.

When the Indian meets his parents, wife, or family again after a long absence, he offers no kiss or affectionate word or phrase or even a look. He merely lets out a sort of grunt, half cough, half laugh, and when his wife gives him chicha, he laughs angrily and unpleasantly.

The Indian is not seduced by beauty, nor does he desire a pretty woman, perhaps because he lacks an aesthetic sense. It is enough that a woman should be a good worker and have good teeth for masticating chicha. He never reproves nor punishes his children, paternal authority being nonexistent among them. It is doubtless because of this that, from the age of reason, they learn to fight by beating their parents. Fighting is very common during the drinking feasts, for the Indian only fights when he is drunk. Fortunately, they do not understand even the rudiments of boxing, because if they did, there would be many deaths. They grasp each other and fall to the gound, scratching and biting, the real victim being the clothes they happen to be wearing. These are ruthlessly destroyed, their owners being left completely naked. Their fights are very noisy; they insult each other, threaten each other with sorcery, roar ferociously like tigers and other wild beasts, compensating with their mouths for what they cannot do with their hands. Needless to say, the disagreement does not outlast the feast and it is very common, on the following day, to see two contestants who the evening before wanted to kill each other eating and laughing together in complete harmony.

Lack of Hygiene

In matters of hygiene all Indians are as dirty as it is possible to be. Although they bathe daily in pure water, the rags with which they cover their bodies remain untouched up to the time when they fall in tatters from their wearers' bodies. The rubber extractors have made heroic efforts to force the Indians to wash their clothes. When their clothes lose their natural color and become earth-colored through dirt, they do not wash them but dye them with *sani*, a leaf which produces a dark purplish coffee color, and this is the color they retain until they are no longer usable. As they never wash with soap, they all exude a rank, unpleasant odor which they call *chompeto*. A woman who lacks this odor lacks attraction, since I have heard them, when talking about whites, single out as one of the white man's faults that he does not smell like a *runa* [Indian], but only of soap.

Both men and women have very tangled hair which they hardly ever comb, and which become the breeding grounds for large numbers of lice which they raise as one would a domestic animal, for in their spare time they delouse each other and eat each other's lice. Mothers will sometimes purposely put lice into their children's hair, since delousing sessions (*husa micuna*) are considered to be one of the finest activities for an Indian. Husbands and wives regularly eat each other's lice, but it is commonest between women for whom it is a private and mysterious time during which they exchange confidences, tell each other secrets and acquire great intimacy. Consequently, the relationship of mutual trust between two women is referred to as *husa micuc pura* [between louse eaters], this being the literal translation, but the real significance of the phrase is actually: "between those who have eaten each other's lice."

On one occasion in Archidona, I saw an Indian who had put his feet in a pigsty in which there were many maggots. "Get out, imbecile!" I said to him. "Can't you see how many maggots there are?" He replied: "That is exactly what I want, because there are none in my house and I am going to take them back and breed them there." As a result I am convinced that the maggot, like the louse, is used by the Indians for sustenance and food, since it is taken off meat (when the latter is ripe) and eaten greedily. They do the same thing with the mosquitos and horseflies which suck their blood. They collect them when they are full and eat them. Asked why they do this they reply sharply: "*Randi*" [revenge], that is to say, they apply the rule of tit-for-tat.

There are other aspects of their disregard for decency and hygiene which I shall not enumerate here because they seem to me to be too repugnant.

At home men and women never eat together. The women form one circle and the men another. Between the two, banana leaves are spread on the floor and on them are placed the spoils of meat and cooked bananas with a large *callana* [pan] in the middle full of sauce or plantain mush, and beside it a smaller one of ground chili. When everything has been set out, they sit down on the floor and begin the meal without a single spoon between them. The men are not as dirty as the women. They devour the pieces of meat dipped in chili and the cooked banana in a similar way and pass the container of sauce or mush to each other, everyone taking three or four mouthfuls straight from it and passing it on to his neighbor. But the women seize the banana and knead it in their hands until it forms a sort of paste which they then dip into the sauce or mush, stirring it round inside the container until it has absorbed enough of the liquid. They then transfer this to their mouths, licking their sauce-drenched hands up to the wrist. They normally wear bracelets of beads or shells which they never take off and which therefore become bands of total filth with bits of dirt clinging, apparently symmetrically, to the decorations. Many diseased hands are put into the vessel as well, but the Indian never shows any repugnance for his own kind, and believes that the fear of contagion is the best way of ensuring it. This is not entirely true for the women for, if anyone is affected by leprosy or is similarly diseased, they inoculate that person immediately, in the manner I have described. This belief is doubtless responsible in large measure for the spread of leprosy, which is very common among the Indians of Oriente.

Betrothal

No Indian girl knows who her husband will be until she has been asked for and then she is made to marry, whether she wants to or not, the first man who asks for her hand. The bridegroom-to-be never asks the woman herself, but points out the woman of his choice to his parents or closest relations, who then have the task of asking for the girl's hand. This process is an involved one and difficult for an outsider to follow. The "askers" approach the girl's parents and, on their knees, recite a long and convincing discourse which can last up to seven hours or more. The girl's parents like to be pleaded with as much as possible and often the asking procedure has to be repeated three or as many as seven times at a stretch. When asking for a woman in marriage, the procedure must never be initiated during the day, but only after nightfall, and as the girl's distant relations must be asked as well as her parents, as many as eight or ten nights may be spent on this task.

The asking procedure never takes place unless there is a good supply of aguardiente, since the words are alternated with reciprocal gulps of it, and if the man or his intercessors do not obtain consent for the marriage, the cost of the drink has to be paid for as part of the intercessors' duty. As soon as consent is obtained from everyone, the marriage (*boda*) is fixed for a certain day. Sponsors assume the responsibility for the marriage petition, and once the match has been arranged, they start their preparations, making enormous vats of chicha and distilling large quantities of aguardiente.

The Wedding

On the day of the wedding, drinking begins very early in the morning. The sponsors arrive at the bride's house to "dress" her. They remove the clothes she is wearing, and make her put on a skirt. They cover her shoulders with two shawls joined together, the ends of which serve to cover her face completely during the dance, and they place a red or blue band around her head. Most brides, however much they want to be married, run away when the time comes for them to be dressed and hide in a yucca or banana patch, feigning a repugnance which they do not feel. Failure to do this will lay them open to bitter criticism from the other women. What I have described is the bride's full outfit. The sponsors dress like the bride, especially the godmother, who is dressed exactly like the bride except for the band around her head, which is the particular symbol of those about to be married. She wears the same red shawls which she uses like the wings of a bird, sheltering, underneath the right one, the red-faced, embarrassed bride so that the latter may feel less embarrassment.

Having dressed the bride, the procession makes its way to the bridegroom's house where he awaits them wearing the accepted clothes: white shirt and trousers; long stockings with the toes turned up like leggings; a hat with a blue or red band; a white poncho of fine woven cloth, and on the poncho the classic red shawl, the symbol of matrimony. The sponsor is dressed like the bridegroom (with the exception of the hatband) and he leads his protégé, under the right wing of his colored shawl, to the trial dance. At the end of this, they all go before the officiating Indian or white man who makes them join hands, and, after much ceremonial, gives them his blessing, and initiates the festivities. There is a terrific noise, produced by more than twenty drums, a song which is not really singing but a monotonous whining which is repeated always on the same note and with little variation in the words, and a violin which does not harmonize — and all this is combined with the shrill and unharmonious blast of the *pingullos* [whistles], which produces a sound capable of bursting anyone's ears and which has not even a rudimentary resemblance to music. Then to the dance: the women stand in lines of six or eight with the bride and her sponsor in the middle and the men form a parallel line in the same way. Then the slow shuffle of the dance begins. As the line of women advances, the line of men recedes and vice versa, and they spend days and nights doing this until the three days of the wedding have passed.

I shall not speak of the custom which they call *chaucha* in order not to offend the modesty of my readers, for it is a savage and horribly immoral rite which surpasses the limits of the worst type of corruption. All the participants in the wedding take part in this brutal rite. The bridegroom's sponsor has the ill-judged responsibility of initiating the wife in her marital duties, and the bride's sponsor has the same responsibility with respect to the bridegroom. This means that the bride has to begin her married life by belonging to the man who was sponsor at her wedding, and she feels that she owes more to him than to her husband since it is he who has paid the expenses for drink, and has worked hard in presenting her husband's petition. After the sponsor comes the father-in-law, since it is he who has "raised a male child, expressly to be given to her as a husband," and then comes the sorcerer who has allowed the marriage to take place, and who has promised to preserve the bride's life and health so that she could get married. In this way, an Indian woman who gets married becomes the sponsor's wife, her father-in-law's wife, the sorcerer's wife, and finally, her husband's wife. These customs are all recognized as sacred and religious precepts. To put it more clearly, marriage is the beginning of polyandry.

Enemy of the White Man

Generally speaking, the Indian is totally resistant to civilization, hating even the language we speak, his favorite word for it being *supai-shimi* [language of the devil]. In order to convince them of the superiority of the white man over the Indians, by reason of our customs and knowledge, and to rid them of their hatred of the Spanish language, a neighbor of mine on this river, a rubber man, employer of many laborers, called together all the Indians one day and showed them a figure of Christ. "This is God," he said to them. Then he added: "Is it not true that he is a *viracocha* [white man] with a beautiful beard?" All the Indians admitted that he was a *viracocha*, adding that he was the *amo* [lord] of everything. "Well then," said the employer, "you say and teach your children to believe that Spanish, our language, is the devil's language. A man who dies before learning to speak Spanish has no hope of entering heaven, since, although he has a right to go there, God does not understand Quechua. St. Peter, who is the doorkeeper, still less, and, moreover, he is old and irritable and will surely send to hell anyone who confuses him with a language he does not understand. You cannot expect any help from the other saints for they are all white with the exception of St. Martin who is black but also speaks Spanish." It seems that he succeeded in convincing the Indians, and, chastened and ashamed, they ceased to criticize *supai-shimi* and put no obstacles in the way of those wanting to learn it.

If an Indian's child has a white godfather, he will first have him baptized with another Indian as godfather, then another, and only the third time round will the white man be asked. The belief is that if a child has only a white godfather it will surely go to hell. There are Indians who have had their children baptized six or seven times, mostly as a form of speculation since the godparent has an obligation to clothe the child who therefore has the opportunity to be well looked after and have all his clothes provided.

Envy is one of the principal causes of the mortal hatred which the Indian feels toward the white man. They see that even the worst of the white man's customs are less corrupt than their own. They see that whites are stronger and more intelligent, and they feel a deep hatred which they spread and transmit through a thousand lying fictions in order to keep their race separate from ours, and prevent theirs from becoming civilized or from mixing with ours. Moreover, they know what Indian women are like, how they love comfort, luxury, and the like, and they estimate that if an Indian woman attached herself to a white man who could provide her with some comforts, she would be unwilling to regress to her natural state of abject misery and, with other women following her example, Indian men would have either to abandon their laziness and acquire by hard work the same comforts which a white enjoys or give up the idea of having wives. They know how limited their intelligence is, and know that they have no aptitude for competition. Yet they cannot, or must not, admit that they are beaten. On the contrary, they believe that they are superior, and keep their race even more aloof by inculcating this dogmatic hatred toward the whites. It is lost effort. As if streams which come from the same source and flow into the same sea could flow in the same bed without mixing, simply because the water of one of them is clean and that of the other dirty.

I have had in my house female Indian servants, selected when they were young, and I have sought to tame them, molding them to our ways. I have sought to eradicate their own beliefs and to teach them our language. I have employed various methods, some gentle, some severe, but without success. They learned the language but only after a fashion, but on the question of forsaking their beliefs, of accustoming themselves to a good life and forgetting their hate for our race, never. I raised one from the age of four and in thirteen years I have not civilized her. She hides her beliefs, but she cannot hide her devotion to her own race. Someone asked her one day whom she believed knew more, her employer or an Indian. Without hesitation, she replied: "The Indian!" At first appearance she seems a rational woman: she speaks Spanish perfectly and dresses like a white woman. So it is that a white man who takes Indians into his house with the idea of civilizing them, inculcating new habits, and more, is only succeeding in opening his home to rabid enemies whom he maintains and clothes. I, for example, as honorable man and father of a legal family born in matrimony, have as servants in my house Indian women of various ages in whom I do not tolerate prostitution. As they have been brought up in an atmosphere of unbridled license and with exaggeratedly immoral customs, and as they have been corrupted since they had eyes to see and ears to hear, they yearn for their disreputable life. They are carried along by their instincts and their passions. But I forbid anything of this kind since to allow it would be to corrupt my own family. They see that I am the only obstacle preventing them from enjoying what they believe to be their happiness, and they hate me mortally.

Some employers, believing erroneously that they must keep their servants contented, allow them full liberty. They permit them to attend drinking sessions and tolerate prostitution. They only succeed, not in remedying the situation, but in aggravating it, since hatred, far from burning itself out, increases. Their "captivity" become more painful to them, and they try to achieve their liberty by any means. They go to the feasts and there lie about their employers and slander them, inflaming the other Indians, and even going so far as to ask them to kill the employers.

Many assassination plots which have been discovered have been started in this way. Let it not be believed that this discontent of the *cholas* [Indian women servants] is the result of ill-treatment because, here, Indian women servants have considerations which they do not deserve, since our Spanish women who live here have come to believe that having an Indian servant is a great boon and therefore clothe and feed them as well as possible and seek to make them as contented as possible. They are discontented because they do not have complete freedom. If they are allowed to attend the feasts, this is only an occasional privilege, and they no longer live among the other Indians, in an atmosphere of corruption where they are free day and night, to go with whom they please, do what they like, and to be wife to all and sundry even when they are not married to anyone.

I believe that all employers of *cholas* have observed the Indian women's aversion to civilization, and have perhaps had setbacks similar to mine, and would have to admit that I am right. The tolerant as well as the intolerant find that their servants are a group of enemies who would like to see their employer in the middle of a fire. This is because they believe instinctively, as far as the white man is concerned, that his object is to repress them in some way or even to hide them away, or subject them to rules, whereas, as free women they could indulge in adultery and untrammeled prostitution. Some poor employers consider it a great boon to have in their houses four or more Indian women, infected with the hereditary leprosy of their race, who serve them very unwillingly and do more damage than service. Yet these employers do not see these women as their enemies, as assiduous spies who observe their employers' smallest actions, who slander them viciously, and corrupt their families. These poor men kill themselves to clothe these women decently and even luxuriously, and give them superfluous things without considering that the Indians' services are out of all proportion to the employer's sacrifice in inculcating moral sentiments, correcting defects, and, in a word, rationalizing them, at the risk of his own life. This sacrifice is always useless, since, given the limited intelligence of the Indian, his character and inclinations, seeking to civilize him is like trying to float upon water an object heavier than the water itself.

REFERENCES

ANONYMOUS
  n.d.a   "Los Indios civilizados." Unpublished manuscript, Rome.
  n.d.b   "El Oriente: la población blanca." Unpublished manuscript, Rome.
CÁCERES, R.
  1892   *La provincia oriental de la república del Ecuador: apuntes de viaje.*
         Quito: Imprenta de la Universidad.
DE CIEZA DE LEÓN, PEDRO
  1554   *Parte primera de la chronica del Perv* .... Antwerp.
DE ORTEGÓN, DIEGO
  1577   "Relación del estado en que está la gobernación de los Quijos, Sumaco
         y La Canela." Archivo General de Indias, Audiencia de Quito 82:71, 1,
         28. Manuscript, Quito.
JIJÓN Y CAAMAÑO, JACINTO
  1941–1947   *El Ecuador interandino y occidental antes de la conquista Castel-
         lana,* four volumes. Quito.
JIMÉNEZ DE LA ESPADA, MARCOS, *editor*
  1881–1897   *Relaciones geográficas de Indias,* four volumes. Madrid: Minis-
         terio de Fomento.
LEMUS Y DE ANDRADE, CONDE DE
  1881   "Relación de la gobernación de Quijos," in *Relaciones geográficas de
         Indias,* volume one. Edited by Marcos Jiménez de la Espada, c–cxii.
         Madrid: Ministerio de Fomento.
MAGALLI, JOSEPH M.
  1896   *Voyage d'exploration d'un missionaire dominicain chez les tribus sauv-
         ages de l'Équateur.* Paris.
OBEREM, UDO
  1967   *Los Quijos: historia de la transculturación de una tribu indígena en el.
         Oriente Ecuatoriano.* Madrid.
OSCULATI, GAETANO
  1850   *Esplorazione delle regioni equatoriali* ... Milan.
RAMÍREZ DE AVALOS, GIL
  n.d.   "Expediente de personas particulares." Real Archivo de Indias de
         Sevilla: Audiencia de Quito. Unpublished manuscript, Seville.
RIVET, PAUL
  1924   "Langues de L'Amérique du Sud et des Antilles," in *Les Langues du
         monde.* Edited by A. Meillet and Marcel Cohen, 639–712. Collection
         Linguistique. Paris: Société Linguistique de Paris.

s.,l.l.
1894   *La misión del Napo.* Quito: Universidad Central.
SIMSON, ALFRED
1882   Notes on the Napo Indians. *Journal of the Royal Anthropological Institute* 12:21–27.
STEWARD, JULIAN H., ALFRED MÉTRAUX
1948   "The Quijo," in *Handbook of South American Indians*, volume three. Edited by Julian H. Steward, 652–656. Bureau of American Ethnology Bulletin 143. Washington, D.C.: Smithsonian Institution.
TESSMANN, GÜNTER
1930   *Die Indianer Nordost-Perus.* Hamburg: Friederichsen, de Gruyter.

The Growth and Structure of a Provincial Community of Poncho Weavers, Belén, Argentina, 1678–1869

ESTHER HERMITTE

The northwestern region of Argentina has historically been the center of the country's traditional industries. These industries originated during the crisis in international trade in the seventeenth century which was caused by conflict between the Spanish agricultural and industrial producers on the one hand and the colonial consumers on the other. During this crisis, industries developed in the colonies to fill the gap produced by the conflict. From Mexico to Argentina, sawmills, vineyards, and small manufacturing industries arose to satisfy the growing market of the region.

When the crisis was resolved in the second half of the century, the population had increased to such an extent that these new industries were able to maintain themselves. It was only well into the eighteenth century that the removal of imperial restrictions finally allowed Spain to resume supplies to American markets. In spite of this, many of the colonial industries had secured markets which allowed them to compete not only with Spanish products but also with contraband imports, especially from England.

One of the classic centers of local industry was the province of Catamarca in the northwest of present-day Argentina. In that area, the textile industry had developed apace, consisting mainly of the manufacture of articles in cotton and in sheep, llama and vicuña wool.

One of the most important weaving centers was the town of Belén in the west of Catamarca. Although of relatively late foundation (1678),

This article forms part of a research project on "The social organization and economic system of a community of northeastern Argentina," directed by Esther Hermitte, Center for Social Research, Instituto Torcuato Di Tella. We should like to thank Zulma R. de Lattes and Alfredo Lattes who read a first draft of this work and made valuable suggestions for the demographic analysis. We also thank Martha Barciela, a graduate student who copied the national archive's 1869 census data.

toward the middle of the eighteenth century it emerged as an outstanding producer of textiles. Its predominance in this field was confirmed in the nineteenth century, and even today, the majority of its economically active population is involved in the manufacture of ponchos and shawls of vicuña and llama wool.

The purpose of this article is to describe the demographic growth of this famous textile center and to determine its fundamental social structure given the unusual nature of its work force. Unlike most colonial industries, weaving employs predominantly, almost exclusively, female labor. This feature, which still characterizes Belén, means that it is a place where special conditions prevail. We hope to analyze these later.

The material which has enabled us to reconstruct the historical process consists of documents which describe the population from the time of Belén's foundation to the nineteenth century, and of censuses of the town carried out in 1756, 1770, 1812, and 1869.

BACKGROUND TO THE FOUNDATION OF BELÉN

In the seventeenth century the western part of Catamarca was inhabited by Indians. The need to establish defenses against their warlike depredations was one of the decisive factors in the founding of some settlements in the area. In addition, the possibility of recruiting Indians to work on the large estates was not entirely unconsidered in the plans to establish settlements in this frontier zone.

The first Spanish settlement on the site of present-day Belén took place in 1607, the year in which Captain Gaspar Doncel established, for the third time, the city of Londres. The site of this town had changed several times, and it only lasted in this particular spot for a few years before being abandoned. The reason for the failure of the attempts to establish Londres lay in the insecurity caused to the Spanish settlers by Indian attacks. When the governor of Tucumán, Don Alonso de Ribera, decided on the foundation of 1607, he did so because of the need for a permanent settlement in the extensive region of west Catamarca, which had had none since the destruction of an earlier Londres in the sixteenth century.[1]

The definitive establishment of the present-day town of Belén dates from 1678 when the priest Bartolomé de Olmos y Anguilera sent a petition to Don José del Garro, governor of Tucumán. In it he says:

---

[1] At the same time as the 1607 foundation of Londres, the bishop Trejo y Sanabria appears to have established the curacy of Londres. This curacy covered 60,000 square kilometers and included under its jurisdiction the present-day districts of Santa María, Tinogasta, Fiambalá, and Antifagasta de la Sierra. Historical sources describe it as a wilderness dotted by small clusters of settlement (Olmos 1957:58).

this boon I beseech you in the name of His Majesty, who will be well served therein, since I am at present dedicated to the service of both Majesties, the Divine and the Human, and there is no danger of interference since it is evident that it is more than thirty years that this site has been deserted and abandoned and without an owner of any kind (Larrouy 1915).

Spanish perseverance in creating settlements in western Catamarca, in spite of many failures, was due not only to a desire to control the frontier with the Indians but also to the strategic value of the area. In effect, Belén is situated on the route which led from Santiago del Estero to Copiapó in the north of Chile, and also the only one which ran from north to south without going through the mountains. The junction of these two roads with the trails used by the mule trains made Belén the most important commercial center of the whole of western Catamarca.

There is only the scantiest information on production in the region before the foundation of Belén in 1678. We suppose that the cultivation of maize and wheat must have been important and that these two cereals provided the essential ingredients for food. On livestock to provide the settlers with meat, and on other types of cultivation there is little known. Larrouy and Soria mention, without giving many details, the existence of some agricultural and stock-raising settlements in Aldalgalá, Pisapanaco, and Pomán before 1630 (1921:7). Similarly, the mention of vines in Pomán in 1671, to the south of Belén, suggests that this plant, which was later to acquire economic importance, was already a feature of the local landscape.

The Spaniards who went to the west added the products which they had brought with them to the traditional, indigenous ones. Emilio Coni, referring to the introduction of European plants, says:

The introduction of all the European plants took place almost all at the same time, between 1526 and 1575. . . . Military expeditions, as well as settlers, carried in their wagons seeds of wheat, barley, oats, maize, and cotton; vegetables of various kinds like garlic, onions, beans, pulses, and so on; fruits like oranges, plums, quinces, peaches, sweet limes, cherries, apples, figs, walnuts, olives, and so on; and the famous vine shoots. Every expedition also carried droves of all types of livestock (Coni 1939:253–254).

Belén, at the crossroads between Chile and Bolivia (Alto Perú), must assuredly have received many of these plants.

THE FOUNDATION

Given the strategic position of the new settlement, it was inevitable that it should eventually become permanent. Don Bartolomé de Olmos y Aguilera, in his petition to the governor of Tucumán, based his case as much on geographical and religious arguments as on those related to mere subsistence.[2]

De Olmos y Aguilera states in his petition that there was already one settler in the vicinity of the site he had chosen. It was Captain Gerónimo de Artazar, who had settled on the left bank of the river. The other settlers could be situated mainly on the right bank.

The chief judge, Don Gregorio de Villagrán, gave legal possession to Olmos who set out immediately and traveled through the territory in question ordering those already there to get out — not that there were many. There were only Gerónimo de Artazar and Hernando Enriquez as far as Spaniards went, and a few Indians, including Don Antonio, cacique of the Tinogasta pueblo, Juan, an Indian of the Aimogasta pueblo, and Marcos Joseph, an Indian from Tinogasta.

The energetic priest threw himself enthusiastically into the organization of the new settlement. Three years later, on December 2, 1681, at the dedication of lands to the Virgin of Belén, he declared:

[as] Pastor of Souls, Ecclesiastical Judge, having jurisdiction over tithes in San Juan Bautista de la Rivera de Londres, in the parish of Our Lady of Belén, I have performed these duties up until now. . . . I have peopled the said parish, built a decent church, constructed an expensive canal, set up plantations and introduced livestock, built houses (Larrouy 1915:115).

This dedication of the lands of Belén to the Virgin so that it could be incorporated into the emphyteutic system provides us with valuable information. In the first place there was a fairly systematic procedure for the distribution of land and water, in the sworn devotion to the cult of the Virgin and in the inhabitants' obligation to contribute in terms of taxes and alms. Moreover, the system of emphyteusis introduced certain limitations on the possession of land which were to last for more than two centuries.[3]

The initial number of settlers in Belén was small: "I have opened this door to more than thirty souls whom I observe to be poor and scattered" (Larrouy 1915:120). To add to these poor folk, isolated and thinly scattered, Olmos suggested that there should be added those who would be available for imperial service in time of war and who would also increase the tithes and comport themselves like Christians.

The new settlement comprised thirteen parcels of land allocated in the following manner:

[2]   "Inasmuch as I need to assist in this benefice and the area is extensive, to be centrally placed and to maintain myself, I need a portion of land on which to build my house, grow my food, and keep my horses, in order to exercise jurisdiction over Londres, to administer the sacraments which by my office, I am bound to do" (Larrouy 1915).
[3]   In 1889, the then incumbent of Belén, Father Benildo Fierro, initiated the sale of church lands to private individuals.

one to Doña Juana Perez de Hoyos, another to Bernardo Dominguez de Tejada, another which has been set aside for the Holy Virgin of Belén, two others to the priests, another to Julián de Herrera, another to Alférez Joseph de Matos Nerón, another to Nicolas de Matos Nerón, another to Antonio de Araya, another to Santos de Acosta, another to Lorenzo de Luna, another for the relief of a daughter of Julián de Herrera, another for another daughter of Santos de Acosta (Larrouy 1915:120).

The settlers who received the grants of land were obliged to pay an annual rent of two pesos to the Virgin and a tithe of four reals to the priest who said Mass during the novena. The senior stewards of the guild were responsible for the collection of the tribute.[4]

To avoid the risk of defaulting from the stipulated contributions, the relevant sanctions were outlined from the very beginning:

And if any owner of property should fail to give the two pesos of tribute to the Virgin or the four reals to the priest with evil intent for the space of four years, he will cease to have possession, by the authority and will of the Lord Bishop who will have been previously notified and given reason. This will be done by the priest invited for the feast who will take note of what is lacking and will see that this complement is made up since it is offered by the people as a sign that they are the servants of the Blessed Virgin (Larrouy 1915:120).

The new settlement, as an oasis and watering place, like all communities of this type, had to confront the problems of the distribution and use of this precious but limited resource. The founder, in the same document cited earlier, included the conditions which would regulate the consumption of water (Larrouy 1915:119). The water from the canal was to be divided among the allocated parcels of land on a pro rata basis, and the inhabitants were to be responsible for maintaining these canals and ensuring that they were not blocked.

The fact that Belén would grow and that it would be necessary to adopt measures in keeping with the increase in population did not escape the notice of its founder, who, in the beginning, decided that:

The aforesaid poor who have hitherto joined us and who in future will join us, will have included in this our writ and in the original despatches of the government, the details of their land allocation, in the same way as those who possess them at the moment, and when the number of land allocations exceeds twenty, those over this number will have to have their feast, on January 14, to the Holy Image of the Blessed Christ of the Miracles, in the same way and with the same fee as for this guild [that of the Virgin of Belén] with the same intention and style on the holy day in the name of Jesus (Larrouy 1915).

A document of 1724 reflects the continued preoccupation of the people and authorities of Belén, which had now become a city. It is a writ from

---

4   Those responsible for collecting these taxes were first named on February 28, 1683.

chief judge and captain, Don Estaban de Nieva y Castilla, who specified new rules for the allocation of land. Thus the four parcels on each side of the plaza could only be allocated singly, no one person having more than one of them. He also introduced a distinction between the payment of the tax to the Virgin, which continued to be two pesos annually for land held in perpetuity, and the leasing of land for annual sowing, the cost of which would be confirmed with the guild and the church (Lafone Quevedo 1879).

ECONOMIC AND SOCIAL CHANGES UP TO THE MIDDLE OF THE EIGHTEENTH CENTURY

A few years after the foundation, it began to be clear that Belén would have considerable economic importance, and, correspondingly, a process began which would change its original character as a settlement for "poor and plebeian" inhabitants, and crystallize it into a class society. The factor which determined its economic importance relates to the livestock trade between the provinces of La Rioja, San Juan, and Mendoza with Bolivia. This trade necessarily passed through the main square of Belén.[5]

The growth of the new settlement was also aided by the fact of its position "in the middle of a valley, joined, by easy lowlands, to the settlements of Pomán and, to the north, to the ranches of Malfin, Santa Maria, and San Carlos de Austria, with its mining operations and other facilities" (Guzmán 1969). According to the same author, another factor which explains the growth of the town and which, in our opinion, is an element in the process of social differentiation, is the fact that inhabitants of the failed settlement of Londres, "the most important of whom appeared to be Carrizo de Andrada, returned to the new settlement and united themselves in marriage with the inhabitants of that place" (Guzmán 1969).[6]

Apart from these Londrinos who moved to Belén and occupied high positions there, there were officials of the crown — field marshals, captains, and sergeant majors who, with the former, formed the local elite.[7]

---

[5] As early as 1688, the drivers of mule trains had to pay a tax which was meant to help defray the expense of defending the frontier against the Chaco Indians. It was collected by an important settler in these parts, Bartolomé de Castro, future founder of the city of Catamarca (Larrouy and Soria 1921:23).

[6] At this time, there was, situated about 14 kilometers from Belén, where Londres is today, the ranch of Santos Carrizo de Andrada, known as Santa Gertrudis la Magna. In 1689 it already had a well-appointed chapel. The same Carrizo de Andrada affirmed that he had founded "a settlement called Londres, planting vines and trees and building a chapel, dwelling houses, and a mill" (Olmos 1957:82).

[7] See below regarding the censuses of 1756 and 1779 when reference is made to the criteria by which this elite was defined.

There is information dating from the same period of a small group of Indians living in the area. On the left bank of the river, opposite the site on which Belén was founded, was a small settlement of Indians,

who were not natives of the place but were originally from Tinogasta whence they were brought, around 1680, by their trustee, Juan de la Vega y Castilla, to his lands in Belén, a portion of which he gave over to them. The chiefs of La Banda [left bank of the Belén river] belonged to the same family as those of Tinogasta and had the same surname, Chanampa (Larrouy and Soria 1921:39).

The bishop, Monsignor Joseph de Zeballos, corroborates the fact that the number of Indians was declining in 1736:

The said population of Belén, on that side of the river where the church of Our Lady of Belén is situated, consists of Spaniards, thirty or forty households altogether, and, on the other side, is an Indian settlement, so small that it appears to be no more than six families. They do not work for the land trustees but are under the control of the crown and their administrator at this time was Don Francisco de Cubas, from the city of Catamarca (Larrouy and Soria 1921:appendix, p. xxv).

But if the numerical importance of the Indians in the population was slight in the early years, it must have been very different at other times and in other parts of this extensive parish. In 1691, the priest, Baltasar de Vargas Machuca, had to be transferred because "although he is a very good person (declares the bishop of the diocese), I understand that he does not speak Quechua, the so-called 'lingua franca,' and, to the great shame and distress of the people, their confessions have to be interpreted" (Larrouy and Soria 1921:23).

One condition laid down by de Olmos y Aguilera in the governing principles of the new settlement confirms our view that certain distinctions were implanted then which contributed to the future establishment of a class system: ". . . and if the Indians want to celebrate their feasts let them do so when the Spaniards have had theirs . . ." (Larrouy 1915:119).

Regardless of the number of Indians who lived in the settlement of Belén or in the surrounding areas, it is clear that, already in the first decades of the life of the town, we have the classic dual social pattern of Indians on one side and whites on the other, with intermediate colored groups in the middle.[8] These groups, blacks and mestizos, increased during the eighteenth century but during the nineteenth century there were measures which produced a process of homogenization as we shall see when we analyze the first national census of 1869.

[8] This early settlement of Indians in Belén is interesting especially as they are not included in the first census (1756). We can suppose that this was an omission since the continued and increased presence of Indians is seen from later censuses until the process of homogenization began in the nineteenth century.

The beginning of the eighteenth century marked an important phase, inasmuch as there were Indian risings in the west of Catamarca, and these had an effect on the social and economic life of this vast region. The victory of the Spaniards meant, apart from the possibility of establishing new settlements, the loss of manpower by the victors since many Indians were exterminated or driven far away into lands which were not part of viceregal territory. This state of affairs has been described as a volte-face which obliged the Spaniards to participate in all forms of essential activity in a direct manner (Lizondo Borda 1939:289–290). According to this author, Catamarca and La Rioja, "marginal cities," were distinguished by having a large number of landowners who had only a single Indian each, the latter working like a tenant farmer alongside the landowner. This was enough for the landowner to get along and gave the Indian a certain importance.

The ruralization of Catamarca and La Rioja may be attributed to the fact that their inhabitants, who were mostly Spanish peasants and Creoles, could not aspire to live by trade, except in the cultivation of vines, which came to be the chief economic activity of the region. The soil of the area was eminently suitable for this.

Belén therefore seems to be a town that is atypical of the area. Let us then examine the preceding interpretation in the light of what was really taking place in the town which is the subject of this analysis. It is clear that when Belén was settled by poor people and peasants it was envisaged that Spaniards would be involved in agricultural work. Moreover, the only large landowner was settled on the opposite bank of the river and the Indians were not subject to him but to the crown. That is to say that if ruralism existed it was not due to changes in the available Indian work force, but derived rather from the very nature of the place as determined by those features which have already been mentioned. Belén did not share the commercial quietism characteristic of Catamarca. The active mule traffic, the rearing and wintering of them in the ranches of the district, the transport of goods and people must, surely, have given rise to a number of activities derived from trade which were reflected in the local economic scene.

THE CENSUS OF 1756

The first census of Belén dates from 1756 and was carried out by the alcalde of the holy brotherhood by order of the cabildo of the city of Catamarca. As the demographic information contained in the four censuses which we will analyze (1756, 1770, 1812, and 1869) reflects different census criteria, it is necessary, in dealing with each, to describe briefly the type of data which it contains.

The population investigated by the census of 1756 was of the order of 422 inhabitants including, apart from those living in Belén proper, the estates of Londres and Malfín (today Hualfín). The unit of information is the dwelling-place, following the social differentiation which was already a prominent feature of the community. The only names and surnames which appear are those of the heads of households, and although the sex of everyone is noted, there is no information on the age or occupation of any of the inhabitants. Civil status is mentioned exclusively for the heads of households and the family relationship is specified for the members of the nuclear family and sometimes for other relations who live in the same dwelling, but in the case of "retainers" it is impossible to say for certain whether they have any blood relationship to other members of the household or not.

As mentioned earlier, this census clearly shows the social stratification of Belén. In the foreground are the most important families, usually of officials of rank in the colonial administration or of those heads of households which contain, apart from the nuclear family, other members, like kinsmen, adopted children, and slaves.

Top of the census list is the field marshal, Don Ignacio Herrera. Then follow the four sergeant majors and then nineteen captains, some of whom live on the ranches of Malfín and Londres. Next come six households whose heads are entitled to style themselves *Don* (or *Doña*, as the case might be). These thirty households, with 261 inhabitants, constituted Belén's elite.[9]

Then come the households whose heads have no title or special style of address. They are the common people and the members of the household are, basically, members of the nuclear family.

Last of all come unmarried mothers who, clearly, in the highly religious and narrow society of the rural parts of colonies were considered to be of the very lowest status.

The increase in the population, the introduction of slaves, the taking up of residence by many colonial government officials, all contributed to the hardening of social distinctions. This can be seen from the mention in the census of twenty heads of families with posts in the government, and is equally apparent in the different composition of the various families. That is to say that the important families, those which head the list, are those which have the greater number of members in the categories of retainers, slaves, and adopted individuals (see Table 1). According to Guzmán (1969) the category of "retainers" consisted of poor relations,

[9] It may appear surprising that we refer to as an elite a group of individuals who comprised the majority of the population in 1756. The criteria followed for doing this are based on the range of characteristics which distinguish them from other sections of the population, as is made clear in the text. Furthermore, if we subtract from the total of the elite the numbers of adoptives, slaves, and "retainers" who form part of their households, their number is considerably reduced, to 136.

Table 1.   Family structure in Belén in 1756 (including Londres and Malfín)

Type of family	No. of persons	No. of families	Average census household size	Average no. of retainers, adoptives, slaves, and kinsfolk per household*
Elite	261	30	8.7	4.2
Common people	130	24	5.4	0.2
Unmarried mothers	31	7	4.4	0.1
Total	422	61		

* This category includes 83 kinsfolk and retainers, 32 adoptives, and 16 slaves; 79 (95%) of kinsfolk and retainers, 30 adoptives, and all the slaves pertain to the elite.

the mothers and mothers-in-law of the heads of families, widows, and child-orphans, who occupied an intermediate position in the household between the owners who kept them and the genuine servants.

An examination of Table 1 shows that the average size of the household varies greatly from one social group to another: from 4.4 to 8.7. This difference can be explained almost entirely by the presence of retainers, adoptives, and slaves, since without these groups the figures average between 4.3 and 5.2.

Looking at some of the households in more detail one finds, for instance, that in the household of the captain Baltasar Romero were his wife, his son, and fifteen retainers — seven men and eight women (total 18); in that of the captain Juan de Castro were his wife, his nephew, his slave, his retainers Domingo Ortiz and his wife, his mother-in-law, and twelve others, including her children, nephews and nieces, and grandchildren — five males and seven females (total 19); in the household of Doña Mariana de la Maza, a widow with two children, a son and a daughter, were a slave and four female retainers (total 8); and in that of Don Santiago de Aibar were his wife, a son, a nephew, a slave and his wife, and five retainers — three men and two women (total 11).[10]

Later in the census list there are no slaves, adoptives, or retainers; there are simply nuclear families. Last of all, as has been mentioned, there are women living alone and unmarried mothers.

The census of 1756 provides us with important data on the social reality of the period. According to Guzmán, the notable increase in population was due in part to new settlers arriving from Catamarca and La Rioja. Guzmán, with his deep knowledge of the history of Catamarca, affirms that the majority of the important citizens of the place came originally from the two cities mentioned. Migrating thus to settle in Belén denoted for them a loss of social standing although in their new community they established themselves in the upper echelons (Guzmán 1969). A com-

[10]   There is a total of 16 slaves for the district, only one being an Indian, a woman, Inés, registered in the household of the captain Antonio Liendo.

parison of the figures given at the time of Belén's foundation with those of this census corroborates the view that immigration was the principal factor in population growth.

Of the total population of 422, the bulk resided in Belén, seat of the district and commercial center of the region. By looking at the census of 1770 which we shall analyze later, we can calculate, for the town itself, a population of 316 in 1756. The other 106 lived on the ranches of Malfín and Londres.

To summarize: the demographic and social process which took place in the 78 years between the foundation and the first census was character- ized, in the first instance, by a notable increase owed mostly to immigra- tion. In the second instance (i.e. socially), there is a marked degree of differentiation reflected in the composition of households, in the incorpo- ration of slaves, and in the numerous officials of the crown who carry out duties in the area. The causes behind this double process are to be found in the economic importance of Belén and the area under its jurisdiction, a region of gentle pastures, rich in wheat and maize and in herds of llama and vicuña, centrally situated in the west of Catamarca, and capable of supplying a much greater area.

THE CENSUS OF 1770–1771

In 1770 and 1771 a new census (Acevedo 1965) took place in the whole region of Catamarca, the object being chiefly the need to set up a Mercedarian convent in the capital city. This census followed the same criterion of social stratification as that of 1756. Thus the elite come first, that is to say, the officials of rank, followed by those members of the community entitled to use *Don* as a form of address. Then come the common people, the Indians, and last of all, mulattos. In this census, ages and occupations are also given. The changes which can be seen between this census and the previous one concern the inclusion of the names of wives of heads of households, the separate treatment of Indians and mulattos, and the failure to specify the sex of children, kinsfolk, retainers, and adoptives.

The census gives a total of 737 inhabitants (Table 2). Unlike 1756, there is a separate census for the neighboring settlements of Malfín and Londres, which were found to have 122 inhabitants. Fourteen years earlier these had been included with Belén. If we assume that in this period of time these had remained in the same place of residence, this would mean that the population of Belén, which was 316 in 1756, had more than doubled in a very short space of time. If we calculate a rate of natural increase of 10 per 1000, a reasonable figure for a pretransitional population, this means that at least 75 percent of the growth was due to immigration. Moreover, an examination of the surnames of residents in

Table 2.   Family structure in Belén in 1770–1771

Type of family*	No. of persons	No. of families	Average census household size	Average no. of retainers, adoptives, slaves, and kinsfolk per household
Elite	134	18	7.4†	4.9
Common people	312	66	4.7	0.2
Indians	167	39	4.1	0.3
Mulattos	124	23	5.1	0.7
Totals	737	146		

* The category of unmarried mothers disappeared in 1770.
† The size of the elite family has been inflated by adding the retainers, adoptives, and kinsfolk. Without these, the average census size of the elite family is 2.7.

the two censuses confirms the arrival of various families between 1756 and 1770.

The numbers of "principal houses," those having retainers and adoptives, are lower than in the first census. There are two exceptional cases: the household of the captain Juan de Castro, married with one child, 19 adoptives, and 16 retainers (38 persons in all) and that of Doña Inés de la Masa, single, with 8 retainers and 15 adoptives (24 in all).

In the rest of the population the number of adoptives and retainers is no more than two or three. In the last section in particular, there are only nuclear families. In the section on the mulattos, there is a single family with four adoptives and it is, surprisingly, that of Lucas Balboa, presumably the bastard descendant of the captain Lucas Balboa who figures in the census of 1756. He is the only Balboa to appear in this census, although this family, residing in Belén, came to wield great political, economic, and social power in the whole western part of Catamarca in the first half of the nineteenth century.

The number of adoptives and retainers is higher for the elite families than in the previous census. In the case of the Indian and mulatto families there are no adoptives except in the case mentioned earlier. This is important because the ability to house, in a state of semidependence, a considerable number of individuals, is directly related to the means of the head of the family. This leads us to another aspect of the census which is significant for the light it throws on the living conditions of the community. Although in 1756 there is mention of only one Indian woman, fourteen years later, 167 Indians are listed occupying 39 households. It might be supposed that the Indians from the left bank of the river had moved to the right bank, but the facts suggest that this increase was also due to migration. In effect, the surname Chanampa disappears and new ones arise, like Cusapa (the name of the cacique), La Jampa, and Chacana. There are also other individuals classified as Indians but having Spanish names like Carrizo, Cabrera, Rodriguez, Martínez, and so on. The number of mulatto families is given as 23. There is no record of slaves. Demographic data complemented by a document from the period allow us to draw a picture of what Belén was like at the end of the eighteenth century with an elite who controlled agriculture, textiles, and trade and a large lower stratum which depended for its existence on the work provided for it by the minority. The ownership of great stretches of land, for example, was fixed by the system of emphyteusis. That is to say that only the left bank of the river and sections to the south and the north of the town remained outside the emphyteutic system. And land was a capital asset if one wanted to sell crops outside the parish. In addition, trade and the transportation of goods, for which mule trains were required, presupposed the wherewithal to secure the animals and staff to attend them. A document of 1772 confirms that it was the elite who were actively involved in traveling. It is the same document that petitions for the status of the place to be raised to that of *villa* and, in it, it is stated that the request was supported by all the most distinguished citizens whose names did not appear because they were all "away on their travels."

The mention of this petition is important since it provides us with further information. The inhabitants of Belén had acquired an awareness of the importance of their settlement and on April 3, 1772, the priest and citizens petitioned the governor of the Tucumán for the creation of the *villa* of Belén. The intention is clearly to acquire greater political and administrative control since a *villa* was almost the equivalent of a city. To support their request, they describe the area's products. Thus, they say that wine and wheat are the most important crops, which they supply to Salta and Tucumán, and they also mention the "growing trade in vicuña." Evidently, the products of Belén now went beyond the limits of western Catamarca and were already entering into an important region of the northwest.

THE CENSUS OF 1812

Toward the end of the colonial period, the stability and economic importance of Belén were much in evidence. Between 1770 and the next census in 1812, the population increased from 737 to 1,276, that is to say, there was a mean annual rate of increase of 13 per 1,000. The census of 1812, the motives for which are not at all clear, was meant to include the area covered by the whole viceroyalty of La Plata. This objective was not realized (Maeder 1968–1969:217–249).

The demographic information contained in this census is more detailed than that of the two previous ones. For the first time, the ages of all the inhabitants are given (there are no cases of ages being unknown). Civil status and place of origin are also given as are occupations of males. In the case of females, the only occupation recorded is that of servant. The population is grouped into classes according to whether they are

Spaniards, freedmen, or slaves, and in a section headed *"pardos* and *morenos"** there are mestizos, negroes, mulattos, and Indians.

Unfortunately it is virtually impossible to distinguish one household from another. The list is so composed that there is no notion of family continuity; surnames are frequently repeated, and it is not often possible to decide if groups of two or three persons constitute a separate household or are retainers in another. Nevertheless, the criterion of stratification is maintained, given that at the head of the census list appear the large Spanish households with numerous slaves and adoptives, while the mestizos and free mulattos are given in the final section.

Despite the limited nature of the data, and in view of the fact that age and sex are recorded, we are able to deduce from this census that the importance of the textile industry had been clearly established and that, because of this, Belén had acquired a predominantly female population, a characteristic which was to be maintained in all subsequent censuses.

As can be seen in Table 3 under "index of masculinity" there is a high percentage of women. When the age pyramids are analyzed it is also clear that the surplus in the number of women between the ages of 20 and 29 is

Table 3.   The age of the population of Belén (by sex) in the census of 1812

Age groups	Men (*M*)	Women (*W*)	Index of masculinity (*M/W*)
0–9	212	196	103
10–19	134	168	80
20–29	91	174	52
30–39	66	82	80
40–49	26	41	63
50–59	23	24	96
60–69	10 ⎫	17 ⎫	
70–79	7 ⎬ 18	3 ⎬ 21	86
80 and over	1 ⎭	1 ⎭	
Total	570	706	82

an indication of female immigration. The high proportion of women in the key age categories for employment is a reflection of the economic drawing-power which the textile industry exercised over the workers of the region. This predominance of women naturally has an effect on the number of marriages (see Table 4). It can also be seen that the population of Belén was an extremely young one, as might be expected in a pretransitional period when both the birth and death rates were high. However, even here, in important differential percentages, the effect of women's immigration can be seen (see Table 5).

---

* The words *pardo* and *moreno*, for which English has no exact equivalents, indicate degrees of racial mixing in which the individual is more than half white. — *Translator.*

Table 4. Civil state of the population aged 15 and over, by sex, Belén, 1812

Civil state	Men		Women		Total	
	No.	%	No.	%	No.	%
Single	143	51.4	213	49.9	356	50.5
Married	124	44.6	152*	35.6*	276	39.1
Widowed	11	4.0	62	14.5	73	10.4
Total adults (15+)	278	100.0	427	100.0	705	100.0
Children (0–14)	292		279		571	
Total	570		706		1276	

* The greater number of married women as opposed to married men can be attributed to temporary absence of men in connection with the selling of goods.

Table 5. Distribution of the population according to age, Belén, 1812

Age	Men		Women		Total	
	No.	%	No.	%	No.	%
0–14	292	51.2	279	39.5	571	44.8
15–54	251	44.0	399	56.5	650	50.9
Over 55	27	4.8	28	4.0	55	4.3
Total	570	100.0	706	100.0	1276	100.0

Maeder, in his study of the demographic situation in Catamarca in 1812, made the following comments with regard to the province:

The decline of the colored population (as had also taken place in Córdoba) together with the parallel increase in whites suggested a levelling off of ethnic terms, a progressive "whitening" that was making inroads, given the weight of prejudices and restrictions still in force. This decline occurred notably in the rural areas and amongst the "free" individuals in that the number of slaves had increased in small proportion over the figures of 1778 (Maeder 1968–1969).

We do not have the corresponding data for Belén for 1778, but a comparison with the census of 1812 clearly shows a process of "whitening" as indicated by this author (see Table 6).

The distribution of male occupations, according to figures from the same

Table 6. The distribution of population by ethnic group, Belén 1812

Group	No. of men	No. of women	Total	
			No.	%
Spanish	69	93	162	12.6
Indian	44	41	85	6.7
Mulatto	169	221	390	30.3
Mestizo	282	344	626	49.4
Black	6	7	13	1.0
Total	570	706	1276	100.0

census, is interesting in that it shows a relative lack of diversification with a high percentage of men involved in agricultural work (see Table 7).

Table 7.   Distribution of male occupations, Belén, 1812

Occupation	No.	%
Farmers	64	22
Laborers	204	70
Others*	22	8
Total	290	100.0

* This category includes 7 shoemakers, 2 silversmiths, 3 carpenters, 3 merchants, 1 painter, 1 hatmaker, 3 blacksmiths, and 2 taverners.

THE CENSUS OF 1869

The first national census differs further in the type of demographic data which it contains. Apart from name, age, surname, sex, civil status, place of birth, literacy, and legitimacy, it records, for the first time, the distribution of both male and female occupations. This last serves to confirm the overwhelming importance of weaving in the economy of the area.

From what we have shown of the demographic structure as reavealed by the census of 1812, it is possible to see that this was substantially maintained in the decades that followed. In 1869 there is the same numerical superiority of women, although Belén had had a sustained growth. In the 57 years between these two censuses, the rate of growth per annum was 15 per 1,000, but the index of masculinity is almost identical to that of 1812. Nevertheless, as can be seen from Table 8 and Figure 1, there are some changes in the age structure of the female population. The greatest change can be seen in the fact that the age range recorded by the 1869 census can be depicted much more in the form of a normal pyramid. This

Table 8.   Ages of the population of Belén according to sex, 1869

Age groups	Men (M)	Women (W)	Index of masculinity (M/W)
0–9	445	511	87
10–19	376	415	91
20–29	199	303	66
30–39	161	213	76
40–49	93	140	66
50–59	46	67	69
60–69	32 ⎫	38 ⎫	
70–79	11 ⎬ 52	18 ⎬ 73	71
80 and over	9 ⎭	17 ⎭	
Total	1372	1722	80

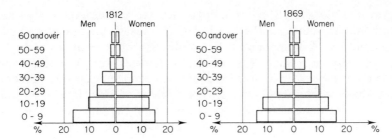

Figure 1.   The age and structure of the population of Belén, 1812 and 1869

could be attributed to the fact that the census was more carefully conducted, but equally it suggests that female immigration had come to an
end (Table 9, Table 10).

Table 9.   Distribution of the population according to age, Belén, 1869

Age	Men		Women		Total	
	No.	%	No.	%	No.	%
0–14	680	49.6	718	41.7	1398	45.2
15–54	625	45.5	911	52.9	1536	49.6
Over 55	67	4.9	93	5.4	160	5.2
Total	1372	100.0	1722	100.0	3094	100.0

Table 10.   Civil status of the population over 15, by sex, Belén, 1869

Status	Men		Women		Total	
	No.	%	No.	%	No.	%
Single	388	56.0	576	57.4	964	56.8
Married	273	39.5	307	30.6	580	34.2
Widowed	31	4.5	121	12.0	152	9.0
Total adults (15+)	692	100.0	1004	100.0	1696	100.0
Children (0–14)	680		718		1398	
Total	1372		1722		3094	

The ending of immigration could have been due to the growth of the
town and the relative stability of the textile industry. We could argue that
the population, higher now, and with improved productivity, was enough
to satisfy the needs of this traditional industry. A synthesis of the annual
rates of growth between all the Belén censuses, even allowing for errors
and regarding the figures as only approximate, makes it necessary to
single out the enormous difference between the rate for the period
1756–1770 and those of later periods. The fact is that, in the 14 years
between the first and second census, the annual rate was 57 per thousand,

between 1770 and 1812 (an interval of 42 years) the rate was 13 per thousand, and between 1812 and 1869 (57 years), the rate was 15 per thousand. An examination of the distribution of occupations makes it immediately clear that 75.3 percent of females were in occupations directly to the textile industry is composed of spinners, *teleras* [general that a high proportion (77 percent) of women and girls 10 years old and over was economically active, while for men of the same age range the proportion was 72 percent (see Table 12). Both represent very high rates of employment.

The figure of 75.3 percent for females in occupations connected directly to the textile industry is composed of spinners, *teleras* [general workers], and weavers responsible for different stages in the cloth-

Table 11.   Distribution of female occupations, Belén, 1869

Occupation	No.		%	
Teleras	239 ⎤		25.7 ⎤	
Spinners	385 ⎬ 700		41.4 ⎬ 75.3	
Weavers	76 ⎦		8.2 ⎦	
Seamstresses	115		12.4	
Servants	36 ⎤		3.9 ⎤	
Laundresses	33 ⎬ 94		3.5 ⎬ 10.1	
Cooks	25 ⎦		2.7 ⎦	
Bakers*	9		1.0	
Others†	11		1.2	
Total	929		100.0	

* Or "kneaders," women responsible for preparing the dough for the household's bread.
† This category includes 3 tradeswomen, 2 "nurses," 2 servants, 2 bakerwomen, 1 potter, and 1 vendor.

Table 12.   Distribution of male occupations, Belén, 1869

Occupation	No.	%
Laborers	354	52.7
Day workers	61	9.1
Drovers	43	6.4
Firewoodmen	40	6.0
Shoemakers	32	4.8
Peasants	25	3.7
Traders	24	3.6
Carpenters	14	2.1
Hatmakers	10	1.5
Servants	9	1.3
Others*	60	8.8
Total	672	100.0

* This category includes: 7 butchers, 5 tavernkeepers, 5 masons, 5 blacksmiths, 4 tailors, 3 shepherds, 3 employees, 3 plaiters, 3 butlers, 3 priests, 2 silversmiths, 2 textile workers, 2 spinners, 2 ranchers, 2 teachers, 1 miller, 1 *petaquero* (*petaca* is a leather trunk for carrying articles), 1 miner, 1 baker, 1 violinist, 1 bleeder, 1 cooper, 1 gardener, and 1 foreman.

making process. One of the first tasks, the spinning of llama, vicuña, or sheep wool, was done, and continues to be done, by hand, using a spindle. Another, the weaving, was performed on rustic, Creole looms, which are also still in use today. Cloth artisans could specialize in one or the other. The *teleras* were the nonspecialists who worked at various stages in the textile production process.

Of the male population 62 percent are engaged in agriculture (see Table 12). Characteristically, this distribution of the labor force has predominated until today. Even though women were controlling almost all aspects of textile production (if less of the distribution to which we will refer again later), men were working in small irrigated lots or as day workers in the few latifundia of the zone.

The census data of 1869 on the work structure show Belén to be a typical rural town with an exceptionally high rate of female employment, this last feature being its distinguishing characteristic. The small number of male occupations, besides agricultural work, indicates that it was through the textile industry that the inhabitants provided for their basic needs of food and clothing. But Belén, from its foundation, had always been a community with an external orientation and the bustling commercial and trading scene is described in detail in the almost contemporary account of Federico Espeche (1875), an expert on the region. He attests to the high degree of commercial activity in the second half of the nineteenth century, as well as to the importance of the weaving trade in the community:

The products of the soil and those of the hand of man are known even in the neighboring provinces. Flour is exported to the fort of Andalgalá and Tucumán. Alcoholic beverages go to Bolivia; dried fruit, sweets, and so on, to the ranches of Santa María and the province of Salta; and fresh fruits, grapes, and peaches are transported in sacks of soft straw (*chiguas*) on the backs of mules. In exchange, Belén receives money, cows, sheep, wool, and dried meat.

Bullocks and sheep are exported to Chile, after wintering in the alfalfa fields around Belén. Mules and donkeys are sent to Bolivia and Peru. Manufactured goods are bought from Chile and Andalgalá. Hides go to Tucumán in exchange for leather and shoes (1875:346).

The same author praises the high quality of the textile products of Belén:

The textiles of Belén are known even in Europe. The highly-valued mantles of Catamarcan vicuña wool come from this region whose woven goods are unsurpassed by those of any other province of the interior or the north of the republic. Articles in other wools are equally good. Here they weave the famous *cordillate*, a sort of cashmere. Everyone who has seen this material has desired to possess a suit of it.

The quality of the wool in this part of the province and the skill of the women weavers of Belén almost compensates for the lack of facilities for the manufacture of these products, which is achieved using totally inadequate procedures. [This is a reference to hand-spinning and weaving on rough, homemade looms, both of which make the manufacture of cloth a long and tiring process.] This dominant industry is completely in the hands of women (1875:347).

The population of Belén which, throughout this period, had a class structure characterized by marked social differences, also secured luxury articles for itself. In the eighteenth century the so-called "merchant-dealers" were already traveling to Belén and widely throughout the northwestern region, supplying a wide range of products, as well as slaves, from Buenos Aires, Chile, and Peru. Guzmán mentions several of them who resided in Belén and regarded it as their center of operations. The list of articles available is interesting:

They bring jewelry, pearls, gold bars, silver in all forms, expensive books, Spanish guitars, English violins. . . . Apart from materials and goods from Spain, Italy, England, Holland, and so on, they also bring patterns which show us, down to the smallest detail, the latest dress fashions for both men and women. They also sell arms, firearms like shotguns, blunderbusses, and pistols, as well as swords, dress swords, cutlasses, and daggers (Guzman n.d).

Although we have information on economic activity and on the persistence of the textile industry, the historical sources do not include descriptions of the social system of Belén during the second half of the nineteenth century. In this regard, a social anthropology study (Hermitte and Herrán 1970) carried out in the community allows us to reconstruct certain features of life in Belén at this time. By this time textile production had become specialized and consisted of products made of llama and vicuña wool. Cotton products were no longer made because of competition from imported articles together with the high cost of freight to and from the markets. *Cordillate* suffered the same fate shortly afterward.

The principal markets for textile products were Catamarca, Tucumán, and Salta, and the vast distances between them meant that distribution costs were very high. The journey to Salta took twelve days, that to the city of Catamarca five days. The journeys by mule were difficult in winter because of the intense cold, but it was the only season of the year when any travel was possible in the north because the summer temperature was almost intolerable.

The organization of these trips was in the hands of a small group, mule-train owners, who were able to meet the cost of equipment, feeding the animals, payment of taxes, maintenance of attendant staff, and so on. Equipping a profitable trading expedition meant that there had to be a large enough quantity of products to ensure that the cost of the enterprise did not exceed receipts from their sale. Informants tell us that up until the beginning of the twentieth century, only a small number of "wealthy gentlemen" were able to become involved in the running of these uncertain ventures. These men, in addition to being merchants and landholders, also employed and controlled a considerable dependent work force consisting of peasants who spun and wove vicuña and llama wool and laborers who worked the land. The growing value of textile products, and the fact that nearly the whole output was marketed outside the community, meant that they soon became the principal source of revenue, trade, and wealth in Belén.

The nature of the system of production and distribution of textiles cemented a system of patronage, which, with certain modifications, continues to this day. The raw materials for weaving, vicuña skins and llama wool, come from the animals' natural habitat in the mountainous regions to the north of the district of Belén. The difficulty of access to these raw materials as well as the marketing of finished products in distant places meant that the craftswoman was dependent on someone who could take care of both these aspects. She also came to rely on the support and material security (for example, in providing food and so on) which characterize patronage systems. The *patrón*, for his part, had access to the skills of the textile worker, her chief resources, and thus to a product of immense value which could be exchanged for articles which Belén needed.

We have, therefore, a class system with a small number of landowners/farmers simultaneously involved in business, and a large majority of workers dependent on them. The independent weaver was almost nonexistent if we exclude certain women of good social position who wove themselves but also employed peasants. We have collected from the area accounts of journeys to the city of Catamarca at the end of the nineteenth century in which the wives of leading men of the town took part with the object of selling vicuña shawls there. This upper class also included some descendants of early settlers who owned large estates and who, let us repeat, were actively involved in business, and some recent arrivals who had succeeded in making money quickly and, by marrying the daughters of the local upper class, had reinforced their status in this provincial society. The fact that both names and surnames were recorded in the national census allows us to establish who was who in the community at this time.

The continued production of goods which could not be replaced by imported articles ensured overall demographic and economic stability in the period with which we are concerned. Only toward the end of the nineteenth century was there any marked exodus of men when the sugar industry in Tucumán became important and started to recruit labor from outside that province. The twentieth century has seen a growing tendency toward male emigration, many of the men taking up permanent settlement in Buenos Aires or in Comodoro Rivadavia.

Several conclusions emerge from this examination of the demographic and social history of Belén:

1. Although it was a colonial settlement of late establishment, with the usual stratification of whites, Indians, mestizos, and negroes, it rapidly evolved into a homogeneous Creole settlement by the end of the eighteenth century.

2. Its central position for interregional trade turned it into an important distribution center for western Catamarca. By a happy coincidence this favorable economic situation was combined with the fact that the region of Belén was the home of herds of vicuña and llamas. This contributed to its emergence as one of the most important textile towns of the region.

3. The dryness of the climate, which makes land cultivation very risky, together with the dedication of lands to the church, functioned as a brake on local agricultural enterprise and made the importance of the textile industry still more decisive.

4. The concentration of textile production in the hands of women gave rise to a very special situation. In the first place, this skill allowed women to enter into patron–client relationships. Although it is the case that not all the clients were women, they nevertheless formed a high percentage of those dependent on the support and mediation of patrons of privileged status.

5. Throughout its history, Belén's cultural tradition has accepted that weaving is a specifically female activity, while agriculture and other occupations are defined as belonging to men.

6. Men's traditional activities, restricted by ecological limitations and the existence of favorable alternatives for them outside Belén, meant that there was no incentive to redefine masculine as opposed to feminine occupations within the community.

7. It was the presence of craft industries which brought an important section of the population to Belén in the first place. Yet the exodus of men from the community has been characteristic of all historical epochs and, from the end of the nineteenth century, it increased as new centers of work developed outside the town.

8. Textile production, characterized by a system of tied labor up to the beginning of the twentieth century, has been modified into many different forms of patronage allowing some independence, however relative, to many weavers.

9. The numerical importance of households headed by women and composed of blood relations is not accidental in this economic system, given that a domestic group centered round a single mother and her daughters is a very viable unit of production in which the more or less sporadic presence of the man does not fundamentally alter the mother's dominance.

We have chosen to close this analysis with a look at the first national census of 1869, since, by this time, the economic and social system which this study describes had been definitively established in Belén. The continued importance of textile work and patronage, somewhat modified, but still in force to this day, has been the subject of a study which we have summarized briefly here to illustrate some of the salient features of the social system as it now exists (Hermitte and Herrán 1970).

Belén is the chief town of the department of the same name. Its population, according to data contained in the national census of 1970, is 6,100. As far as its economy is concerned, the cultivation of some crops, especially cereals, and a few other crops like cumin, anise, and pimento grown commercially, and the weaving of ponchos and shawls of vicuña and llama wool continue to be important. This last industry still principally involves female labor, although there are a few male weavers, and takes place within the household. The peons of the past who went to their employer's house and were there given the wool for their day's weaving have virtually disappeared. There is, without doubt, a great variety in the level, quality, and rhythm of production, depending on access to markets. The producers can be summarized in three broad categories. The first corresponds to the least favored position in the stages of production and marketing — those weavers who work for others and perform one or more tasks in the textile process. Having no capital, they are totally without access to raw materials, and the problem of marketing does not exist for them because at no stage are they the owners of the product. The second includes a large group of craftswomen who could perhaps be subdivided still further although the differences within this category do not fundamentally alter the stages of production or marketing. We include within this group those weavers who have access to labor inside their own domestic circle, where clearly a larger number of females would make for greater productivity. They may also have family contacts outside the community who could help with the obtaining of raw materials and the marketing of the finished product. In spite of all this, the great mass of products is sold to local monopolists who then supply the credit necessary to continue production and to acquire basic necessities. The third group consists of a minority, who could almost be defined as "weaver owners," who have access to labor from outside their domestic circle. Consequently, their rate of production is much higher and they compete directly in the national market where they have stable clients. They are also able to secure bank credits, a facility beyond the reach of the small-scale producer. This type of textile worker does not depend on local monopolists in any way. The fringes of these categories are not rigid and upward mobility, although difficult, can occur when there is a convergence of other circumstances which allow greater production and better marketing. The opposite process, downward mobility, also occurs.

Marketing of textile products on a national scale presents distribution problems similar to those of the last century. This situation restricts the small producer whose need to establish contacts explains the persistence of the system of patronage. However, different factors have brought about changes which point to cracks in the system, as, for example, the increase in the number of patrons per individual and growing differentiation in the social origins of patrons. This results in greater freedom, albeit still partial, in the marketing of textiles. As far as the need for more than one patron is concerned, it is easy to understand how the growing complexity of life in the town has meant that the needs of producers have been increased. New requirements, of greater complexity and variety, for the circulation of goods and services have resulted in a system of plural patronage, since a single client may need more than one patron in order to obtain the services previously supplied by a single individual. The strategic positions for the assumption of this role have been modified and some professionals whose services are indispensable and an increased number of business men resident in Belén have entered the ranks of those who sponsor textile production.

REFERENCES

ACEVEDO, EDBERTO OSCAR
1965   "Situación social y religiosa de Catamarca, 1770–1771," in *Primer congreso de historia de Catamarca con motivo de la fundación de la ciudad de Londres de Catamarca, 1558—1596*. Edited by the Junta de Estudies Históricos de Catamarca. Catamarca.
CONI, EMILIO
1939   "La agricultura, ganaderías e industrias hasta el virreinato," in *Historia de la nación Argentina*, volume four, part one. Edited by Ricardo Levene, 357–371. Buenos Aires: El Ateneo.
ESPECHE, FEDERICO
1875   *La provincia de Catamarca*. Buenos Aires: M.Biedma.
GUZMÁN, GASPAR H.
1969   Los comienzos de Belén y el censo de 1756. *Diario La Unión*. June 15. Catamarca.
n.d.   "Catamarca en el siglo XVIII: mercaderes tratantes y Portuguesas." Unpublished manuscript.
HERMITTE, ESTHER, CARLOS HERRÁN
1970   ¿Patronazgo o cooperativismo? Obstáculos a la modificación del sistema de interacción social en una comunidad del noroeste Argentino. *Revista Latinoamericana de Sociología* 6 (2):293–317.
LAFONE QUEVEDO, SAMUEL
1879   "Pueblo de Belén: institución para su fundación y disposiciones de la comisión del poder ejecutivo." Tomadas del las Publicaciones Oficiales. Catamarca. Unpublished document.
LARROUY, ANTONIO, *compiler*
1915   *Documentos relativos a Nuestra Señora del Valle*, volume one: *1591–1764*. Buenos Aires: Compañía Sudamericana de Billetes del Banco.

LARROUY, ANTONIO, MANUEL SORIA
1921 *Album de autonomía Catamarqueña.* Catamarca.
LIZONDO BORDA, MANUEL
1939 "El Tucumán de los siglos XVII y XVIII," in *Historia de la nación Argentina*, volume three. Edited by Ricardo Levene, 389–419. Buenos Aires: El Ateneo.
MAEDER, ERNESTO J. A.
1968–1969 "El censo de 1812 en la historia demográfica de Catamarca," in *Anuario del Instituto de Investigaciones Históricas*, volume ten, 217–249 Rosario: Facultad de Filosofía, Universidad Nacional de Rosario.
OLMOS, RAMÓN R.
1957 *Historia de Catamarca.* Catamarca: La Unión.

An Ecological Perspective of Socioterritorial Organization Among the Tehuelche in the Nineteenth Century

E. GLYN WILLIAMS

The purpose of this paper is to reinvestigate the socioterritorial organiza-tion of the Tehuelche in the light of some new historical evidence and the recent rapid theoretical advance in the study of hunting and gathering cultures. An ecological approach is employed and " sense" is made out of the available historical information. In contrast to earlier statements about the Tehuelche it is concluded that the population was divided into six major units which in turn consisted of about four small bands number-ing about seventy. Patrilocal residence and patrilineal inheritance applied only to the caciques and it would appear that the remainder of the popu-lation followed a bilateral affiliation and were extremely fluid in their band membership.

Among the most neglected areas of the study of native cultures in the Americas is that which pertains to the southernmost part of the continent. Within what is commonly known as Patagonia there existed until recently a variety of cultures which subsisted mainly by hunting and gathering. Among them were the nomadic Tehuelche who occupied most of what now constitutes the Argentine provinces of Chubut and Santa Cruz. While a considerable body of information exists in the writings of the early European explorers of Patagonia, the anthropologists who have made use of such information in an attempt to recreate a picture of the culture prior to its disappearance have been slow to write a comprehen-sive ethnohistory of the native people of the region. Among the most notable exceptions was John M. Cooper who wrote extensively about the Tehuelche (1925, 1946). Yet Cooper was writing at a time when our theoretical knowledge about the social structure of nomadic hunting and gathering societies was limited. In this paper I would like to consider two aspects of Tehuelche culture, their territoriality and their acculturation with the neighboring Araucanian population in the light of recent theoretical insights about these concepts, and in so doing I would also like to draw upon ethnohistorical information that has come to light in recent years.

Since 1965 several volumes containing the fruits of recent research into hunting and gathering societies have emerged (Leeds and Vayda 1965; Lee and DeVore 1968; Bicchieri 1972) and several themes appear in the contents. Among the most prominent of these themes are, on the one hand, the relationship between hunting and gathering as an economic mode and the nature of the physical environment; and on the other, the development, out of this relationship, of specific forms of social and territorial organization. Clearly the focus of such an interest involves an ecological stance which emphasizes the continual process of human adaptation in response to variations in the physical resource base. Since there is a tendency for studies to refer to hunting and gathering as a spatially diffuse but specific mode of production it is not surprising that the above themes have been given predominance. Furthermore, in attempting to reconstruct models of society on the basis of historical documentation it is this type of material rather than that pertaining to factors such as religious or kinship organization that is invariably the most reliable and most extensively documented. In light of the theoretical sophistication and the resultant clarification of the adaptive response involved in hunting and gathering it is appropriate to reconsider the historical documentation available about such societies. An attempt will be made to create a generative model that will account for some of the elements of social organization and culture that derive from the specific adaptation.

PHYSICAL ENVIRONMENT

The area occupied by the Tehuelche at the end of the eighteenth century appears to have extended from the Río Negro in the north almost to the Strait of Magellan in the south (de Viedma 1836:42; d'Orbigny 1839:vol. 2, p. 95). Within this area the main ecological distinctions are found on an east–west rather than a north–south axis. In the east lies the Patagonian plateau with only the deeply entrenched river valleys interrupting the seemingly level plain. Some 550 kilometers inland in the north, and some 400 kilometers inland in the south, a series of low hills are encountered but the vegetation remains little changed until one reaches the Andean foothills where, in a matter of 50 kilometers or less a change from dry scrub to lush alpine vegetation is encountered.

It should therefore be clear that the region is broadly divided into two climatic zones, the semiarid east and humid west. The aridity of the east is partly a result of its location within the Andean rain shadow, but more importantly it is the result of the cold offshore Atlantic current which tends to cool the impinging air masses to the extent that it inhibits the possibility of rain when the cyclonic storms pass over the land mass. As a result, the average annual rainfall is of the order of 204 mm. (Galmarini and Raffo del Campo 1965), showing little variation between north and south. In some years the contact of the western and eastern air masses produces a series of long-lasting frontal storms which drastically affect such "average" figures.

To the west the warm Pacific current produces a land-sea pressure variation which produces moist air masses that move eastward, their ascent over the Andes producing extremely heavy relief rainfall. To the east of the Andean range rainfall incidence drops off rapidly, the eastern pre-Andean depression having about 600 mm. of rainfall annually, although this figure is subject to considerable fluctuation. In contrast, the mountain peaks may receive as much as 4,500 mm. of rain annually (de Aparicio and Difrieri 1958:74).

The offshore currents have an ameliorating effect upon Patagonian temperatures, serving to reduce annual temperature variation in such high latitudes. The average summer temperatures vary from 10°C to 15°C while the equivalent mean winter temperatures range from 0°C to 5°C. There is a difference of about 5°C between the average annual temperatures of northern and southern Patagonia. Within the pre-Andean depression the average annual temperature is of the order of 8.8°C while the average maximum temperature recorded for January and July were 6.6°C and −0.9°C respectively. On average, 102 days of frost are recorded annually. These temperatures are influenced by the wind system with the mild temperatures in such a southerly latitude resulting to a great extent from the weakness of the polar winds. Yet the winds tend to be extremely strong and, blowing as they do predominantly from the west, they have been compared with foehn winds.

The relationship between rainfall and vegetation is particularly apparent within the region. The arid areas are characterized by what is known as "shrub steppe" with the scrub cover being fairly dense in places. The grey-brown sandy loam of the Patagonian plateau supports a high proportion of shrubbery growth which can achieve a height of five feet although it is usually only about two or three feet high. The shrubs consist predominantly of Compositae or Leguiminosae with the following being among the more common species: *Prosopis strombulifera, Cassia iphylla, Lepidophyllum, Verbena tridens*, and *Nardophyllum kingii*. Within the incised valleys the *Berberis* species (*B. boxifolia, B. heterophylla*) are common as are the *Stipa* grasses.

Within the pre-Andean and Andean zone little if any virgin vegetation remains on account of the recent burning practices of the native population. Within the low-lying *Festuca* zone the vegetation is characterized by short grass steppe which includes such species as *Stipa speciosa, S.*

hueritis, *S. chrysophylla*, *Poa lihularis*, *Mulinu spinosum*, and *Berberis empetrifolia*. To the east the vegetation deteriorates in quality and quantity with distribution becoming so sparse that only about fifty percent of the soil surface is covered by vegetation at longitude 71°. However, to the west vegetation increases in density with altitude. Between 1500 and 3000 feet one finds the southern beech (*Northofagus dombeyi*) while the species *Northofagus piemilio* grows above 3000 feet. Invading the *Northofagus* zone are smaller bushes of *Libocedrus* which serve to increase vegetation density (Rosevane 1948; Davies 1940).

The wild-animal population responds to this variation in the physical environment. Some have their ecological niches while others move over the entire range of environments in response to seasonal changes. It was this response together with the availability of vegetative food sources that patterned the temporal movements of the Tehuelche. Most important of the land fauna to the Tehuelche were the guanaco (*Lama guanicoe*) and the rhea (*Rhea darwin*). The guanaco tend to migrate in small herds consisting of an adult male and four to thirty females, in small herds of young males, or more rarely in larger herds of about 100.[1] Variation in number results from a tendency to group by sex during the breeding season. It seems that a stronger male attempts to protect a large number of females, while weaker males form small bands until the mating season when they attack the major bands and carry off a few females each, only to lose them again later in renewed fights with stronger males (Musters 1871:131).

The young guanaco were born during October, this being the time when they were most widely sought by the Tehuelche. The rhea often moves among the guanaco and here again one also finds groups consisting of several females and a single male migrating together. The male incubates the eggs which usually number over twenty, being produced by several females.

Among the other animals sought were the puma (*Felis concolor*),[2] which, being a predator, tended to follow the guanaco and rhea; the armadillo (*Zaedyus unicultas*); the huemal (*Hippocamelus bisulcus*); the wild cat (*On. aloffroyi*); the fox (*Ps. gracilis patagonicus*); the quirquincho (*Zaedyus pichiy*); hares (*Dolichotis patagonica*); animals called *cuyaconicha*, *chines*, and *xuimps*; and grouse. Many of these were restricted to the cordilleran zone and were not very important as food sources (UCNW Library n.d.:ms. 7668). This was also true of wild cattle which appear to have sought refuge from the hunters in the Andean forests during the first half of the nineteenth century (Musters 1871:160). The horse also appears to have been the source of considerable meat on

[1]   Referring to the Santa Cruz area Darwin (1836) commented on guanaco herds ranging in size from 50 to 100 animals with one large herd of 500 being noted.
[2]   In addition to eating the meat of the puma its skin was regarded as ideal for making saddles, mantles, and leg coverings in that it was held to be extremely water-repellant.

vital occasions (de Viedma 1836:65). In terms of products related to the commercial contact with the European population the mountain cat, skunk, and ostrich appear to have been most important (Vignati 1936:605). During the summer in the Andean zone the eggs of various lacustrine fowl, including the upland goose (*Chloëphaga leucoptera*) and yellow-billed goose (*Cygnus caseotoba*), were consumed (Musters 1871:102).

A considerable amount of the food supply derived from vegetative sources but the information in the various historical documents is not always sufficient to facilitate exact identification. Furthermore, it is impossible to ascertain an accurate ratio of food derived from animal and vegetative sources, especially since this varied from time to time during the year. A variety of tuberous roots were gathered, one of the most important of which was *yareta* (*Bolax* and *Azorella* species), which was eaten roasted and boiled. Vignati (1941) claims that *Bolax gummifera* was employed to make a form of bread, and he is supported by evidence that the seeds of some vegetables were roasted and ground into a flour. Also important was the potato (*Solanum tuberosum*) which abounds in the precordilleran zone. Among the other identified plants which were gathered are *Chenopodium quinoa*, chalia (*Tropaeolum patagonicum*) pambay (*Cymnera seabra*), kelhala (*Azorella glebaria*), macachi (*Arjona tuberosa*), molle (*Schinus molle fotus primatus*), ugui (*Myrtus boxifolia*), colius (*Aundo* species), boighe (*Winterania antartica*), theyge (*Salix chilensis*), chamar (*Lucuma spinosa*), huancu (*Ceratonia chilensis*), abedul (*Betula antartica*), mushrooms (*Cyttarium* species), chivivia [parsnip] (*Pastinaca sativa*), *Scirpus tatora*, and *S. riparius*. Other plants have been described in European terms and include spinach, parsley, celery, dandelions, and rhubarb. Although this by no means exhausts the range of plant food consumed it does serve to demonstrate the degree of diversity.

In season, fruit was also an important supplement to the diet with the *calafate* (*Berberis boxifolia*) being the most sought after since it was not only eaten raw but mixed with water as a drink. Also employed to make a drink was the *dropas del incienso* (*Schinus* species), while the rind of the algarroba, the honey mesquite (*Prosopis* species), was alleged to have been ground and mixed with water to make a form of cake. Vignati (1936:602) refers to the use of crushed and fermented apples to produce a wine but in all likelihood this was a later trait adopted from the Araucanians. The other fruits consumed included strawberries (*Fragaria* species), algarroba (*Prosopis denudans*), algorrobito (*Pr. campestris*), a fruit resembling the blackberry called *con*, the myrtle berry, which was called *yamgar*, and another resembling the cranberry which went under a variety of names including *col*, *potenc*, and *belco*. As in the case of the many root crops, these were restricted to the precordilleran zone during the months October, November, and December.

ECONOMY

The nomadic nature of the Tehuelche was related to their movement in search of the game, vegetable plants, and fruit which served as the basis of their subsistence (see Table 1). Thus not only did the nature of their diet vary from one season to another but it also depended upon the exploitation of a variety of ecological settings. The various ecological settings were to a great extent dictated by the manner in which the animal population migrated in search of its own subsistence.

The main animal food source derived from the hunting of the guanaco and the ostrich, both of which also contributed considerably to essential nonfood resources. The severity of the Andean winters drove both species eastward to the milder plateau areas, this being primarily responsible for the nomadic patter of the Tehuelche life-style. Other food sources, important though they were, were supplementary to guanaco and rhea meat.

Rhea meat was preferred to that of the guanaco (Pritchard 1902:100), and the guanaco was not eaten unless the stay was long or the rhea scarce (Musters 1871:78). Much of the pursuit of guanacos was related to the use of their skins to make *quillangos*, the skins of about 13 young guanacos being required to make a single *quillango*. Since these were exchanged with Araucanian Indians for important commodities, including horses (de Viedma 1836:50), or were essential in their European trade, a considerable importance was placed upon guanaco hunting. Similarly in the nineteenth century the hunting of the rhea became increasingly related to the demand for rhea feathers, with as many as 150 rheas being killed for this purpose in a single hunt (UCNW Library n.d.:ms. 7668).

The skins of the young were preferred to make the *quillangos* and they were even removed from the guanaco womb prior to birth (Musters 1871:131). Thus the hunting of the guanaco for this purpose was restricted to the months October to December, that is, soon after the birth of the young guanaco (Pritchard 1902:95). The skins of the young guanaco tended to become too woolly to be employed for the making of *quillangos* after the turn of the year (Musters 1871:219). This was also the period when the rheas were extensively hunted, although it was during September and October that rhea eggs became the main item of consumption (Musters 1871:19; UCNW Library n.d.:ms. 7668). At the end of September fat rheas became scarce (Musters 1871:96) and the armadillo came into season serving, with rhea eggs, as the major feature of the diet (Musters 1871:96, 107, 131). The eggs of the various lacustrine fowl of the Andean glacial lakes were also consumed at this time, and both root and berry crops were gathered during the months of the stay in the cordilleran zone prior to the turn of

	Jan	Feb	Mar	Apr	May	Jun	Jul	Aug	Sep	Oct	Nov	Dec
Group movements	Andean migration		Eastward migration to coast; bands separate		Permanently resident in coastal valleys; bands unite		Westward migration to cordilleras; bands separate			Leisurely migration in cordilleras; bands separate and converge		
Men's subsistence activities	Rhea hunts		Hunting hare and skunk; gathering armadillo		Gathering salt; periodic hunting sorties		Collecting pigments, stone, etc; hunting			Pasturing horses; hunting fox, puma, wild cat, skunk, etc., for skins; guanaco hunting; making various articles of stone, leather, etc.		
Women's subsistence activities	Cutting poles for *toldo*; making mantas		Loading horses, collecting firewood, some gathering		Gathering vegetative foods and making food		Loading horses; collecting firewood, some gathering			Dressing skins, sewing mantas, gathering roots		
Relative subsistence hardship	Relative abundance		Relative scarcity		Scarcity at times		Scarcity at times			Relative abundance		
Availability of water	Water abundant in Andes		Water deficient except in permanent streams		Rainfall significant; water in streams		Water in streams and waterholes			Water and rainfall abundant		
Season	Summer		Autumn		Winter		Spring			Summer		
Rate and nature of migrations	Leisurely		Rapid and meaningful		Negligible		Relatively rapid			Leisurely		
Main food sources	Young rhea, root crops, berries		Puma, guanaco (rarely)		Puma, skunk, guanaco (rarely); various root crops		Root crops, puma, guanaco, rhea			Rhea eggs, fat female rhea, puma, young guanaco, armadillo, roots, berries, eggs of lacustrine fowl		

the year (H.M.S. *Amethyst* 1884; Outes 1905:253; UCNW Library n.d.:ms. 7668).

The advent of more severe weather in the cordilleras brought the growing season of the vegetative sources to an end, not only for the human but also for the animal population. This prompted the eastward migration of the guanaco and the rhea and with them the puma (UCNW Library n.d.:ms. AX14). During the winter months game would gather in favored sheltered locations within the deep coastal valleys. Their movement east would begin about the end of February (Musters 1871:59) and would end in the arrival at the coast in mid-April where two or three months would pass prior to returning westward following the most severe part of the winter in July. By the time they returned to the cordilleras the growing season was again in full bloom, offering an abundance of the essential food sources.

Clearly the temporal–spatial aspects of Tehuelche nomadism related to the need to pursue the above economic resources. The range of migratory routes pursued by the Tehuelche population of Chubut during the nineteenth century is shown in Map 1 and the time of year when they occupied the different ecological zones is shown in Map 2. During the annual cycle both the rich, narrow zone of the cordilleras and a narrow coastal niche, where marine resources (for example the molluscs — *Patellas* and *Mytilus* species)[3] and the concentrated population of guanacos and rheas were exploited, constituted important resource areas at either end of the climatic cycle. The broader niches of the Patagonian plateau were of secondary importance, relating primarily to intermediate periods associated with migration between the two primary zones. Map 1 shows most of the major *paraderos* [resting places] and it is clear that these are associated with the existence of water resources in water-deficient environments and favored grazing areas for the animal population in the more favorable areas. Movement across the plateau followed the main eastward-flowing streams, the Chubut, Senguerr, and Chico rivers, or other available water sources such as springs and river headwaters. Considerable care was taken in selecting the migration route in order to guarantee the capture of sufficient game and the acquisition of pasture for the horses. Most of the movements were undertaken at a leisurely pace with even the crossing of the plateau being undertaken at a rate of about ten to twelve kilometers a day. The movements were not only related to the gathering of food resources and skins but also of other necessities such as the stone from which the bolas were made and which was acquired in the southwest of Chubut (Musters 1871:89), or the color pigment used to make green, red, blue, and white paint, that derived from locations such as the confluence of the Chico and Chubut rivers (H.M.S.

[3]   An abundance of marine food sources are found in coastal archaeological sites but there is no evidence as to the dates to which they pertain.

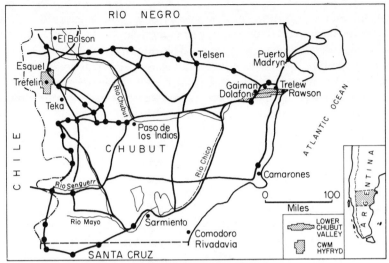

Map 1.   Tehuelche migratory routes in the nineteenth century

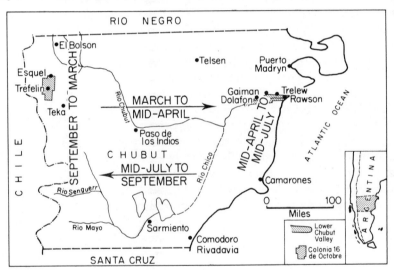

Map 2.   Tehuelche occupation zones in the nineteenth century

Cracker 1871). Salt also was obtained, from the salinas of the coastal locations. In addition to stops made to gather such essential resources the band might spend several days in a location that offered pasture for the horses, abundant game, or vegetable foods. They appear to have covered an area of about five miles radius from the camp in search of food (Matthews 1894:135). This is in accordance with the existence of about ten stations employed in crossing the four hundred miles of plateau, even though de Viedma (1836:66, 72) claimed that they never traveled more than four leagues (twenty kilometers) at one time and that 70 leagues

(350 kilometers) were traveled in twenty days, and Musters (1871:78, 203) claims a general daily journey of eight miles but with forty miles a day being traveled at certain times. The major distance between two stations involved a day-and-a-half's riding and sufficient water was carried for such a journey (Bormida and Casamiquela 1958–1959:175). However this was not always necessary since preferred routes followed the valley bottoms, although semipermanent streams such as the Chico, which is dry during January and February, were also followed. Following river courses, unlike waterholes, had the added disavantage of rendering hunting more difficult because of the dispersion of the game along the continuous water source. Furthermore, traversing the plateau was hampered by the effect of the stony surface and scrub vegetation. Under such circumstances it was essential that all available water sources be known and areas such as that between Rankiwaw and the Valdez peninsula where water was scarce were never traversed even though the distance does not appear excessive (UCNW Library n.d.:ms. AX14).

While these were the sources of information accumulated and the physical restraints associated with traversing the plateau they were by no means consistent. The westward journey which was undertaken during July, August, and September was undertaken at a time when water in the streams and springs was plentiful whereas the return journey at the beginning of the year was undertaken at a time when the streams were relatively dry. Thus both the routes and the distance traversed each day must have been subject to considerable variation. Food was obtained en route by hunting and gathering although there are references to guanaco meat being smoked and stored for emergencies (Coan 1880:84).

Although the information is somewhat confused as a result of Musters's associations with different bands his journey during the 1860's affords additional information about band movements among the Tehuelche (Musters 1871).[4] The winter camp occupied by several bands was located at the mouth of the Santa Cruz river. The movement inland commenced at the beginning of August and followed the course of the Chico almost to the Andean foothills. The two hundred or so miles were traversed at a fairly rapid rate of seven miles a day for about a month. During this time the occasional stop for a day or two was made but generally the movement was continuous. The stops were usually associated with the abundance of a food source or the occurrence of a ritual. Once the Andean foothills were reached at the beginning of September the northward movement continued at a similar rate until mid-October, about 300 miles being traversed in forty days. It was with the advent of the young guanaco hunting season and the nesting season of the rhea

---

[4] It should be emphasized that the migration of Musters's account was undertaken once every three years and was related to the new demands of their ecomonic relationship with Patagones.

that periods of several weeks were spent at single locations and the movements became more leisurely. It was also at this time that bands tended to regroup. Later, if the game became scarce at a specific location the bands would divide for a while, only to regroup at a later date.

SOCIOTERRITORIAL ORGANIZATION

There appears to be support for the relationship between availability of resources and some aspects of social organization. The overall population density for the Tehuelche was low. While there is considerable disagreement over the total population it would appear that the most reliable estimates (de Viedma 1836:79; Muniz 1918:213; FitzRoy 1839:vol. 2. p. 231) give a figure of about 4,000 exploiting an area of about 690,000 square kilometers. Certainly the evidence pertaining to Chubut prior to the "conquest of the desert" (Davies 1872:44; Parish 1836:159; UCNW Library n.d.:ms. AX14) suggests a population of 1,500 within an area of 200,000 square kilometers. The distribution of this population appears to have related to the necessity to travel the entire area in a series of moves, but, as suggested above, the exploitation of a radius of five miles from each camp offered abundant resources. Thus from the standpoint of food gathering it seems that a fairly large population density could be supported.

However, with reference to the guanaco and the rhea, population may well have been determined by herd size. Here we must consider such factors as hunting techniques, size of herds, and their population increase potential.

While there are potentially several methods of hunting the guanaco and rhea, the method employed should relate to the availability of human and technological resources. It seems that in the eighteenth century, tame young guanacos were employed as decoys (Pigafetta 1906:pt. 1, p. 52), feathers were worn as camouflage, and it is also possible that nets were employed (Fletcher 1854:41–42). Such techniques would have been advantageous prior to the advent of the horse during the first half of the eighteenth century. Indeed de Viedma (1836:67–68) mentions that the more southerly Tehuelches were virtually without horses as late as 1782 and that this was a great disadvantage in hunting. He also suggested that the game was more abundant and less mobile in areas where they were hunted on foot. Presumably a greater emphasis was placed upon gathering among such populations who had fewer trade contacts with northern cultures and thereby less need for skins as the basis for trade.

The use of the horse gave an increased mobility which was a distinct advantage in hunting. The general hunting pattern became one in which several hunters scattered in pairs in opposite directions, and circled before closing in upon the prey. They were accompanied by dogs and fires were lit to mark their positions. The animals were felled by the use of bolas, one hunter being responsible for felling the animal and the other for killing and taking charge of it. It seems that the guanacos rarely defended themselves and became bewildered when approached from different directions.

While this was the general hunting method it varied according to location, time of year, and the species hunted. In areas that were inaccessible to the horseman fire was employed to drive out the game (Musters 1871:61, 76; UCNW Library n.d.:ms. 7668). Interestingly the Tehuelche held that the guanaco had originated at Pecheckaik, southeast of Lake Buenos Aires in Santa Cruz, and the rhea at Genua, near Epuyén, both being places which abounded in game on account of their inaccessibility to horsemen (UCNW Library n.d.:ms. 7669). Similarly wild cattle retreated to the forested Andean slopes where mobility on horseback was difficult. During the rainy season the rhea, in a quest for increased mobility, retreated from the tall grass to sandy ground but even so the moisture made their feathers wet, thereby weighing the animal down and making capture easy (n.d.:ms. 7668). In winter on the other hand the tendency would be to drive the rhea to a river or wet ground, where, after becoming wet, ice would form on their feet and would slow them down (Musters 1871:53). Rheas were not hunted until they were two years of age unless food sources were scarce, and the older rhea was preferred during the nesting season when the females tended to be at their fattest (Musters 1871:131) and were easy prey.

Given the above method of group hunting it seems that ten to fifteen men were required to constitute a hunting group (Matthews 1894:137; UCNW Library n.d.:ms. 7668) although smaller groups were possible. With a ratio of 4.5 women and chidren for each male (de Viedma 1836:23),[5] this would give a band size of between 55 and 82. Thus a *tolderia* [small band] consisted of about five *toldos* [dwelling units] (Musters 1871:71; Pritchard 1902:101; UCNW Library n.d.:ms. 7668) although it may have included as many as nine (UCNW Library n.d.:ms AX14). Each *toldo* was occupied by up to three or four families, each of which had an average of five persons (Sánchez Labrador 1936:119). These units would migrate separately when game was dispersed, that is, while crossing the plateau during the months March to April, and July to September.

At other times of the year, often coinciding with the grouping of game in favorable ecological niches, several bands would unite. These larger units appear to have consisted of about twenty *toldos*, or about four bands. Thus a group of about two hundred or more people would unite periodically (Musters 1871:71, 117). Several examples of such groupings

---

[5]   Further demographic information is not available. The 1895 census might have thrown more light on this issue but was compiled after military conquest.

exist in the literature. Musters describes a group of 75 men together with their "women, children and relatives" in twenty *toldos* (1871:71). In 1866 two groups of seventy Tehuelches housed in twelve *toldos* camped in the lower Chubut valley opposite another similar group (Williams 1962:107; UCNW Library n.d.:ms. 7668). A few years later four bands with a total population of about 300 occupied the same location (H.M.S. *Cracker* 1871). De Viedma reported a group of 300 at San Julian in 1782, and another occasion when 400 gathered at the same location (1836:27). Borgatello (1924:20) claims that there were never more than twenty *toldos* (about 400 people) to be found in one camp. These larger units would gather in the coastal locations where the game tended to group in the sheltered environs of the incised river valleys. Thus the larger number of animals afforded sufficient food resources for a large number of people. Several bands were accustomed to uniting at Kichocle near Gan Gan in December after the season for hunting young guanaco (UCNW Library n.d.:ms. 7667). Other gathering places were at Lago Colnua Huapi during the winter months, thirty kilometers east of Lago Fontana at the end of December, at the confluence of the Chico and Chubut rivers, and at Esquel in mid-February (UCNW Library n.d.:mss. 7667, 7668).

There is evidence to suggest that five bands exploited the Chubut territory prior to the "conquest of the desert". A band under the leadership of Sagmata centered upon the Gualjaina area (*Buenos Aires Herald* 1907) while Kilesamal's band centered upon the source of the Tecka river. Another band under the leadership of the cacique Galach occupied the Chico river area through to lakes Buenos Aires and Fontana, while the northern area together with a portion of what is now southern Río Negro was under the cacique Chicichano (UCNW Library n.d.:mss. 7667, 7668). Each of these bands of course had access to the full range of ecological niches. The sources are unclear about territorial rights but there are suggestions that each unit had a crudely defined area as its own hunting territory (FitzRoy 1839:vol. 2, p. 131; d'Orbigny 1839:vol. 2, p. 98), or in de Viedma's words, each cacique had ". . . a determined territory under his jurisdiction, no Indian or his group can enter the territory of another headman without seeking the permission of the latter" (1836:73). On the other hand Bormida and Casamiquela (1958–1959:173) claim that this was not the case and that hunting territory was open to anyone without needing to seek permission from anyone. The contradiction appears to arise from a confusion about the population unit under discussion. In all likelihood territoriality was restricted to the larger units as de Viedma recognized but that the bands were not restricted to individual territories, although this is by no means clear. However, the degree of fluidity of band membership would make band territoriality relatively meaningless except that it could allow each cacique to gather a band around his territorial authority and also ensured that locations were not overpopulated.[6] Thus de Viedma identified six major groups within Patagonia at the end of the eighteenth century and also related them to their territories. In the extreme south was the cacique Ono's group numbering about 150 who moved primarily on foot. North of them was cacique Camopan's group occupying an area that extended as far as the (Santa Cruz) Chico river which was the southern extremity of the group, headed by Gamelo (or Julian as he was known to de Viedma), which occupied a territory that extended to Río Deseado and numbered about 400 people. Twenty-five days journey or 425 kilometers to the north was another river, presumably the Chubut or its tributary the (Chubut) Chico; the intervening territory was occupied by the groups of caciques Ayzo and Cocnoros. A further thirty-five kilometers to the north, in all likelihood at the Chubut, the territory of cacique Camen commenced. This was some 350 kilometers south of the Río Negro and was probably the most northerly of the Tehuelche groups although de Viedma's informant also mentions a group of Indians who "are bad" under the leadership of cacique Chanel (1836:42). However, they occupied 44 *toldos* (1836:52) and therefore numbered about 750 people. In all likelihood they were either of a different cultural affiliation or were Tehuelche who had been subjected to acculturative contact with the Araucanians. A picture therefore emerges of a culture subdivided into six territorial units most of which numbered about three to four hundred people and occupied an area of about 120,000 square kilometers and included the entire range of ecological niches from east to west. These units were subdivided into four or five bands during the period of major migration and in adjustment to available resources.

Each *toldo* was occupied by a patriarch, his wife or wives, his children and his relatives, and occasionally the spouse and offspring of his children (de Viedma 1836:76). The other *toldos* in the *tolderia* were occupied by other kin of the "subaltern cacique," as the band leader was described by de Viedma, including his sons and daughters with their families (de Viedma 1836:76; Borgatello 1924:19–20; UCNW Library n.d.:mss. AX14, 7668).[7] This suggests an ambilocal postmarital residence while other evidence suggests a preference for patrilocality (Steward 1946: 410–411), although this may be a response to the need for some band members to marry out of the group in order to keep its size constant. One source (Bormida and Casamiquela 1958–1959:182) claims that marriage

---

[6]   Thus the band is akin to what Naroll (1964:286) called a "territorial team" and which he defined as "a group of people whose membership is defined in terms of occupancy of a common territory and who have an official with a specific function of announcing group decisions — a function exercised at least once a year".

[7]   When visited by Moreno (1879:11) Shaihueque's *tolderia* consisted of ten large *toldos* where his kinsmen and "allies" lived.

was endogamous with reference to the *tolderia* and that initial postmarital residence was within the wife's *toldo*, a new *toldo* close to that of the wife's parents being constructed soon after marriage. What does appear to be clear is that caciques entered into marriage with either a daughter or sister of another cacique (de Viedma 1836:74), suggesting a trend toward a hereditary status (Steward and Faron 1959:411). Furthermore, since the preferred marriage seems to have been restricted within the lineage this would suggest band endogamy at least between headmen, which is reminiscent of the discussion concerning the strategic symmetrical exchange of women (Evans-Pritchard 1965; Lévi-Strauss 1949; Ardener 1972).[8] Yet apart from this specification, the evidence suggests that women were free to choose their husbands, although FitzRoy (1839:vol. 2, p. 152) reports child marriage.[9] Since inheritance seems to have been patrilineal, and territoriality associated with the headman, it is clear that, as least for the cacique, postmarital residence was patrilocal. However, if Vignati's comment (1936:623) that, although inheritance was from father to son, if no son existed the nearest relatives inherited, *preference being given to the female sex*, is correct, it is conceivable that the territorial inheritance could pass outside the band. Polygamy was practiced, primarily by the "wealthier" members but it rarely extended beyond bigamy (Bormida and Casamiquela 1958–1959:18). Given this, the reporting of both cousin marriage and the levirate, marriage among the caciques appears to have functioned as a means of solidifying band relationships. In all likelihood therefore the *tolderias* consisted of minor units the amalgamation of which produced the larger lineage groups.[10] Thus although territoriality was ostensively associated with band membership rather than kin group membership, the two were often synonymous.[11]

[8] Musters (1871:113) gives evidence of an exchange of men with the son or brother of a cacique being exchanged for a similar person at a time when the bands merged.

[9] A further restriction of marriage choice relates to the incest taboo. De Viedma (1836:74) mentions that one could "sell a wife to a relative other than the son or brother or the original seller" while Vignati (1936:623) states that only sexual relationships with "the son or sister of the wife" were regarded as incestuous. Both statements suggest that an incest taboo extended to include kin of first degree.

[10] Since children were often named after the location of birth and since the nomadic movements of all lineage members was restricted to the sum of the territories of the bands of the lineage, the name served to identify a person with his lineage.

[11] There is a suggestion (Moreno 1879:234) that kinship terminology was employed with reference to all group members without restriction to consanguinity or affinity. That the terminology did not correspond to specific position as in the *estancia* system which the European observers were familiar with suggests that an alternative terminology existed in which every affine was a kinsman of some kind. Schmid's early work (1910) on Tehuelche vocabulary at one point indicates the term *con* for "mother," *canco* for "father," and *canelecan* for relatives in general and in this source the only other apparent kinship terms refer to brother and sister. However, he refers to the vocabulary of the northern Tehuelche as including terms which distinguish between generation, consanguinity, and affinity, if not extensively by sex. However, far more work along these lines, possibly as "salvage ethnography" is necessary, especially in order to distinguish between Tehuelche terminology and kinship terms adopted from the Araucanians.

While it seems clear that band patrilocality applied to the caciqueship it is equally clear that for the remainder of the population there existed a considerable degree of band fission and realignment.[12] It is this as much as anything which confuses our understanding of the kinship system. The fluidity of band membership was partly associated with the population–resource ratio and the need for a tension management system. De Viedma (1836:74) has described the process in relation to leadership roles. The band cacique, as a result of his position, was obliged to protect and support the members of his band. In terms of physical protection this depended upon his ability to establish effective relationships with other bands, primarily through marriage exchange, and the reciprocal exchange of goods and visits. Material support on the other hand depended upon the cacique's ability to direct the hunting operation, not only in terms of the hunt itself but in directing the migration route toward available food resources. It is clear that his primary, and usually his only, authority was associated with "directing the march of the *tolderia*" (Muniz 1918:212) and thereby in determining the economic success or failure of the band.[13] In the nineteenth century when the horse became the dominant prestige item and was obtained by trading the skins acquired in the hunt, his ability became even more important. Several authors (e.g. Musters 1871:75; de Viedma 1836:71) attested to the cacique's oratory in announcing the day's activities at the beginning of each day and eloquence was one of the prerequisites to inheriting caciqueship (Vignati 1936:621).

Failure on the part of the cacique meant that band members "go off and seek another cacique" (de Viedma 1836:74), apparently leaving the cacique and the remnants of his band open to invasion by neighbors, which probably meant that the obligation of nonmembers to seek permission to enter the territory would be ignored in the light of the occupants' reduced ability to defend territorial rights. Yet even though the size of the band might diminish, the cacique and his immediate family maintained the territorial rights and the band could be built up in subsequent years. In effect, this inheriting group formed the "core unit" of the band beyond which the interband mobility, which was restricted to the lineage, gave a variety of kinship affiliations within each band. It is probable that, as Helm (1965, 1968) has suggested in discussing band composition, married couples always joined bands in which a sibling, parent, or child of one of the spouses was already resident. There is a suggestion that descent was bilateral (Bormida and Casamiquela 1958–1959:182) and it is possible

---

[12]   This is not always appreciated and the Tehuelche are often exclusively classified as patrilocal. See for example Martin (1969:246). In all likelihood residence was ambilocal within the confines of the multiband lineage.
[13]   De Viedma (1836:71) claimed that the cacique's jurisdiction was absolute with reference to hunting and the movement of the camp.

that the order that existed was not imposed by employing resident and descent rules but by bilateral affiliation.

As a safeguard against economic failure there was a tendency to relinquish caciqueship at a relatively early age (de Viedma 1836:74). However, much of the failure must have related to resource deficiency with fission being an adaptive response to such localized shortages. This suggestion becomes meaningful when one considers the manner in which the spoils of the hunt were distributed. As stated above, men hunted in groups which consisted of pairs and if one felled the animal the other took charge of it. Although the animal "belonged" to the captors in reality they were obliged to share the spoils in a predetermined manner.[14] The feathers and the body of the rhea from the head to the breastbone and one leg belonged to the captor, the remainder to the assistant. With the guanaco, the man responsible for the felling took the better half. When the animal had been cooked the back part, which consisted of the desired edible fat, was divided among members of the party and this was subsequently subdivided, with the captor retaining little or none for himself. However, the greatest portion was reserved for the cacique, or alternatively the nearest friend or relative (?) of the owner (Musters 1871:77–78). Clearly limited success in hunting would affect every member of the band and each one must have had a definite notion of what was a reasonable share that could be expected.[15] Muniz (1918:204) mentions that caciques tended to distribute possessions among band members in an attempt to maintain their affiliation.

Fission or band realignment also related to an attempt to avoid disharmony (Musters 1871:182) and was possible because of the lack of exclusive band membership and its relationship to exclusive rights to resources. The circumstances which prompted a threat to harmony may well result out of tension related to overpopulation, and the resulting fission served as an effective realignment of the population structure.

It should be clear from the above that many of the customs are related either to limiting population growth or to guaranteeing a population–resource ratio that was conducive to maintaining an expected standard of living. If, as Muniz (1918:206) claimed, the postpartum sex taboo lasted three to four years,[16] it is in line with the average spacing of children among hunters, which is about four years (Whiting 1968:249), and since women married at the age of fifteen to eighteen (FitzRoy 1839:vol. 2, p. 152; Vignati 1936:619), this would give a figure of about six children per

---

[14]   This apparent anomaly has been discussed by Dowling (1968).
[15]   Rhea eggs were divided among all of those who arrived on the scene before they were removed and they presumably redistributed them (Musters 1871:93).
[16]   Even accepting Moreno's figure (1879:445–446) of a one-year postpartum prohibition or Vignati's suggestion (1936:617) of a two-year prohibition the average number of children per mother is not large.

mother. However, since there is no indication about the average life expectancy among the women it is impossible to adjust this figure accurately, but in considering the presumed high infant mortality and abortions resulting from horse riding (Bormida and Casamiquela 1958–1959:163), it is unlikely that there would be much of a population surplus in each generation. Certainly Sánchez Labrador's figure (1936:119) of five members per family and de Viedma's ratio (1836:213) of 4.5 women and children for each male tend to substantiate such an argument. This latter figure of de Viedma's also suggests a slight imbalance in the male–female population ratio. This may relate to the deaths associated with warfare and vengeance killings related to witchcraft, and both of these may in turn be a reflection of the stress induced as a result of excessive population density within a strictly defined territorial base. However, after contact it was epidemics, particularly of smallpox (Parish 1836), which caused most of the deaths among the Tehuelche.[17] It was claimed during the nineteenth century that for every natural death there were six deaths from other causes (UCNW Library n.d.:ms. 7668) and of the eighteen men in the band which Musters accompanied in 1867 only eight lived to reach their destination (1871:71).

ROLE AND STATUS DIFFERENTIATION

In the preceding discussion there is a hint of status differentiation and yet, as Lee and DeVore (1968:12) have suggested, the nature of the nomadic economy limits the amount of personal property that can be transported, thereby limiting economic differentiation. This was true of the Tehuelche prior to the acquisition of the horse and extensive contact with the European population, but as we shall see, it became less apparent in later years.

The most obvious role differentiation is related to the division of labor by sex. In addition to hunting, the men sought wild horses which they broke and trained. They also spent considerable time making hunting and fighting implements as well as saddles, harnesses, and objects of silver. Most European observers have regarded the work of the women as far heavier and more time-consuming. They were responsible for gathering; fetching wood and water; cooking and preparing the food; looking after the children and the *toldo*; dressing, sewing, and painting skins; making clothing, and caring and preparing for migration.[18]

---

[17]   The cacique Antonio in a letter to the Welsh colonists mentioned that he was unwilling to go to Buenos Aires to confer with the Argentine authorities because of a fear of the diseases which killed his people (*Correspondence* 1867).
[18]   Women were afforded subservient status and were not allowed to speak among men unless questioned (de Viedma 1836:79).

More specific role differentiation involved specialized positions. As suggested above each cacique had a certain amount of authority and apparently wore more elaborate adornments to signify his position (Vignati 1936:607), but by and large, apart from his control over the planning of hunting, migration, and warfare, his authority was disregarded by members of the band, and was relatively ineffective in cases of dispute. It seems that his senior wife, the relative of another cacique, held priority over any other of his wives, who were obliged to attend her (Vignati 1936:617). The aged were respected and there appears to have been an avoidance practice between a man and his father-in-law in that he was not allowed to look toward him when in conversation with him (1871:184).[19] A position which appears to have more effectively distinguished the holder from the remainder of the population was that of shaman. Shamanism was open to both sexes and the selection appears at times to have been associated with physical or mental deviance, including male homosexuality and transvestism (Coan 1880:158; d'Orbigny 1839:vol. 4, p. 220). Falkner (1774:117) claimed that the shaman was always a male homosexual who wore women's cloths and was selected when a child because of signs of effeminacy, but Outes (Muniz 1918:207, footnote 4) denies this and claims that Falkner's observation referred to the Araucanians. The shaman possessed special ability and knowledge that was essential for a variety of functions including the various rites of passage, curing rituals, and general witchcraft practices (Musters 1871:80, 201, 206; d'Orbigny 1839:vol. 2, pp. 177–178; de Viedma 1836:78). Yet in other contexts the shaman played customary economic and social roles.

Economic differentiation was minimized. The redistribution of the spoils of the hunt between members has already been mentioned, although since most of such food had to be consumed within a short time it was not a commodity that was capable of accumulation. More important was the destruction of items of prestige in ceremonial contexts. De Viedma (1836:78) mentions the ritual killing of the horse in a variety of ceremonies associated with marriage, death, loss of teeth among children, female puberty rites, bad illnesses, difficulty encountered in hunting, preparation for combat, and placation of the gods. He further claimed that this was the primary reason for the limited number of horses and why such an emphasis was placed upon exchanging skins with the Araucanians for them. It does seem that some element of accumulation was necessary to facilitate some such rituals, and particularly that of marriage. However, it is necessary to distinguish between rituals associated with the entire band as opposed to those associated with the individual or *toldo*. Of

---

[19] Sweetser (1966:304) has suggested that men will avoid their parents-in-law when unilineal affiliation is an important basis on which social relationships are organized, and yet residential family groups are fragmented and impermanent.

the latter, marriage assumes a particular relevance since the groom was obliged to give gifts to the bride's father or parents who in return were obliged to give gifts of equal value (Musters 1871:177–178). The wedding feast included an abundance of mare's meat although it is unclear who was responsible for providing it. Finally, the destruction of all personal property on the death of the owner (Muniz 1918:213; de Viedma 1836:79; FitzRoy 1839: vol. 2, p. 156) meant that the accumulation of wealth through inheritance was impossible.

It would appear therefore that the social organization involved little role or status differentiation other than that based on sex and possibly age. Since the economy was based upon mutual interdependence and involved little work specialization economic relations were not separated from other social relationships. Much of the economic process was related to wider social implications including political, ceremonial, and religious festivities. Yet a limited amount of accumulation was essential in order to undertake certain essential transactions and for the individual to safeguard his interests, especially in relation to the supernatural. By and large however, it was an essentially egalitarian society.

From the above description one should be able to consider a model that could be compared with a general model of hunting and gathering societies. A picture emerges of a hunting and gathering culture consisting of groups that are flexible and composite with individuals exercising a high degree of choice from among a variety of situations. Much of the social organization and the decision making was related to the ecological setting since it determined the availability of resources. The nomadic pattern was related to the manner in which the animal population which they hunted was itself obliged to migrate in search of subsistence. The manner in which the hunting was undertaken and the size of the herds appear to have been instrumental in influencing band size and it was only during periods of abundance that the bands united. This fluid population context was superimposed upon an apparently rigid territoriality which focused upon a hereditary leadership. Thus a structure that was recognized by members of the culture extended throughout the entire area occupied by the Tehuelche.

TEHUELCHE DECULTURATION

The process of cultural and social change among the Tehuelche must have increased in intensity after contact with the European population. and reached its peak during the period under scrutiny. Undoubtedly a major agency of change was the horse, which was introduced during the first half of the eighteenth century (d'Orbigny 1839:vol. 2, p. 100), which was still not employed by all groups at the end of the century (de

Viedma 1836:67). The increased mobility must have had a profound impact upon the socioterritorial organization. Despite the use of dogs as beasts of burden the territories of the various bands were restricted and it is quite possible that in the north of Patagonia the bands did not have access to the entire range of ecological regimes. It is also clear that the horse had a profound impact on the manner of hunting and the success of the hunters. Thus the earlier bands were either smaller in number or placed a far greater emphasis upon gathering.[20]

Contact with other groups was also enhanced by the adoption of the horse and it seems clear (Cooper 1925:405) that a large number of Araucanian traits were assimilated into the Tehuelche material culture. These involved changes in diet, technology, and consumption of material items on the part of the Tehuelche. A more recent source (Priegue 1966) has suggested that the Tehuelche penetrated far further north than has thus far been suspected, having relatively early contact with the southern frontier of the European settlements. However in all probability this was a result of employing the horse to establish trade relationships with the Europeans. The northerly orientation associated with trade carried groups across traditional territories and appears to have been one of the primary reasons underlying group conflict.

It seems that the adoption of the horse took about 150 years (Cooper 1925:407), and it is highly likely that this process contributed to variation and convergence among the Tehuelche as a culture. Increased mobility and contact between the different Tehuelche groups must have served to produce a degree of universal conformity. On the other hand the cultural lag associated with differential stages of adoption of the horse between northern and southern Tehuelche may well have been responsible for the contrasts noted between these two subgroups.

What is clear is that after the middle of the eighteenth century the process of change among the Tehuelche intensified. This involved increasing contact with other native groups such as the Araucanians, the Pampas, and the Puelche. Furthermore both direct and indirect contact with the European settlements also had its impact during the early postconquest period.

Later contact with the European population and its diet and technology had equally profound effects upon the Tehuelche. The first permanent European settlement was established in Patagones in 1778, although a significant amount of contact had been established by early European explorations. Perhaps the most important consequence of the contact was the establishment of an economic relationship between the two cultures. It was not until 1865 and 1868 that subsequent settlements

---

[20]   In all probability they were far more localized, and less involved in hunting. We know that their migratory movements changed after the adoption of the horse. Future work may outline the nature of this change.

were established in the lower Chubut valley and at Puerto Deseado respectively. It is clear that contact with the European population prompted the development of a strong dependency by the native people on European consumer goods, especially liquor. This was probably a major reason for an expanded tendency to adjust the migration patterns to involve crossing group territories in moving northward to establish contact with Patagones. Despite the recognition that they were being exploited by the European traders (UCNW Library n.d.:ms. 7668) the Tehuelche felt that it was to their advantage to tolerate the occupation of their territory by European settlements. In a letter written by Antonio, cacique of the territory between the Negro and the Chubut, to the Welsh colony on the lower Chubut valley in 1865 it was stated that the settlements should communicate with him rather than with the Argentine government, but that he was willing to accomodate them if they agreed to trade fairly (*Correspondence* 1867). By 1880 the value of trade in the spoils of Tehuelche hunting that passed through the lower Chubut valley annually amounted to £6,800 (H.M.S. *Garnet* 1880) — this despite the Welsh reluctance to trade liquor. This trade had a distinct effect upon the exploitation of the natural environment, especially the guanaco and rhea, to the extent that it would have taken but a few years to reach a stage of severe depletion.

More serious from the Tehuelche perspective was another context of the contact with the European population. Prior to 1810 the Spanish had refused entry to foreigners through Buenos Aires but after 1812 the new government encouraged immigration (Leiserson 1971:62). Thus by 1869 the national population had increased to almost two million and during the following decade immigration was proceeding at the rate of 32,310 per year (Alsina 1933:63). The resultant internal population growth created a demand for land, a demand which was resisted by the native people. The same process was in operation in southern Chile where pressures were placed upon the Mapuche (Willis 1914:295–296). The confrontation resulted in the "conquest of the desert" (Hasbrouck 1934; Páez 1971), in which the native population was hounded and methodically subdued. Although most historians restrict this event to an area north of the Río Negro and to a period which culminated in 1884, it continued for several years beyond this date and extended deep into Patagonia.

The main facet of Tehuelche culture after the "conquest of the desert" was its rapid deculturation resulting from depopulation and assimilation. The pressure of a northern incursion was felt early and it is likely that the pressure of European settlement upon the Chilean Araucanians resulted in their settlement of the Andean areas of Neuquen and Río Negro (Cooper 1946; Canals Frau 1953). Here they practiced a form of transhumance based upon the use of the precordilleran lakes in winter and the

Andean streams to the west during the dry summers (Parish 1836). Their economy involved cultivation of maize and potatoes among other crops, and the rearing of sheep, cattle, and horses, but it would appear that their movement eastward had resulted in the adoption of hunting as a supplement to their pastoral and agricultural economy (Gardin 1968).[21] There is some evidence to show that the encroachment of the Araucanians into Tehuelche territory had produced a violent confrontation at the beginning of the nineteenth century and that the superior armory of the northern group had imposed a serious defeat upon the Tehuelche (Escalada 1949:264–265). It certainly seems clear that by the mid-eighteenth century the Araucanians had occupied the area between Mendoza and south of Lake Nahual Huapi (Sánchez Labrador 1936:30–31), having occupied the Andean cordillera between latitudes 34 and 37°S by 1806 (de la Cruz 1836:36), and that they were rapidly being driven south by 1870 (Mansilla 1877).[22] Musters (1871:116) also commented upon hostility between the two groups and mentioned that an uneasy alliance had been established in an attempt to deter the more belligerent Pampean cacique, Calficura, from attacking the European settlement at Patagones.

Following the "conquest of the desert" the native people were interned at various centers before the men were drafted into the army or navy for six years while many of the women and children were taken as slaves by the families of the soldiers and frontier families (Jones 1898:115–116). They were eventually allowed to readopt their former life-style but within a restricted territory (Davies 1892:27). However, most of those who had been assimilated as labor into Argentine families were prevented from returning and others chose to remain in Patagones. A substantial number must also have died of the various diseases that troubled them at the internment camps. Certainly the number of nomadic Indians was greatly reduced and was estimated at 1,500 during the late 1880's (UCNW Library n.d:AX14; Davies 1892:44) and "a few hundred" which existed in five localities during the following decade (Pritchard 1902:88). This is substantiated by a fairly detailed census that was undertaken in 1896 accounting for only 735 speakers of an indigenous language in Chubut. Of this number 125 were children younger than six years of age, a further 147 were between the ages of six and fourteen, 73 between the ages of fourteen and eighteen, and 234 male and 156 female adults (*Y Drafod* 1899). This male–female imbalance contradicts earlier estimates (Muniz

[21] This readaptation to hunting has its parallels among the Siriono of Amazonia (Holmberg 1950) and the Veddas of Ceylon (Seligman and Seligman 1911).
[22] The Araucanian cacique Sagmatta and his followers had occupied the Gualjaina area of northern Chubut as early as the 1840's (UCNW Library n.d:ms. AX14), and by the 1880's the belligerence of the government forces had driven both he and the cacique Inakayel as far south as the Senguerr (H.M.S. *Amethyst* 1884).

1918:213) and was probably the result of assimilation of the females into the domestic labor force following internment.

The above-mentioned territorial restriction was presumably related to the desire on the part of the government to colonize the Andean foothills and this may have been partly responsible for the increased contact between Araucanian, Puelche, and Tehuelche people, although other factors including contact during captivity must also have been important. It seems that by the early 1890's almost all of the nomadic groups were an admixture of members of the three cultures (UCNW Library n.d.:ms. 7668) and soon thereafter it was claimed that "the Indians that visit the lower Chubut valley are so mixed that cultural classification is impossible" (n.d.:ms. AX14). Certainly it seems that non-Tehuelche traits were being assumed, the main tendency being toward an increased Araucanization (Hughes 1927:51). As one observer commented "the effect of rubbing against other nationalities is gradually obliterating the native customs but as long as they remain nomadic they will retain some of their old customs" (UCNW Library n.d.:ms. 7668). Araucanian traits were apparent, among them the use of woven *mantas* as adornment for the *casa linda*, the dependence upon cattle as a major part of their subsistence, the search in the sierras for wild cattle which they tamed, and the use of wine presses (n.d.:mss. 7667, 7668).

The livestock resources of the Araucanians gave them an enhanced ethnic status with reference to the Tehuelche and Puelche. Their caciques had contracted with the government to receive substantial tribute in return for refraining from attacking the frontier. Thus, for example, in 1860 the caciques Rwanke, Namuncura, and Sayhueque each received at Patagones 4,000 head of cattle per quarter from the government (Jones 1898:114), substantially more than that received by any of the Tehuelche caciques. Musters (1871) suggests that the status differentiation existed at the time of his journey in the 1860's. This was important when contact between members of the two groups intensified, in that it was partly responsible in determining the direction of flow in the acculturation process with the Araucanian language being quickly assimilated by the Tehuelche (Jones 1898:114). Furthermore, band flexibility and lack of internal control mechanism meant that the Tehuelche were free to join a more prestigious group.

The main mode of interaction appears to have been through intermarriage, with marital ties between Tehuelche, Puelche, and Araucanians assuming a degree of fluidity that served to break down cultural barriers. Such circumstances, involving limited lineage or cultural endogamy, tended to promote assimilation into the numerically and economically superior groups. Musters (1871:118) mentions that Janakachel's group, while consisting of a mixture of Puelche and Tehuelche, had a predominance of Puelche males and that the cacique was himself a Puelche. Since the groups led by Tehuelche caciques had little or no Puelche or Araucanian membership this tends to suggest female assimilation associated with Puelche patrilocality.

By the end of the century European colonization of Patagonia was well under way. Large tracts of land were granted or sold both to immigrant groups and families, and to commerical ventures such as the Southern Land Company which acquired 300 leagues at Leleque in 1888 (UCNW Library n.d.:ms. AX14). Among the land grants were token parcels allocated to the native population. For example, 89 lots, each measuring 625 hectares were allocated at José de San Martin; units of similar size were allocated at Genua (n.d.:ms. AX14) and further land was made available at Epuyen and El Bolson in 1896. Much of this land was allocated to Araucanian groups, most of them having been relocated from Neuquen, although it is possible that they included Tehuelche and Puelche members. Thus Sayheque received twelve leagues in Chubut (Páez 1971:113); and it was estimated in 1912 that the Andean valley south of Bariloche held a population of 3,500 of which more than 2,000 had entered from Chile, that is, they were in all likelihood Araucanians (Willis 1914:295–296). The Araucanians extended as far south as the Senguerr, where Sacmata's group comingled with a Tehuelche population (Escalada 1949).

This allocation of land together with expansion of European settlement virtually ended the possibility of the Tehuelche pursuing their traditional life-style. Around 1902 about two to three months a year were spent hunting rhea and guanaco; the rest of the year they were "totally inactive" — and the authorities were determined to end their nomadic existence (Anchorena 1950:50). By the 1920's all nomadic pursuits were impossible and it was estimated at this time that some fifty Tehuelche families remained in Chubut (Hughes 1927:48). Escalda's work in southwest Chubut during the 1940's indicated that 135,000 hectares were claimed by 785 native people; tenancy was extremely insecure, to the extent that only 87,500 hectares were actually occupied. It appears that only about two hundred were regarded as Tehuelche, with even Sacmata's group having lost the language and intermingled with the numerically superior Araucanian population.

In Escalada's opinion the deculturation process had been extremely rapid, the admixture between Tehuelche, Araucanian, and European populations having deprived the natives of their traditions and customs, including their language and religion (Escalada 1949). In no way did they constitute vigorous ethnic units. In all probability this is an over exaggeration but the implications of his observations are clear. He further claimed that each generation revealed greater "ethnic degeneration" to the extent that in a few years the deculturation would be complete.

Associated with the deprived economic condition was an extremely high infant mortality, with more than half the children dying before reaching two years of age. Adults were also prone to illness, with goiter and rickets being cited and prominent. Their poverty and inability to counteract the effects of the imposition of European "vices" led to general disillusionment and a negative self-concept which was evident in their relationship with the national society. The traditional role of the cacique was eroded, his prestige having been undermined by the low status of the ethnic group. Thus their contact with the authorities was conducted from a position of weakness which did nothing to develop confidence in those authorities or in commercial contacts. The authorities, especially the police and legal administrators, conducted themselves in much the same way as the *comerciantes*, being totally unfair and exploitative in their relationships with the native people. This lack of support both in material and administrative terms, together with such factors as diet deficiencies, sickness, and general poverty resulted in a psychophysical degeneration which in turn promoted the development of a detrimental cognitive orientation. Escalada (1949) emphasized that this general low social status emanated from a lack of state action, especially with reference to education.

Between 1966 and 1968 an indigenous census was conducted in Argentina (*Censo indígena nacional* 1966–1968). Almost 9,000 native people existing in fifty-two groupings were enumerated in Chubut. Of these all but two are classified as Araucanian groups, the remaining two being an admixture of Araucanian and Tehuelche, although no one was reported as speaking the Tehuelche language. The province of Santa Cruz was the location of the only Tehuelche speakers of whom there was a total of fifty-two. The distribution of the native population is related to government policy, with those of the cordilleran zone being integrated, those of the interior being isolated, and those of the coast having disintegrated.

The economy of the remaining population involves a constant struggle to balance a high population against limited and depleting resources. Most of this involves livestock rearing on a limited transhumant pattern, the cultivation of a few small patches of crops, the weaving of *mantas* and, where it is essential to ensure survival, the hunting of a few of the remaining wild animals. There is little security of land tenure and their land is constantly diminishing as a result of a variety of strategies employed by the local *hacendados* to deprive them of it. This is known as *corrida de alambrado* and in addition to the moving of fences it involves a variety of other devious and often illegal methods. Under such circumstances migration is often the only solution, movements being either to work on local ranches where they constitute the cheapest regional labor, or to the *barriadas miserias* on the outskirts of the larger towns.

Associated with the general poverty is an acute medical problem that is partly related to diet deficiencies but which must also be related to the rapid change in diet patterns resulting from the change in life-style. Among the most common diseases are tuberculosis, especially the osseous form, and rickets among children. Some of the illnesses appear to be hereditary and related to genetic deterioration associated with alcoholism.

These are but a few of the problems faced by those that remain of the Tehuelche, who in a span of about eighty or ninety years have been reduced from a thriving culture of several thousand members which for centuries had successfully pursued their hunting and gathering life-style to a handful of survivors who exist in a condition of abject poverty and misery.

REFERENCES

ALSINA, JUAN B.
  1933   *La inmigración en el primer siglo de la independencia*. Buenos Aires: F. S. Alsina.
ANCHORENA, AARON
  1950   "Excursión a la Patagonia y a los Andes," in *Numero especial del Diario Esquel*, 49–53. Bahia Blanca: Jornada.
ARDENER, EDWIN,
  1972   "Belief and the problem of women," in *Interpretation of ritual*. Edited by J. S. La Fontaine. London: Tavistock.
BICCHIERI, MARCO G.
  1972   *Hunters and gatherers today*. New York: Holt, Rinehart and Winston.
BORGATELLO, M.
  1924   *Nella Terra del Fuoco*. Turin: Società Editrice Internazionale.
BORMIDA, M., R. CASAMIQUELA
  1958–1959   Etnografia Genua-Kena: testimono del ultimo de los Tehuelches septentrionales. *RUNA: Archivo para las Ciencias del Hombre* 9(1–2):153–194.
Buenos Aires Herald
  1907   *Buenos Aires Herald*. September 3.
CANALS FRAU, S.
  1953   *Las poblaciones indígenas de la Argentina*. Buenos Aires: Editorial Sudamericana.
Censo indígena nacional
  1966–1968   *Censo indígena nacional: resultado provisorios y definitiva*, four volumes. Buenos Aires.
COAN, T.
  1880   *Adventures in Patagonia: a missionary's exploring trip*. New York: Dodd, Mead.
COOPER, JOHN M.
  1925   "Culture diffusion and culture areas in southern South America," in *Proceedings of XXIst session of the International Congress of Americanists*, volume two, 406–422. Gothenburg.
  1946   "The Patagonian and Pampean hunters," in *Handbook of South American Indians*, volume one. Edited by Julian H. Steward, 127–168.

Bureau of American Ethnology Bulletin 143. Washington, D.C: Smithsonian Institution.

Correspondence

1867   *Correspondence respecting the establishment of a Welsh colony on the river Chupat in Patagonia.* London: Her Majesty's Stationery Office.

DARWIN, CHARLES

1836   *Journals of researches into the natural history and geology of the countries visited during the voyage of H.M.S.* Beagle. London: H. Colburn.

DAVIES, C.

1892   *Patagonia: a description of the country, and the manner of living at Chubut colony, also an account of the Indians and their habits.* Treorchy: D. Davies.

DAVIES, D. S.

1872   *Y Cymro: sef llyfr y wladfa Gymreig* [The Welshman: the book of the Welsh community]. New York: Taylor and Barwood.

DAVIES, W.

1940   *The grasslands of the Argentine and Patagonia.* Bulletin 30. Aberystwyth: Imperial Bureau of Pastures and Field Crops.

DE APARICIO, D., A DIFRIERI, *editors*

1958   *La Argentina: suma de geografia*, volume two. Buenos Aires.

D'ORBIGNY, ALCIDE DESSALINES

1839   *L'Homme américain*, five volumes. Paris: Pitois-Levrault.

DE VIEDMA, F.

1836   "Memoria sobre ... los establecimientos projectados en la costa Patagonica," in *Coleccion de obras y documentos relativos a la historia antiguo y moderna de los provincias del Río de la Plata*, volume six. Edited by P. de Angelis, 3–81. Buenos Aires: Imprenta del Estado.

DOWLING, JOHN H.

1968   Individual ownership and the sharing of game in hunting societies. *American Anthropologist* 70 (3):502–507.

ESCALADA, F. A.

1949   *El complejo Tehuelche: estudios de etnografia Patagonica*, Buenos Aires: Coni.

EVANS-PRITCHARD, E. E.

1965   *The position of women in primitive societies, and other essays in social anthropology.* New York: Free Press.

FALKNER, T.

1774   *A description of Patagonia and the adjoining parts of South America.* London: T. Lewis.

FITZ ROY, ADMIRAL ROBERT

1839   *Narrative of the surveying voyages of His Majesty's Ships* Adventure and Beagle, three volumes. London: H. Colburn.

FLETCHER, F.

1854   *The world encompassed by Sir Francis Drake.* Hakluyt Society 16. London.

GALMARINI, A. G., J. M. RAFFO DEL CAMPO

1965   *Investigación sobre la existencia de posibles cambio de clima en Patagonia.* Buenos Aires: Consejo Federal de Inversiones.

GARDIN, C. J.

1968   El camaruco de Aneson Grande, provincia de Río Negro, Republica Argentina. *Etnia* 7:27–31.

HASBROUCK, ALFRED
1934   The conquest of the desert. *Hispanic American Historical Review* 15; 195–228.
HELM, JUNE
1965   Bilaterality in the socio-territorial organization of the Arctic drainage Dene. *Ethnology* 4 (4) 361–385.
1968   "The nature of Dogrib socioterritorial groups," in *Man the hunter*. Edited by Richard B. Lee and Irven DeVore, 118–126. Chicago: Aldine
H.M.S. *Amethyst*
1884   Report of H.M.S *Amethyst*, Admiralty Records Office 147/1, Public Records Office, London. May 19.
H.M.S. *Cracker*
1871   Report of H.M.S. *Cracker*, Admiralty Records Office 147/1, Public Records Office, London. July 3.
H.M.S. *Garnet*
1880   Report of H.M.S. *Garnet*, Admiralty Records Office 147/1, Public Records Office, London. April 21.
HOLMBERG, ALLAN R.
1950   *Nomads of the long bow: the Siriono of eastern Bolivia.* Publications of the Institute of Social Anthropology 10. Washington, D.C.: Smithsonian Institution.
HUGHES, W. M.
1927   *Ar lonnau'r Camwy* [On the banks of the Camwy]. Liverpool: Y Brython.
JONES, LEWIS
1898   *Hanes y wladychfa Gymreig* [History of the Welsh settlement]. Caernarvon: Cwmni'r Wasg Genedlaethol Gymreig.
LEE, RICHARD B., IRVEN DE VORE, *editors.*
1968   *Man the hunter.* Chicago: Aldine.
LEEDS, ANTHONY, ANDREW P. VAYDA, *editors.*
1965   *Man, culture and animals: the role of animals in human ecological adjustments,* American Association for the Advancement of Science Publication 78. Washington, D.C.
LEISERSON, ALCIVA
1971   *Notes on the process of industrialization in Argentina, Chile and Peru.* Politics of Modernization Series 3. Berkeley: Institute of International Studies.
LÉVI-STRAUSS, C. LAUDE
1949   *Les structures élémentaires de la parenté.* Paris: Presses universitaires de France.
MANSILLA, L. V.
1877   *Una excursión a los indios ranqueles.* Leipzig: F. A. Brockhaus.
MARTIN, M. KAY
1969   South American foragers: a case study in cultural devolution. *American Anthropologist* 71 (2): 243–261.
MATTHEWS, A.
1894   *Hanes y wladfa Gymreig ym Mhatagonia* [History of the Welsh community in Patagonia]. Caernarvon: Mills and Evans.
MORENO, F. P.
1879   *Viaje a la Patagonia austral 1876—1877.* Buenos Aires: Imprenta de la Nación.

MUNIZ, R.
1918   Observaciones etnograficos de Francisco Javier Muniz editado por Felix F. Outes. *Boletin de la Sociedad Physis* 3: 197–215.
MUSTERS, GEORGE CHAWORTH
1871   *At Home with the Patagonians.* London: J. Murray.
NAROLL, RAOUL
1964   On ethnic unit classification. *Current Anthropology* 5 (4): 283–312.
OUTES, FELIX
1905   La edad de piedra en Patagonia: estudio de arqueologia comparada. *Anales del Museo de Historia Nacional de Buenos Aires* 12(3):203–574.
PÁEZ, J.
1971   *La conquista del desierto.* Buenos Aires: Centro Editor de América Latina.
PARISH, W.
1836   Account of a voyage to explore the river Negro . . . .*Journal of the Royal Geographical Society* 6:136–167.
PIGAFETTA, A.
1906   *Magellan's voyage around the world.* Cleveland: A. H. Clark.
PRIEGUE, C. N.
1966   Extencion hacia el norte de los Guennaken. *Etnia*, 3:5–9.
PRITCHARD, H.
1902   *Through the heart of Patagonia.* New York.
ROSEVANE, G. M.
1948   *The grasslands of South America.* Bulletin 36. Aberystwyth: Imperial Bureau of Pastures and Field Crops.
SÁNCHEZ LABRADOR, J.
1936   *Los indios pampas, puelches, patagones segun Joseph Sánchez Labrador S. J.* Buenos Aires: Viau y Zona.
SCHMID, T.
1910   "Two linguistic treatises on the Patagonian or Tehuelche language," in *Actas del XVIIº Congreso Internacional de Americanistas*, volume one. Edited by Robert Lehmann-Nitsche, appendix. Buenos Aires: Coni.
SELIGMAN, C. G., B. Z. SELIGMAN
1911   *The Veddas.* Cambridge: Cambridge University Press.
SERVICE, E. R.
1962   *Primitive social organization: an evolutionary perspective.* New York: Random House.
STEWARD, JULIAN H., *editor*
1946   *Handbook of South American Indians*, seven volumes. Bureau of American Ethnology Bulletin 143. Washington D.C.: Smithsonian Institution.
STEWARD, JULIAN H., LOUIS C. FARON
1959   *Native peoples of South America.* New York: McGraw-Hill.
SWEETSER, D. A.
1966   Avoidance, social affiliation, and the incest taboo. *Ethnology* 5(3):304–316.
UCNW LIBRARY
n.d.   Manuscripts 7667, 7668, 7669, and AX14. Library of the University College of North Wales, Bangor.
VIGNATI, M. A.
1936   "Las culturas indígenas de Patagonia," in *Historia de la nación Argentina*, volume one. Edited by Ricardo Levene. Buenos Aires: El Ateneo.

1941 El "pan" de los Patagones protohistoricos. *Notas del Museo de la Plata: Antropología* 6(23):321–336.

WHITING, J. M.
1968 "Discussion of Pleistocene family planning," in *Man the hunter*. Edited by Richard B. Lee and Irven DeVore, 248–249. Chicago: Aldine.

WILLIAMS, R. B.
1962 *Y Wladfa* [The community]. Cardiff: University of Wales Press.

WILLIS, BAILEY.
1914 *Northern Patagonia: character and resources.* New York.

Y Drafod
1899 *Y Drafod*. Trelew, Argentina. April 10.

PART TWO

Ecology and Economic Systems

Introduction

The natural diversity of the South American continent in topography, climate, flora, and fauna provides a wide range of settings for human habitation. Each ecological biotope offers opportunities and obstacles to subsistence and the acquisition of economic surpluses, and challenges the technological and cultural resources of the society.

Anthropological studies of economic systems in South America have generally dealt with microcosms: the relatively isolated tribe, and the organization of production and distribution of goods among peasant communities. The papers in this section reflect the dominant themes of economic studies of the region and provide case material from a variety of ecological settings. Traditional systems of production and distribution are documented, with an emphasis on technological, social, and cultural change. There is an increasing interest in systems of land holding and their relationship to social and political structures at various levels of organization. Other topics include the various modes of land reform, industrialization, information flow, and technological change in rural areas. With the rapid pace of development on the continent, such a concern is inevitable.

The emphasis of Moran's paper is methodological. Drawing on data from Wagley (1964) and Carneiro (1957), Moran shows how an "energetics approach" is useful in organizing information on economic systems. He argues that the application of systemic models in the field can lead to more thorough collection of essential data, thus yielding more productive and representative models.

Camino's study of the Upper Urubamba contains a detailed description of the local ecology in a tropical forest area. After outlining the traditional methods of exploitation, he discusses a succession of factors contributing to a powerful thrust toward change, including such elements as the demand for rubber by outside markets, large-scale internal migrations, the planting of new cash crops, and the influence of missionaries from the Summer Linguistic Institute. As a consequence of these pressures, traditional social and cultural patterns have begun to disappear in the area and are being replaced by new ones.

Partridge provides a detailed analysis of the interrelationships among the subcultural groups involved in the production, use, and distribution of the narcotic cannabis in northern Colombia. As in Camino's study, historical events are shown to have modified this cultural complex and Partridge takes into account the establishment and departure of the United Fruit Company, and the demographic effects of the civil war (*la violencia*) of the late 1940's and 1950's.

Flores focuses on subsistence techniques in a coastal environment, tracing the fishing technology of coastal Venezuela from preconquest periods to the present. He documents the changes introduced during the colonial period, and analyzes the effects of modern commercial trusts on the fishermen who are marginal to the lucrative internal market.

REFERENCES

CARNEIRO, ROBERT
    1957   "Subsistence and social structure: an ecological study of the Kuikuru Indians." Unpublished doctoral dissertation. Ann Arbor, Michigan: University Microfilms.
WAGLEY, CHARLES
    1964   *Amazon town: a study of man in the tropics*. New York: Macmillan. (Originally published 1953.)

An Energetics View of Manioc Cultivation in the Amazon

EMILIO F. MORAN

An energetics approach, such as is presented in this paper, combines qualitative descriptions with the potential for quantification. This approach begins with whole systems considerations, before undertaking specific analyses. It is especially useful in studying the interactions between man and the environment. The natural system consists of energy flows in which certain natural compartments capture dispersed solar energy and utilize it for self-maintenance and growth. Likewise, man's culture is a system. It is a premise of cultural ecology that man's primary adaptive system, culture, has taken shape in response to the need to collect the energy captured by the cultural system more efficiently (White 1949).

The approach presented here is different from traditional anthropological approaches. It does not automatically posit culture as the most powerful factor. It includes many nonsocial elements, such as weather, soils, stress factors, storages, and multiplier effects. In short, it attempts to be holistic in practice. Its method calls for acquaintance with the relevant literature, not only in the cultural field, but also in agronomic, botanical, and other fields relevant to an understanding of man–environment flows. This approach can sharpen our understanding of a social system by forcing us to focus on processes and causal factors.

The energetics approach also allows one to analyze ethnographic data critically. For the sake of clarity, two Amazonian ethnographies have been chosen because they have substantial sections on the cultivation and utilization of manioc. Carneiro's data on the Kuikuru (1957) and Wagley's 1953 data on Itá, in Paraguay (Wagley 1964), are among the best available on the region. Even today, little so far has been produced to surpass their work. This paper suggests that there is another way to organize one's reading and field research. While this approach has not yet yielded fruit comparable to that of traditional approaches, it is herein suggested that it can serve researchers in the future by focusing their attention on the "system" rather than its "parts."

In the sections that follow, this paper will discuss the advantages of searching for a common denominator, energy, in man/environment studies, using the data on manioc in an Indian and a modern peasant community. The energy language will be explained through diagrammatic models of the two Amazon communities.

MODELING AND ENERGETICS

Modeling before undertaking research offers a number of advantages. First, it serves to direct one's reading, by setting priorities. Usually a problem is in mind. How much one wants to know about different things is monitored by the need to understand some things rather than others. If, for example, one has in mind the study of the nutritional status of an Amazon population, one needs to start with broad understandings of the tropics, tropical plants, tropical agriculture, the nutritional content of Amazon plants, dietary patterns, the level of population, the amount of rainfall and sunlight, the availability of outside foods, seasonal variations in diet, days lost due to sickness, and capital available. There are many other questions such as diet preferences, intake of nutrients, cooking methods and their effect on nutrients, and so on, that are also important. Thus by a "problem" orientation, modeling tends to set up a list of items toward which reading at home is oriented. Of course, there will be no data about many of these items, and when that is the case, the need is noted and this becomes an early goal in field research. The aim is to develop a diagram of the flows through a system that explains the structure and functioning of that system. As reading progresses, the diagram will need revision and redrawing.

Secondly, modeling tends to identify the type of unit that will be most useful. It is not uncommon for field-workers to spend many hours gathering data and then having to spend many more hours converting such numbers to some usable standard. In identifying data gaps, one also decides on the most useful units to use. The hours spent in conversions could better be spent in analyzing the data.

Modeling, therefore, aids the researcher in organizing data in such a way that it is more generally useful to other scientists. Systems analysis is growing in applications and cultural data is beginning to be included in models made by scientists outside the cultural field. It would be useful to provide data in terms that can be used by others. An energetics approach should also aid anthropologists in the achievement of that ever-elusive goal of cross-cultural comparison. By identifying major factors and sim-

plifying the broad elements in a man/environment system, one can eliminate the detail that so often clouds attempts at comparison.

One thing that an energetics approach does is to overcome the inertia
of staying within one's discipline. It is natural to be reluctant to go outside
one's field of special competence, but the understanding of most problems calls for a consideration of many topics in other disciplines. Modeling beings with the understanding that one must retrieve whatever knowledge is required to understand a system. This aids the researcher in
broadening his information base as well as in directing him toward approach-
ing scientists in other disciplines for help. If the researcher goes to a fellow
scientist with a model of what he wants to know, this sets up a common
ground of understanding and the introductions are less fumbling.

To sum up this discussion so far, modeling leads one to make qualitatively descriptive diagrams based on available literature. In this manner,
knowledge is summarized and gaps identified. This model of ethno-
graphically established relationships stands until data is obtained that
contradicts them, and alters the model. In other words, the model is a
hypothesis that is tested time and again as new data come in.

TROPICAL MAN AND MANIOC

When the Portuguese discovered Brazil in 1500, they found the native
populations making great use of the plant manioc.[1] Within a decade the
Europeans had taken this plant to the Cape Verde Islands, then to Africa
and later to Asia. Manioc is today a pantropic staple. In its native region,
it is a plant with an infinity of uses. The Europeans and mestizo populations that later came to inhabit the tropical Amazon forest adopted the
cultivation and processing models of the aboriginal population.

Manioc is a plant that is ideally suited to the tropics. It stores in the
ground for up to two years, an important factor in an area where rainfall
and humidity make preservation difficult. Manioc is resistant to pests and
grows well in acid soils (Rogers and Appan 1971). It produces best in
areas of abundant rainfall, while it is capable of surviving drought conditions. Yields compare favorably with those of other starchy staples. Five
to ten tons per hectare can be expected, using traditional technological
methods. Under experimental conditions, manioc has yielded up to 65
tons per hectare (Moran 1974).

A general ignorance of the function of manioc in the cultivation–
utilization complexes of tropical areas accounts for its bad reputation.

[1] Manioc is also known as yuca, cassava, and mandioca. In this paper we will use manioc
throughout. It is now accepted to be *Manihot esculenta* Crantz, with "bitter" and "sweet"
varieties being descriptive of the content of prussic acid, rather than of a difference in
species.

Temperate-zone researchers, when faced with this unusually productive plant, find it either exotic or repulsive. At best, most of them would claim that it cannot compare with the far more beneficial crops from temperate areas. This imposition of taste preferences has served to harm research on manioc overwhelmingly. In this paper we will suggest how future research on manioc in the Amazon may be organized so as to lead to more balanced development and improved nutrition.

While the people of Itá (Wagley 1964) are a mestizo population, the folk culture of the Amazon adopted the indigenous subsistence system with but few modifications. Cultivation of the crop is relatively easy. After the cycle of slash-and-burn activities has been carried out (see e.g. Conklin 1957) the fields are planted from cuttings. Thereafter there is little need for maintenance work until eight months or more have passed, when the tubers are ready for picking. However, it is in processing the tubers that the major expenditures of energy occur. This aspect, then, may lend itself to greater technological improvement.

The preparation of manioc flour basically involves the removal of prussic acid and the conversion of the raw tuber into a dry, storable form. There are two widely used methods to accomplish this. The first includes peeling, grating, and then squeezing the pulp in a tubular basket (*tipiti*) to remove the poisonous juice. Then this mixture is toasted on a large griddle until a coarse, mealy substance is obtained. The second method involves soaking the unpeeled tubers until a point of near decay, at which time they are peeled and squeezed to remove the poisonous acid. The pulp is then roasted as in the first method. It takes a man and his wife a full day to process thirty kilos of farinha. This labor input is more than occasional since an Amazonian peasant family of five consumes over two kilos of farinha daily (Wagley 1964:66). It may be noted that among aboriginal peoples, the processing of farinha was entirely women's work.

The Amazon population hunts and fishes for most of its protein and until recently populations have been concentrated on river banks where this supply is assured. Their slash-and-burn fields give the appearance of a young forest due to the variety of growing cultigens. The population also gathers seasonal fruits that most surely are important. As might be expected, the ethnographies concentrate on manioc when discussing Amazon populations. To understand the grasp of the environment by these populations, however, more attention needs to be paid to the other foods as well.

Figure 1 and Figure 2 are energy flow diagrams made from Carneiro's and Wagley's ethnographies (Carneiro 1957; Wagley 1964). These are followed by Table 1 which summarizes the data presented. As can be seen from the table there are many areas that were not documented. This list was made following a third diagram, a generalized manioc model (Figure 3). Table 1 and Figure 3 illustrate the first stage of research,

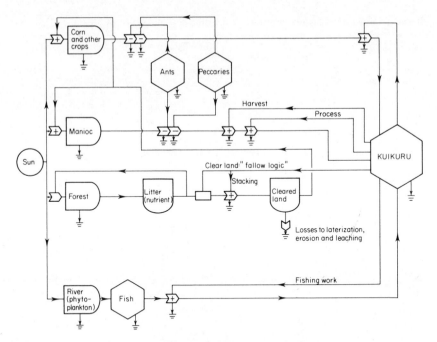

Figure 1.   Energy flow diagram: Kuikuru model (Carneiro 1957)

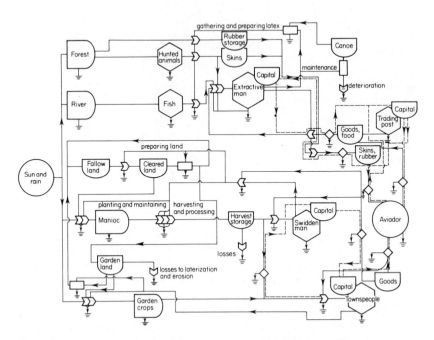

Figure 2.   Energy flow diagram: "Amazon town" model (Wagley 1964)

Table 1.   Energetics factors necessary to the model of manioc cultivation

Factor	Kuikuru (Carneiro 1957)	Itá (Wagley 1964)	Comment
Solar input	–	–	Available in meteorological literature
Rainfall pattern	?	?	Available in meteorological literature
Manioc biomass	344,451,200 kg	? plus 350,000 kg imported	
Other crops biomass	no studies	–	No accurate estimates made
Forest biomass	no studies	–	Approximations available
Labor inputs (manioc)	657 man/hours/year	168 man/days/year	How many hours in a man/day? Includes walk to field?
Labor inputs (other)	?	?	
Fishing labor	1.5 hours daily	no accurate figures	
Hunting labor	rare	seasonally	
Yields (manioc)	4–5 tons/acre/year	5,300 kg/4 tarefas	Tarefa = 3,906 m²
Yields (other)	no figures	no figures	
Average plot size	1.5 acres	2.7–2.9 tarefas	
Length of fallow	25 years	6 years	
Losses to pests	high	no comment	Important: some data in the literature
Size of population	145	500 (or 2,000)	
Manioc consumption	127 million calories	720 kg/family	calories or kilocalories?
Other food consumption	general comments	general comments	
Biomass marketed	none	4,680 kg/year	
Price obtained	not applicable	variable	
Losses in storage	no comment	no comment	
Losses to laterite	soil studies	frequent	
Losses to erosion	general	occasional	
Capital inputs	–	–	
Capital outputs	–	–	
Losses of time to disease	–	–	

summarizing what is known from the literature and identifying gaps, thereby avoiding duplicating studies where data saturation has already been reached in favor of collecting data on aspects that have never been understood. This list was then applied to our two sample ethnographies and the resulting gaps may be seen. These omissions could be a function of the difficulty of collecting some of this type of data, as was certainly the case when both Wagley and Carneiro did their research. Now there are few spots on Earth, including the Amazon, where an anthropologist is

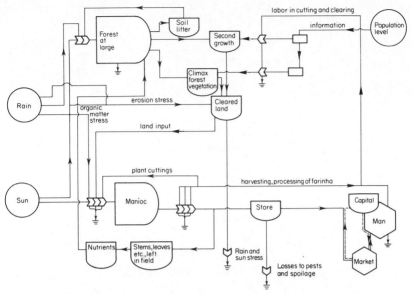

Figure 3.   Energy flow diagram: generalized manioc model

so isolated that he cannot obtain outside help in collecting data outside his field of competence. But he has to know precisely what he wants. This is where these energy diagrams are useful; by modeling what is understood, and knowing what data one can collect for oneself and what one cannot do, the proper cooperative behavior can be planned.

Figure 4 is the key to the symbols in the energy flow diagram. These symbols are like morphemes in language; it is necessary to know them to be able to communicate, but such knowledge quickly expands our capacity to communicate new ideas as well. Everything that occurs on Earth involves a flow of potential energy from some *source*, in this case usually the sun, or rain, but it can be population level. The label source is fairly self-explanatory. What is of interest in modeling is that its own inner functioning is of no significance to the rest of the model. Only its input to the system under consideration is of importance, and such values can be obtained from meteorological tables. The symbol for sources is a circle.

The source is understood to be "outside" the system under consideration but the output from the source *is* evaluated. Energy from the source moves through *pathways*, which identify the energy flows through a system and their direction. In most systems, energy is unidirectional, due to the law of entropy. Once a flow has occurred, there is a major portion of that potential energy lost as heat; these heat loss centers are termed *heat sinks*, and are symbolized as downward-pointing arrows. The presence of heat sinks prevents any return to a previous state. The pathways form a configuration: certain configurations or patterns, such as the prey–

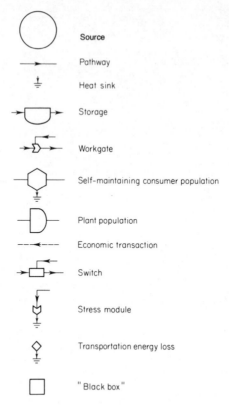

Figure 4.   Symbols used in energy flow diagrams

predator relationship, have been noted to occur repeatedly in man and nature. This is important because it can lead the researcher to otherwise unnoted similarities.

Next to be considered are the *storages*. A passive storage shows the location within a system of actions such as moving potatoes into a storeroom, fueling a tank, or the collection of litter on the forest floor. No new potential energy is generated by such action and some work must be done by some other unit in moving energy in and out of the storage. In Figure 2, for instance, we have marked storages for gathered rubber and skins of prized animals, as they are "stored" until taken to market. Capital, fallow land, cleared land, garden land, storage of harvest, and the canoe, as potential producers or procurers of goods, are also storages, until acted upon by some other energy flow.

Unspecified functions not having a standard symbol to describe them could have been indicated by a simple square, a "*black box*." This is basic practice in modeling for things which are important but whose functioning we do not clearly understand. Unfortunately much of culture has to be put into a "black box" at this point, although in the future some of these unknowns may be understood. However unless these unspecified functions detailed in ethnographies as "black boxes" are visualized, their inner functioning is unlikely to be investigated. I have, nevertheless, eliminated the potential black boxes in Figure 2, since it deals only with subsistence, and a great deal of the cultural behavior is omitted.

The *workgate*, indicated by an outlined arrow, can express as simple an action as a person turning a valve, as well as such complex processes as the action of a limiting fertilizer or the multiplicative effect of man's labor inputs on production of food for himself. In a workgate, a flow of energy, from a *control factor*, which is indicated as entering the workgate from the top, makes possible another flow of energy. For example, at the top of Figure 2, man's energy in gathering and preparing latex is indicated as a control factor in determining the amount of rubber obtained. Without this flow or control factor, the rubber would remain in the trees. If man did not fish, he could not eat fish, and they would just go on swimming and reproducing without interference. Without man entering the scene and actively interfering in the natural development of climax forest vegetation, production by the forest environment for man would be nearly zero (Odum and Pigeon 1970). Man himself acts as a control factor as he burns and cuts a field for his use. The amount of labor in this control factor also determines the output of the field. If man clears one hectare of land, all other factors remaining equal, his yield will be less than if he clears five hectares. Thus the actions of man in clearing a field resemble those of a man turning a valve: the more he turns the valve, the more water will come out, up to a certain point. But land, like valves, has limits on output, regardless of increasing inputs; there is a point of diminishing returns.

A *self-maintaining consumer population*, indicated by a hexagon, is a combination of a storage and a workgate, by means of which potential energy stored in one or more sites within a subsystem is fed back to work upon the self-maintenance and growth of that unit. In this symbol are included animals, man, industries, and cities. In the case of the Kuikuru model (Figure 1) the symbol is applied to the Kuikuru populations as a whole. In Figure 2, however, the population is subdivided into its natural classes: extractors (extractive man), shifting cultivators (swidden man), and townspeople. The interactions between each group and their environments are clear: extractors deal with the forest as if they were predators. The shifting cultivator has closer dealings with the townspeople and is somewhat dependent on them, dealing with the forest only as a source of land for farming. The townspeople have little direct dealing with the environment as such, and rely on their status positions and capital to mediate in their acquisition of inputs, and to process the outflow of capital from the town. The trading post is important in that, for the extractor, it mediates in the marketing of his rubber and other forest products. The trading post is a consumer and not a producer: like cities it serves to organize inputs and outputs for others.

A *plant population*, indicated by a D shape, is a reservoir of plants capable of transforming solar energy into tissue; these make up a major proportion of the larger symbols. The green plant receives the wave energy of the sun and produces tissue that is then consumed by other animals in the food chain. In the case of forest climates this maintains a near equilibrated or closed nutrient cycle, demonstrating the saying that the forest "feeds on itself." The essential relationships then, on the earth, develop from the flow of solar energy, which is transformed into plant tissue by the plant producers, which are in turn acted upon by the consumers, who in various ways cycle the materials of the producers back to the earth and the air.

A whole-systems approach must consider that in some societies man engages in *economic transactions*; these are indicated by a broken line which is arrowed in the direction of the money flows involved. The unbroken line, the pathway, describes the flow of energy. Money flows in the opposite direction to the flow of energy, and the concept of price proportionately adjusts one flow to the other. Equivalences of goods to money vary from situation to situation but in each case the goods-for-money exchange holds true. In Figure 2 the flows involving money occur as the forest provides products to the trader, who returns capital to the extractor, who then buys goods with it.

Under certain circumstances, "on-and-off" states occur. For example, a symbol is needed to indicate that under a system of shifting agriculture, after perhaps three years the farmer will move from one piece of land to another. Unlike the workgate, where the control factor determines the *amount* of output, in the *switch*, indicated by a small rectangle, the situation described is one in which the control factor simply determines whether there *is* output or not. Other factors then determine the amount of the output. Ceremonial complexes are capable of providing this sort of unequivocal signal: following a certain feast, it is time to start cutting the forest for next year's crops. In Figure 2 man turns cleared land into land planted in manioc through his work and decisions. Another switch in the diagram is the turning of garden land into fallow land. In this case the logic of the switch is probably a certain known period of time after which gardening is less rewarding on a particular plot of land. The switch is activated by a *signal*, which is represented as entering the long side of the rectangle.

The last symbol that we will present here is the *stress module*. It defines the drain of energies from a flow caused by a stress factor, such as too much rain on unprotected soil, crop failures on human nutritional status and health, and pests upon crops. When a system is stressed, the potential energy that was available to do work is lost. The stress symbol is, then, a workgate, pointing downward, with energy from the system being drained into a heat sink by an environmental (or social) stress factor. Figure 1 includes a rain and sunlight stress (high soil temperatures destroy soil humus and rainfall on uncovered tropical soils leads to leaching of nutrients).

Following Figure 1 through may clarify exactly how to read energy models and how to use them in describing systems. The sun (source) is the general motor of the producers (plant populations) that are, in this case, manioc, corn and other crops, the forest, and phytoplankton in the water of the river. The Kuikuru (self-maintaining consumer population) interfere in the natural forest cycling of nutrients by clearing land, stacking wood, and turning the land to manioc and corn production. Ants and peccaries (self-maintaining consumer populations) take a toll of the crop (as negative multipliers or workgates). The Kuikuru harvest and process the manioc and corn and consume this product themselves. They also fish for their food.

There is no market activity to influence the production–consumption system. As Carneiro (1957) explains, at sufficiently low population levels this system may remain relatively sedentary for very long periods. There is, therefore, no need here to include a signal to migrate, but in a general case it might be accurate to provide a signal (switch) for out-migration when certain population levels are reached in the area. This signal is provided in Figure 3 and is signified by "population level."

The "manioc model" (Figure 3), as indicated before, is a generalized model to guide the initial stages of research. It includes more agronomic data requirements than most anthropologists would be willing to research. But if the social data is to be useful to other scientists, more specific physical data is needed. The population signal is included since it is potentially important in a shifting agricultural system. A market is also included (a factor not included in the Kuikuru model). This diagram differs from the other two in its generality, as only manioc is of interest here. In the field this could be greatly modified. The goal of this sort of model is to identify the broad areas in which data is essential. Thereafter, more details and cultural considerations can be included to fit the specific problems that one needs to answer.

THE ADVANTAGES OF ENERGY MODELING

As we have seen, this form of organizing research is diagrammatic. It uses both qualitatively and quantitatively descriptive models to summarize knowledge or understanding of a system. In this way it affords a tool to ease the growing gap between traditional descriptive anthropologists and the more quantification-oriented breed of today. The traditional researcher can easily learn to use these symbols and start speaking a "systems language." The quantifiers can understand and accept what he wants to say more easily than if he tries to engage them through the anecdotal technique. Understanding essential system relationships is a language which any scientist should be able to speak since it involves the search for interconnections and causes.

At the same time this approach permits the more quantification-oriented group in the profession the opportunity to fill in the lines with mathematically formulated data (e.g. Lugo et al. 1972; Odum 1971; Patten 1971) that will permit simulations on analog and hybrid computers. This extension of the systems approach, originated in departments of environmental engineering, may be one important contribution toward joint research languages and understandings of man and the environment.

The energy language is not finished. There is a need to add "cultural morphemes" to explain the special processes of cultural behavior. This will be the primary contribution of the anthropological scientists. The ecologists have given us a language adapted to study of natural factors and the essential man–environment encounters, but to understand the functioning of man's choices, values, and actions we need to develop sharper concepts of the functioning of the cultural factors themselves. The energy language approach is therefore an expandable system. Not only can it accept the addition of cultural morphemes but it can grow from very broad whole-systems diagrams (such as the manioc model) to specific models to describe and explain the relationships between the parts of a smaller unit. Thus the size of the researcher's unit of study is not limited by the use of energy language, and smaller diagrams can be linked to give a detailed view of a more complex unit.

Cultural ecology without measurements is like philosophy without logic, but not all measurements are worth taking. The energetics approach offers the potential of guiding a researcher toward a processual mentality, toward a visually useful organization of his data, and, in conjunction with other scientists, to the identification of essential agronomic data that will permit precise description of the agricultural systems of the world.

An energetics approach is not a panacea for mediocrity. The researcher still may do poor or excellent research after defining his problem and his goals. What this approach does, however, is help the investigator organize himself before, during, *and* after his field trip, so that optimal results will come out of his experience. A picture is worth a thousand words, and modeling is the logical extension of this proverb. Traditional approaches have contributed a great deal to our present knowledge. It is time to take this data and identify the areas where enough data is already available, so as to proceed to new areas left untouched by members of the discipline.

REFERENCES

CARNEIRO, ROBERT
 1957 "Subsistence and social structure: an ecological study of the Kuikuru Indians." Unpublished doctoral dissertation. Ann Arbor, Michigan: University Microfilms.
CONKLIN, HAROLD C.
 1957 *Hanunóo agriculture: a report on the integral system of shifting cultivation in the Philippines.* Forestry Development Paper 12. Rome: FAO.
LUGO, ARIEL, *et al.*
 1971 *Models for planning and research for the South Florida environmental study.* Gainesville, Florida.
MORAN, EMILIO F.
 1974 Energy flow analysis and *Manihot esculenta* Crantz. *Acta Amazonica.*
ODUM, HOWARD T.
 1971 *Environment, power, and society.* Environmental Science and Technology. New York: John Wiley and Sons.
ODUM, HOWARD, T., R. F. PIGEON, *editors*
 1970 *A tropical rain forest.* Springfield, Virginia: United States Department of Commerce.
PATTEN, BERNARD, *editor*
 1971 *Systems analysis and simulation in ecology,* volume one. New York: Academic Press.
ROGERS, D. J., S. G. APPAN
 1971 Cassava-based nourishment-generating system capable of functioning in ecologically and economically impoverished areas. *Tropical Root and Tuber Crops Newsletter* 4:13–18.
WAGLEY, CHARLES
 1964 *Amazon town: a study of man in the tropics.* New York: Macmillan. (Originally published 1953.)
WHITE, LESLIE
 1949 *The science of culture.* New York: Grove.

Sociocultural Change in Upper Urubamba, Peru

ALEJANDRO CAMINO D.C.

In Upper Urubamba, in the Peruvian province of Cuzco, the traditional subsistence patterns of the native Machiguengans have been transformed in the last ten years. These changes have been caused by the introduction of cash crops and manufactured goods brought in from other parts of the country by immigrating Andean peasants. In this article I shall explain some of the factors of these changes, with specific reference to the Monte Carmelo settlement in the Upper Peruvian *selva*, or forest (see Map 1 and Plate 1).

This situation is also occurring in the other valleys of the upper *selva* throughout Latin America. Except where native settlements have withdrawn to remote gorge areas, they have started to become an integral part of the national economy. The natives either become salaried workers or grow cash crops for sale. The case of Monte Carmelo is one of the latter.

The Machiguengans are an ethnic group of the Arawak linguistic group, with an estimated population ranging from 3,500 to 12,000 inhabitants (Ferrero 1966:18; Varese 1972:173). They inhabit the banks of the streams and tributaries of the Upper Urubamba river starting from Echarate, the right shore of the Manu and its tributaries, the Yavero and its tributaries, and the right-hand tributaries of the Tambo river. This represents an area of approximately 30,000 square kilometers.

Since pre-Columbian times these natives have been influenced by the

This article is based on fieldwork carried out in September–November 1972 with the assistance and under the auspices of Dr. Allen W. Johnson of Columbia University. I am most grateful to Dr. and Mrs. Johnson for their invaluable collaboration and counseling. I should also like to express my appreciation to the inhabitants of Upper Urubamba, without whose assistance and hospitality this study would not have been possible. My special gratitude goes to Dr. Enrique Mayer, of the Universidad Catolica del Perú, for his advice in the final section of this report.

legendary cannibals, the Chonchoites, the Piros, rubber planters, missionaries, and migrant Andean peasants. There appear to have been links with the Inca empire, although little is known about this relationship. After the conquest of Peru, the Upper Urubamba region began to undergo economic changes caused by the expansion of the European capitalist economy.

During the eighteenth century, the Piros came up the upper Urubamba in fragile canoes, carrying off Machiguengan women, children, and goods. They would go to the August fair in Santa Rosa, Rosalino (Spanish

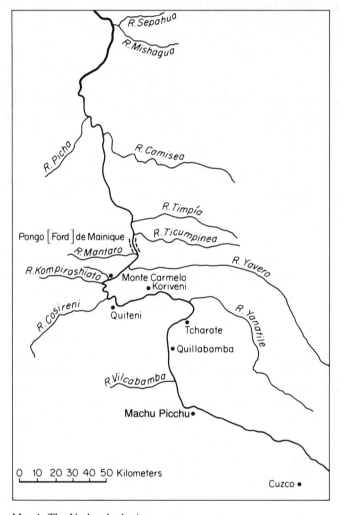

Map 1. The Urubamba basin
Source: Based on Daniel W. Gade (1972)

hacienda), where products such as cinchona bark, were exchanged (Gade 1972:206). It appears that the French demand at this time for cascarilla bark (for the manufacture of quinine) affected the Piros as much as the Machiguengans. It is possible that the introduction of iron instruments (knives and machetes) dates from this period.

Plate 1. Monte Carmelo

The first missionary attempts also begin in the eighteenth century, but without great success. When independence from Spain was achieved, these missions were closed (Ferrero 1966:46–48).

The nineteenth century is one of isolation for the region, though during this period the first estates (haciendas) of mestizos or Creoles begin to form between Echarate and Palma Real. Toward the end of this century the rubber boom occurred in the Amazon region. Some rubber planters came through the Lower Urubamba, and others from Cuzco, organizing "raids" to capture natives to work on the rubber plantations. Although the end of the boom marked the abandonment of the region by these fortune hunters, the effects on the native economies were long range.

When the rubber era ended, Fidel Pereira, the son of a rubber planter and a Machiguengan mother, remained permanently (see Plate 2). The importance of this man and his children in the history of the Upper Urubamba is so great that the explorer novelist Matthiessen, after making a trip to this region in the sixties, has called it "Pereira Country" (Matthiessen 1968:186).

Fidel Pereira, who to a large extent belongs to the Machiguengan culture, lived in isolation for some decades, first breeding livestock and subsequently growing cocoa and coffee. He had up to forty Machiguengan families in his service, and took several natives as wives at various times. The many children resulting from these unions were essentially brought up within Machiguengan cultural patterns.

Plate 2. Fidel Pereira

In 1952, the year in which the missionaries from the Instituto Lingüístico de Verano, the Summer Linguistic Institute, entered the region, Pereira divided up "his" Machiguengan families among his four grown sons (his children are mainly Machiguengan speaking). The latter settled throughout the Upper Urubamba, between the Kompiroshiato river gorge, near Mainique Ford (*Pongo*). Soon three more children were added.

The present article is based principally on the fieldwork carried out in one of these settlements: Monte Carmelo. Eighty-five Machiguengans live in this community of scattered dwellings. They include Fidel Pereira (eighty-eight years old) and his wife Doris, the teacher in charge of the Escuela Evangélica Bilingüe [Bilingual Evangelical School]. The Machinguengans are distributed in thirteen family houses over an area of some nine square kilometers, linked by paths which cross the small farms and woods. The huts, made of palm bark and leaves, generally shelter a single family, consisting of the father, one or two wives, and children. Polygamy is not common (in 1972 there was only one case).

Monte Carmelo is two days' travel by horse from Quiteni, the end of the Cuzco–Upper Urubamba highway. Quiteni is the commercial center where migrant peasants and occasionally Machiguengans sell their products and buy manufactured products and other goods. Two launches run by peasants (one belonging to a private merchant and the other to a production cooperative society) make irregular trips between Quiteni and Pongo Mainique. On these trips they ferry passengers, purchase regional products, and sell manufactured goods.

TRADITIONAL SUBSISTENCE PATTERNS

The Machiguengans use of resources has its frame of reference in a multiple system of organized information which falls, fundamentally, into three aspects:
1. The variety of species (fauna and flora) and inorganic materials of the tropical woods.
2. The ways and life forms of these species.
3. The complex relationships between the various species and elements.
This information represents the basis of the subsistence techniques available to the settlers of the Upper Urubamba. Survival depends on the use of this "science of the concrete."

Subsistence activities centered on food production may be divided into four categories: agriculture, hunting, fishing, and gathering. I shall explain each of these groups in turn.

Agriculture

Agriculture and hunting constitute the main sources of energy for the Machiguengans. The ecological peculiarities of the tropical woods, together with the importance of agriculture, require that the greater part of working hours be devoted to this activity. No attempt shall be made to give a detailed account of the tropical forest ecological system. For such the reader is referred to the valuable works of Meggers (1971:6–38) and Geertz (1971).

Like other ethnic groups of the Latin American tropical woods, the Machiguengans use the agricultural system known as swidden, or slash and burn. The family's subsistence depends on establishing a small farm (known as a *chacra* or *samarintzi*). The *chacra* is usually located near the house (this is no longer the case in Monte Carmelo). Around May or June the father of the family determines the place where he will establish his *chacra*. Generally speaking, during his hunting expeditions, the Machiguengan is always inspecting the land. He digs up earth with his machete and examines its texture and quality, while evaluating the slope of the land, the vegetation present, etc. By the time he must choose the site of his *chacra*, he has a good knowledge of the surrounding land.

The natives I met explained that they distinguish only three types of land: black, sandy river banks, and red, in that order of desirability; the black earth of loose texture, with few stones and little slope, is the best. The packed, strong, deeply sloping red soil is the worse, and is feared as being inhabited by evil gods. Sandy lands, annually renewed with nutritional matter, are highly valued, even though the Machiguengans are afraid of sudden rises of the river.

In regions with a low population density, the average Machiguengan has a relatively wide choice for his *chacra* site. But in the high, wooded mountains with their slope and stones, the possibilities decrease considerably.

Previous *chacra* sites (of the past twenty-five to fifty years), on which there are now only secondary, or *purma*, woods, are avoided because of their low fertility. A *chacra* established here would have a poor, short producing season, and the native requires a three-year yield.

Preliminary investigations estimate that only 33 percent of all land is usable (Johnson, personal communication). Personally, I would place the figure at under 25 percent. Thus we see that *even* in conditions of low population density (as the region was before the increasing influx of the Andean peasantry), the task was never easy.

Once the site is determined, land clearing starts around May or June. First the branches and shrubs are removed. Then the father, using an ax,[1] gradually fells the trees located in the elevated areas. The trees are carefully selected so that in falling they will knock down other trees in their path, often as many as ten. Old, weak, and top-heavy trunks are eventually isolated and then knocked down by the wind.

---

[1] There is no information as to when axes were abandoned. Ax heads have been found in many parts of the Upper Urubamba, as well as in the Upper Peruvian *selva*. Some have been exhibited in the small museum of the Dominican convent in Lima. It is possible that the use of metallic instruments goes back to pre-Columbian times. Coming from the Andean area, they possibly reached the hands of the Machiguengans through a long chain of bartering.

The sons remove the roots and smaller plants. Dry or rotten trees are not felled, but are taken care of during the burning.

It is difficult to determine the average amount of energy which is required for the felling process, as composition and size of the different trees varies so greatly. The task is undoubtedly a difficult one, and at times takes up to two months, depending on the extent of the area and the daily working hours.

The size of the *chacra* varies considerably, especially in Monte Carmelo. Here the introduction of cash products (coffee, cocoa, peanuts) has profoundly altered traditional agricultural patterns. Nevertheless, for the more traditional families, I estimate the *chacra* size at between one-fourth and a little over one-half hectares per family. The *chacra* extends over irregular plots of land, often circular in shape. Concerning the size difference of the *chacras*, some natives claimed that this depended basically on the farmer's desire to work; others maintained that it depended on family needs.

Except in situations where cultural patterns have greatly deteriorated (as in Monte Carmelo), *chacras* are separated by considerable distances. This is due to the limitations of the environment: the absence of large areas of good quality land; low population density; and the need for large areas of forests near the house to provide hunting, privacy; etc. The very slash-and-burn system, which presupposes a low population density, requires for its stability the strict observance of established patterns concerning *chacra* proximity. In Monte Carmelo the erosion of these traditional patterns has created serious problems.

The burning process takes place in July, August, and September, when the river level is at its lowest. Once the cut vegetation is dry, the Machiguengan waits for a dry, windy day which has been preceded by at least nine or ten days without rain. These factors guarantee a good burn. The wind direction will determine the point where the burning starts. At times sudden rainfalls or unexpected changes in wind direction prevent a good burn. Then a second attempt is made a few days later. The charred wood continues smoldering days after the burn. Charred trunks are left everywhere; the Machiguengan uses them as paths. The small, clear areas between the burned trunks are covered by ashes. If the land is on a slope, the first rains wash away this cover.

Now the sowing begins, a task in which the whole family participates. The different crops intermingle on the *chacra*. Without regard to any apparent order, they sow yucca or bitter manioc (*tsekatsi*), maize (*shinki*), unkucha or taro, bananas, and the like, using the spaces between the trunks. The Machiguenga takes care to maintain the distances between plants of the same species as well as between different species. These distances, established traditionally, are made "by estimation" during the sowing process. The first crops sown are yucca and maize.

Stalks rather than seeds are used for sowing yucca, the basis of the Machiguenga diet ("yucca" and "meal" are designated by the same word in their language). The bare stalks are obtained from the previous *chacra* harvest or may be provided by a nearby relative.

I did not have an opportunity to see the selection of stalks for reproduction, but it is recognized generally that in Monte Carmelo many varieties of yucca known to the "old Machiguengas" are being lost. The selection of stalks at present, especially in the Pereira area, seems completely haphazard. But the interest and knowledge shown by a more traditional settler, when asked about varieties of yucca, makes one suspect that stalk selection is still carried out among these more traditional members. This is confirmed by the fact that some families, who consume large quantities of *masato*, made of fermented yucca, know which varieties lend themselves best for preparation of this drink. These families still basically retain the traditional Machiguengan diet.

The yucca stalks are cut into small stems fifteen to twenty centimeters long. These stems must have a considerable number of nodes (four to eight) from which emerge the buds that give rise to a new plant. While sowing methods differ for new *chacras*, in all cases one to three stalks are placed diagonally into the earth with the nodes pointing upwards, about twenty centimeters deep and with one end uncovered. On old *chacras* the hole left after the removal of the rhizomes of earlier yucca plants is used.

The criteria determining the number of stalks sown are basically (1) the quality of the soil, (2) the quality of the stalk and the number of its nodes, and (3) the variety of plant. A single, well-noded stalk is sufficient in black, fertile soil with few stones. But risks increase as the quality of the land decreases; thus, two to three stalks will be used in red and stony lands. The second criterion, i.e. the quality of the stalk and the number of its nodes, is of secondary importance. A thick, well-noded stalk reduces risks and under good conditions may be sown alone. Thin stalks with few nodes are sown in pairs or in groups of three.

The varieties of yucca[2] have different growth rates. Some, such as *kemarigáneri*, mature after six to eight months, others require longer. The varieties most valued in Monte Carmelo are those whose growth takes longer, as for example *oegánire*.

Yucca may be sown throughout the year as each plant is harvested, using the holes left by previous plants. The removal of the rhizomes takes place after six months to a year, depending on the variety of plant, soil

[2]   The term "variety" as applied to Machiguengan yuccas constituted a problem during my field work. My lack of botanical knowledge made it difficult for me to distinguish apparently similar yuccas with different names.

It is also possible that often it was not a question of varieties, properly speaking, but of "family plants"; that is, certain superior plants have been repeatedly selected for reproduction, gradually giving rise to new varieties. This process, which may extend over several generations, could help us to trace the historical origin of the human groups themselves.

type, and degree of ripeness desired. Black, stone-free earth will produce good yuccas at the end of six or seven months. Stony and red soils delay the development of the rhizomes for another five or six months.

The removal of the rhizomes depends on four factors: (1) plant "variety," (2) soil quality, (3) desired ripeness of the rhizomes, and (4) consumption needs (the "larder" is close to the house and one may "harvest" what is required for a few days[3]). First the stalks and branches are cut and placed in a heap to one side. Then the soil is loosened with a machete and the rhizomes are carefully removed.

Yuccas are sown no more than three consecutive times on one *chacra*; some natives do not sow more than twice. Further sowings would only produce small yuccas with little flavor.

Preliminary investigations indicate that the Machiguengan sows more yucca than necessary; it is rarely scarce. This may respond to a wish for security against plant failure.

The sowing of the yucca takes two to eight days and is carried out by the father and his oldest sons. It is also their job to sow maize, usually after the yucca has been sown.[4] Maize is first sown close to where the first shoots of the yucca are beginning to appear. The shoots serve as a guide in spacing the different species. Distances are carefully maintained, although without apparent order. A hole about ten centimeters deep is made with a stick held in the right hand. Two to four maize kernels are sown in each hole (the criteria used to determine the number of kernels are similar to those used for yucca). This work requires some effort, depending on the texture of the soil. The task is repeated until the whole farm is covered, a process which may take some days. The harvest takes place after three months, if unripe maize is desired, or the maize is left to dry on the ear for another month. This last method produces chicken feed. Unlike yucca, maize is generally only planted once in a *chacra*. As maize is an important source of proteins, a new *charcra* must be sown annually.

After the maize, the next crops are the tubers (*sachapapa* or *ongo*), the sweet potato (*koriti*), pineapple, and others. These crops are planted by the women, who mix them with the earlier crops in the *chacra*. Generally speaking, these crops are limited to small areas.

Pineapple (*tsiriandi*) in its many known varieties is planted along the entire perimeter of the *chacra*; the Machiguengans maintain that its spiny leaves prevent the yucca from being eaten by animals. Preliminary investigations suggest that the motive for this practice is rather the desire for privacy (Johnson, personal communication).

[3] The yucca plant, once harvested, remains in usable condition for two to five days. To delay deterioration, it is often buried in a hole beside the house.
[4] Occasionally the maize precedes the yucca. On other occasions a small amount of yucca is sown before the burn, guaranteeing an early supply (Johnson, personal communication).

Other crops gradually added in small quantities and of minor importance are: bananas, achiote (*poxoti*), sugarcane, *shonate, poe* (tuber), *magona, bingoki* (a small tree which produces pods with edible seeds), *shounaki, makato, kiemi* (a sweet squash), a few cotton plants, *pamoko, rimangona,* and some others, including medicinal plants such as the various *ibengikis.* Papayas (*ti'ndi*) grow from seeds dropped by the people working in the fields, and from seeds carried by birds. A certain variety of common bean is also sown.

Although a *chacra* farm will yield yucca for up to three years, the growth of underbrush and grass (cleared every four to six months), plus the growing invasion by insects, gradually reduce output. When there are no more suitable lands in the area (a common occurrence after four to six years), the Machiguengan will move his home, erecting a new house and *chacra* in a relatively uninhabited region. *Chacras* very far from the home are not desirable.

The *chacra* provides not only vegetable foods. Some insects and larvae are associated with the plants (e.g. the *kororo* larva, which lives between the stalks of the yucca). The *shigopa* larvae is allowed to grow in trunks of banana trees or palms which have been felled for the purpose. Firewood is also available on the *chacra*, from partially burned trunks.

Hunting

Hunting constitutes one of the central activities; it is a principal source of proteins and is the natives' favorite pastime. Hunting expeditions occur throughout the year, although the heavy downpours of the rainy season interfere. May is regarded as the best time for hunting. This is when the *shima-shiri* tree flourishes and the monkeys are fat. The men go out in groups of two or three, often accompanied by their sons; the former carry guns and the latter generally use bows and arrows.

Machiguengan bows and arrows are an engineering feat of proportions, balance, and accuracy. The bows are of hard, flexible wood, and the arrows of reed with various tips (appropriate for each animal to be hunted).

Hunting expeditions last hours or even days. They may be nocturnal, aided by flashlights, but generally take place during the day. The Machiguengans travel far from the home into the woods. There are numerous, crisscrossing paths which have been created by the constant expeditions.

The Machiguengans travel in silence, alert for animal sounds or tracks. They sometimes station themselves in trees over places frequented by animals and wait hours for their arrival. When the prey is sighted, it is approached cautiously. When it is within range, it is shot. If the prey does not fall, a long pursuit starts, during which time the hunting paths may be left behind. Traps are sometimes used. They are not common in Monte Carmelo, although they appear to be so elsewhere (Ferrero 1966: 125–127). In Monte Carmelo they are used mainly by children to hunt small birds.

The most valued prey include the *huangana* (*sandabiri*), the *sachavaca* or tapir (*kemari*), the *sajino* (*shíndori*), the *majaz* (*samani*), the grey-coated *sajino* (*keitiarikiti*), the *ronsoco* (*ibeto*), and others. Monkeys are also abundant and prized: the spider monkey (*osheto*), the black monkey (*komaguinaro*), the howling monkey (*yaniri*), and others. Among the birds, all are eaten, except for turkey buzzards and birds of prey, but those with white meat are preferred: the turkey hen (*kenari, sankate*), trumpeters (*séyoni, tsacami*), and toucans (*oe, pishiti*). Deer (*maniro*) are not eaten because of the belief that they possess a diabolical female spirit. Neither do they eat serpents nor most insects.

The Machiguengan is very familiar with animal behavior, tracks, and places frequented, such as watering places (*tsimi*). He also knows their vulnerable points and the most effective arrow tip.

The animals bagged are carried by the older children. On occasion they return without game. However, hunting expeditions are also occasions for collecting food. Various types of insects and edible wild vegetables are gathered up on their way: larvae, certain types of ants, fruit, palmetto (the bark of certain palm trees), *magona*, etc. Some are consumed en route, while others are wrapped in leaves and carried home.

Upon returning, if the hunt has been very successful, the game is shared among the adults who participated in the hunt, and the rest is sent as a gift to neighboring relations. This guarantees a constant supply of meat from a variety of animals. The first parts to be eaten will be the innards, boiled or roasted. A portion may be preserved, cured, or smoked.

Fishing

Fishing is another important source of protein among the natives of the Upper Urubamba, when hunting in the forests is inadequate.

Fishing methods differ, depending on the state of the river waters. Between December and April the river rises and the waters become muddy. In this case a small net is normally used; at times the fish are also caught by hand in shallow waters. Muddy waters make a large haul possible. When the river is flowing clearly, the bow and arrow are used, especially in bends of calm water. The fishhook is also used, but the haul is then usually smaller.

At certain periods (every two to four months), two or more families join together to practice another method, poisoning. The roots of a stout weed, the *kogui*, are mashed, yielding a poisonous juice. The *kumo* plant is also used. Then a small tributary is closed off with reed mats (see Plate 3). Its preparation takes a whole day, and at daybreak on the following day a group heads for the source of the tributary, where the poisonous substance is dumped.

A short time later, the dazed fish are carried along by the current and trapped in the reed curtain. This method allows a large catch, shared among the participating families. Edible and valued varieties include: *cobĭri, omani, charába, mámori, pangotsita, contsi, tsegori,* and *máboro*, the number exceeding thirty species. The fish is often cured or smoked for preservation.

Plate 3. Preparing reeds for making straw mats

Gathering

Although gathering does not constitute an organized activity, it is carried out on a large scale. For example, on every hunting expedition gathering occurs. At the *chacras*, the insects which live among the crops are collected. During frequent "walks" through the woods, mothers and children consume a large number of larvae, fruit, etc. Visits to relations are also an occasion for gathering food en route (see Plate 4).

Among the items collected are: larvae of butterflies, cicadas (*tsigueiri*), the larvae and honey of wasps and bees (*sahni*), ants and termites, toads and frogs, and land and water snails (*pomboro, sánkiro, isorábaki*).

Among the plants gathered are: wild fruit, palm hearts, rhizomes and tubers, berries, grains, nuts, and mushrooms and toadstools.

Such customs, added to the seasonal variability of the products, make it difficult to determine the amounts and types of food gathered throughout the year. But their importance in the diet is unquestionable, especially if we consider the high protein value of many of these types of food.

Plate 4. Catching grasshoppers and cicadas (*tsigueiri*)

FACTORS OF CHANGE

Excluding intertribal conflicts in the region, there have been three main causes of social and ecological changes occurring in the Upper Urubamba in the last eighty years: (1) the rubber era, (2) the Andean migration, and (3) the Instituto Lingüístico de Verano.

The Rubber Era and Its Consequences

The exploitation of rubber through the use of native manpower produced demographic disturbances in settlement patterns (Varese 1972). The introduction of infectious and contagious diseases, which caused a massive reduction of the native population, dates from those years.

Many Machiguengans who apparently inhabited the tributaries of the Upper Urubamba at that time were abducted in "raids" and forced to work extracting latex. The rubber planters usually made use of the headman (*curaca*), stationed at the mouth of the tributary, for controlling the natives. Payment for goods, if any was made, was effected through the *curaca*, who redistributed the products given to him: large chests containing knives, machetes, fabrics, mirrors, necklace beads, pots, mosquito nets, etc.

When the rubber boom was over (approximately 1912), Fidel Pereira remained in the region and, along with his children, retains this method of labor control. In 1950 he had forty native families working for him through the intermediary of the *curaca*. In exchange for goods, the natives sowed and harvested coffee, cocoa, and, during a short period, cotton. They gathered green vanilla and incense for Pereira. These were sold, along with other products, downstream up to 1920–1930, and later upstream. The natives also took care of Pereira's forty head of cattle and thirty hogs and at one time they were also employed (unsuccessfully) in wood exploitation.

It is difficult to analyze the relationship between Pereira and "his Machiguengas." As he himself had a Machiguengan mother and spoke Machiguengan, he usually took the daughter of his *curaca* or any other woman from "his" families as his wife. Relationships of kinship exist between the Pereiras and almost all the natives.

In 1952 Pereira divided up his forty families between his three grown sons, keeping ten families for himself. Years later, one more son and two daughters had the same number of families in their service. The service of these families was at the constant disposal of the Pereiras.

This labor system characterizes Machiguengan life in the Upper Urubamba today. Besides working their own farms, the native families work the Pereira farms, especially for the coffee and cocoa crops. Working under the same conditions as the Pereiras, they receive products in exchange, although presently payment is usually in cash.

This method of working has caused the formation of communities or more densely populated regions, as in the case of Monte Carmelo, where a variable number of native families revolve around one of the Pereira families.

It should be pointed out that the Dominican missions, which played so important a role in the history of the Machiguengans of the upper part of

Upper Urubamba (as well as in Lower Urubamba), had little influence over the region where the Pereiras settled (between the Kompiroshiato river and Pongo Mainique), although Fidel Pereira's children did pass through the Quillabamba mission schools.

The Andean Migration

Since colonial times, large estates (haciendas) were formed in the highest part of the Upper Urubamba (from Santa Ana to Cocambilla). This was a border zone between the Andean ethnic group and the Machiguengan. Coca appears to have been an important crop, probably obtained in Inca times through the formation of human "islands" which attempted a vertical control of various ecological recesses (Murra 1972).

But these migrations acquired a massive nature only after the 1940's, and especially after the guerrilla activities of Hugo Blanco (1961–1963). The Andean peasants were pushed by a population explosion, the scarcity of land, and poor working conditions. They were soon established throughout the Upper Urubamba and along its tributaries.

These impoverished peasants in search of a better future devote themselves to commercial agriculture on a large scale. On small *chacras* which are gradually expanding, they plant coffee, cocoa, fruit trees, tea, and coca, which they sell at market prices in the new settlements. The money acquired is used to purchase tools and other industrial and manufactured goods sold in these towns. Part of the money is used for the education of their children in the schools of the provincial and departmental capitals (Craig 1969).

Their intensive agriculture on a permanent site is not prospering in many cases. The limiting ecological conditions of the tropical woods require the abandoning of the farm after a few years of use; before this time the peasant gradually begins to use the adjoining land. Vast areas have been deforested, with the consequent erosion and soil impoverishment. Before this occurs, the advance of peasants in search of virgin lands increases, leaving behind the devastating traces of their costly contacts.

Meanwhile, the Machiguengan natives are invaded by the undesirable *puñaruna* (loosely translated as "foreigner," the name they give to the Andean). Some flee, taking refuge in the upper parts of the tributaries. Others (generally those linked with the Dominican missions) eventually hire out to the Andean bosses. Working conditions in these situations are very bad and many abandon the boss after a time. At the same time the Machiguengans lose many women to the peasants, who abduct them for cohabitation.

In spite of these problems, the Machiguengan who has to some extent adapted to the new culture sees in coffee and cocoa two possible sources of money, and therefore of manufactured goods. Added to this is the status and prestige offered by farming these products.

The Influence of the Linguistic Institute

The advent of the missionaries from the Instituto Lingüístico de Verano (Summer Linguistic Institute) dates from 1952. Following the existing grouping of native families, they set up bilingual schools and are attempting the "Peruvianization" and evangelization of the native.

The first school, established in Pangoa in 1952, has been discontinued. A second, founded in Monte Carmelo in the sixties, attracts pupils from the whole Pereira area (see Plate 5). A precarious landing strip for small airplanes serves as a link between the institute and the teachers.

Plate 5. Monte Carmelo students dressed especially for the visit of the Quillabamba authorities

One of Fidel Pereira's daughters, trained by the institute at its base in Yarinacocha, Pucallpa, is in charge of the school. She provides bilingual training in Spanish and Machiguengan for the primary grades. The institute's work includes the training of a local native to handle medicines.

Through training bilingual teachers, the North American missionaries inculcate the natives with an overvaluation of work and an ethic within the canons of the "American way of life." Tobacco, intoxicating drinks, and drugs for ceremonial use are prohibited. The teacher embodies a

Protestant work ethic that impels him to grow cash crops. Considering himself as the leader of the community and supported by the institute missionaries, he applies his energies to growing coffee and cocoa, crops which acquire a symbolic prestige value. The bilingual teacher usually has the largest coffee and cocoa farms. (This observation appears to be corroborated by investigations made among other native groups of the Peruvian forest area [Mayer 1971]). Working hours are doubled, and increasing coffee, cocoa, and other crops (recently peanuts) becomes the objective of the evangelized.

Cash crops imply profits, and money must be saved or used. The Protestant work ethic in Upper Urubamba advocates a greater consumption of foreign manufactured goods, ranging from machetes and clothing to milk and canned tuna fish. The institute supports the formation of a community store, usually run by the teacher. The goods are delivered by the institute's airplane, and the natives gradually increase their consumption of goods.[5] Acting as a training center, the school succeeds in inculcating the new work ethic among new Machiguengan generations: cash crops become a matter of prestige and the consumption of foreign goods a necessity.

The Gregorian calendar is introduced, and observance of religious festivals is expected. Time is divided into hours and minutes, and this is reflected in the strict observance of the daily routine: breakfast, school, lunch, work, dinner, etc.

In Yomentoni (a new settlement of peasants six hours by road from Monte Carmelo), there is another school run by the state, attended by a few Machiguengan children.

SOCIOECOLOGICAL CHANGES

The above factors have caused many changes among the Machiguengans of Upper Urubamba. New elements have been variously rejected, reformulated, or completely accepted.[6] But the effects of these new elements are increasingly alerting the foundations of native culture. Technological innovations and participation in a commercial agrarian economy, with prices established by the mechanics of a capitalist market, are changing the character of this society. A transition from tribalism to peasantry is occurring, under the most disadvantageous conditions.

[5] The institute missionaries set up these shops for a protectionist motive over native economies. Swindling is characteristic of economic relations between mountain dwellers and natives of the forests, to the detriment of the latter.
[6] Here the creative factor begins to operate: "The process of adaptation to local factors is a creative one, in which the agriculturist transforms the environment in the process of adapting to it" (Johnson 1972:154).

At the agricultural level, it is no longer only the Pereiras who farm cash crops. Traditionally, the Pereiras were the only Machiguengans who regularly planted coffee (2,000 to 8,000 bushes), although without consistent success. The teacher in Monte Carmelo, assisted by native manpower, had 7,000 coffee and 4,000 cocoa bushes in 1972. She obtained 35 bags of coffee in the harvest. Her father, Fidel Pereira, annually obtains 20 to 30 bags of coffee and 5 to 10 of cocoa. There are five more Pereiras in the region engaged in this type of production.

More traditional natives, as well as the first graduates of the school, attempt to sow cash crops as the Pereiras have done, as soon as they marry. They are motivated by a desire to increase consumption of foreign goods, or to acquire status and prestige. In any case, they are few in number and possess 20 to 300 bushes. (There are also those who do not participate in this new trend.)

In preparing the new *chacra*, following the advice of the *puñarunas*, the natives mix coffee and cocoa plants with traditional crops. Keeping the advised distances, they plant all or part of the *chacra* with coffee (most frequently), cocoa, or both. Andean peasant techniques are put into practice with disregard for the adaptive efficiency of traditonal techniques. I have seen Samuel, the teacher's husband, sow maize in rows in the manner used on farms in temperate climates. But studies prove the adaptive effectiveness of sowing without any apparent order as a system for counteracting erosion in tropical zones (Meggers 1971; Geertz 1971).

The slash-and-burn system is being abandoned without regard for the great risks this implies:

The fact that it is the only agricultural technique that can be practiced indefinitely without permanent damage to the land accounts for its widespread occurrence throughout the tropics. Its success in conserving the fertility of the soil carries with it a price, however, in the form of relatively low concentrations of populations and permanency of residence (Meggers 1971:23).

The *chacra* of traditional crops is abandoned or is of secondary importance at the end of three years, just when coffee is beginning to bear fruit. The natives have tried to resolve this difficulty by making new *chacras* with traditional crops (where they will once again mix them with the new products) near their homes.

Considering the present family concentration in Monte Carmelo, finding suitable land not far from the home already constitutes quite a problem. In the face of this situation, the native who tries to make money by planting coffee may be obliged to abandon his newly flourishing bushes, a dilemma that has occurred in Monte Carmelo. Cocoa farming is even more serious, since the first fruits do not appear until the fifth year, and the plant requires intensive care during its period of growth.

Muro's studies in the Upper Peruvian *selva* reveal a 50 percent reduction in harvest for soils in an advanced state of laterization (Muro and

Platinius 1949). Preliminary data on the Upper Urubamba area also reveal a significant decrease in land fertility after the second and third year of consecutive use (Johnson, personal communication). Frequent use for permanent agriculture in tropical woods does not succeed: ". . . clearing of rain forest destroys the mineral cycle in the forest. Subsequent agriculture on this soil is disappointing; and after abandonment of the field, shrub and land of low productivity takes the place of the highly productive rain forest" (Witkamp 1971: 101). This limiting factor prevents population concentration within the framework of a subsistence agriculture (see Plate 6).

Plate 6. Three contiguous areas of frequent use

Besides the agricultural problems mentioned, the formation of settlements causes other serious difficulties. Firewood, which generally comes from partially burned trunks of the *chacra* or surrounding area, is scarce, giving rise to the need for a substitute fuel, kerosene (bought in the teacher's store).

Good-quality palm trees, necessary for house construction, are scattered — at times days' travel away. The grouping of houses makes the task very difficult and inferior quality trees must often be used instead. A house lasts from four to eight years, depending on the variety of palm tree used. In regions of great population density, this represents a difficult obstacle to permanent settlement.

The gradual loss of traditional farming techniques is only one aspect. The vast knowledge of edible plants of the traditional settlers contrasts with the limited knowledge of the new generations. This is also true regarding the knowledge about crop spacing, soil selection, and general botanical, zoological, and ecological knowledge of the tropical forests.

The introduction of firearms dates from the rubber period. They were used by few people, perhaps only by the Pereiras, because of their high cost and scarcity. But the last few years have seen a proliferation of firearms, which are gradually replacing traditional weapons. Firearms are borrowed by those who do not have them in exchange for a share of the prey captured. The use of these weapons has increased hunting effectiveness, and many species have considerably decreased in the last ten years as a result. Some previously abundant species are now scarce; others are almost extinct. The resulting ecological imbalance has repercussions in the forest (Brown and Orians 1970).

The disappearance of animals has made hunting a very difficult task. Today it is common for a group of hunters to travel many kilometers for an entire day and return home empty-handed. This situation is worse in the more modernized regions (for example, Koribeni), where most proteins now come from the market rather than the woods.

The forests adjacent to Monte Carmelo are the source of proteins for thirteen families. If we add to this the increasing flow of Andean migrant peasants from the mountains and their precarious settlements, we see that the problem is more serious. Highway construction (such as the Quillabamba–Quiteni) has practically eliminated the remaining animals. In Monte Carmelo the use of dogs in hunting is growing.

The resulting scarcity of game has forced the Machiguengans to eat animals which used to be scorned (like the armadillo) or feared and considered taboo (deer). A second solution is the breeding of domestic fowl. There is practically no family in the area of Monte Carmelo which does not have a few chickens, hens, and a rooster. In 1972 the teacher had more than sixty, plus fifteen ducks, and two cashew birds (*crax pauji*). The meat from these birds is only used on rare occasions, in times of prolonged scarcity of game or fish.

Eggs are seldom eaten (except by the Pereiras, who have done so on several occasions). The eggs are hatched or sold. The sale of eggs is carried out through the teacher, who acts as intermediary between the merchant from the launch and the natives. Because she is the most familiar with the "national culture" and speaks Spanish, she sells their products. Her house and school constitute the center of Monte Carmelo's market economy.

A third source of proteins is purchased at the small stores in the towns of the Andean migrants. There they buy canned fish, plus other items such as candy, brown sugar, bread, butter, oil, noodles, chocolate, carbonated drinks, and cookies. Most of the profits from the sale of coffee and cocoa are spent for these products. The quality of the purchased proteins is not high, and the presence of intermediaries results in excessively high prices for all goods.

The formation of new riverside settlements has caused a scarcity of fish. In the face of a game shortage, the people go to the river, and if the yield is not sufficient, new fishing techniques are used. In the short term, dynamite is effective, and, although illegal, it is easy to obtain in the immigrant settlements; but in the long run its use is seriously threatening the river fauna.

Changes are also occurring at the level of food gathering, though these are not as great. The increase in the time devoted to cash crops and school results in the loss of knowledge of the flora and fauna. The old generations and more traditional natives have a vast repertoire of botanical and zoological knowledge that is no longer being handed down.

Parallel with this, the influence of the attitudes of the Andean migrant and of some missionaries operates against the consumption of certain species. Larvae and insects are not viewed as a suitable food source by these people, and their consumption causes great loss of prestige.

In summary, changes in agriculture, hunting, fishing, and food gathering have produced significant changes in diet.[7]

The introduction of new fruit trees and other products have also caused changes in the diet. Oranges, mandarin oranges, lemons, avocados, rose apples, and the breadfruit are now eaten on a small scale, as is rice, which has recently been introduced but is not popular. The Pereiras are the only people who consume coffee and cocoa.

The changes in the traditional subsistence system have altered the structure of economic relations. As we saw earlier, the use of native labor is characteristic of the mastery of the Pereira family, and natives are being incorporated into the national economy with this family as intermediaries. But the conditions of this domination have changed. The natives no longer wish to work for goods, demanding the payment of a daily wage. Furthermore, as we have seen earlier, the teacher purchases native products, such as coffee, cocoa, achiote (*Bixa orellana*), rice, maize, peanuts, and eggs; and for her personal use she buys maize and *teirigoki* (seed used to feed chickens). She keeps sun-dried animal skins, also bought from the natives, in expectation of a visit from a foreign skin trader. Occasionally she will resell the skins in Pucallpa through the Linguistic Institute. In the store she sells the following goods, brought by plane from Pucallpa: machetes, cloth fabric, clothing, cups, plates, aluminum pans, lamps, torches, thread, needles, fishhooks, shoes, blankets, notebooks and penholders, and firearms (on special request). Other products, brought from Quiteni by the launch at prices which are

---

[7] Some products, such as salt, have a very deep-rooted usage. In the treeless areas of the Sacramento pampas, for example, all salt has been obtained through exchange since pre-Columbian times (Varese 1968).

already inflated, are: kerosene, matches, salt, oil, detergents, batteries, candy, sugar, evaporated milk, etc.

Natives from the whole area occasionally make purchases at the store shop, being served by the teacher or her eldest daughter. From time to time Andean migrants also use the store. In this way Monte Carmelo operates as a center for spreading cultural changes. New products and cultural features gravitate to Monte Carmelo, and from here they are disseminated among all the natives. New attitudes and desires are created through the school.

The system of Machiguengan kinship is also gradually being altered. New categories are created and new distinctions established, while others are disappearing. Spanish designations are beginning to replace native words. The impoverishment of the habitat and the Christian ideology operate against polygyny.

The traditional drunken native festivals are avoided by those who have been evangelized. Among the others, however, alcoholism is affecting native families, creating psychosocial conflicts that erode the bases of Machiguengan culture.

The traditional cosmology — a universe of beneficent and malefic gods — is beginning to disintegrate. As it is associated with knowledge of the habitat and traditional culture, the mythology is losing its meaning, being regarded as belonging to the "old Machiguengans." Traditional social institutions, such as puberty rites, food taboos, shamanism, games and amusements, etc., are being abandoned.

The native Machiguengan of Upper Urubamba, assuming the role of a peasant, in the national economy, seeks equal treatment with his migrant neighbor but fails to achieve it. Converted into a peasant, but unable to manage any element of the national culture, he is at the bottom of a dominating hierarchy (Fuenzalida 1970: 69). He either flees from the Andean invasion or is exploited by these impoverished immigrants. The closed existence of the native settlers is passing away. Those who have adapted to the national culture are becoming part of a "peasant lumpen" of the Upper Latin American forest. Others, fleeing to the less accessible streams, are making a last effort to retain their ethnic identity.

REFERENCES

BROWN, JERRAM L., GORDON H. ORIANS
1970   "Spacing patterns in mobile animals," in *Annual review of ecology and systematics*, volume one, 239–262. Edited by R. F. Johnston. Palo Alto, California: Annual Reviews.
CONKLIN, HAROLD C.
1969   "An ethnological approach to shifting agriculture," in *Environment and*

cultural behavior. Edited by Andrew P. Vayda, 221–233. New York: Natural History Press.

CRAIG, WESLEY W.
1969 "The peasant movement of La Convención," in *Latin American peasant movements.* Edited by Henry A. Landsberger, 274–296. Ithaca, New York: Cornell University Press.

FERRERO, P. ANDRÉS
1966 *Los machiguengas, tribu selvática del sur-oriente Peruano.* Lima: OPE.

FUENZALIDA, FERNANDO
1970 "Poder, raza y etnia en El Perú contemporáneo," in *El indio y el poder en el Perú.* Lima: Instituto de Estudios Peruanos.

GADE, DANIEL W.
1972 "Comercio y colonización en la zona de contacto entre la sierra y las tierras bajas del valle del Urubamba en el Perú," in *Actas y Memorias del XXXIX Congreso Internacional de Americanistas,* volume four, 207–221. Lima: Instituto de Estudios Peruanos.

GEERTZ, CLIFFORD
1971 *Agricultural involution.* Berkeley: University of California Press.

JOHNSON, ALLEN W.
1972 Individuality and experimentation in traditional agriculture. *Human Ecology* 1 (2): 149–159. New York.

MATTHIESSEN, PETER
1968 *The cloud forest* (second printing). New York: Viking.

MAYER, ENRIQUE
1971 *Vida y cambios, cultura ashaninka.* Programa Académico de Ciencias Sociales, Area de Antropología, Oficina de Trabajo de Campo. Lima: Universidad Católica del Perú.

MEGGERS, BETTY
1971 *Amazonia: man and culture in a counterfeit paradise.* Arlington Heights, Illinois: AHM.

MURO, JOSÉ DEL C., HANS PLATINIUS
1949 *Suelos y posibilidades agrícolas entre el Boquerón y Pucallpa.* Tingo María, Peru: Estación Experimental Agrícola.

MURRA, JOHN V.
1972 *El control vertical de un máximo de pisos ecológicos en la economía de las sociedades Andinas.* Huánuco: Universidad Hermilio Valdizán.

SCHWERIN, KARL H.
1970 "Apuntes sobre la yuca y sus orígenes," in *Boletín informativo de antropología.* Caracas: Asociación Venezolana de Sociología.

VARESE, STEFANO
1968 *La sal de los Cerros.* Lima: Universidad Peruana de Ciencias y Tecnología.
1972 "Las sociedades nativas de la selva," in *Diagnóstico socio-económico preliminar del área rural Peruana.* Lima: SINAMOS.

WATTERS, R. F.
1968 *La agricultura migratoria en Perú.* Mérida: IFLAIC.

WITKAMP, M.
1971 "Soils as a component of ecosystems," in *Annual review of ecology and systematics,* volume two, 85–110. Edited by R. F. Johnston. Palo Alto, California: Annual Reviews.

Cannabis and Cultural Groups
in a Colombian Municipio

WILLIAM L. PARTRIDGE

The anthropological contribution to an understanding of cannabis seems to lie in three distinct but related areas: (1) studies of the nature of the culture and community in which the phenomenon is present; (2) translation of concepts, models, and methods into applicable forms for testing in the field of social and cultural realities in which the phenomenon is immersed; and (3) ethnohistorical study. The work reported here falls mainly within the first of these three divisions, a community study in the tradition of social anthropology (Arensberg and Kimball 1965).

The objective of the study, begun in July of 1972 in a *municipio* on the north coast of Colombia, South America, is the description and analysis of the subcultural units connected to the cannabis cycle, cultivation, marketing, and consumption. The paper will focus on the subcultural groups associated with cannabis in relation to their position and function in the larger community, following a brief ethnohistorical review.

I. ETHNOHISTORY

The introduction of cannabis into Spanish South America is not well documented. Patiño (1967, 1969) indicates that hemp was introduced not once but several times by the Spanish: experiments were attempted in Peru, Mexico, Chile, and Colombia, but only Chile developed the capacity to export hemp to Spain (Patiño 1969). In Colombia reports from 1607, 1610, 1632, and 1789 indicate that repeated introductions failed to

The research is supported by the National Institute of Mental Health Predoctoral Research Fellowship number 1F01MH54512–01 CUAN and the supplementary grant number 3F01DA54512–01S1 CUAN.

produce a hemp industry for the rigging of the Spanish fleet. Silvestre (Vergara y Velasca 1901) in his 1789 description of the viceroyalty of Santa Fé de Bogotá indicates that hemp was introduced in the savanna of Bogotá, but failed so completely that no seed was available for further experimentation. He urged the reintroduction of hemp cultivation near Santa Marta or Cartagena and also that seed be shipped from Spain (Vergara y Velasca 1901). In Silvestre's opinion hemp could replace *cabuya* or the fiber of *Fourcroya foetida* (Patiño 1967) in Colombia, indicating the most telling reason for the former's failure in South America. *Fique, pita*, or *cabuya* was collected in tribute from the indigenous peoples of Colombia by the first Spanish colonists (Reichel-Dolmatoff 1951). As late as the early 1800's *cabuya* was a Colombian export (Vergara y Velasca 1901). *Cabuya* replaced hemp in the manufacture of such items as sandals, rope and cordage, sacks, harnesses, and fishnets (Patiño 1967). Another native fiber, cotton, replaced hemp in even such basic items as candlewick, used in huge quantities in the mines of South America, which in Europe had been made of hemp or flax. It appears that native fiber-producing plants acted as a barrier to the diffusion of hemp. As late as the present century experiments continue in Colombia (Patiño 1969), but no hemp industry has ever existed in Colombia compared to that which existed in North America (Seale et al. 1952).

The use of cannabis products as intoxicants is still another question. Linguistic evidence indicates West African slaves brought cannabis to Brazil as the earliest route of diffusion (Patiño 1969; Aranújo 1959). The adoption of cannabis smoking by indigenous people of Brazil seems to confirm the antiquity of diffusion in that part of South America (Wagley and Galvão 1949), but the spread of the custom to Spanish America is less well known. It should be noted that cannabis competed with available indigenous intoxicants, narcotics, and hallucinogens.[1] Of these, only tobacco was adopted by Spanish colonists, which with coca had the widest distribution and popularity in the New World. Tobacco was snuffed for headache, chewed for toothache, smoked for "cold humors," and mixed with rum and *aguardiente* and applied to mosquito bites. Negro slaves and Spaniards were reported to use it for working because it reduced fatigue. Due to this property tobacco was allotted as part of the workers' rations on a Jesuit hacienda (Patiño 1967). Perhaps we have here another barrier to diffusion of cannabis in South America.

It seems certain that smoking cannabis is a relatively new innovation in the region with which we are concerned. Ardila Rodriguez (1965) and Patiño (1969) suggest the Magdalena river valley as the route of penetra-

---

[1] *Erythroxylon coca, Banisteriopsis* species, *Phyllanthus mexiae, Opuntia* species, *Datura arborea, Methysticodendron amesianum, Nicotiana tabacum*, and *Clibadium surinamense*.

tion into Colombia, from the ports of Santa Marta, Barranquilla, and Cartegena, originating in the Antilles and Panama. Specifically, Ardila Rodriguez (1965) suggests that the spread of the use of cannabis as an intoxicant dates from the work on the Panama Canal and the "intense human interchange" which resulted among circum-Caribbean countries. This interpretation is given weight by the observation that both Costa Rican and Colombian laws concerning marihuana date from 1927 and 1928 respectively (Patiño 1969; Ardila Rodriguez 1965; Torres Ortega 1965), when the movement of *braceros* and *marineros* was a fact. Nevertheless, it was not until around 1945 that the Colombian press began reporting clandestine marihuana plantations on the Atlantic coast and in the Cauca valley (Patiño 1969).

II. RESEARCH COMMUNITY BACKGROUND

The *municipio* lies at the base of the western slopes of the Sierra Nevada de Santa Marta, between two of the six rivers which flow to the Ciénaga Grande. Within its boundaries are found vast swamplands and the highest mountain peak in Colombia. The town in which the research was based is the *cabacera* of the *municipio*, at a distance of about 90 kilometers from the city of Santa Marta. The areas of dense settlement are the nonflooding lowlands at the base of the mountains and the highland valleys of the rivers. The two areas are ecologically and culturally distinct, each inhabited by a distinct subcultural population, although each is articulated politically, economically, and ritually with the *cabacera* of the lowlands.

Neither of the ecological-cultural zones was of much interest to the Spanish colonists of the sixteenth century: Spanish efforts on this part of the coast consisted mainly in exterminating the native population. A high price in blood was paid for a territory left uncolonized until the present century (Alarcon 1963).

The *municipio* is an excellent example. Governor Garcia de Lerma instituted a scorched earth policy in the region in 1529, burning towns and fields between Santa Marta and the River Magdalena. By 1600 there was no native population in the region. The land was mostly swamp. As late as 1898 a Colombian geographer notes that the region is densely forested, subject to frequent floods, and sparsely populated (Vergara y Velasca 1901).

Beginnining in 1896 however, this picture started to change dramatically, when the United Fruit Company began operations in the future *zona bananera*. By the second decade of the twentieth century, banana plantations blanketed the lowlands from the mountains to the Ciénaga Grande. The *municipio* was a center of this development. The company put in production some 10,000 hectares, and at the height of productivity a total of 30,000 hectares were under cultivation (Kamalaprija 1965; Comisión de Planificación 1964).

Development was spectacular. By 1938 the *municipio* had sprouted a population of 15,861 persons. United States capitalists, French, English, and American engineers, and a work force recruited from all over the coast founded several such towns, straightened the course of rivers, built a drainage and irrigation system, paved roads, installed bridges, completed a railroad from the docks in Santa Marta to the southern limit of the banana zone, and built work camps and employee housing on vast banana estates. Church records from 1914 to 1925 indicate that about half of the marriages performed united persons from different regions of the coast. This pattern continues to the present.

The influence of the banana company upon the organization of life in the region was felt in four ways: (1) the local elite composed of original settlers was transformed into a wealthy elite; (2) a middle sector was created by recruitments of employees from the coastal cities; (3) the traditional social relationships among landowners and laborers were altered; and (4) the nature of the social relationships among laborers themselves was changed.

Landowners who were operating tracts of cattle and sugarcane quickly converted to bananas. Some sold their land and moved to the cities, but many built fortunes selling bananas and purchased homes in the coastal cities. They sent their sons and daughters to the capital, to Europe, and to the United States for education. They held political offices at the departmental and national levels where the aristocratic cattle barons of ancient Spanish towns had previously dominated political life.

The middle sector comprised employees of the company: estate managers, clerks, commissary directors, secretaries, fruit selectors, and labor supervisors. They received single family dwellings with running water and indoor plumbing, furniture, mules and horses, coupons for shopping at the company store, medical treatment in hospitals staffed by United States physicians, and a monthly salary. Their sons and daughters were given scholarships to study at universities. Several of these families also built fortunes during the banana heyday.

Workers were provided with three rooms of a row house, running water and indoor plumbing, reduced train rates, hospital services deducted from their pay (2 percent), a machete, work clothes and boots, coupons for shopping at the company store, and a cash wage higher than that paid to workers on the coast today.

Traditional patron–client relations existed among landowners and their laborers. On the coast this relationship entailed the following responsibilities for the landowning employer: lending several hectares to his client to plant crops, credit reference at a store in town or an estate commissary, providing a degree of security in times of life crisis or illness as well as small cash gifts. Wage labor destroyed this relationship; workers demanded money in return for labor on the model of the company relationship with workers, rather than the beneficence of a patron. Landowners charged the company with "ruining the workers."

Among the workers themselves the industrialization of agriculture naturally included industrial forms of organization. The workers became quite specialized, working in groups at specialized tasks. Significantly, there were no peasants in the *municipio* during the development of the banana zone[2] as all land was devoted to the plantation production of bananas.[3]

Other subcultural groups present in the *municipio* during the early twentieth century included Middle East immigrants who opened stores, bars, and brothels, a small number of West Indian immigrants who worked as day laborers, and Americans living in the *quinta* or group of manor houses on the other side of the railroad tracks.

The picture painted by Gabriel García Márquez of this period in his novel *Cien años de soledad* is for the most part accurate (García Márquez 1970). The small hamlet was indeed transformed into a boom town, with accompanying street brawls and deaths by machete. Many informants repeat the tales of "happy drunks" on Saturday nights burning pesos to light their cigars. The elite founders were the prime movers and beneficiaries of the boom; they drank scotch, played poker, and grew rich with the Americans.

From 1915 to 1943 the company exported to the United States all the fruit it could buy or produce. In 1928 the first labor strike in Colombia began in the banana zone resulting in the massacre of thousands of workers by the Colombian army, on the morning of December 6, 1928, a fact often cited as the reason for the ultimate departure of the United Fruit Company (Montaña 1963; Fluharty 1956). On the contrary, production rose after the strike, reaching a high in 1930 and leveling off at prestrike levels. Production continued high until 1943 and only then fell drastically. During the world war no ships called for bananas at the port of Santa Marta. When the company reopened its operations in 1947, it found the land had been invaded by both wealthy private producers and landless laborers (Kamalaprija 1965).

The elaborate road system constructed by the company provided channels for invading workers, who founded several small hamlets that exist today, and colonized smallholdings nearby. In like fashion, but on a

---

[2]   This pattern changed during World War II with the invasion of the lands of the United Fruit Company by landless workers who then became peasants exploiting a few hectares. These peasants are now being offered title to the land by INCORA, but many refuse as they wish to avoid taxes. Still others desire title so as to qualify for loans with the Caja Agraria for cash crops, animals, or more land.

[3]   Original maps used by the United Fruit Company were kindly made available by the offices of INCORA in Sevilla, Magdalena.

grander scale, wealthy landowners annexed lands. The company negoti-
ated a new policy with the Colombian government. Contracts were signed
which gave the wealthy squatters the status of *arrendatarios* [tenants]; the
peasants were simply ignored. The tenants in turn agreed to sell all
bananas produced to the company and to pay US $1.00 for each hectare
not producing bananas. By the year 1949 exports were higher than the
highs of 1930.

But at this time the company began liquidating its holdings in Colombia
as a result of the changed world market. The company landholdings were
reduced until by 1964 it owned no banana-producing land. They were
concentrated to the north and the banana industry of the town and
municipio died.

With the exit of the company the *municipio* saw the exit of wealthy
plantation owners, much of the middle sector of employees, and hundreds of workers. Many families of the elite and middle sectors were
ruined. The workers lost an income that provided the impetus for migration, an income that was high compared to today's wage.[4]

Today the lowlands are devoted primarily to rice, cattle, and cattle
products. Some 48,964 hectares are devoted to pasture while only 23,195
are in agricultural crops (Departamento Administrativo Nacional de
Estadística 1971:23). Of the lands in agricultural production perhaps
only 3,000 hectares are in *pan cojer* [maize], manioc, and *plátano*, the
staple foods consumed by the population (Comisión de Planificación
1964:99). Of total lands being exploited 683 persons own farms of
between 1 and 50 hectares (Departamento Administrativo Nacional de
Estadística 1971:12).[5] In short, the *latifundia* devoted to cattle dominates
the landscape, a cultural value with an ancient pedigree in this region of
Colombia.

Concomitant with the departure of the company another process of
change was set in motion. In 1948 the civil war called *la violencia* began in
the interior regions of Colombia (see Dix 1967, Fluharty 1956). The
effects of this bloodletting, which Eric Hobsbawn (quoted in Dix

---

[4] At the exchange rate of 1.02 pesos to the dollar in 1925, the worker earning 1.30 pesos a
day received about US $1.30 a day. Today the worker makes 25 pesos a day (some as little as
15 or 20), and at the exchange rate of 23.00 he earns the equivalent of US $1.05 a day.
(Wage levels collected from former workers for the United Fruit Company. Exchange rates
taken from Kamalaprija 1965.) It should also be noted that food and goods available in
company stores were much cheaper than that available for persons not working for the
company.
[5] These figures are based on the Department of Statistics' concept of a "unit of exploitation" which is all the land within a *municipio* exploited by a single producer, individual, or
corporation. It should be noted, however, that the land-use pattern in this region of
Colombia is different from that observed in other regions (e.g. Fals Borda 1956; Fluharty
1956) where holdings are widely scattered. Land holdings in this region tend to be concentrated in a single farm. Exceptions are generally *lafifundistas* who have holdings scattered
over the *municipio* and often in several *municipios* and departments.

1967:361) has characterized as "the greatest armed mobilization of peasants in the recent history of the western hemisphere, with the possible exception of some periods during the Mexican revolution," are many and varied. The one that concerns us here took place in the *municipio*. Families of Andean peasants, mainly from the departments of Santander, Norte de Santander, and Cundinamarca, fleeing the spreading mania, migrated to the foothills of the Sierra Nevada, an area similar ecologically to the ones they had been forced to abandon. Study of the origins of these families indicates that the move was generally made between the years 1950 and 1953. Most of them directly cite *la violencia* as their motive for moving. They brought their wives, children, parents, siblings, and other relatives and staked out 50 to 200 hectares of land in the low-altitude valleys at about 400 to 500 meters. The coastal label for these new colonists is *cachacos*, meaning persons from the interior of Colombia. With them came *cachaco* storekeepers buying up stores, bars, and brothels.

Between 1947 and 1964, therefore, the entire fabric of community life underwent dramatic change, affecting every element of the community. The transition was not easy or peaceful.[6]

III. SOCIAL GROUPS AND PARTICIPATION IN THE CANNABIS CYCLE

The *cachacos* and *costeños* form the major division within the community; foreign nationals have departed, except for the *turkos* or Arabs who have been incorporated through marriage. Each subculture has a distinct social and economic organization, a distinctive heritage, and interacts socially and ritually apart from the other. Within each subculture there are further subdivisions.

The *cachacos* are composed of the highland peasants living on dispersed individual family farms and the storekeepers who live in town and are gradually acquiring large herds of cattle; the two groups form an interdependent relational system. The peasant subsists mainly upon crops he himself produces (corn and yucca or sweet manioc being the staple foods), in addition to which cash crops, rice, beans, and corn, are sold to storekeepers in town. The storekeepers grant clients credit and contracts for raising cattle on the highland farms. The peasant can there-

[6] The legend of *cachaco* violence persists to the present. Some Antioquia *cachacos* migrated into the *municipio* at the start of this century to work for the company and were responsible for the deaths of several coastal men in razor fights, according to informants. One night in 1914 the coastal townspeople dispatched the entire immigrant group with machetes. No other *cachacos* came to the *municipio* until the 1950's. While no incidents occurred at this time, the *cachacos* are perceived as violent and dangerous as evidenced by *la violencia* in the interior departments from 1948 to 1968.

fore acquire two sources of income: cash-crop sales and from the share of cattle he may fatten for a storekeeper patron. But the majority of Andean peasants have only the former option, as there are a limited number of *cachaco* patrons and cattle.

An additional source of income is provided by the cultivation of cannabis. The sparse settlement of the Sierra Nevada and the rugged terrain permit some protection and the legend of *cachaco* violence prevents too many inquisitive intruders. Cannabis is grown as a cash crop; it is not consumed by the *cachacos* who cultivate it, nor by those neighbors who do not. The sale of the crop is arranged through coastal middlemen who live in the towns and cities. *Cachaco* storekeepers do not deal in cannabis. Contracts are often made before the crop is planted and buyers sometimes treat their clients in traditional paternalistic fashion, giving gifts of rum, *aguardiente* and money. But such contracts seldom bind either party for more than one growing season. Cash cropping of cannabis appears to be the best of all possible incomes for a peasant: a kilo of coffee, the best of cash crops in Colombia, brings 12.50 pesos whereas a pound of cannabis will net from 100 to 300 pesos, depending on the quality. But it is a business that takes *pateloncitos* [guts], as one farmer said. Yet at the time of this writing no peasant in this region has been bothered by police investigation or arrest. Most highland peasants are aware, however, that pressure from the United States has produced arrests for cultivation of cannabis in other regions of Colombia.

The *cachaco vereda* [rural neighborhood] is an ethnocentric homogenous, politically cohesive unit (Fals Borda's 1955 definition applies equally well to these immigrants as it did to peasants in Boyacá). The various highland *veredas* are linked together by filial and affinal kinship ties of ritual obligations and ties of common origin. The work unit which exploits the land is composed of male members of the extended household, a man, his oldest sons, sons-in-law, and any other male relatives present. The household head directs all farming activity and even adult sons will consult with him before setting out to the field to work. Few residents of the *vereda* have family in the town or in the rural areas of the lowlands, but all have family in their *municipios* of origin. When a death occurs relatives and neighbors of the *vereda* come for the nine-day wake and the first-anniversary wake. In several cases, families living in the highlands have migrated from the same *municipio* in the interior and settled near each other. But the males of different families do not work cooperatively, except in hunting *ñeke* and other wild meat. Wage labor is absent from the highland *vereda*, excepting the police commissioner who is recruited from among the peasants. The current officeholder cultivates cannabis for cash sales. Aside from his familial and friendship ties, this may be another reason he has never arrested anyone for cultivating cannabis.

The *cachaco* storekeepers are an important economic force in the *vereda* and the town, and are clearly part of the *cachaco* subculture. They willingly sell rum and *aguardiente* for coastal fiestas such as Carnaval but do not themselves participate. Although they are part of the highland *vereda*, they play no role in the cannabis cycle.

The coastal subculture is more complex in structure and is perhaps best described as a series of subsystems. The first of these is the estate system, including landowners, estate managers, estate employees, and wage laborers. The employees on the estate sometimes live in outbuildings left by the company, but frequently they live in the better town *barrios*. They receive only slightly higher wages than the day laborer, but they have the security of steady employment, often the use of two or three hectares for planting, and the higher status of machinery operators. It is the estate employee who drives the tractors, combines, trucks, and other farm equipment. When landowners have estates in several different parts of the *municipio*, or in other *municipios* or other departments, the employees usually work on all of his holdings and thus travel widely. The day laborers, on the other hand, are recruited from the landless poor of the town and country. None live on the estates where they find work. The day laborer obtains work on a contract basis and is often called a *contractista*. He is hired by the job, for a certain task over a certain period of time, and then released: to clean an irrigation canal, to cut and clear brush from a field, to dig ditches that carry water to the crop, to fumigate a field to keep weeds down, to herd cattle, etc. Thus, the work group in the coastal subculture is composed of male nonkin. It is from this group of day laborers that the cannabis consumers come. Cannabis in the form of cigarettes is consumed among groups of day laborers while working; it is generally purchased as they have no land on which to grow their own.

The landed gentry live in the coastal cities, in contrast to the days of the banana zone when they constituted a town landed gentry. An estate manager has the responsibility of running the estate, including hiring and firing workers, directing day-to-day operations, operating a commissary for employees, and traveling to the city to consult the owner and receive money for paying workers and expenses. The managers form a minor elite in the rural lowlands and are generally recruited from an educated minority in this and other coastal towns. In many cases they are the offspring of former employees of the United Fruit Company.

Identification of commercial buyers of cannabis is a tricky and dangerous process. Contacts are difficult to maintain when one is not buying. But those who are known are drawn entirely from the upper sector of the community. Given the crisis which enveloped many of these families upon the departure of the company, it is logical that they would be drawn into lucrative trade activity in an effort to retain their newly won status and income. Not only in the case of cannabis but in the bustling contraband trade with Venezuelan black marketeers, members of the upper sector play principal roles. It is they who staff the patronage government customs posts and the smuggling operation. Cannabis traffic has been accepted as merely another contraband activity, one of the more lucrative specializations. Members of the best families are involved in contraband activity and in the towns and cities the upper-sector families are avid consumers as well. Thus, professionals, landowners, and businessmen of the coastal subculture form the commercial buyers of cannabis.

The third subsystem of the coastal subculture is that composed of coastal peasants and coastal shopkeepers. The Arab-owned shops on the market square are the focus of this subsystem, just as the highland shopkeepers of the town are the focus of the *cachaco* subculture. Credit is granted to the coastal peasant and he markets some of his produce to pay his bill where he has credit. Similarly, coastal peasants sell fruit and vegetables to street vendors. The coastal peasant generally has less land than his Andean counterpart, sometimes only two or three hectares. The coastal peasant also raises fewer cash crops than his *cachaco* counterpart, and depends upon *plátano* as his staple food more than on corn or manioc. He frequently lives in a poor *barrio* in town, commuting by burro or by foot to his farm where he may stay for several days. Typically, the coastal peasant has had years of experience as a wage laborer on other people's land. Through saving, establishing a good reputation as a *padre de familia*, and obtaining credit through a *fiador* [cosigner] he has been able to purchase his own land. He himself and his neighbors consider him a successful man.

Unlike the highlanders, the coastal peasants are consumers of cannabis, which they frequently grow for their own use and for petty trade with landless day laborers. Cannabis grown in small quantities in the lowlands is used by the long-term cannabis user. Highland commercial growers produce for the urban internal and international markets in large quantities on a hectare or more whereas the coastal peasant often grows no more than a few plants.

In summary, the cannabis production-distribution-consumption cycle involves groups drawn from both the major subcultures of the community. Andean peasants in the lower altitude valleys of the Sierra Nevada are the commercial cultivators. Consumers are drawn from the wage laborers and coastal peasants; the latter also being small-scale cultivators and the former frequently petty merchandisers. Large-scale merchandisers are members of the upper sector of the coastal subculture and among the most respected of townspeople. The place of these groups in the organization of community life is best demonstrated by Figure 1. It is important to note that these groups are not drawn from deviant, parasitic, or marginal elements of the community.

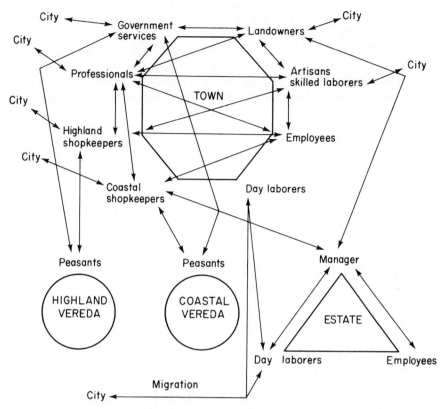

Figure 1.   Reciprocal social and economic relations between town, estate, highland *vereda*, and coastal *vereda* (including the exchange of personnel, goods, money, and services)

IV.   THE CANNABIS CYCLE

Cultivation

Today cannabis is farmed in secret; the peasant generally plants his seeds just as the March rains begin, usually on an isolated part of his farm hidden by dense underbrush. Commercial growers in the highlands first germinate their seeds in a germination box made of four logs placed in a square surrounding well-cleaned and mixed soil. Seeds are simply scattered on the surface of the prepared soil. A thick layer of commercial ant-killer is spread around the perimeter. The plants are thinned, selected, and transplanted in about 15 or 20 days to the peasants' *rosa*. The *rosa* is a mixed garden plot, always located on the steep hillsides, and moved every few years in the pattern of swidden land use. When cannabis is included in the *rosa* it is planted at the lowest point on the hillside, below the tall corn plants, far from the numerous paths which crisscross the ridge tops, to conceal the growing crop.

Coastal peasants do not utilize the germination box; they simply plant cannabis seeds in the same way they plant corn. A hole is poked in the prepared soil with a machete and covered with the foot after several seeds are inserted. Several weeks later the smaller of the plants are thinned out, leaving the healthiest looking plants to grow to maturity. When asked about this difference in planting techniques coastal informants explain that the *cachacos* use a germination box because they are all from Norte de Santander. In that region tobacco is an important cash crop, and since tobacco seeds are quite small a germination box is needed. But there is no need for this with cannabis. The coastal peasants conclude that *cachacos* plant as they do out of habit.

Peasants classify the parts of the plant in two categories: *la mona*, a mixture of resin and small leaves from the tops of the mature female plants, and *la hoja*, the larger lower leaves of both male and female plants. *La mona* is sold for around 200 to 300 pesos a pound and *la hoja* brings about 100 pesos a pound. The merchandiser usually doubles the prices paid to the peasant when the product is retailed. The growing season runs from March until August or September, or five to six months, to obtain *la mona*. Consumers universally prefer *la mona* for smoking.

It should be noted, however, that *la mona* is a generic term for cannabis as well as the terms *la amarilla* and *marihuana*.[7] Consumers usually refer to cannabis simply as *la mona* or *ella*, regardless of the category being consumed. One never hears the Spanish *cáñamo* [hemp] applied to cannabis in the *municipio*; *cáñamo* signifies a lasso of *cabuya* fiber in this region of Colombia.

Harvesting the cannabis crop takes several days of intense labor. The plants are first girdled by cutting off a ring of bark around the circumference of the trunk. In a few days the leaves begin to fall off. These are either gathered and packed for sale as they fall or are picked just before falling. When all the leaves have fallen the tip of the female plant, called *la mota*, is harvested. In this fashion the leaves are air and sun dried before sale or consumption. This process of harvesting is believed to increase the potency of the marihuana: by girdling the trunk, informants state, one conserves the *leche* [sap] of the plant and this is believed to rise to the tip of the plant since it cannot flow to the roots.

At least two varieties of cannabis are recognized by highland commer-

---

[7]   The word cannabis is frequently heard among the offspring of upper-sector families who experiment with cannabis and other drugs. A discussion of this group is omitted here, since the phenomenon is related to the influence of American and European hippie groups and clearly not related to the customary patterns of long-term use in the lower sector of the *municipio*. For similar reasons, a discussion of cannabis smoking by lawyers, dentists, agronomists, and other professional people in the urban centers is also omitted.

cial growers and lowland consumers and petty merchants. Samples of these varieties have been collected for botanical and chemical analysis.[8]

Some commercial growers report a variety of cannabis they call *patagallina* [chicken foot]. This is said to be an inferior grade, but in reality appears to be *Hibiscus cannabinus* L. or *kenaf* (Pate et al. 1954). During the 1950's a landowner in the *municipio* operated a fiber industry under contract with the United States Department of Agriculture. This operation was closed down in 1961, but plants can still be found in the area. *Patagallina* seems to resemble cannabis in leaf form and stature only, which does not preclude its sale as cannabis. This mistaken identification of *kenaf* as cannabis and the inappropriate cultivation techniques imported from the interior of the country both point to the *cachaco* cultivators as relatively new innovators. While the presence of cannabis among coastal people seems traditional, it is probably a market-induced phenomenon among the highlanders.

Distribution

There are two separate distribution systems which correspond to the two systems of cultivation. The first is the market-induced system, involving highland commercial growers and wealthy coastal buyers and retailers. This system moves large quantities of marihuana to the cities of the coast, often for export to the United States.[9] The second or local system involves no wealthy upper-sector middlemen but is specific to lower-section day laborers and coastal peasants. The coastal peasant produces cannabis in small quantities and day laborers who are consumers also purchase some for resale to fellow day laborers in the town and countryside. A single plant may produce two pounds of *la mona* and up to twenty pounds of *la hoja*, so that a peasant who grows around ten plants will frequently be able to sell several pounds and still conserve enough for his own needs.

The homes of day laborers who act as distributors are often centers where users assemble to smoke marihuana, talk and gossip, and make small purchases. Such sites are called *caletas* which means small bays or coves in nautical terminology. Since these sites are frequented by a number of people, informants were asked how secrecy and some degree of security from law-enforcement officials was maintained. They explained that the police are frequently consumers of cannabis, and that

[8]   Professor Richard Evans Schultes, Harvard University, has agreed to examine samples collected by the author from the plantations in the Sierra Nevada de Santa Marta. Chemical studies of these plants will also be undertaken in the near future.
[9]   Quantities of marihuana are confiscated by the police in the major cities of the coast as reported by *El Tiempo*, May 8, 1973; *El Espectador*, April 12, 1973; *El Espectador*, January 5, 1973; *El Espectador*, November 19, 1972; *El Tiempo*, June 13, 1973; *El Diario del Caribe*, May 26, 1973.

those who are not accept bribes quite readily. Secondly, the petty merchant usually gets on well with his neighbors because he gives them small loans of perhaps five or ten pesos, which are seldom repaid. Such a good-neighbor policy is considered a business cost to be absorbed.

Consumption

Table 1 shows the varieties of cannabis use in the *municipio* and the groups in which each form occurs. These will be discussed separately.

Table 1.   Forms of cannabis use in the *municipio*

Forms of cannabis use	Subcultural groups
Mixed with rum or *aguardiente* and applied to the skin for pain of joints and muscles	All groups of the coastal subculture
Smoked to reduce fatigue during work	Day laborers and peasants of the coastal subculture
Smoked to relax and socialize with friends	
Smoked to augment sexual intercourse	
Smoked in a program of health maintenance	
Green leaves crushed and rubbed on the skin for treatment of pain	
Boiled with water and raw sugar and given to infants for excessive crying	
Not used in any form	Highland subculture

There is widespread belief on the efficacy of cannabis mixed with rum or *aguardiente* and applied to the skin for pain of joints and muscles. The practice is present throughout the coastal subculture. A puzzling fact is that this mixture and its use for relief of pain is absent from the treatments reported by coastal *curanderos* or herbalists. The practice of mixing various plant parts with rum or *aguardiente* is common for the treatment of pain, snakebite, and to stop bleeding; but in all cases the mixture is to be drunk, not applied to the skin. Perhaps the explanation is to be found in the fact that herbalists are specialists, for example, in snakebite treatment or protection from evil curses. In contrast, the knowledge that cannabis can be used for treatment of pain is widespread and not the unique property of the *curanderos*. *Curanderos* normally keep their formulas secret. And it will be remembered that the use of tobacco in this form is quite old on the coast, and the medicinal use of cannabis might derive from this practice (Patiño 1967).

The use of cannabis for health maintenance is also reported (Fabrega and Manning 1972). Cases cited involve men of advanced age who smoked all their lives and have enjoyed excellent health; they state that smoking marihuana is generally good for one's health. The green leaves are crushed and rubbed on the skin for treatment of minor pain and cannabis is mixed with water and raw sugar and brewed as a tea given to infants to stop excessive crying.

Smoking cannabis is restricted to the lower sector of the coastal subculture, composed of landless day laborers and peasants as reported for the Caribbean (Rubin 1975; Comitas 1975). In all cases cannabis is smoked in cigarette form. It is first air and sun dried; green cannabis is said to "inflame the head." It is smoked pure, unmixed with other substances. The cigarette is rolled in commercial tobacco cigarette paper, other kinds of paper burning too hot, and it is generally short and thin. Probably no more than a gram is contained in these cigarettes.

The coastal work group is composed of unrelated males, the exact composition of which may change from week to week; it is in this group that marihuana is consumed. A group contracted to clean an irrigation ditch, for example, will assemble in the morning on the estate after catching rides or walking from town. They assemble to sharpen their machetes, talk about girls, dances and drunks, and to smoke a marihuana cigarette.[10] The cigarette is shared among the men just as tobacco cigarettes are often shared. They receive work directions from the estate manager and set about their task. Around ten in the morning they may pause again for another marihuana cigarette; they continue working until noon. They bring with them in their *mochilas*, woven carrying bags of *cabuya*, several nesting aluminum pots with a hot stew prepared in the morning by wives, sisters, or daughters. After lunch they stretch out under the branches of a tree for siesta. Work resumes around 2:00 P.M. and another marihuana cigarette is smoked. Around 4:00 or 5:00 P.M. they will start for home. In the evening they may meet neighbors and friends at a bar for beer, rum, or *aguardiente*. But the friends with whom they drink may or may not be the same with whom they spent the daylight hours working.

Marihuana cigarettes are not always consumed by the workers. This depends upon the availability which in turn depends upon limited resources. But some informants report that they are unable to work without smoking marihuana; they have no *fuerza* [force] and they lack the necessary *ánimo* [spirit] for working. Not all workers smoke, nor are they encouraged to do so. I have never heard disapproval of the practice expressed in work groups: "he is an addict" nonsmokers will say, but they

---

[10]   The marihuana cigarette is called a *cigarrillo* just as are tobacco cigarettes. There is little evidence of a special argot among cannabis consumers.

do not avoid smokers in town or treat them in any special fashion. At work it is impossible to tell one who is a smoker from one who is not, unless consumption is observed.[11]

On the basis of interviews and observations, from five to seven marihuana cigarettes are consumed in a day; only one is smoked at a time. These are not passed from person to person, but each individual smokes the same way he normally smokes a tobacco cigarette, no effort apparently being made to retain the smoke in the lungs (Partridge 1973). Coastal peasants consume cannabis in the same manner and in the work context, but they smoke alone on their farms since they are no longer working in a nonkin male group. One old man is locally known as the *Rey de la marihuana*. He is an adobe brick maker who uses cannabis during his work; he is said to be the best brick maker in town by consumers and nonconsumers alike, turning out more bricks faster than any other brick maker. Smokers credit this to the effects of cannabis: to *quita el cansancio* [reduce fatigue], to increase *fuerza* [force], to make a man *incansable* [tireless], and to give *ánimo* [spirit] for working. Such words and phrases are the most frequent responses to questions regarding the effects perceived by the user. A few informants report that they smoke marihuana to relax, to think about and resolve some problem that is troubling them, or to go to sleep at night, but these are not mentioned as frequently as those connected with work. Laborers on construction sites in coastal cities are also reported to smoke marihuana in the morning before going to work and during their *agua de panela* [water mixed with raw sugar] breaks during the day.

While most informants also report using marihuana for leisure activities such as fiestas, I have not observed this with any frequency. Several informants who live and work in the *municipio* confirm the report that in Cartagena where they were born, there are social clubs for smoking marihuana and for leisure activity (U.S. Department of Health, Education and Welfare 1972). And in fact all the female smokers interviewed were born and grew up in the city of Cartagena or in the department of Bolívar. In the department of Magdalena, in which the *municipio* is located, the incidence of female smokers is quite low, and there are no social clubs where cannabis is smoked during leisure activities.

In reality, alcohol is the drug of choice on festive days in this region of Colombia, being an essential element in the reciprocal relationships among male laborers (Gutierrez de Pineda 1958). Informants mention that cannabis is cheaper than alcohol and is preferred for this reason. They also report that cannabis is better than alcohol for sexual relations because the former does not inhibit sexual desire or capability in contrast

[11]   Dr. Joseph Schaeffer has pointed out that detailed study of videotapes made of smokers and nonsmokers in Jamaica reveal that there are subtle behavioral modifications among the smokers. But this can not be detected by the observer (Schaeffer 1975).

to alcohol, but the same informants can often be found drinking at the stores and bars in town.

Female smokers are rare in Magdalena; however, one female informant reports that women habitually smoke greater amounts of cannabis than do men. She informed me she smoked up to twenty marihuana cigarettes, each day, every day. Little information is available at present concerning the socialization of females into cannabis use patterns.

Males are socialized into use during late adolescence, with the initiation of adult work patterns. Informants report learning to smoke in the male work group; only one learned in the context of a fiesta activity. Such learning seems to depend largely upon individual interaction patterns and friendships, since most informants are the only adult males in their families who smoke cannabis. No informant reported that his father used the drug. This is not surprising giving the nonkin composition of the male work group where socialization takes place.

Informants began smoking cannabis between the ages of 12 and 22, and have between 11 and 31 years of experience; all are male heads of households which they support entirely. Those informants who are coastal peasants are all former day laborers, as is typical of the group. Through saving and obtaining a cosigner they have been able to establish credit and buy a piece of land or they are *colonos* who for years have successfully supported a family from the land they took over and planted. For these peasants, socialization into cannabis use patterns began in the nonkin male work group. Cannabis consumers are thus best described as nonkin networks of landless day laborers, some of whom eventually obtain land.

Informants report that a person who is *debil en la cabeza* [weak in the head] should not use cannabis. They observe that the drug often "turns people crazy," but these are said to be people with "weak heads." Only one informant reported experiencing negative effects which he described as a feeling of sleepiness; he recommended cold water poured over the head, eating green bananas, and drinking hot black coffee as remedies. No informant reported visual distortion, seeing strange things, or having hallucinations while smoking cannabis. This is remarkable given the belief, common in the United States, that cannabis grown in this region of Colombia is one of the most potent varieties. One informant reported that the novice often feels hunger, as if he could eat a "whole cow." But this passes when one learns the effects of the plant.

Consumption patterns of other drugs should also be considered, given the high correlation reported in the United States between the use of alcohol and tobacco and cannabis (U.S. Department of Health, Education and Welfare 1971; U.S. National Commission on Marihuana and Drug Abuse 1972). Alcohol is easily the most popular of all drugs used by all subcultural groups in the *municipio*. There are four patterns of use: (1)

reciprocal buying and mutual consumption among friends and business associates at cockfights, during the sale of animals, at leisure at stores and bars, etc.; (2) individual consumption by peasants and coastal day laborers in the morning before going to work, and to a lesser degree during working hours; (3) two-to-three-day *borracheras* [drunk feasts] during fiesta days, family celebrations, or on a whim; and (4) ritual drinking to the point of stupefaction at weddings, during the nine-day wake, and at other life-crisis events.

The first pattern is part of a wider system of social and economic reciprocal relationships. The sale of a cow by a storekeeper to a peasant demands that the former buys drinks for the latter. A landowner attending a cockfight who meets one of his employees will purchase drinks for both as part of the patron–client relationship. A peasant who had been given good manioc or corn seed will partly repay his peer with a bottle which they can share at a store.

The second pattern is largely confined to agricultural workers and peasants. Alcohol is consumed with the morning black coffee. Infrequently laborers will consume a bottle during the day while working; this is shared among their fellows who are expected to reciprocate later. And a few laborers are so fond of *aguardiente* that a ration of it is part of their contract with an employer.

The third pattern of use is confined to the upper sector of the coastal subculture, since the poor have few resources for binges. The wealthy are famous for drunken feasts; stories are told and retold of conspicuous alcohol consumption, pranks such as chicken stealing, putting soap in food for a wedding party, and extended stints in local brothels.

The fourth pattern is present throughout the highland subculture. Life-crisis events are generally drunken affairs; the wake and the first-year anniversary observation of the death of a relative are the most outstanding, calling for the consumption of quantities of food, *chica* [maize beer], and *aguardiente*.

Tobacco is also consumed by all groups but it is seldom used habitually as in the United States. Rather, cigarettes are frequently purchased one or two at a time. One may go for days smoking only once or twice and then at a fiesta or during an evening of drinking, consume an entire pack with friends. At upper-sector feasts tobacco cigarettes are provided together with food and drink for the guests, and on such occasions persons who normally do not smoke tobacco may indulge. Females of all groups in the *municipio* use alcohol and tobacco only rarely; upper-sector females take both during fiestas and private parties at home. Females of advanced age in all groups of the coastal subculture smoke tobacco cigars, with the burning end inside their mouths as is the coastal custom.

V. LEGAL PROHIBITION AND SOCIAL VALUES

There are legal and social sanctions against the cultivation, sale, and use of cannabis in Colombia. Decree 1699 of 1964, Article 23, dictates from two to five years of incarceration for cultivation, elaboration, distribution, sale, use, or possession of cannabis. Article 24 prescribes one to four years of incarceration for the same offenses regarding any kind of *estupificante* (Torres Ortega 1965). In the *municipio* it is recognized that cannabis is totally prohibited by law. Moreover, social tradition conceives of a *marihuanero* as a lazy, often criminal, vagabond. To be called such is to be called a bum. Neither of these sanctions seems to deter cultivation or use.

Most townspeople, public officials, and growers simply wink an eye at cultivation and say that it brings United States dollars into Colombia. Cannabis cultivation and marketing are placed in the same class as contraband, in which most upper-sector persons play some role. As one upper-sector woman laughingly told the observer, "[name of *municipio*] produces the best marihuana in the world." Contrary to what might be expected, the commercial growers are drawn from among the most well-off and prosperous of the *cachaco* peasants. Some cultivators are youthful adults, but most are well advanced in age, well-established, and highly respected household heads.

Consumption of cannabis is another matter. Smoking is a lower-sector activity. All instances in which I have heard persons called *marihuaneros* have involved upper-sector families reprimanding their offspring or gossiping about other families. One never hears the word in lower-sector families. This label appears to be a stigma applied to poorer persons in general by upper-sector families, since the people they gossip about and label *marihuaneros* are often not cannabis consumers. And the true identities of long-term users are well known in the *municipio*, by everyone from the mayor to the police.

Such negative stigmas, however, tell us little about what people actually value. For this reason the anthropologist examines values as they are reflected in social interaction, rather than ideology, spoken and written words, and formal law (Kluckhohn 1954). We have seen that many lower-sector males value cannabis as a supplement to work, leisure, sex, for the treatment of pain, and in health maintenance.

Analysis of the interaction patterns typical of each subculture brings into sharp focus the significant differences between them. The subculture in which the consumer lives is characterized by a mobile subsistence pattern, nonkin male work groups, stem family structure, and wage labor. The subculture which does not contribute consumers (although there is ample opportunity since they produce tons of cannabis) is characterized by a sedentary subsistence pattern, the kin-based male work group, the three-generation extended family structure, and swidden agriculture.

These are only the central differences, many others exist. Perhaps the most telling difference is that of mobile versus immobile settlement patterns. The coastal subculture concentrated in the towns and cities is an urban-oriented population. Even when living in the rural area geographical mobility is normal and urban work experience is common. The nonkin male work group, adolescent peer groups, and the stem family are all structures which conform well to the migratory subsistence pattern. In contrast, the highland subculture scattered about on dispersed individual family farms offers little opportunity for mobility, cooperation among nonkin, the formation of adolescent peer groups, or the budding-off of nuclear units. Mobility data from the *municipio* confirm this pattern. In a rural hamlet surveyed, only 2 of 25 male household heads and only 5 of 25 female mates were born in the *municipio*. Only 4 household heads had worked solely in the *municipio*, whereas 21 had worked in other *municipios* and other departments. Of the latter, 10 had worked in cities of the coast. In a town *barrio* surveyed, 23 of 76 household heads were born in the *municipio*, and 36 of 76 mates were born in the *municipio*. Of 76 household heads, 26 had worked in other departments of the coast and 33 had worked in the cities.

The process of migration begins in the late adolescence or at about the age of 18 when a young man frequently leaves home and obtains wage labor where his travels lead him. Typically, the worker settles down with a mate some years later. He is brought in and out of contact with his family members, reciprocal relations with nonkin evolving as he travels. Almost always he will come home for fiestas and holidays, traveling 100 or more kilometers.

Socialization to cannabis use takes place during this migratory phase in the life of a coastal worker. All informants have histories of wage labor in other departments and cities. Several have had a few years of experience working in the banana zone; some have been able to save money, maintain a good reputation, and obtain credit and are now landowners living a sedentary existence. Others merely acquired mates and children and settled in one of the towns discovered during their youth. They all learned to smoke cannabis as young wage laborers.

Since not all coastal peasants and day laborers consume cannabis we must ask what are the differences observed among users and nonusers. Briefly, none have been observed. Studies of other Colombian user populations have pointed to factors such as mobility, single marital status, marginality, unemployment, concubinage, criminality, lack of housing, lack of children, low salary, low productivity, illiteracy, family disintegration, and segregation from the larger society as characteristic of cannabis users (Ardila Rodriguez 1965). Interestingly enough, nonusers and users of the day laborers and coastal peasants are more alike with regard to these factors than different. About half of all day laborers live in concubinage, more than a third are illiterate, and the rest have only one to three years of primary schooling; all earn low wages and have no resources of productivity aside from their backs. All workers in the coastal subculture are mobile early in life; unemployment is generally confined to the aged and is absent among cannabis informants; criminality is rare and no cannabis informant has ever been in jail; and cannabis consumers are no more segregated from society than are nonusers. Lack of housing is atypical of users and nonusers and some users have more than one house. Single marital status is not typical of any group in the *municipio* and a lack of children is unheard of. "Marginality" and "family disintegration" are concepts that cannot be compared among populations without definition. If marginality means an absence of the social and economic reciprocal relationships typical of the community, then cannabis consumers are not marginal. If family disintegration means some form of family life other than that typical of the community, cannabis consumers do not live in disintegrated families. In short, cannabis consumers and nonconsumers have more in common than in contrast by the light of these characteristics. The fact is that Ardila Rodriguez (1965) depends mostly upon Colombian police records, since there has been no scientific work on cannabis in Colombia.

Some investigators in the United States have posited a relationship between social and psychological stress and cannabis (Ausubel 1970; Partridge 1973). Since the community discussed in this paper has experienced significant social and economic changes that are generally stressful, we should consider this interpretation. Abandonment of the banana zone produced a grave economic crisis throughout the coastal subculture; upper-sector families were probably the hardest hit, since they had developed considerable wealth and status due to the presence of the United Fruit Company. It is likely that this crisis is a factor in explaining their present involvement in the internal and international drug traffic. The workers, on the other hand, experienced no dramatic social mobility. It is true that the worker is worse off than at any time during this century, but he did not experience the relative deprivation of upward mobility followed by economic crisis. Moreover, about 11 of 25 families in a rural hamlet had some member working for the company, while in the town *barrio* only 16 of 76 families had a similar experience, and most day laborers and peasants had worked with the company for only one to five years, unlike the grandparental generation in which thirty and more years experience is not uncommon. Cannabis users frequently have had work experience with the company, but never unbroken by other employment and never for more than a few years. We might relate cannabis consumption to stress if the exit of the company affected the present generation of coastal workers in general and cannabis consumers in particular, but work histories are varied and rarely dominated by experience with the company.

In conclusion, the following generalizations are supported by the data:[12]

1. Cannabis cultivation, marketing, and consumption seem to be relatively recent innovations on the north coast of Colombia.

2. Cannabis cultivators, merchants, and consumers are integral members of the community in which they live, involved in typical community systems of social and economic reciprocities.

3. Long-term cannabis consumption (more than ten years) is not observed to engender indolence, parasitism, or marginality, in that the oldest and most experienced consumers have often bettered their social and economic position during their lives.

4. Cannabis consumption is related to mobile patterns of subsistence early in the life of the coastal day laborer, in which there is contact with users and socialization to cannabis use.

5. Cannabis consumption occurs in the context of the nonkin work group, although users continue to consume the drug alone when patterns of subsistence change.

6. Cannabis consumption does not appear to be related to stressful conditions produced by severe social and economic change in the history of the community.

7. Cannabis merchandising does appear to be related to stressful conditions produced by severe social and economic change in the history of the community.

8. Cannabis merchandising is governed by two distinct systems of contribution, a market-induced system involving Andean peasant growers and wealthy upper-sector coastal buyers, and a local system involving small vendors among the day laborers and peasant growers of the coastal subculture.

9. Alcohol is the traditional and actual drug of choice for business negotiation, social relations, and religious celebration. Since a bottle of alcohol costs a full day's wage for a day laborer, cannabis may be related to economic deprivation resulting from exploitative wage levels.

10. The use of tobacco for treatment of pain and reduction of fatigue are traditional, and cannabis has been adopted to serve these same functions; this suggests that cannabis use may be related to tobacco use in the coastal subculture, and may have been substituted for tobacco at some time in the past.

---

[12] These conclusions must be considered preliminary, as full analysis will not be possible until all data collection has been completed.

REFERENCES

ALARCON, JOSÉ C.
1963   *Compendio de história del departamento de la Magdalena de 1525 hasta 1895.* Bogotá: El Voto Nacional.

ARANÚJO, ALCEN MAYNARD
1959   *Medicina rustica.* São Paulo: Compañia Editora Nacional.

ARDILA RODRIGUEZ, FRANCISCO
1965   "Aspectos médico legales y médico sociales de la marihuana." Doctoral thesis, Facultad de Medicina, Universidad de Madrid.

ARENSBERG, CONRAD M., SOLON T. KIMBALL
1965   *Culture and community.* New York: Harcourt Brace Jovanovich.

AUSUBEL, DAVID P.
1970   "The psychology of the marihuana smoker," in *Marijuana.* Edited by Erich Goode, 17–19. New York: Atherton.

COMISIÓN DE PLANIFICACIÓN
1964   *Plan de desarrollo económico y social del departamento de la Magdalena.* Santa Marta, Colombia: Comisión de Planificación.

COMITAS, LAMBROS
1975   "The social nexus of *ganja* in Jamaica," in *Cannabis and culture.* Edited by Vera Rubin, 119–132. World Anthropology. The Hague: Mouton.

DEPARTAMENTO ADMINISTRATIVO NACIONAL DE ESTADÍSTICA
1971   *Censo agropecuario, 1970–1971,* volume two. Bogotá: Centro Administrativo Nacional via a Eldorado.

DIX, ROBERT
1967   *Colombia: the political dimensions of change.* New Haven, Connecticut: Yale University Press.

FABREGA, HORACIO, JR., PETER K. MANNING
1972   "Health maintenance among Peruvian peasants." *Human Organization* 31 (3):243–256.

FALS BORDA, ORLANDO
1955   *Peasant society in the Colombian Andes.* Gainesville: University of Florida Press.
1956   "Fragmentation of holdings in Boyacá, Colombia." *Rural Sociology* 21 (2):158–163.

FLUHARTY, VERNON LEE
1956   *Dance of the millions: military rule and the social revolution in Colombia, 1930–1956.* Pittsburgh: University of Pittsburgh Press.

GARCÍA MÁRQUEZ, GABRIEL
1970   *One hundred years of solitude.* Translated by Gregory Rabassa. New York: Harper and Row.

GUTIERREZ DE PINEDA, VIRGINIA
1958   "Alcohol y cultura en una clase obrera," in *Homenaje.* Edited by Paul Rivet, 117–168. Bogotá: ABC.

KAMALAPRIJA, V.
1965   *Estudio descriptivo de la estructura del mercado del banano Colombiano para la exportación.* Bogotá: Instituto Latinoamericano de Mercadeo Agricola.

KLUCKHOHN, CLYDE
1954   "Values and value orientation in the theory of action," in *Toward a general theory of action.* Edited by Talcott Parsons and Edward A. Shils, 388–433. Cambridge, Massachusetts: Harvard University Press.

MONTAÑA CUELLAR, DIEGO
1963   *Colombia: país formal y país real*. Buenos Aires: Platina.
PARTRIDGE, WILLIAM L.
1973   *The hippie ghetto: the natural history of a subculture*. New York: Holt, Rinehart and Winston.
PATE, JAME B., CHARLES C. SEALE, EDWARD O. GANGSTAD
1954   Varietal studies of *kenaf, Hibiscus cannabinus* L., in South Florida. *Agronomy Journal* 46 (2):75–77.
PATIÑO, VICTOR MANUEL
1967   *Plantas cultivadas y animales domésticos en América Equinoccial*, volume three: *Plantas miscelaneas*. Cali: Imprenta Departamental.
1969   *Plants cultivadas y animales domésticos en América Equinoccial*, volume four: *Plantas introducidas*, Tomo IV. Cali: Imprenta Departamental.
REICHEL-DOLMATOFF, GERARDO
1951   *Datos historico-culturales sobre las tribus de la antigua gobernación de Santa Marta*. Bogotá: Banco de la Republica.
RUBIN, VERA
1975   "The '*ganja* vision' in Jamaica," in *Cannabis and culture*. Edited by Vera Rubin, 257–266. World Anthropology. The Hague: Mouton.
SCHAEFFER, JOSEPH
1975   "The significance of marihuana in a small agricultural community in Jamaica," in *Cannabis and culture*. Edited by Vera Rubin, 355–388. World Anthropology. The Hague: Mouton.
SEALE, C. C., J. F. JOYNER, J. B. PATE
1952   *Agronomic studies of fiber plants: jute, sisal, henequen, fureraea, hemp, and other miscellaneous types*. University of Florida Agricultural Experiment Stations Bulletin 590. Gainesville: University of Florida.
TORRES ORTEGA, JORGE
1965   *Código penal y código de procedimiento penal*. Bogotá: Temes.
U.S. DEPARTMENT OF HEALTH, EDUCATION AND WELFARE
1971   *Marihuana and health: a report to the Congress from the Secretary*. National Institute of Mental Health. Washington D.C.: Government Printing Office.
1972   *Marihuana and health: second annual report to Congress from the Secretary*. National Institute of Mental Health. Washington D.C.: Government Printing Office.
U.S. NATIONAL COMMISSION ON MARIHUANA AND DRUG ABUSE
1972   *Marihuana: a signal of misunderstanding*. New York: Signet.
VERGARA Y VELASCA, F. J.
1901   *Nueva geografía de Colombia*, volume one. Bogotá: República de Colombia.
WAGLEY, CHARLES, EDUARDO GALVÃO
1949   *The Tenetehara Indians of Brazil*. New York: Columbia University Press.

Changes in the Traditional Fishing Technology of Northeastern Venezuela

JUAN ELÍAS FLORES

Venezuela was perhaps the last region of the New World to be conquered and colonized. The Spaniards, at first, gave most of their attention to Peru and Mexico because of their vast human resources and material wealth.

During the first three decades of the sixteenth century, the conquistadores limited their activities to the slave trade, the search for gold, and oyster-fishing for pearls. The latter came to be the exclusive incentive in eastern Venezuela, particularly in the adjacent islands of Cubagua, Coche, and Margarita.

Santo Domingo was the center for all operations related to the conquest in the Caribbean area as well as the exploitation of the pearl fisheries, the salt works in Araya, and the dried-fish industry. It was also from Santo Domingo that monks of the Dominican or Franciscan orders moved in to establish monasteries along the Caribbean coast where the most important groups of Indian population were located: from Cumaná, westward to Santa Fe, the Píritu islands, and all the way to Lake Maracaibo, the Gulf of Venezuela, and the Paraguaná Peninsula. The headquarters for operations connected with the conquest was transferred to the western part of the country in 1528 (Lieuwen 1964:34–35).

Along the Atlantic coast Indian groups were found in the Gulf of Paria and the Orinoco delta, as well as along the rivers that flow from the plains into the Orinoco.

Since colonial times an economy based on fishing has been established in places where the most important communities of aborigines already existed.

This paper is drawn from materials gathered for a study conducted by the author under the auspices of the Commission for Scientific Development, Universidad de Oriente, Cumaná, Venezuela.

INDIAN FISHING TECHNIQUES BEFORE THE CONQUEST

The accounts left by the historians of the conquest permit us to make a succinct summary of the fishing methods used by the aborigines of the region at that time. First, as regards fishing along the coast, the following techniques are mentioned:

1. The simple gathering of shellfish and mollusks in the mangrove swamps and along the beaches when the tide receded; and diving for oysters (mussels are also gathered nowadays).

2. Fishing with lookouts stationed in high places (they may still be seen in the Gulf of Santa Fe, and are used for fishing jurel — *Caranx hippos*). When the lookouts saw schools of fish, a large number of young people would come down to the beaches and swim a certain distance from shore. They would then swim or walk back keeping rhythm in a sort of dance, striking the water with poles which they handled deftly with their right hands, while, with their extended left hands, driving the fish toward the shore. There they were caught in baskets, in an operation in a way similar to sardine-catching nowadays.

3. Night fishing with torchlight (today kerosene lamps and powerful gasoline lanterns are employed although their use is strictly forbidden). The Indians would wave torches alongside their boats at the places where the largest fish could be found, then, with arrows and spears (nowadays hanging nets are used) they could catch as many fish as they wished since the number of fish attracted by the light was very great indeed (Martir de Angleria 1962:26–27; also López de Gomara 1962:299; de Herrera 1962:50).

The historians also mention techniques used in rivers and in some coastal lagoons (Vila et al. 1965:488–490):

1. Fishing with fences or traps made of sticks, placed in small streams, shoals, or lagoons such as Unare Lagoon. (The fences now in use are made of wire mesh and are placed at the mouths of lagoons.) When the fish were caught within a fenced area it was easy to pick them up (now with casting nets). When the rivers carried a large amount of water the level in the lagoon also rose, and swarms of sea fish rushed into it (Flores 1971:16).

2. Catching turtles along the sandy banks of some rivers and channels of the Orinoco basin when the volume of water was reduced during the dry season (starting in February); and catching alligators during the rainy season.

3. Fishing with barbasco, a poison, in ponds and brooks formed by waters overflowing the banks of swollen rivers (fishing with barbasco and dynamite are now prohibited).

4. Fishing with arrows, spears, and clubs.

Apparently, at the time of the conquest, the Indians were using neither nets nor metal hooks. There is no evidence to suggest they were using fishing rods either. Finally, the boats typical of that period are the canoes (curiaras or cayucos), driven by paddles or poles. Apparently they did not have sailing boats and did not use oars. Canoes are still seen today, particularly on the rivers, around Margarita Island and Unare Lagoon. The large canoes (curiaras) are provided with outboard motors.

SPANISH COLONIAL FISHING TECHNOLOGY

The fishing techniques of the pre-Hispanic era, with the net, sail navigation, and other techniques of Spanish origin added, made possible an increased production of fish to meet the growing demand. Those techniques remained basically unaltered until a few years ago. Colonial organization for fishing activity as well as for the marketing of the product was based on the regional specialization the natives had prior to the conquest. As a consequence the life of the people of the coastal regions became more maritime, while those living inland concentrated on agriculture.

Ruben Carpio attributes the increase in the demand for fish, as well as the improvement of methods and systems of fishing and the valorization of fish-producing regions alongside regions dedicated to other types of production, to the strict observance of religious practices in colonial times, including abstaining from meat during Lent and on Fridays (Vila et al. 1965:498).

Fishing with nets (casting nets and *chinchorros*) was unknown to the aborigines, though they knew how to weave hammocks and baskets. There are a few documents which assert that the Indians used nets, metal hooks, and fishing rods, but they are not dependable (Méndez-Arocha 1963:33). Furthermore the Indians did not know the techniques of using lead and cork to equip fishing nets. Also, they did not have the sailing boats which would have been necessary to take them away from the coast for net fishing. It is impossible to use nets on coral reefs in shallow waters with rocky bottoms. Anyway, the Indians did not have any need to increase the catch of fish before the coming of the Spaniards and the development of colonial life.

Most of the production of fish during the colonial period was dried and sent to the cities and settlements located inland and to the ports of call where ships resupplied.

Since the end of colonial times, fishing has had its commercial capital in the eastern part of the country and a good part of the population of that region has depended on it for a living. In 1822 and 1875, just as for the time of the conquest, mention is made of the large amount of dried fish sold in local markets, of large shipments bound for Caracas and other cities, and even to the West Indies (Vila 1965:209–210). Codazzi mentioned in 1940 that between Peninsula de Araya and the islands of Coche, Cubagua, and Margarita, the catching of mullet was still essential, and that many people were engaged in it, men and women. They established settlements for salting and drying fish. (Vila et al. 1965:499). On the other hand fishing activities along the Atlantic coast of eastern Venezuela, in the villages of the Gulf of Paria and the Orinoco delta region, remained separate from those of the rest of the country because of lack of communications. In this area fishing was limited to barely satisfying the subsistence of the local population.

CHANGES IN TRADITIONAL FISHING TECHNOLOGY

During the nineteenth century and until the death of the tyrant Juan Vicente Gómez in 1935, fishing techniques did not undergo any important modifications. Concern for locating new fishing grounds, along with increasing the productivity of areas already known through the use of improved techniques and tools, is very recent. Within the process of modernization which was initiated in Venezuela in 1936, but which started in earnest after the Second World War, the changes in the traditional technology of fishing, which had remained unaltered since colonial times, ran parallel with those in the traditional customs of Venezuelan society. Therefore, the innovations that occurred in commercial fishing have to be considered in the socioeconomic context which emerges from 1945 on, this context owing much to increasing revenues derived from the oil fields, to the great explosion in population, and to the large-scale collective mobility of the people. All these factors exerted a multiplying effect upon demand for basic goods and services. A severe scarcity of basic goods was felt following the Second World War: in 1947 consumers would pay four times the regulated price for some articles, and a law was enacted against hoarding basic commodities and subsequently speculating in them.

   The drive to develop agriculture and fishing was due to the preoccupation with the diversification of the Venezuelan economy. To help, a policy of credit on easy terms was launched, but in 1958, at the fall of Pérez Jimenez, who had ruled as a dictator for ten years, the country was still importing consumer goods, it being only in the sixties that importation of vegetables and other agricultural products began to be replaced progressively by national production.

   In 1945 the fisheries were faced with the necessity of increasing both production and productivity. Traditional fishing technology had to undergo some important innovations, comparable only to those which occurred during the colonial period when nets and sailing boats were introduced. Outboard or inboard motors, the usefulness of which had been proven by anglers and in smuggling activities, represented obvious alternatives to the sail. Ruben Carpio says that no other activity was so drastically affected by the beginning of oil exploitation in Venezuela as fishing. Lower prices for gasoline made possible the use of motors on fishing boats (Vila et al. 1965:501).

Apparently, Venezuela is the only country in Latin America where outboard motors, originally designed for speed in sporting events, are used for commercial fishing. In fact, the result has not been economical. Outboard motors are expensive; they do not last and they require constant and costly maintenance. They ought to be considered luxuries rather than working tools for poor fishermen. Nevertheless, these motors, with their extreme versatility and their unique ability to be controlled at will, have displaced sailing boats of the piragua and *tres puños* types, whose efficiency depended on the unpredictable wind.

Inboard motors are certainly more convenient than outboard motors, but despite this fact they have never enjoyed the fishermen's preference. This is perhaps due to their cost (about three times greater than the cost of an ordinary outboard motor), and to the fact that the outboard motor takes up less space. It appears that the outboard motor is better adapted to the characteristics of traditional coastal fishing with light boats, the type locally known as curiaras, or other types of boats of Hispanic colonial origin. Finally, loans for the acquisition of outboard motors have been given preference because, for the seller or the bank that extends the credit, the risk is less on account of the lower price of an outboard motor, and, for the usually poor fisherman, small loans are more convenient.

An official survey of the fishing situation in 1957 (Vila 1965:212), gives the following numbers of vessels for the state of Sucre: 30 canoes, 903 boats, 163 pirogues, 5 *tres puños*, and 77 launches, a total of 1,178. In 1963 the forms used to gather data for official statistics did not mention sailing boats, and again, in the inventory conducted in 1967 regarding the socioeconomic aspects of commercial fishing in Venezuela's northeastern region (including the states of Sucre, Anzoátegui, and Nueva Esparta), sailing boats are not mentioned. Only boats with outboard motors, launches with inboard motors, or even boats without motors were taken into account. The total number of fishing craft for Sucre was 1,416 (Comisión para el Desarrollo de la Región Nor-Oriental de Venezuela 1968).

Fishing loans granted between 1945 and 1948 contributed mainly to the expansion of the use of the outboard motor. In the communities the first to use motors were those of a higher economic status and some immigrants.

In 1964, commercial fishing was providing employment for a bare two percent of the national labor force (25,000–30,000 persons), but subsistence fishing represented a part-time activity which gave employment to a much larger population (Lieuwen 1964:157). In 1951, in the eastern zone of the Caribbean coast there were 4,013 fishermen, of whom 533 personally owned the vessels they were using (Vila 1965:211). And in the 1967 report on the abovementioned northeastern region, Sucre alone accounts for 5,058 professional fishermen (Comisión para el Desarrollo de la Región Nor-Oriental de Venezuela 1968).

Since colonial times, Venezuelan fishermen have come from the poorest levels of the population living in small communities along the coast. In the western part of the country particularly, fishermen of the villages and settlements are mere spectators to the lucrative operations of the large fishing boats. During the first part of the present century fishing operations were already organized in *trenes*. At the time, a few investors, who owned the tools for fishing, had a large number of employees. The existence of a similar fishing organization in the eastern side of the country is referred to in a study of Manicuare (Ginés et al. 1946). Apparently, this type of organization still exists in the west, but on a much smaller scale than formerly. In the nineteenth century, the *trenes* had an average of 200 workmen; nowadays, such teams are considerably reduced, to an average of only ten persons, who are fishermen in partnership to a certain degree with the owner of the equipment (nets, boats, and motors). They also share, according to their ability, in the profits produced by the enterprise (Ginés et al. 1946:196–197).

Another important innovation in the traditional fishing technology occurred in the sixties, when nets and lines made of vegetable fiber were rapidly replaced by nylon nets and plastic lines. The landscape has since changed on some beaches. The net weavers have disappeared, and the palisades where thread nets were put to dry are no longer seen. However in the twentieth century the fishing gear of colonial origin is essentially still the most abundant, though other new elements, such as the vivarium inside the boat for keeping the bait alive, the *palangre* [boulter], and some new types of fishing baskets, have been introduced in the course of recent decades.

During the first half of the twentieth century, other changes related to the fishing net took place in Venezuela and modified the traditional technology. In effect, ring nets were introduced in Venezuela in 1940 by the *Pesquerías Vascas del Caribe*, and dragnets by Italian fishermen in the late forties (Lundberg et al. 1970:4). Later on, the dragnet was used extensively for shrimp fishing, particularly in the western part of the country. Shrimp production began at 91 tons in 1951, but as early as 1965 it had reached 5,360 tons (Ministerio de Agricultura y Cría 1970:545).

It is possible that the use of the ring net in eastern Venezuela contributed to the vanishing of the so-called "line *chinchorro*." This was a big sweep net or dragnet, with a fine mesh of about three centimeters, thirteen meters high and a kilometer long, which was pulled ashore by a great number of men, women, and even children. It was used specially for catching mullet.

In the course of the fifties, the Ministerio de Agricultura y Cría (MAC) forbade the use of ring nets and dragnets within five miles of the coast. It also enacted a series of norms concerning the rational construction of fishing gear and the regulation of fishing methods. The fishery law was decreed in 1956 (Méndez Arocha 1963:52).

The nets being employed now are smaller than those used in the past: *bolicheras*, *chinchorros*, and *mandingas* are disappearing quickly. The types of nets being used most at present are encircling nets: ring nets (*máquinas*) and seines; drive-in nets; gill nets; trammel nets; and combinations thereof.

The survey conducted in the northeast in 1967 shows that in Sucre there were 900 nets used with motor boats, 92 used on boats without motors, and 24 for which it is not specified as to whether they were used on motorized boats or boats without motors. The total of 1,016 nets was distributed as follows: 409 *chinchorros*, 352 gill nets, 219 encircling nets, and 36 nets whose type is not specified (Comisión para el Desarrollo de la Región Nor-Oriental de Venezuela 1968:1–36).

In 1957, 441 *chinchorros* were mentioned in Sucre, but this should be interpreted as a total for all types of nets (Vila 1965:213).

With progressive improvement of land communications in eastern Venezuela, refrigerators and refrigerated trucks began to be used. The stocking and marketing of fresh fish became possible, and even the traditional dried-fish trade became easier. Communications were difficult and freight costs high until the late fifties, but from that time on, the eastern region, which had been peripheral to the important centers of the national market, began to be integrated into them at an accelerating pace. Distances which nowadays are covered in one hour on good highways would have required three hours on the old roads and three days by horse trails. Sucre, Anzoátegui, and Monagas are now connected by excellent highways.

In 1959, Sucre had 724.7 km of highways, of which 133.8 km were paved with concrete or asphalt, 402.1 km were graveled, and 188.8 km were of compacted soil. In 1963 the highways totaled 764 km, 548 km of which were paved with concrete of asphalt, 177 km graveled, and 39 km of compacted soil. Table 1 shows the road distances between Cumaná and various places in 1944 and 1963. It is clear that even if average speeds are held to have remained constant the times for the journeys were considerably reduced.

In 1964 there were already a number of cold storage lockers in Sucre. They received, stored, and distributed fresh fish. In 1958, there were only three ice plants. Their daily sales in 1959 were 51 tons, which left an idle

Table 1. Road distances and journey times from Cumaná (average speed 40 km/h)

	1944	1963
Caracas	901 km (22.53 h)	392 km (9.80 h)
Carúpano	178 km (4.45 h)	130 km (3.25 h)
Güiria	316 km (7.90 h)	234 km (5.85 h)

capacity of 42 tons. A salt refinery was installed in 1959, with a capacity for producing 30 tons daily but having monthly sales of only 150 tons (Vila 1965:231–232, 240–241).

A modernization process has been operating in Venezuela since the end of the Second World War. The traditionally different sectors of the country have been adapting to new living conditions. As regards fishing, what has already been mentioned may be summarized as follows:

1. Motor boats have substituted for sailing boats.
2. Nylon nets have substituted for those made of vegetable fibers.
3. Some types of nets have disappeared as others have been introduced.
4. Techniques for storing and transporting fresh fish have been improved.

Nowadays northeastern Venezuela is outstanding for its coastal fishing activity along with its sardine and tuna-canning industry. This region contributes more than half of the national production of fish. Notwithstanding, the fishing communities are dominated by indecision about the change; they are confined within the boundaries of their coastal operations where the resourses of the sea are increasingly harassed and depleted by the indiscriminate efficiency of drag fishing. They have to expand their area of operation constantly, They are furthermore confronted with other dangers like the ecological changes triggered by dumping industrial wastes into the sea. Pollution is manifest in Lake Maracaibo and in the Gulf of Cariaco.

Since the end of the Second World War, Venezuelan fishing production has greatly increased (Table 2). This increase is due fundamentally to the following factors:

1. Mechanization of the fishing fleets of long-line lighters and trawlers;
2. Establishment of plants for freezing and canning fish;
3. Recent development of the international port of Güiria on the Atlantic side of the northeastern region;
4. Easy extension of government loans, particularly to offshore and trawler fishing (Ministerio da Agricultura y Cría 1970:537–538, 542–543, 545).

On the other hand, the indexes of productivity for coastal fishing are considered low in northeastern Venezuela, only about two tons per man-year (Méndez Arocha 1963:17; see also Comisión para el Desarrollo de la Región Nor-Oriental de Venezuela 1968).

Table 2. Venezuelan fish production (tons)

	National	Northeastern region	Sucre region
1945	54,000	n.a.	n.a.
1950	61,000	n.a.	n.a.
1955	70,000	n.a.	n.a.
1960	85,000	n.a.	n.a.
1965	112,000	74,000	39,000
1970	122,000	85,000	38,000

With the introduction of Hispanic colonial technology, fishing activities in Venezuela were insured for a long time. But now despite the partial modernization of the traditional technology, the adoption of the motor, new types of nets, and cold storage lockers where fish is kept fresh, the same is not likely to happen. Rather, the fishing trade is confronted with new difficulties. Some of them come from the complete mechanization of new fishing technology which emerged at the end of the Second World War. Although the techniques employed by tuna and shrimp-fishing boats do not represent the best of contemporary technology, they have made possible an increase in production and productivity.

The so-called fishing *roscas*, that is, fishing trusts, control the large-scale production and marketing of fresh fish and shrimp in Venezuela. Their productivity is small compared to that of the Japanese, American, and Cuban fishing fleets operating in nearby international waters, but they control both the national marketing of daily consumption and the exportation of shrimp to the United States. They also supply, together with traditional coastal fishing, the demands of the fish-canning industry.

The coastal fishermen have only a marginal participation in the lucrative internal market because of a chain of intermediaries. Nevertheless, the fishing communities still control the traditional dried-fish market, whose most important consumers live far inland, in the small towns or in the country, but it is a market of poor consumers of dried mullet, a cheap fish. There is no demand for mullet as a fresh fish.

The transition from local traditional economy to a modern economy on a national scale is accompanied by progressive substitution of different manifestations of the precapitalist economy, despite the low income level and the great unemployed or underemployed human potential of the fishing communities, despite the retention of some traditional patterns of behavior not rationally congruent from an economic standpoint, and finally, despite the low productivity of coastal fishing. All these factors, combined with a process of accumulative causation, are driving the traditional fishing economy into a bottleneck. To break this stranglehold the credits that now benefit the influential businessmen should go to the fishing communities, so that they can participate in modern fishing technology. On the other hand, sea farming should receive more attention;

experimental growing of mussels and shrimps has given good results. Finally, new investments in traditional coastal fishing should not be encouraged, since they would only tend to perpetuate existing conditions. Such a solution is not even considered in the fishing communities. For them, fishing goes on being traditional and routine. Modern fishing technology remains something foreign to them, as well as does the concept of big capital investments. They do not take advantage of available credit facilities, not even of official credit set up to promote development of different regions of the country. The policy of credit now in effect would have to be reoriented to take coastal fishing activity out of its present impasse.

REFERENCES

COMISIÓN PARA EL DESARROLLO DE LA REGIÓN NOR-ORIENTAL DE VENEZUELA
  1968   "Inventario y características socio-económicas de los puertos – base de pesca," in *Diagnóstico socio-económico de la región nor-oriental*, 1–80. Caracas: Oficina France-Venezolano de Estudios.

DE HERRERA, A.
  1962   "Historia general de los hechos de los Castellanos en las islas y tierra firme," in *Venezuela en los cronistas generales de Indias*, volume two, 11–147. Caracas: Academia Nacional de la Historia.

FLORES, JUAN ELÍAS
  1971   "La pesca en la laguna de Unare." Paper presented to the Seminario sobre el Desarrollo de las Lagunas de Unare y Pirítu, Puerto La Cruz, Venezuela.

GINÉS, H., *et al.*
  1946   Manicuare. *Memoria de la Sociedad de Ciencias Naturales La Salle* 16: 157–200.

LIEUWEN, E.
  1964   *Venezuela*. Buenos Aires: Editorial Sudamericana.

LÓPEZ DE GOMARA, F.
  1962   "Historia general de las Indias," in *Venezuela en los cronistas generales de Indias*, volume one, 285–306. Caracas: Academia Nacional de la Historia.

LUNDBERG, H., *et al.*
  1970   *La flota de arrastreros de Venezuela en 1968*. Caracas: Ministerio de Agricultura y Cría/Food and Agriculture Organization of the United Nations.

MARTIR DE ANGLERIA, P.
  1962   "Décadas del Nuevo Mundo," in *Venezuela en los cronistas generales de Indias*, volume one, 3–39. Caracas: Academia Nacional de la Historia.

MÉNDEZ AROCHA, ALBERTO
  1963   *La pesca en Margarita*. Caracas: Fundacion La Salle de Ciencias Naturales.

MINISTERIO DE AGRICULTURA Y CRÍA
  1970   *Anuario estadístico agropecuario 1969*. Caracas: Ministerio de Agricultura y Cría.

VILA, MARCO AURELIO
  1965 *Aspectos geográficos del estado Sucre*. Caracas: Corporación Venezolano de Fomento.
VILA, PABLO, *et al.*
  1965 *Geografía de Venezuela*, volume two. Caracas: Ministerio de Educación.

PART THREE

Culture and Ethnicity

SECTION A:
THE LOWLANDS AND MONTAÑA REGION

Introduction

Identification, classification, and differentiation of individuals and groups occur within and between all societies. In some contexts the difference between two individuals is the significant one, while in others, the extended family, village, barrio, or ethnic group is the important category. The analytical problems involved in the relationships between culture and social organization in Latin America have been the basis for some important theoretical arguments in anthropology. Redfield's formulation (1947, 1953) of a model of folk society, and the critical discussion which followed (e.g. Foster 1953, Miner 1952, Mintz 1953–1954), are benchmarks in the anthropology of Latin America. Writings by Beals (1953), Wagley and Harris (1955), Wolf (1955), and Adams (1967) have contributed to the classification of sociocultural units and to our understanding of many issues related to ethnicity, class, power, and social structure in Latin American societies.

Recently, the question of boundary maintenance has come to occupy the attention of anthropologists working in Latin America (e.g. van den Berghe 1968; Whitten 1974), and contributions to this volume by Whitten, Albó, and van den Berghe are examples of anthropological research on this problem. Their studies, along with the others in this part, are based on fieldwork in areas where ethnic integrity is being threatened by the forces of internal colonialism under the banner of national development. Such pressures are being met with various strategies in which native languages and a reevaluation of ethnic categories play an important role. While bilingualism is increasing substantially among indigenous groups, this development does not necessarily lead to a shift in ethnic identification and may, as Whitten suggests, force ethnicity to intensify.

At the present time the outcome of the struggle of ethnic minorities to maintain their cultural integrity is difficult to predict. Ethnicity is essentially a problem for those in the marginal and lower economic categories who have little influence on those who formulate national policy. Though these minorities are making themselves heard and have some support among liberals and intellectuals, their present strategies are essentially defensive in nature. Unless programs of national development which allow for cultural pluralism are formulated and implemented with and by members of ethnic communities, there seems little hope for their eventual survival outside isolated zones of refuge.

The articles which follow deal with questions of classification, personal and cultural identity, social organization, and boundary maintenance. Ramos's article covers the topic of individual identity and social classification among the Sanumá of the northern Amazon basin. She presents a detailed analysis of the situational aspects of personal names and shows how the Sanumá system of classification relates to levels of self, lineage, and residence.

De Friedemann focuses on a single event, a local Catholic religious festival, as a basis for examining interethnic relationships among the black and Indian populations of western Colombia. She describes the role of the blacks as cultural brokers, the content of the local cultural stereotypes and the way in which the fiesta serves to perpetuate them, and some of the economic aspects of the event. Her description of the Indians, the Emberá, returning to their villages suggests they maintain a strong sense of their own identity which is reinforced by the character of the ethnic interactions during the festival.

Siverts discusses the relationship between ethnicity and headhunting among the Jívaro Indians of Ecuador. He looks at how the common ideology of ceremonial headhunting was important to the formation of temporary "corporations" which are a central feature of the highly flexible Jívaro social organization. Siverts cites some of the recent changes that have occurred in the Jívaro region and considers their prospects for survival as an ethnic group with no heads left to hunt.

Whitten provides a detailed analysis of indigenous adaption to technological change and internal colonialism in eastern Ecuador. He discusses the evolving nature of ethnicity among mestizos migrating from the highlands and the indigenous groups in the montaña region. Whitten documents the major struggles between populations as the highland migrants seek to expand their territorial, political, and economic control over the indigenous inhabitants, and he examines the differential access to resources of each group. His analysis of the situation in Ecuador has global implications for those concerned with problems of internal colonialism and ethnocide.

REFERENCES

ADAMS, R. N.
1967   *The second sowing: power and secondary development in Latin America.* San Francisco: Chandler.

BEALS, R. L.
1953   Social stratification in Latin America. *American Journal of Sociology* 58:327–339.

FOSTER, G. M.
1953   What is folk culture? *American Anthropologist* 55:159–173.

MINER, H.
1952   The folk-urban continuum. *American Sociological Review* 17:529–537.

MINTZ, S. N.
1953–1954   The folk-urban continuum and the rural proletarian community. *American Journal of Sociology* 59:136–143.

REDFIELD, R.
1947   The folk society. *American Journal of Sociology* 52:293–308.
1953   *The primitive world and its transformations.* Ithaca, New York: Cornell University Press.

VAN DEN BERGHE, PIERRE L.
1968   Ethnic membership and cultural change in Guatemala. *Social Forces* 46:514–522.

WAGLEY, C., M. HARRIS
1955   A typology of Latin American subcultures. *American Anthropologist* 57:428–451.

WHITTEN, NORMAN E., JR.
1974   "The ecology of race relations in Northwest Ecuador," in *Contemporary cultures and societies of Latin America* (second edition). Edited by D. B. Heath, 327–340. New York: Random House.

WOLF, E.
1955   Types of Latin American peasantry: a preliminary discussion. *American Anthropologist* 57:452–471.

Personal Names and Social Classification in Sanumá (Yanoama) Society

ALCIDA R. RAMOS

This study attempts to show the interaction existing between the naming system of the Sanumá Indians of northern Brazil and their social system, and the need for reference to both these systems in the identification of the individual. The naming system, besides locating specific individuals in the social matrix, functions to provide an idiom for group classification. In order best to demonstrate how the Sanumá naming system operates in this connection, it is necessary to characterize the social structure, at least in those aspects that bear a direct relationship to the subject.

The Sanumá are a subgroup of the Yanoama (Yanomama)-speaking group, which occupies a territory in South America contained between the equator and 5° north latitude and 61 and 67° west longitude. Their villages are found in the northern part of the Amazon basin in Brazil and in the southeastern part of the Orinoco basin in Venezuela. The Sanumá number approximately 2,000 people (Migliazza 1967:160–165), living mostly on the heavily forested mountain range that divides the two river basins and serves as a natural boundary between Venezuela and Brazil. Their territory is located in the northernmost portion of Yanoama country.

The research on which this study is based was conducted jointly with Kenneth I. Taylor, and lasted for two-and-a-half years from April 1968 to September 1970. Twenty-three months were spent in Indian villages. The project was financed by a National Science Foundation predoctoral grant. The bulk of the data collected during this field trip has been organized and presented in the form of doctoral dissertations to the Department of Anthropology, University of Wisconsin, Madison (see Taylor 1972; Ramos 1972). I am very grateful to Dr. Taylor for his most useful suggestions on this work, and to Dr. Roberto Cardoso de Oliveira for having read and commented on it.

The Sanumá live in semipermanent settlements which they occupy fairly continuously during the rainy season (May–October). In the dry season it is common for a whole village or parts of it to go on camping trips in the forest, mainly for the purpose of hunting and gathering, but also for some fish poisoning. They make fields on the slopes of hills by the slash-and-burn technique, growing primarily bitter manioc and a great many varieties of bananas. Trade within and between groups is extremely important. With exchange of goods there is also intensive exchange of news from village to village. Unlike other Yanoama subgroups, such as the Yanomamö,[1] the Sanumá do not build their houses in the typical circle around an open inner plaza. They live in small rectangular thatched houses that contain from one to four hearths. Each hearth is most frequently occupied by an elementary family or by a polygynous family although the presence of aggregates of various sorts is not uncommon. Of the eight settlements we have information about, the number of houses per settlement varies from one to six.

Information collected on the naming system was mostly elicited from specific informants. Name secrecy greatly inhibited the people from talking about the subject, and thus systematic questioning on naming practices had to be restricted to the few individuals willing to ignore this secrecy.

THE SANUMÁ SOCIAL SYSTEM

The sanumá are organized in a series of named, patrilineal, exogamous sibs that are found dispersed throughout a wide area.[2] Each sib is subdivided into a number of lineages, also named, patrilineal, and exogamous.

Some fifteen sibs were recorded for the eight settlements about which information is most accurate. Of these fifteen sibs, data are most complete for three whose members became better known to us than others. These three sibs and their respective lineages are shown in Table 1.[3]

These three sibs are widely dispersed, especially the *higiadili* and *koima*. The greatest concentration of *higiadili* is in five settlements which make up the northern portion of Sanumá territory in Brazil. Among these are four of the eight settlements of the study. *Nimtali* sib members are present in two of these eight settlements. Most of the other *nimtali* people

[1]   See especially Chagnon (1968a); Biocca (1971); Becher (1957); and Barker (1953).
[2]   For greater detail on the Sanumá social system, see Ramos (1972).
[3]   Sanumá vowels are mostly closely pronounced as Spanish vowels (a, e, i, o, u). A tilde over a vowel (e.g. $õ$) indicates nasalization. The sound symbolized by "ɨ" indicates a high central vowel that roughly approximates the vowel in the English word bɨrd. The consonant *s* changes to *sh* before or after the vowel *i* as in English feet. The consonants *p*, *t*, and *k*, when intervocalic, are in free variation with *b*, *d*, and *g*, respectively.

Table 1.   Sanumá sibs

Sib	Lineage
higiadili	azagosi kadimani sabuli sobositili lalawa
nimtali	omawa sogosi puluidili pukumatali
koima	wisa mamugula

are either to the south or to the north of the international boundary. In any given settlement one finds representatives of a variable number of sibs. For the eight settlements referred to, the number of sibs represented in each varies between one and twenty-seven.

Members of the same sib acknowledge each other by the possession of a common name (patronym) and by kinship terms that denote a consanguineous relationship and which vary according to sex, age, and generation. But there seems to be no reference to a common ancestor, albeit unknown and untraceable. It is rather by general consensus that common membership is acknowledged.

Given that Sanumá sibs are dispersed, noncorporate units, the membership of which never comes together for joint action, it would be more appropriate to refer to these units as social or kin categories, as distinct from kin or descent groups, such as the lineages. Sanumá lineages should be understood in the context of their developmental cycle. They emerge, grow, and segment during a time period that covers more than three generations, but usually no more than five. This process of segmentation seems to occur along predictable cleavage lines. One of these appears at the death of a lineage (and village) headman, and the subsequent transmission of headmanship to the next generation. As a rule, the position is passed on to the headman's eldest son, but in cases where there are still living brothers of the deceased headman, these tend to compete with their brother's son for the headmanship. In the case with which we are most familiar, and which seems to represent the usual outcome of this kind of situation, the headmanship was transmitted to the son, and the deceased headman's brother, who up until then lived in the same village, moved away with his wives and children to the village where the husband of one of his sisters is the headman. It is very likely that his children will initiate a new lineage.

Perhaps the most common way in which a lineage segments is the separation of groups of uterine siblings resulting from polygynous marriages. One of these sibling groups tends to remain in the village, while the other (or others) moves elsewhere. The group that stays represents the children of the senior wife of the lineage leader, whose death may precipitate the separation. This sibling group constitutes the core of the lineage that becomes thus dispersed. The uterine sibling group that moves away may settle down in another village as a whole, or its members may disperse further, thus becoming scattered throughout several villages. As a result, lineage affiliation will eventually be lost and the next generations will have individuals without lineage membership. In fact, about half of the population of the eight settlements for which we have data show no specific lineage affiliation although they maintain their sib membership.[4]

At the village level one normally finds a localized lineage or a segment of a dispersed lineage[5] whose members are married either to individuals from other lineages or to people who do not belong to any lineage. The practice of bride service brings the groom to his in-laws' house, at least temporarily. Parent-in-law avoidance is strictly observed. This avoidance is also observed for cross-relatives of generations other than that of ego.

The kinship terminology reflects the type of organization described by Needham (1958) as a two-section system, with bilateral cross-cousin marriage and a clear separation between kin and affines. There is a preference for village endogamy whenever demographically possible. The existence of groups of coresident siblings of opposite sex maximizes the chance of eligible spouses, that is, of cross-cousins of opposite sex, within the same village.

The village is the most meaningful corporate group beyond the level of the domestic group. Food, particularly meat, is shared among villagers, and defense and attack are also a common concern of all members of a village. There is a consensus that village territory boundaries should be respected, especially concerning hunting grounds; and although there seems to be no explicit demarcation, adjacent villages by and large avoid trespassing into the hunting grounds of others.

Villages are named after the prominent lineage resident in it. This prominence derives both from the larger number of members and from the figure of the village headman, who is also the head of the lineage.

---

[4] Recently separated branches of existing lineages retain the lineage name for at least another generation. Contacts are frequent and friendly until eventually the two subgroups drift further apart.
[5] This basically corresponds to Leach's concept of "local descent group" (1961:56), and has been described by Chagnon for another Yanoama subgroup (1968a:68–70).

THE NAMING SYSTEM

Among the Sanumá, two basic types of names are used for human beings: personal names and patronyms. Both are required in the binomial which is necessary for individuation. In the case of the Sanumá, patronyms are the names of sibs and lineages as applied to their individual members. Both types of names are surrounded by secrecy. Although Sanumá name secrecy does not reach the extremes that have been reported for other subgroups of the Yanoama (Barker 1953:471–472; Biocca 1971:129; Chagnon 1968a:209), it nevertheless requires a long stay among the group for the subject to be treated with a certain ease. This secrecy seems to be a way of expressing respect for other people, a form of etiquette that consists of not pronouncing their names in their or their close relatives' presence. Breach of this etiquette is rarely seen except among children. In general, secrecy is more severe with regard to personal names and less so concerning patronyms. Teknonyms, also a common practice, fall within the category of personal names and are the least secret of all.

Personal Names

Personal names can be acquired at any age, and it is possible for an individual to have more than one name, sometimes as many as three or even four. This fact, however, is not readily admitted, and informants tended to deny that people have multiple personal names. This attitude considerably restricted data collection on multiple naming, which remained limited essentially to those occasions when additional names were overheard in conversations about specific individuals. In this, as in other respects, children were by and large more cooperative sources of information.

There are several ways in which an individual may acquire his personal names. A brief summary of the different procedures of name giving follows.[6]

When a child is born, the father goes on a ritual hunt with the specific purpose of finding an edible animal, the name of which species will be given to the child. Associated with this naming procedure is the acquisition by the child of a certain spirit of the animal killed, which enters the child's lumbar (or coccyx) region. But although this is the basic naming procedure, statistically it represents less than half the names in circulation in the population of the eight Sanumá settlements for which data are available. The reason for this discrepancy has to do with a series of

---

[6]   The acquisition of personal names and how these reflect and emphasize the Sanumá two-section system are the subject of a separate paper (Ramos n.d.).

precautions and observations surrounding the ritual-hunt naming procedure. The father only goes on a ritual hunt if physical and social conditions are normal. Even when a ritual hunt is successfully completed, the child may not necessarily receive the name of the animal, for basically the same reasons, i.e. those having to do with physical health and social normality. Failure to give the child a ritual-hunt name starts the process of choosing an alternative name. One or more of the following procedures can be selected:

1. Names based on body or behavioral characteristics;
2. Contingent names based mostly on events or circumstances at the time of the birth or later in life;
3. "Personalized" patronyms; and
4. Teknonyms.

These procedures can be used to give a child its first name or to provide individuals with second or third names. A physical state or condition of an individual can be the source of inspiration for his personal name. These names are usually acquired in early childhood but can also be given to an older child or to an adult. They can refer to a permanent state such as "small," "brown eyes," "big penis," or to a temporary condition, for example, "weak," "feverish." Also in this category are personal names that are animal names, but are no longer acquired by means of a ritual hunt. The information conveyed by these names is of a different kind; they represent analogies between the characteristics of an individual and those of an animal, a tree, or another sort of being. For example, a child was named Kazu because it was as big as a *kazu* [capybara].

By "contingent names" is meant those which indicate that an individual was named after an event, place of residence, or place of birth. For example, a boy was called Waikia because he was born at the time of a visit by the Waika people to his family's village.

"Personalized" patronyms are names which, although they designate kin categories, are, nevertheless, used secondarily as personal names. There are very few instances of these (all sib, not lineage) names (e.g. *sadali*, *koima*). They are equally applied to children and adults, males and females.[7] I know of no explanation for this particular usage. They differ from other usages of patronyms in that they are applied apparently in the same fashion as personal names. For these individuals the standard evasive answer "No name" to the question "What is your name?" never occurred. It is conceivable, however, that these names operate as safeguards against disclosure of the individuals' real personal names. For reasons that are still obscure to me, the names of certain individuals seem to carry a greater degree of secrecy than others.

---

[7]   It has been reported that among the Yuma, women use sib names as their personal names (Daryll Forde, quoted in Spier 1953:336).

Teknonymy is a widespread practice among the Sanumá. I have extended the term to cover all primary relatives of the individual whose personal name forms the base of the teknonym. Thus, one finds people named "father of ——," "younger brother of ——," or "wife of ——." This naming procedure seems to result in the conceptual isolation of the elementary family from the rest of the kinship web. I shall not discuss here all the intricacies and implications of this naming practice, only mentioning that this systematic application of teknonymy seems to occur in the case of a minor branch of a dispersed lineage.

The same personal name can be used for several different individuals. These names cut across sex, kin group, and village affiliation. We find, for instance, three people named Wasi [capuchin], who belong to different sibs and different settlements: two are males, one is female. Even within the same sib there can be recurrence of the same personal name. Within the same lineage, however, such repetition does not seem to occur. The relevance of this name repetition to the process of individual specification will be elaborated later.

Patronyms

As has been mentioned earlier, Sanumá lineages and sibs are named. All individuals have one or more patronyms, which are the names of the lineages and sibs to which he belongs. In their usage as names for individuals I refer to these as patronyms, because, whether applied to a male or a female, they are always transmitted through a person's father. Married women never relinquish their original patronyms.

The origin of lineage names is known and can be explained by the people, whereas, for the most part, the origin of sib names remains obscure. This is due, no doubt, to the fact that lineages are named after their founders, and since genealogical depth rarely exceeds three generations above adult members, lineage eponyms are either still alive or have died only recently and are known or still clearly remembered. In the case of sibs, on the other hand, whatever it was that they were named after or on account of has, in most cases, been forgotten. If asked, for example, why the *higiadili* people or the *azatali* people are called by these names, informants say that there is no reason, they are "just names." For some sibs, though by no means all, certain physical characteristics are associated with their names. The members of the *koima* sib are said to be hairy, from *kōi* [hair]; the members of the "hazatagidili" sib (most of its members live in Venezuela, far from the eight settlements discussed here) are described as being tall, this probably being a reference to the deer (*haza*) from which their name seems to derive. For most sib names, however, informants are unable to provide an explanation beyond the usual statement that so-and-so is called such-and-such following his father, who was already called by that patronym.

Lineage names always derive from a personal name of the founder, whether he is living or dead. The personal names of these founders, which are then used as lineage names, come from one of the naming procedures described earlier. Teknonyms are never used as lineage names, nor are strictly female names, because lineage eponyms are always male. Of the nine lineage names for which there is a clear explanation, five were names given to the founder in his adult life, and four while he was a child. When it is the case that more than one personal name exists for the founder, one only of these names is used to identify his lineage. For instance, the founder of the *kadimani* lineage was named Sɨbidili [unknown] before the neighboring Maiongong (the only Carib-speaking group in close contact with the Sanumá) first called him Kadimani. Although his other name, Sɨbidili, persisted as a personal name, it was never used to designate the lineage he founded. At another village, known as Sogosɨ, the founder of the "sogosɨ" lineage is also known as *Patasi*, but his group is known only as "sogosɨ."[8]

In terms of secrecy patronyms are not so zealously concealed as personal names. When certain personal names become patronyms, following their transformation into lineage names, they lose much of their secret character. These names are mentioned much more freely than strictly personal names, for now they belong to the public domain. Nevertheless, a stranger is not told lineage names unreservedly, or, for that matter, village names, which are, in most cases, coterminous with the name of the local lineage from which the village headman originates.

Unlike personal names, which are not the prerogative of a single individual, patronyms (both sib and lineage names) are never repeated. No two social units (sib or lineage) bear the same name. There is only one *kadimani* lineage, only one *koima* sib, and so forth. Kin groups and kin categories are thus "individualized" by means of specific, exclusive names. As collective entities, they congregate a number of individuals and thus operate as "classifiers," that is, they group individuals into contrasting "classes." But in terms of their own nomenclature, of their identity vis-à-vis each other, they no longer display this classificatory quality. When contrasted with other such units, sibs and lineages maintain their own individuality and are not open to confusion or ambiguity. As will be seen later, this individuality of kin groups and categories is an important element for the individuation of their specific members.

---

[8]   "Sogosɨ" is an abbreviated form of *soko ose* (*soko* [collared anteater]; *ose* [young]). This is a common practice among the Sanumá and is used to designate a person by reference to his older brother (or sister). Thus, Sogosɨ is a younger brother of Soko.

Village Settlement Names

Villages are identified by the name of their headman's lineage. All members of a village, whether they belong to its lineage core or not, can thus be referred to by outsiders as members of such-and-such village, regardless of lineage affiliation. For example, everyone living in Kadimani village can be called *kadimani de*.[9] This creates a certain degree of ambiguity, since both *kadimani* lineage members and other people such as their affines of the *koima* and other sibs (apparently with no lineage affiliation) are in this way grouped together under the same generic name.

The lineage lends its name to the village and not the other way around. For example, the *kadimani* lineage, before its present state of dispersal, lived a few miles to the southeast of its present location. At that time its village was already known as Kadimani although the composition of its non-*kadimani* lineage members was different from what it is now. Five or six years later, after the separation of two or three branches of this lineage, and in a new location with new members attached to it, the village where the main branch of the *kadimani* lineage lives is still called Kadimani.

The ambiguity in the identification of individuals by village name is a consequence of the interplay between the principle of descent and residence in Sanumá society. When descent and residence coincide, as is the case of the *kadimani* lineage members resident at Kadimani village, identification, at this level, presents no particular problem. If, on the other hand, a man is identified as *koima* by virtue of belonging to the *koima* sib and, on the other hand, as *kadimani* by virtue of living at Kadimani village, an ambiguous situation obviously ensues. This ambiguity can be partially resolved by the specification of both descent (or kinship) and residence affiliation. For example, the individual in question may be more specifically referred to as *kadimani de koima* [a *koima* from Kadimani]. In this way the possibility of a man belonging to the *kadimani* lineage is discarded because he cannot belong to both the *koima* sib and to the *kadimani* lineage since the *kadimani* lineage is a branch of the *higiadili* sib with which the *koima* sib is in contrast.

The ambiguity of village names in referring to people who are not members of the core lineage is sometimes resolved by the use of another designation which is socially neutral. Villages may become known by the salient geographic feature of their site. For example, the Lalawa village is also called Kisinabidulia, after the Kisina Biu stream nearby; the Mamugula village is also known as Wanabidulia, after the Wanu Biu stream on the banks of which the village is located. In both cases all the

---

[9]   Alternative singular forms are *de* and *a*; "dibi" indicates the plural.

residents, regardless of lineage affiliation, can be referred to as "kisinabidili dibi" and "wanabidili dibi" respectively.[10]

INDIVIDUATION

It is quite clear that identification of specific individuals is not provided automatically by the use of personal names among the Sanumá. As has been mentioned, the same personal name may be given to several different people regardless of sex, village, or sib affiliation. There are several possible ways of achieving this identification. One can refer to another existing personal name of the individual in question, for chances are that no two individuals have the same set of personal names; or one can always fall back on some kind of teknonymous arrangement, even when the combination that results (personal name plus kinship term) is not one of the person's recognizable personal names but simply a reference device. The use of circumlocutions to identify specific people is also common, for example, some outstanding deed such as a fight, or recent event such as a successful hunt that distinguishes the individual from all the others. But these alternatives depend on rather fortuitous factors that may not always apply. A more systematic mechanism of individuation is available to the Sanumá who make frequent use of it. This is the combination of personal name and patronym in a fully individuating binomial.

Depending on the place of the individual to be identified in the arrangement of sibs and lineages, the binomial will be formed by his personal name plus lineage patronym or sib patronym. In the case of two individuals with the same personal name and who belong to different sibs, it is sufficient to state the sib patronym to set them apart. For example, there are two men named Soko, one from the *nimtali* sib, the other from the *koima* sib. Although one of the two is a lineage member ("sogosi" lineage), in order for him to be unambiguously distinguished from the other man named Soko, all that is necessary is to state the sib names. Thus, Nimtali a Soko is differentiated from Koima a Soko, and both men are then identified. The binomial in this case is formed by sib patronym plus personal name.

It is possible for two individuals within the same sib to bear identical personal names. In this case the process of distinguishing them has to be done at a lower level than that of the sib. In such situations, it seems to be the case that at least one of the individuals in question is affiliated to a

---

[10] It is of interest to point out that Chagnon reports for the Yanomamö, another subgroup of the Yanoama, that they name their villages "after their garden sites, and the people take the name of their gardens" (1968b:150). But according to Chagnon's informants, the Shamatari (a group of Yanoama villages south of the Orinoco river and neighboring parts of Brazil) take their name from one of the headmen (Chagnon 1966:29).

lineage. For instance, there are two individuals named Manomasi [bald] who are from the *higiadili* sib. In this case the message conveyed by the sib name carries very little information. In fact, all it achieves is to exclude other sibs from consideration without actually distinguishing the specific individuals within the same sib. It is thus necessary to add another item to the chain in order for the individuals to be clearly sorted out. In the present case, one of the men named Manomasi, in addition to being a member of the *higiadili* sib, also belongs to the *kadimani* lineage. In order for him to be distinguished from the other Manomasi, it is sufficient to state that he is Kadimani a Manomasi. Neither in his lineage nor in his village is there anyone else named Manomasi. Given that lineage and village can be referred to by the same name, it is conceivable that the distinguishing name in the example above may indicate village and not lineage. However, I suggest it is the lineage that is the referent on the basis of the following case. At Mamugula village, the head of the local branch of the *kadimani* lineage is called Paso [spider monkey], and so is also a man who lives elsewhere. Both men belong to the *higiadili* sib. In order for the first man to be distinguished from the second, he is said to be Kadimani a Paso and not Mamugula a Paso. Thus, reference is made to his lineage and not to his village, in spite of the fact that, considered as logical possibilities, either alternative would be equally satisfactory. In these two cases, the binomial is no longer sib patronym plus personal name but lineage patronym plus personal name. This binomial, however, applies to only one of the two namesakes involved, the one who is a lineage member. The other man, when referred to, is distinguished from his namesake by a teknonym of sorts which then provides a unique combination. For instance, the non-*kadimani* Manomasi is referred to as Amisi a ulubu [son of Amisi]. Chances are that nowhere in Sanumá territory is there another man named Manomasi whose father was named Amisi and belonged to the *higiadili* sib. In summary then:

1. When two namesakes belong to different sibs, the contrasting sib patronyms are the distinguishing features, and the binomial for individual identification is sib patronym plus personal name.

2. When two namesakes belong to the same sib, at least one of them usually belongs to a lineage. In this case, the lineage member can be distinguished by the binomial lineage patronym plus personal name. The second person of the pair, however, is always distinguished from the first by means of indirect reference such as a teknonymous form, if not by a second personal name. If both namesakes belong to two different lineages, then binomials referring to their respective lineage patronyms are sufficient to identify both individuals.

3. Personal names within a lineage are always in contrast, i.e. there are no namesakes within the same lineage.

4. Although lineage and village names coincide, it is the lineage name

that is used as the referent in the binomial, which is established at a lower level than that of the sib. It is the combination of lineage patronym plus personal name, rather than village name plus personal name, that is significant for the purpose of identification of individuals.

INTERPLAY BETWEEN LEVELS OF CLASSIFICATION

As has been seen, one way in which lineages may come into existence is through a process of segmentation. A group of uterine siblings or a dissident member of the main lineage branch may start a new independent lineage. New lineage segments eventually become separated from the main core of the parent lineage both physically and conceptually. They become known by the personal name of their founder.

This process of emergence of new lineages reveals the double role of names in the social classification of Sanumá groups and individuals. It is in connection with the naming of new lineages that the interaction between personal names and the names of social units becomes well-defined. One of the possibly several personal names of a single individual (the founder and eponym) becomes the specific name for a newly formed lineage. From then on, this lineage name reverts to the individual level, now as the single lineage patronym shared by a group of individuals, the members of the lineage. Thus, the naming system provides labels for the categorization of social groups by bringing personal names to the level of kin groups. These labels, turned into patronyms, are called back to the individual level as a means to provide one way for specification of namesakes. Individuation is, for most people, achieved by means of a binomial consisting of patronym and personal name. This feedback interaction between the level of descent groups and that of the individuals is illustrated in Figure 1.

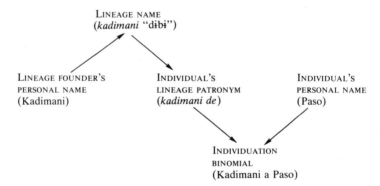

Figure 1.   Sanumá individuating binomial (Sanumá names in parentheses exemplify the phenomenon)

It should be noted that lineage patronyms (unlike some sib patronyms) evidently do not return to the pool of individuating personal names. Were they to do so, this would involve the chance of repetition of lineage names at the kin-group level because it would entail the probability that an individual with such a "short-circuit" name might become the eponym of a new lineage, and thus the same name would designate two different lineages: the emerging one and the eponym's parent lineage. This is not a viable possibility. The ambiguity produced by one name referring to more than one kin group would certainly create communication problems. The advantage of having each kin group and category designated by a specific name becomes apparent in certain contexts. These distinct sib and lineage names are conveniently used, for instance, in defining groups in terms of marriage exchanges, food prohibitions, and village affiliations.

CONCLUSIONS

The Sanumá case reflects a social phenomenon that has often been referred to, particularly in recent years.[11] Concern with naming systems as mechanisms to classify groups and individuals has led Goodenough to assert that "naming customs and modes of address appear to counterbalance the effect that the workings of the social system tend otherwise to give to people's images of themselves and of others" (Goodenough 1965:275). In societies that stress group action at the expense of individual identity, it is expected that individuality will be expressed in some other form. Among the Truk islanders, it is the naming system that provides the individual with his identity, as there are no two individuals with the same name. In contrast to Truk, Goodenough shows that in Lakalai, another Oceanian society, the individual is much less bound by group obligations and finds mechanisms for individual expression within the parameters of the social structure itself. Thus, their naming system does not operate to stress individuality but, on the contrary, displays a cyclical pattern which emphasizes certain social relationships.

Reflecting neither type in particular, the Sanumá situation presents the case of a naming system that, at one and the same time, provides opportunities for individualization and for categorization. Thus, the Sanumá naming system also differs from the "paratotemic" systems of metaphoric naming, for example the Osage system discussed by Lévi-Strauss, but shares with the Wik Munkan system, as interpreted by Lévi-Strauss, the recourse to individuation by means of a binomial or a trinomial (Lévi-Strauss 1966:183–188).

[11] See, for instance, the case of the Desana as described by Reichel-Dolmatoff (1971:140–141), and of the modern Truks described by Spencer (1961:205–218).

Perhaps the situation that most closely resembles the Sanumá naming system in its capacity to individuate and categorize is that described by Collier and Bricker for the Mexican Zinacanteco.

Every Zinacanteco has a surname that identifies the lineage to which he belongs, and most lineages are further subdivided by nicknames that identify individuals belonging to lineage segments. . . . Lineage segmentation can be measured by the distribution of nicknames, and this index has social structural correlates (Collier and Bricker 1970:290).

Besides a nickname, each Zinacanteco has a personal first name, a Spanish surname, and an Indian surname. None of the last three types of names has the power to individualize, as identical combinations can occur often enough to the point of redundancy. As the authors point out, "Zinacantecos themselves have difficulties differentiating people on the basis of first names and surnames alone" (Collier and Bricker 1970:292). In this respect, Sanumá kin-group names have a greater capacity of specification than seems to be the case among the Zinacantecos. Ultimately, "specification of individuals is most efficiently realized by a combination of first name and nickname" (Collier and Bricker 1970:291).

The Zinacantecos, as well as the Sanumá, recourse to a binomial consisting of personal name and group (or category) name that ultimately achieves individuation. In both societies group names derive from the level of individual names, are transformed into patronyms (or surnames) and as such return to the individual with a new function, that of individuation.

It is true to say, then, that the Sanumá and the Zinacantecos have a naming system which provides a classification of the individual by expressing his specific position in the taxonomy of the social groups that constitute the society as a whole. This type of naming system locates the individual in the social matrix within the context of a feedback relationship between the nomenclature of the social groups and that of their members.

REFERENCES

BARKER, J.
  1953   Memoria sobre la cultura de los Guaika. *Boletín Indigenista Venezolano* 2:151–167. Caracas.
BECHER, H.
  1957   Bericht über eine Forschungsreise nach Nordbrasilien in das Gebiet der Flüsse Demini und Aracá. *Zeitschrift für Ethnologie* 82:112–120.
BIOCCA, ETTORE, *editor*
  1971   *Yanoama: the narrative of a white girl kidnapped by Amazonian Indians*. Translated by Dennis Rhodes. New York: E. P. Dutton.

CHAGNON, N. A.
1966 "Yanomamö warfare, social organization and marriage alliances." Unpublished doctoral dissertation, University of Michigan, Ann Arbor.
1968a *Yanomamö: the fierce people*. New York: Holt, Rinehart and Winston.
1968b "Yanomamö social organization and warfare," in *War: the anthropology of armed conflict and aggression*. Edited by M. Fried, M. Harris, and R. Murphy, 109–159. New York: Natural History Press.

COLLIER, G. A., V. R. BRICKER
1970 Nicknames and social structure in Zinacantan. *American Anthropologist* 72:289–302.

GOODENOUGH, W. A.
1965 "Personal names and modes of address in two Oceanic societies," in *Context and meaning in cultural anthropology*. Edited by M. Spiro, 265–276. New York: Free Press.

LEACH, EDMUND R.
1961 *Rethinking anthropology*. Monographs on Social Anthropology 22. London: Athlone.

LÉVI-STRAUSS, CLAUDE
1966 *The savage mind*. Chicago: University of Chicago Press.

MAYBURY-LEWIS, D.
1965 Prescriptive marriage systems. *Southwestern Journal of Anthropology* 21:207–230.

MIGLIAZZA, E.
1967 Notas sobre a organização social dos Xiriana do Rio Uraricaa. *Boletim do Museu Paraense Emílio Goeldi*, n.s. 22:1–24. Belém.

NEEDHAM, R.
1958 The formal analysis of prescriptive patrilateral cross-cousin marriage. *Southwestern Journal of Anthropology* 14:199–219.

RAMOS, ALCIDA R.
1972 "The social system of the Sanumá of northern Brazil." Unpublished doctoral dissertation, University of Wisconsin, Madison.
n.d. "How the Sanumá acquire their names." Unpublished manuscript.

REICHEL-DOLMATOFF, G.
1971 *Amazonian cosmos: the sexual and religious symbolism of the Tukano Indians*. Chicago: University of Chicago Press.

SPENCER, R. F.
1961 The social context of modern Truckish names. *Southwestern Journal of Anthropology* 17:205–218.

SPIER, L.
1953 Some observations on Mohave clans. *Southwestern Journal of Anthropology* 9:324–342.

TAYLOR, K. I.
1972 "Sanumá (Yanoama) food prohibitions; the multiple classification of society and fauna." Unpublished doctoral dissertation, University of Wisconsin, Madison.

The Fiesta of the Indian in Quibdó, Colombia

NINA S. DE FRIEDEMANN

The conceptualization of the "Indian problem" as a structural problem arising out of the linkage of the Latin American economies and the international capitalistic system is presently shared by many social scientists. The continual loss of Indian lands over the past four centuries has been the mechanism by which the Indian groups have been reduced to their present state of social inferiority, exploitation, poverty, and lack of education (Frank 1969:36). This present state renders them incapable of manipulating new circumstances which the dominant society elaborates in order to maintain their subordination.

Mariátegui's analysis (1934:27) of the problem of loss of Indian lands is that administrative measures such as building rural schools or opening roads in or near Indian territories become acts of political demagoguery and thus superficial and extraneous attempts to solve the problem. Other scientists assert that the cultural defeat in which the Indians have lived for four centuries would cease only if they could in turn defeat the dominant economic system, a task which no one is inclined to do for the Indian (Frank 1969:141).

On the contrary, cultural mechanisms of subordination are continuously generated by the dominant system to counteract any means of defense that the Indian groups may adopt. There is evidence that these mechanisms are generated nationwide by governmental and religious institutions. A cultural mechanism of subordination is the bringing of Indians into contact with the urban "white" population of the regional

The data for this article are part of the body of data from the research *Studies of black peoples in the Pacific littoral of Colombia* which the author started in 1969.

The author expresses her gratitude to Coleman Romalis of York University, Toronto, for his comments and suggestions, and to Ronald J. Duncan of Universidad de Los Andes, Bogotá, for his suggestions and revision of the English version.

city which represents the dominant national society. The regional city in an intercultural zone is an instrument of domination in the economic relations of the Indians with the national society, as defined by Wolf (1955:456–467) and by Stavenhagen (1970:253, 256).

Under the pretext of encouraging intercultural relations, and with the benign aloofness of the national society, overtly amicable contacts with the Indians are attempted by the encroaching national groups. These usually take place in non-Indian territory, in the context of celebrations and events organized by government and other national institutions. In this manner, asymmetrical cultural situations are created in which non-Indian groups reinforce their socialization to the national image of the Indian, his life-style, and his universe. This "intercultural" contact is administered with the notions of the colonialist cultural heritage. This cultural heritage, still rooted in the nationwide educational system, maintains a stereotype of the Indian as a "savage, irrational, incomplete, uncivilized being, without intelligence, without religion, without culture, etc."

In Colombia, ethnographic evidence continues to confirm the above statements. At the same time, the evidence shows destruction is being perpetrated by the national society against the tribal groups in many different regions. Contacts between the national society and the Indian populations have continuously resulted in disaster for the Indians. The "intercultural" contact events continue to be a fertile field for the cultural and physical eradication of the Indians. Groups and cultures are disappearing rapidly, often in bloody circumstances. The overall program for the "integration of the Indian into national life" rather than solving the "Indian problem" has led to their continuing disappearance.

The Catholic church, a major Colombian institution, played an important role in the so-called "pacification of the Indians" during the Spanish conquest, and today continues to play the chief role in the eradication of Indian cultures. Since 1824 its activities have had the sanction of governmental laws which, according to Arango Montoya (1971:33), have given a legal basis to missionary agreements between the Colombian government and the church, *which have as their special object the Christian civilization of our Indians*. Their ideology of converting and civilizing Indians includes integral elements of the "integrationalist" policy mentioned above, which is being actively pursued in territories at present inhabited by Indians. These lands are legally considered to be waste lands or unoccupied lands. Their natural resources are available for commercial exploitation by national and international big business.

The fiestas held in the honor of saints in the regional cities have been converted into socializing mechanisms that effectively perpetuate the stereotype of the Indian. The Easter week festivities in Quibdó furnish a case study of interethnic relations on the Pacific littoral that shows the asymmetry of this neocolonial situation of exploitation and domination.[1]

Quibdó is a regional city on the Atrato river; it is the capital of the department of Chocó. It has a population of about 60,000 inhabitants who are for the most part civil servants, employees, and merchants. It is situated in an intercultural zone of black, white, and Indian populations.[2] Indians live in the forests remote from the city, near the headwaters of the rivers. They are being driven further inland by the pressure of the growing black population with concomitant loss of their lands.

The cultural mechanism of subordination used to bring Indians into contact with the people of the regional city of Quibdó is the "Fiesta of the Indian" which takes place in Easter week. The Emberá Indian group accepts an invitation to the fiesta and defenselessly enters a territory foreign to their habitat and culture. Their reception by officials and public has been organized for the past forty years with the object of "civilizing the Indians" by dressing them and persuading them to enter the Catholic church. Both blacks and whites do their best to make Indians drunk. The public posture of the white Catholic priests, both Spanish and Colombian, is expressed in the condescending charity of old clothes and public dressing of the recipients in the street. Finally, they select one or two of the Indians who are dressed to be part of the group that acts out the scenes of the Last Supper in the cathedral.

The Indian becomes a comedian who amuses children and adults alike. His personal adornment, his language, his physical traits, his obvious ignorance of the Catholic ritual, which pervades the life of Quibdó during Easter week, become the factors that structure the stereotype of the Indian. The fiesta takes place in a context of general drunkenness in which the blacks and the whites do violence to the dignity, rights, and cultural identity of the Emberá people. It is also the opportunity for

---

[1]   Other regional fiestas of a similar nature are:
a.   *Fiesta de la Candelaria* [Candlemas] in Orocué, on the Meta river, department of Boyacá. Sáliva and Piapoco Indians. February 2 (Jon de Landaburu, verbal report).
b.   *Corpus Christi fiesta* in Barbacoas, on the Telembí river, department of Nariño. Cuaiquer Indians. June. Since the group has been pushed back to the headwaters of the rivers the Indians no longer come to Barbacoas. However, in recent years the blacks in the river port have been symbolically representing the Indians who formerly participated in this celebration (De Friedemann, field notes).
c.   *Day of the Indian* in Caño Mochuelo, on the Casanare river, department of Boyacá. Cuiva Indians. October 12 (Francisco Ortíz, verbal report).
d.   *Indian week* in Mitú and other regional centers on the Vaupés river, commissary of Vaupés. Tukano, Cubeo, Barasana, Wanano, and other Indian groups. December (Horacio Calle, verbal report).
e.   *Christmas fiesta* in Puerto Leguízamo on the Putumayo river, commissary of Putumayo. Witoto Indians. December 24 (Horacio Calle, verbal report).
[2]   "White" and "black" are categories with complex definitions of the Pacific littoral of Colombia. The majority of the population of Quibdó is phenotypically black. Many of these people and other people of white phenotype form the group culturally "white" who behave according to the standards of the dominant social class in Colombia.

reinforcing and spreading attitudes in favor of the cultural ethnocide which occurs in these fiestas.

In other areas of the nation such events support the physical ethnocide of Indians. Evidence of the effect of this socialization complex upon the behavior of Colombian citizens was demonstrated in the declarations of eight "white" colonists who killed sixteen Cuiva Indians with revolvers, axes, and machetes in Hato de la Rubiera, in Arauca, on December 27, 1967.

The colonists' candid explanations for what they had done illustrate two very important points: (1) they had been taught to hate Indians as being dangerous people, and (2) they had been taught that it was not wrong to kill Indians. Private citizens and government employees had done so with no punishment. Moreover, the colonists considered it a praiseworthy deed to kill an Indian. One of them had killed six Indians before.

Following are quotes that appeared in the course of their trial which closed in July of 1972. The jury found the colonists *not guilty* (Castro Caycedo 1972:29–41).[3]

LUIS MORÍN: In Arauca we consider the Indians as wild animals. I was a little boy when I was taught that they were different from us in dress and in every way. I thought it was like a joke to kill them, and that it was not punishable.

RAMÓN GARRIDO: The only thing I did was to kill a little Indian girl and two Indian men. . . . When I was a child I realized that everyone killed Indians; the police, the DAS [Administrative Department of Security] and the Navy. Over there, on the Orinoco, they killed Indians and no one took note of it!

MARÍA ELENA JIMÉNEZ: I think that Indians are like us, because they are people. Only they lack brains. They are not equal to us in intelligence.

PEDRO RAMÓN SANTANA: They taught me this: to hate them, and since out there, there is no civilization. . . .

EUDORO GONZÁLEZ: I killed those Indians because I knew that the Government wouldn't make me pay for it nor punish the crime committed.

ANSELMO TORREALBA: Before this, I killed six Indians in 1960 and buried them in a place called El Garcero.

CUPERTINO SOGAMOSO: I didn't think it was wrong to kill them, because they were Indians.

The violence that traditionally is used in dealing with the Indians is displayed in Colombia in the plunder of Indian lands, through economic exploitation and the extraction of natural resources. Félix Cisneros, a

[3] The verdict is being appealed in spite of statements by authorities such as Carlos Gutiérrez, the chief prosecutor of justice in Villavicencio, site of the trial, who concluded: "The condemnation of these people would not solve a problem that arose in the beginning of our history."

former colonist of the same area in Arauca (Castro Caycedo 1972:40–41), states this clearly:

It is true that colonists who settle here kill Indians to protect their cattle. They kill and pursue the Indians because the Indians are thieves and treacherous. . . . The lands that formerly belonged to the Indians — like the Hato de la Rubiera — are still considered by the Indians as their property.

On the other hand, the Fiesta of the Indian in Quibdó is a joint effort on the part of government institutions and the merchants to attract Indians, who are withdrawing further and further into the tropical rain forest. Their increasing distance has led to a shortage of hunting and gathering goods from the jungle in the Quibdó market. For example, there is a scarcity of nutria and ocelot skins which supply an important leather industry in the neighboring department of Antioquia. Raw rubber, balata, bananas, maize, and basketwork goods are also becoming scarce. The latter articles are used for both the national and international markets in handicraft goods.

It is well-known that the Indians drink heavily, so the townspeople offer free liquor to the Indians as a part of the Catholic celebration of Easter to attract them to closer ties with the town. In 1971 the government of the department of Chocó allotted a sum of money for the organization of the fiesta and approved the use of CARE food for the farewell lunch for the Indians on Easter Sunday. The police and fire brigade loaned vehicles for a special parade of the effigy of Judas, accompanied by Indians. When the black family who organized the festivity appealed for financial support, the businessmen responded with money and clothes and paid the cost of a band of black musicians who were to enliven the parades of drunken Indians dancing through the streets.

During the first years of these fiestas the main feature was an event sponsored by the church in which an effigy of Judas Iscariot was given to the assembled crowd of Indians to be torn apart, hanged, and finally burned. In recent years, the church has withdrawn from active participation, allegedly due to the "debauched" quantity of alcohol consumed during Easter week. Now the church officially ignores the fiesta, although the priests still use the occasion to dress the Indians in the streets and make them enter the cathedral.

On Palm Sunday, Indian families come down the rivers, tie up their canoes, and unload the goods they have brought to sell. Many who come to the fiesta belong to the Emberá group which is one of the largest ethnic groups in Colombia (Reichel-Dolmatoff 1960; Faron 1962). While they are in Quibdó, some of them stay in the homes of black *compadres* to whom they give presents of forest products. In Quibdó and in the forest the black merchant-entrepreneur is the link between Indians and the outside world. Deluz (1970:4) asserts that the black is a barrier between the Indians of Chocó and the whites. At the same time, the whites use the blacks as instruments and as intermediaries for their domination and exploitation of the Indians.

The chief organizer of the fiesta is an old black merchant who, like many others now, used to go up and down the rivers in Indian territory trading cloth, pots, and machetes primarily for animal skins which he then sold to white businessmen in Quibdó. He is also the man who makes the effigy of Judas which is mutilated in the celebration.

The climax of the fiesta is reached on Saturday and Easter Sunday, after the Indians have been drinking all week in the various bars and cantinas. Often the Indian families fall asleep on the sidewalks or in the doorways of houses. When drunken quarrels occur between Indians, the townspeople urge them on in the hope of enjoying a foot and fist fight. Other people load the Indians into jeeps and trucks and drive them through the streets of the town. A high-ranking white government official once condescendingly commented, ". . . these poor Indians simply love to ride in cars."

On Saturday of Easter week, Judas is given to the Indians. The Judas is over six feet tall, with a wooden face, blue eyes, blond hair, and moustache. The body is stuffed with sawdust and dressed in a brightly colored outfit of satin and cotton and leather shoes.

Then the parade begins. Judas is seated in a chair and carried on the shoulders of the Indians in caravan-chair style like that in which the Spanish colonists had themselves carried by Indians in parts of America. The parade passes with jubilant crowds through the main streets of Quibdó to the beat of a black band playing popular coastal tunes of the Pacific littoral. The band is playing trumpets, drums, flutes, and cymbals. The Indians who dance in the parade become foolishly drunk with the *aguardiente* and rum freely given to them by the organizers and other people. The onlookers enjoy the "ridiculous" spectacle made by the Indians. The parade ends only when the exhausted Indians abandon Judas until the next day, when the fiesta reaches its climax with the "burning of the Jew."

A second parade precedes the "burning of the Jew" on the morning of Easter Sunday. In 1971 this second parade included police cars, fire engines, and sirens. Judas was seated in one of the trucks among the Indian women and children who hesitatingly crowded in against the sideboards of the truck. As the truck paraded through the streets of Quibdó, the band and black townspeople who wanted to dance followed the crowd of Indians who were again dancing and drinking. Crowds of spectators lined the balconies and sidewalks up and down the streets. About noon, the Indians were gathered together in the central plaza of Quibdó in front of the great cathedral. Policemen helped to hang the effigy of Judas by rope from the top of a utility pole. With the force of the hanging the body burst open and the sawdust began to fall over the crowd. The black band and the shouts of the crowd enlivened the square. According to custom, the Indians then received the body of Judas and tore it to pieces, amusing themselves by putting on the costume and shoes and dancing with the torn-up pieces of the head and body.

The crowds of townspeople stayed, enjoying the spectacle until the organizers decided to begin the last act of the fiesta and ordered lunch to be served to the Indians. They sat down on the grounds in the same plaza and each received a plateful of rice and beans. The whites and the blacks then left the plaza, and Easter week with its Fiesta of the Indian was over.

The evening of the same day and the following morning, Indian men, women, and children began to leave the town for the banks of the Atrato river. In silence they stowed their provisions aboard. Standing in the prow of the canoes, the men used their paddle tips to cast off from the sandy beaches and slip into the water. Their destination was the peaceful jungle.

Deculturation as a part of the ethnocide that has occurred among Americans Indians can be seen in the circumstances described above. The victims find themselves in conflict with their normal way of life, they become ashamed of their own image and traditions, and they may take any one of many roads to extinction. Some of the Emberá Indians who participated in the Fiesta of the Indian in Quibdó live on the banks of the Munguidó river. One of them, Lucio, related to Eric Isakson (personal communication)[4] the dream he had on his return from the fiesta:

I dreamed I was in a great city, on the other side of the river. It was a city with cars and white people. I myself was no longer an Indian. I was white and dressed in trousers, a shirt and an Antioquian hat [Antioquian businessmen dominate commerce in Quibdó].

The dream of the Indian, Lucio, brought to my memory the sight of him and other Indians abandoning the town streets for their canoes. On the bank of the Atrato river, they also abandoned the old shirts and trousers that the priests and businessmen had made them put on during Easter week.

REFERENCES

ARANGO MONTOYA, FRANCISCO
    1971   *Los indígenas en Colombia: ayer y hoy de los indígenas Colombianos*,
           26–38. Bogotá.

[4]   Eric Isakson is affiliated to the Department of Anthropology, University of Uppsala, Sweden.

214   NINA S. DE FRIEDEMANN

CASTRO CAYCEDO, GERMÁN
1972   La matanza de la Rubiera. *Antropológicas* 1:29–41. Bogotá.
DELUZ, ARIANE
1970   "Emberá: relato de actividades de investigación." Mimeographed paper. Bogotá.
FARON, LOUIS C.
1962   Marriage, residence and domestic group among the Panamanian Chocó. *Ethnology* 1(1):13–38.
FRANK, ANDRÉ GUNDER
1969   *Capitalism and underdevelopment in Latin America.* New York: Monthly Review Press.
MARIÁTEGUI, JOSÉ CARLOS
1934   *Siete ensayos de interpretación de la realidad peruana.* Lima.
REICHEL-DOLMATOFF, GERARDO
1960   Notas etnográficas sobre los indios de Chocó. *Revista Colombiana de Antropología* 9:73–158. Bogotá.
STAVENHAGEN, RODOLFO
1970   "Classes, colonialism, and acculturation: a system of inter-ethnic relations in Mesoamerica," in *Masses in Latin America.* Edited by Irving Louis Horowitz, 235–288. London: Oxford University Press.
WOLF, ERIC
1955   Types of Latin American peasantry. *American Anthropologist* 57(3):452–471.

Jívaro Headhunters in a
Headless Time

HENNING SIVERTS

The Jívaro Indians of the Ecuadorian and Peruvian montaña have for a long time attracted the attention of anthropologists and laymen alike due to their warlike practices and their habit of shrinking enemy heads into miniature trophies.

This paper is an attempt at viewing Jívaro warfare and headhunting as the core of "Jívaroness" and source of ethnic maintenance. More precisely, one could argue that the ideology underlying headhunting represents the basic value orientation of the Jívaro and that the head-hunting itself is one of the diacritical features exhibiting the Jívaro life-style.

Together, the ideological underpinning and the headhunting-war complex constitute the cultural content that the Jívaro as an ethnic group encloses (cf. Barth 1969: 14). The important point, however, is not so much what is enclosed as the process of enclosing, i.e. how ceremonial headhunting becomes the "source of ethnic maintenance." Thus, inter-tribal warfare, including resistance against the white intruders, was and is considered a totally different undertaking from intratribal headhunting raids.

Probably more than 40,000 Jívaro inhabit an area comprising some 60,000 square kilometers.[1] The region has difficult access, characterized by rugged mountains and steep hills covered by dense tropical forest and crisscrossed by swift-flowing rivers and brooks in an intricate fluvial net. Some of the rivers and tributaries are navigable by canoes and balsa rafts but, as Harner (1968) points out, travel by means other than foot is

---

[1] These figures are estimates based on various sources (Guallart 1964, 1970; Uriarte 1971, 1972; Varese 1970). It is further assumed that the Ecuadorian Jívaro groups occupy a territory about the same size as the Alto Marañon region, i.e. some 30,000 square kilometers (Uriarte 1971).

difficult in large portions of the territory, where barely visible trails and paths tie settlements together.

Subsistence activities involve shifting horticulture, combined with hunting, fishing, and collecting of wild fruits and plants. The chief garden crops are yucca or sweet manioc (*Manihot esculenta*) and various species of plantains and bananas.

Although they form a linguistic and cultural entity — an ethnic group — they do not constitute a tribe if we take it to mean a permanent political group or corporation. The Jívaro are rather an aggregate of neighborhoods, called *jivarías* in Ecuador and *caseríos* in Peru, whose members consider each other as ceremonial foes or temporary allies within an all-embracing kin and affinal network. As headhunters, they recognize only Jívaro heads as worth taking and shrinking into *dánda* to be displayed and celebrated at the great victory feast following a successful headhunting expedition. In other words, a Jívaro is a potential *dánda* while all others, including the white people, are just foreigners.[2]

At present when headhunting is no longer feasible and the victory feast cannot be performed, many Jívaro, reared as warriors, feel that their identity is being threatened, that their hallmark as a people is being lost. In spite of the fact that war parties are no longer organized and the concomitant ceremonial reassurance of commonness is a thing of the past, the fundamental values on which these activities were based are still shared by the majority of the Jívaro whether they live in Ecuador or Peru.

The implication of this observation seems to be that the Jívaro are aware of some "ethos," or, rather, a style of life, which they consider exclusively Jívaro. During my fieldwork among the Aguaruna Jívaros on the Peruvian side of the border, the subject of Jívaro unity and diversity was brought up repeatedly, even by the informants themselves.[3] For obvious reasons they showed concern for the future and wondered what would become of them all now that the military had got a foothold in their territory. They had no organizational means by which to mobilize all Aguaruna, not to mention other Jívaro groups, in order to resist the invaders and the colonists pouring into the area.

It is common knowledge that the Jívaro, until the recent past, have been able to unite in large and effective military operations, repelling attempts at conquest both on the part of the Incas, the Spaniards, and later the Peruvians and the Ecuadorians. The Jívaro themselves know this for a fact. That is why they are concerned; and that is furthermore why it seems pertinent to speak about the Jívaro as an ethnic group which is

[2] Transcription of Aguaruna Jívaro words corresponds to phonemization proposals suggested by Pike and Larson (Pike and Larson 1964; Larson 1963).
[3] Fieldwork was conducted in the Alto Marañon area between August 1970 and April 1971 and was supported by the Norwegian Research Council and Smithsonian Institution (Urgent Anthropology Program).

biologically self-perpetuating, shares fundamental cultural values, makes up a field of communication and interaction, and, finally, has a membership which identifies itself, and is identified by others as constituting a category distinguishable from other categories of the same order (cf. Naroll 1964).

The Jívaro do recognize the overt cultural forms signifying unity such as language, dress, house types, and technology. But, what is more significant, they assume existence of a set of common value orientations: "the standards of morality and excellence by which performance is judged" (cf. Barth 1969: 14).

The concept of *kakáham* is a case in point. A *kakáham* is a man who has killed several times, a *valiente*, and the Aguaruna still distinguish between the *kakáham* and other persons. The former is likely to be an influential local leader. According to Harner, "the personal security which the Jívaro believe comes from the killing has some social reality. A man who has killed repeatedly, called the *kakaram* [i.e., *kakáham* in Aguaruna] or 'powerful one,' is rarely attacked because his enemies feel that the protection provided him by his constantly replaced souls would make any assassination attempt against him fruitless" (1962). According to Aguaruna informants the *cimpuí* [special chair] is reserved for the *kakáham* and the *nágki* [war lance] should be touched only by a person belonging to this category.

In other words, *kakáham* provides us with a focal concept by which the Jívaro classify human beings and their actions. As an achieved status, *kakáham* represents a valued end and a measure of success. Not all Jívaro became *kakáham* but they certainly aspired to become one, and indeed a young man was marriageable only after he had proved his ability as hunter and warrior (cf. Stirling 1938: 110). Thus a Jívaro man is by definition a warrior, and the ideal career involves the recognition as *kakáham* and later *wáhiu*, leader of men and organizer of war parties. The designation *kúhak*, derived from the Quechua–Spanish *curaca*, was probably reserved for those influential men who could muster a following among several local groups.

Thus the typical social categories refer to excellence of performance within a pattern of behavior focused on warfare and trophy making. These activities are still emphasized and until recently were made organizationally relevant. But the warrior ideal cannot be maintained much longer as the primary concern of men. The presence of troops, white settlers, merchants, and missionaries prevents the Jívaro from realizing in actual life the most important aspect of the Jívaro male role: being a warrior. Consequently individual men may consider themselves as only "part-time Jívaros," implying a gradual blurring of the image of virility and manliness assumed to underlie Jívaro behavior. "Since belonging to an ethnic category implies being a certain kind of person, having that identity, it also implies a claim to be judged, and to judge oneself, by those standards that are relevant to that identity" (Barth 1969: 14). According to the Jívaro way of arguing, social order is based on moral order, and the latter is composed of a series of demands and obligations derived from a set of beliefs about souls and esoteric power and the way to obtain it. Only Jívaro own the souls and control the power, and killing another Jívaro is a means by which power is attained; hence a claim to be judged as Jívaro is to kill another Jívaro, or in Karsten's words:

It is characteristic of the Jivaros that they especially wage war against tribes belonging to their own race and speaking the same language. To such an extent has this been the rule for centuries that the word, *shuara*, "Jivaro Indian," has become synonymous with the word 'enemy.' 'My enemy' in Jivaros language is *winya shuara* (1935: 276).

Vengeance and blood feuding, then, is the logical outcome, war parties are a natural tactical device, head trophies the overt and highly dramatic symbol of performance according to standards of morality, and military alliances are the long-term strategic solutions by which one may hope to maintain a reasonable balance between peace and war.

It is not clear whether the Kandoshi were included among Jívaro foes. They waged war on each other, but there is no evidence of head taking. Nevertheless, the Kandoshi are reported as fierce warriors and apparently showed great similarity in their war pattern and beliefs (Wallis 1965). In case Jívaro heads were severed and displayed among the Kandoshi and vice versa, we may assume, according to the argument pursued, that the Záparo-speaking Kandoshi and the Jívaro considered each other as participants in the same raiding game, sharing fundamental values about souls and power, i.e. "the assumptions about reality upon which they [the Jívaro] predicate" their warlike practices (Harner 1962). The implication of such a reciprocity would be the inclusion of the Kandoshi in a Jívaro–Kandoshi ethnic group.

One of my young Aguaruna informants offered a simplified "history" of the area to the effect that in the beginning all Jívaro were united against different foreign tribes, including eventually the white people. Then the Huambisa and Aguaruna started warring against each other and ultimately the Aguaruna split up into feuding units. Speculating over this version for a while, without grasping its meaning, it suddenly occurred to me that my friend was actually conveying a message, the interpretation of which might be the following: formerly all Jívaro were potentially united, but, as we can all see, now they are separated in smaller groups. In other words, he tried to reconcile the facts relating to the present situation and the oral tradition referring to the great alliances of the past. A further indication of relative distance in time and space corresponding to some real or fictive alliance is found in the "tribal" designations handed down from an earlier period. All the people beyond the Santiago river were called *patúk*, comprising both the Huambisa and the Ecuadorian Untsuri Shuara. However, the Huambisa reserve the term *wampís* for themselves and apply *patúk* to describe the Ecuadorian Jívaro. The Achual are named *acuág* by the Aguaruna.

Clearly this selection of "names" for peoples may reflect a particular alliance constellation or some vague notion about territorial groups. Dialect differences may also be involved. Indeed, we can expect a proliferation of names as long as every little *quebrada* [river valley] has its name by which also the group of people living there is known.

A temporary grouping of allies was given the name of the war leader or of the river on which he was residing. Thus, the Antipa may well have been an Aguaruna group distinguished from other Jívaro on account of a powerful leader by the name of Antipa. Today, nobody seems to remember the Antipa, but in 1899, when Up de Graff braved the Pongo de Manseriche, the Antipa were a powerful group which had joined forces with another Aguaruna group in order to attack the Huambisa further up on the Santiago river (Up de Graff 1923: 241ff.).

According to Up de Graff, fifty-five canoes containing some two hundred men were heading upriver "bent on a common mission (which needs no explanation)" (1923: 242). Not all raids counted such formidable forces, but apparently the Jívaro of those days were politically rather active, forming alliances and organizing war parties of considerable size. From Stirling's description we get the impression that the extension of influence assigned to any one *curaka* [war leader] varied from time to time, implying the waxing and waning of alliances between smaller units.

The number of households under the influence of a given curaka is subject to a great deal of fluctuation. It frequently happens that a strong curaka will build up a fairly powerful group of warriors about him. A weak curaka or capito may have a blood-revenge killing to attend to but will find himself outnumbered by the enemy to such an extent that he is afraid to attempt a killing with his own group. In this event he is likely to call upon the strong curaka to arrange the killing for him with a gun or a woman. Often, too, a weak curaka, fearing that his group would not be able successfully to defend themselves against an attack from enemies, will voluntarily place himself and his group under the influence of the strong curaka in a loose sort of alliance. In this way the strong group tends to grow and to become even stronger until one curaka may have 8 or 10 lesser curakas more or less under his control. This state of affairs is usually not very permanent. Owing to the loose organization and lack of any real power on the part of the head curaka, the large group becomes unwieldy or develops diverse interests and it tends to split up again into independent units. Consequently, in as little as 2 or 3 years' time, the original head curaka may find that one or more of his former lieutenants are now stronger than he (Stirling 1938: 39).

Neither Up de Graff nor Karsten are specific in their treatment of alliance-forming and social organization generally. We have to rely on the work of Stirling from the 1930's and Harner's from a more recent period. Fortunately Stirling does go into some details on this point, documenting his generalized description of the political process by citing two cases of regional fusion and fission which he personally had encountered during field work in 1930–1931. The first example illustrates how military strength is related to personal power and, by implication, the physical and mental fitness of the leader or strongman.

Four or five years ago there was a strong chief on the Upano River named Tuki, known to the Ecuadoreans as José Grande. In the manner previously described, all of the curakas from Macas on the Upano River to Mendez on the Paute River became subchiefs under him until he was generally recognized as the strongest of all of the Jívaro curakas. However, he was beginning to grow old by this time and some of his subcurakas were strong men in their own right. About 2 years ago, Ambusha, who had been gradually gaining in power and becoming famous for his headhunting activities, split off with his own group, taking several curakas and their men with him. A little later Utita did the same thing. At the time of the writer's visit (1931), although Tuki was recognized by the Government of Ecuador as being head chief of the Macas-Mendez region, actually he had lost all power excepting that over his own family group and was in reality no more than a capito. These divisions of the organization, if it may be termed such, took place apparently without any ill feeling or formal announcements (Stirling 1938: 40).

The second case illuminates the demographical question in a strife-filled society, by simply showing the repercussion of success.

In 1925 the Canga River and the upper Yaupe was very populous and prosperous. The Indians were a warlike group confident of their own strength and much feared by all of the Indians in the neighboring regions. The curaka of the Canga Jívaros was a well known warrior called Cucusha. Anguasha . . . another warlike leader, was head of the Yaupe group. The two had always been close friends and companions. During a period of 10 or 15 years they compiled a notable war record, each being credited individually with more than 50 heads during this time. Their raids extended to all of the tribes in the district and some quite distant, until they became the terror of the region. However, these constant raids under two such aggressive leaders began to take their toll of men. Although many victories were registered, they were constantly losing warriors, until eventually their numbers were appreciably reduced (Stirling 1938: 40).

The flexibility of organization which these excerpts suggest is amply demonstrated in my own material on Aguaruna local groups and the process by which they are established and maintained. Just as the military alliances were subject to a developmental cycle, the house clusters (*caseríos*) and larger neighborhoods change through time in composition and numbers, corresponding to or reflecting ecological and demographical circumstances, individual mobility and independence being concomitant features. Genealogical data reveal that single persons and families have changed house sites several times not only within a settlement, but have also moved from one *caserío* to another far part. In so doing they have attached themselves to relatives and avoided traditional "enemies."

As I have argued elsewhere (Siverts 1971, 1972) the habitat requires mobility, and this moving about in search of suitable house sites, yucca gardens, hunting grounds, and hunting partners is made possible by the linking of houses and settlements through genealogies. This linking of genealogies or rather fragments of genealogies constitutes an underlying framework of organization which, by extension, embraces all Jívaro in a kin and affinal network. Apparently the Aguaruna consider all other Jívaro, whether foe or friend, as somehow related. Personal experiences, implicitly shown in a statement such as, "my mother was a Huambisa," corroborates this notion.

The alliances of *caseríos* (or *jivarías*) were expedient activations of more or less extensive portions of the genealogical network, a measure which, by implication, established relative peace within an area. The lack of persistence of any particular alliance provided for constancy of the genealogical network itself which thereby was left unbroken as an organizational potential: new constellations of *caseríos* could always be established.

In view of the flexibility of organization, permitting the establishment of impermanent corporations, Jívaro invincibility in the past makes sense. The question has been asked how the Jívaro, preoccupied with the taking of each other's heads, could possible muster an effective resistance against intruders. And the answer must be one that takes account of the strategic advantage offered by the habitat itself as well as the military strength presented by the Jívaro as an ethnic group.[4]

It is this latter theme that is intimately related to the main problem of this essay, viz., the process by which "Jívaroness" is maintained and the cultural boundary defended. From the Jívaro point of view this boundary is essentially one which separates *¢án¢as* from non-*¢án¢as*, and its territorial counterpart is recognized only insofar as the headhunting patterns or the conditions for pursuing this activity is threatened. Thus, the Jívaro make no territorial claim and they did let foreigners visit them and establish contact without showing hostility.

It was when they first felt that Spanish settlement and Spanish rule interfered with their own way of life and its esoteric basis that they acted; and they were able to act in concert since the underlying framework was all-encompassing, and potentially permitted the emergency mobilization

---

[4] How strong the striking power was is illustrated by the famous Jívaro revolt of 1559 when perhaps as many as 20,000 warriors under the leadership of Quiruba annihilated the town of Logroño, terminating Spanish rule in the Jívaro territory. Not even the Peruvians or Ecuadorians succeeded in making headway in this area some fifty years ago. At least they never won a decisive victory.

of all able-bodied men in a grand alliance transforming the Jívaro ethnic group into a corporation.

Such a complete fusion of antagonistic, feuding units may be seen as the automatic result as long as blood revenge and war were parts of daily life, the shifts in power continuous, and the alliance forming an ongoing, cyclical process.

Even as late as the 1930's, when Stirling visited the area, the following statement was probably appropriate:

The alliance between nature and the Jívaros has enabled these Indians successfully to repulse for 400 years the most determined efforts of the white man to establish himself in their territory. The many-faceted account of this prolonged struggle against military, theological, commercial, and territorial aggression constitutes one of the most colorful chapters in aboriginal American history (1938: 28).

The bulldozer and the machine gun have changed the situation. It is no longer possible for the Jívaro to control the area by watching the mountain passes or attacking isolated and vulnerable outposts.[5] The highway and the garrisons have put an end to the endless feuds, and prevented the most dramatic expression of "Jívaroness." A further consequence of this state of affairs is the retention of old grievances between former opponents without the natural outlet, leaving the underlying framework obsolete for corporation-forming purposes and hence leading to a situation of political inactivity and indecision.

And this indecision, combined with the distrust of fellow men, has made it easier for the respective governments to launch their colonization projects, forcing the Jívaro, one by one, from their *chacras* [yucca gardens] and hunting grounds. It is symptomatic that the Aguaruna of Alto Marañon are so paralyzed that they have permitted the Peruvian authorities to back up a figurehead, hated by everybody.

There is only one case on record showing signs of political activity and a will to act *in corpore*: a group of armed men gathered in the Cenepa district in order to resist another round of DDT fumigation. For the first time, the "DDT gang"[6] met resolute and concerted action. They fled, and news about the success spread all over the region. Today, the "malaria-agency" people find it difficult to continue working in the area, which means one nuisance less to cope with.

However interesting this instance appears under the circumstances, it may not necessarily herald a new drive or revival of political activity on a

[5]   In 1915 a Peruvian garrison on the upper Morona was routed and practically everybody killed; and in 1925 the village and mission of Cahuapenas on the Apaga river were wiped out (cf. Stirling 1938: 28).
[6]   The "DDT gang" is short for the employees of the *Servicio Nacional de Eradicación de Malaria* (SNEM) (see Siverts 1972).

large scale. It takes more to unite headhunters when there are no heads around to be taken; and in addition the prospects offered for Jívaro survival as an ethnic group are rather gloomy under the auspices of a "headless" minority policy.

REFERENCES

BARTH, FREDRIK, editor
  1969   *Ethnic groups and boundaries: the social organization of culture differences.* Boston: Little, Brown.
GUALLART, JOSÉ MARÍA
  1964   Los Jibaros del Alto Marañon. *América Indígena* 24:315–331.
  1970   "Magia y poesía Aguaruna: poesía magica y poesía lírica entre los Aguarunas." Unpublished manuscript.
HARNER, MICHAEL J.
  1962   Jívaro souls. *American Anthropologist* 64:258–272.
  1968   "Technological and social change among the eastern Jívaro," in *Proceedings of the Thirty-seventh International Congress of Americanists*, 363–388. Buenos Aires.
KARSTEN, RAFAEL
  1935   *The head-hunters of western Amazonas: the life and culture of the Jívaro indians of eastern Ecuador and Peru.* Helsinki: Societas Scientarum Fennica, Comentationes Humanarum Litterarum.
LARSON, MILDRED L.
  1963   *Emic classes which manifest the obligatory tagmemes in major independent clause types of Aguaruna (Jívaro).* Norman: University of Oklahoma Summer Institute of Linguistics.
NAROLL, RAOUL
  1964   On ethnic unit classification. *Current Anthropology* 5:283–312.
PIKE, KENNETH L., M. L. LARSON
  1964   "Hyperphonemes and non-systemic features of Aguaruna phonemes," in *Studies in languages and linguistics.* Edited by A. H. Marckwardt, 55–67. Ann Arbor: University of Michigan Press.
SIVERTS, HENNING
  1971   "The Aguaruna Jívaros of Peru: a preliminary report." Mimeographed manuscript, University of Bergen.
  1972   *Tribal survival in the Alto Marañon: the Aguaruna case.* IWGIA Document 10. Copenhagen.
STIRLING, M. W.
  1938   *Historical and ethnographical material on the Jívaro Indians.* Bureau of American Ethnology, Bulletin 117. Washington D.C.: Smithsonian Institution.
UP DE GRAFF, FRITZ W.
  1923   *Head-hunters of the Amazon: seven years of exploration and adventure.* London: Herbert Jenkins.
URIARTE, LUIS M.
  1971   *Situación de genocidio, etnocidio e injusticia entre las tribus aguaruna y huambisa del Alto Marañon.* Comisión Episcopal de Acción Social, Cuadernos de Documentación 2. Lima.
  1972   "Algunos datos preliminares del censo Aguaruna-Huambisa." Unpublished manuscript, Chiriaco.

VARESE, STEFANO, *editor*
1970   *Estudio sondeo de seis comunidades Aguarunas del Alto Marañon.*
Division de Comunidades Natives de la Selva, Dirección de Comunidades Campesinas. Series de Estudos e Informes 1. Lima: Ministerio de Agricultura.
WALLIS, ETHEL
1965   *Tariri, my story.* Translated from Kandoshi by Lorrie Anderson. New York: Harper and Row.

Jungle Quechua Ethnicity:
An Ecuadorian Case Study

NORMAN E. WHITTEN, JR.

The vast majority of aboriginal peoples living in eastern Ecuador (the Oriente) in 1972 belong to one of two cultural divisions: they are either Quechua, or they are Jívaro. The latter are well known to anthropology and are regarded as bona fide indigenes. The former Indians are the largest aggregate, numbering approximately 35,000 or more (Burbano Martínez et al. 1964). They speak Quechua[1] as a first language and live a tropical

This paper is based primarily on five months of preliminary ethnography undertaken during the summers of 1970 and 1971. The research is sponsored by the University of Illinois, Urbana, and the Instituto Nacional de Antropología e Historia, Quito, Ecuador, and is funded by the National Science Foundation (Grant No. GS-2999). I am grateful to the Director of the Instituto, Arq. Hernán Crespo Toral, for his constant interest and encouragement in this preliminary field investigation. Considerable thanks also are due five assistants who worked at various stages of the preliminary project: Cynthia Gillette, Nicanor Jácome, Marcelo Naranjo, Michael Waag, and Margarita Wurfl. Michael Waag also commented critically on an earlier draft of this paper. Confidentiality promised to the subjects of research now prohibits me from thanking those who helped the most — the Quechua and Jívaro close associates now caught up in the international scheme of "becoming" Indian while confronting cataclysmic changes in their environments.
    The major result of this preliminary research was a proposal to undertake a year of intensive ethnography with the Lowland Quechua, beginning in late August, 1972. This research, a joint project with Dorothea S. Whitten, is also funded by the National Science Foundation (Continuation Grant No. GS-2999) and supplemented by funds for research assistance by the University of Illinois Research Board and Center for Comparative International Studies. The study has three basic aspects. In the first, Dorothea S. Whitten, Marcelo Naranjo, and I continue our study of Jungle Quechua ethnicity and adaptive strategies in the face of rapid change in their natural and social environments. In the second, John P. Ekstrom is completing a year's study of colonist strategies of land acquisition between the Pastaza and Curaray river drainages. The third aspect, designed and now being carried out by Theodore Macdonald, involves continuities in Quechua world view and symbolic domains, particularly as they relate to their position in the indigenous shaman system of highland and lowland Ecuador.
[1] I am using a standard, familiar international spelling for the word "Quechua," Ecuadorian usage prefers *Quichua*, or *Kichua*. In Ecuador the term is pronounced "Keéchuwa."

forest life. Yet they are frequently mentioned only in passing by authors describing the Oriente. Within Ecuador they are often lumped as "Quijos" (e.g. Porras 1961; Ferdon 1950; Peñaherrera de Costales and Costales Samaniego 1961), reflecting their presumed tribal-linguistic origin west of the Napo river along the eastern cordillera of the Andes; or, they are lumped as "Yumbos" (Peñaherrera de Costales et al. 1969; Burbano Martínez et al. 1964), which suggests that they are acculturated highland Quechuas who moved into the tropical forest and there mixed with other groups (particularly the Záparos). When compared to the Cofán, Secoya, Siona (Piojé), Huarani (Auca), Awishiri (Auca), Zaparo, and Jívaro (Untsuri Shuara — see Harner 1972 — and Achuara), the Quechua of east lowland Ecuador are usually regarded as sufficiently assimilated to lowland *blanco–mestizo* culture as to preclude careful attention. All indigenous people of Ecuador contrast ethnically with the category *blanco-mestizo* (defined below in the section on internal colonialism).

The Jungle Quechua of the central Oriente may be linguistically divided into three major dialect segments:[2] northwest, northeast, and southern (Orr and Wrisley 1965). The northwest dialect, called Tena, is found on the upper reaches of the Napo river, and its headwater affluent the Jatun Yacu. The dialect continues through the administrative towns of Tena and Archidona, and on up the sierra to near the present town of Baeza. It runs down the Napo to the settlement of Ahuano and south to Arajuno, cutting across the Puyo–Napo road at Santa Clara. The northeastern dialect, called Napo, goes on down the Napo river, and is spoken on such north-Napo tributaries as the Suno and Payamino rivers. The southern division, called Bobonaza, begins south of Santa Clara and Arajuno and extends to the Pastaza river. Quechua on the Curaray, Bobonaza, Conambo, and Pindo are all of the southern division, though other further dialectical differences do exist. The territory between the Curaray and the Napo is not inhabited by Quechuas — it is exclusively Auca (Huarani, Awishiri) country.

---

[2]   Cultural differences between Jungle Quechua of the southern dialect group and the northern group are extensive, and beyond the scope of this paper to list. Suffice it to say here that the Quechua-speakers of the Bobonaza basin — the "Canelos Quechua" — are Upper Amazonian peoples who have been adapting for centuries to the zone best identified with the Bobonaza river north to the Curaray river and south to the Pastaza river. This is the area carved out as the archdiocese of Canelos. In spite of their proximity to the Andes and their language, they have a fundamentally tropical-forest way of life, which they have applied in some areas to montaña existence. The Canelos Quechua are, in many ways, more similar to Jívaroan speakers in cultural content than to the Quijos Quechuas (Tena dialect). Ethnic derivation is, in historical times, a merger of Záparoan, Achuara Jívaroan, some Jívaroan proper, and, more recently, Quijos Quechua cultures. Achuara and Záparoan are the most important contributors to culture content. Ancient Omagua and Cocama Tupian influence is probable. The exact origin of the Quechua language in this zone is unknown, at this time, but ancient tropical forest derivation cannot be discounted. A general ethnography of ethnic derivation, world view, and contemporary adaptation is now in preparation.

Culturally, the northern and southern divisions of Quechua territories are distinct, and their relationships with highland and other lowland indigenous peoples are also different.[3] The people of the Tena-Napo dialects and Bobonaza dialect regard one another as different; their aboriginal histories and histories of contact are different, and their present socioeconomic status is quite different, though perhaps convergent. The Tena-Napo groups represent expansions around Catholic mission bases from the sixteenth century on to the present (Oberem 1971). Quechua language clearly came from the missions (cf. Steward 1948:509–515). Their history is one of continuous serfdom to the missions and haciendas, and their present socioeconomic position is analogous to that of the infamous highland *Husipungueros*. They are generally called Yumbos, Napos, and Quijos. For clarity and convenience I will refer to them as "Quijos Quechua." For a recent monograph on this culture see Oberem (1971).

Native people of the Bobonaza, Conambo, and Curaray drainages seem to have been buffers between warring groups of Jívaros, Záparos, Awishiris, and others from the time of first contact. Missions may have been built in existing refuge areas, and while such missions may have solidified such refuge zones, it may not be accurate to say that the missions created these zones. Throughout southern Quechua territory internal bilingual and bicultural activities between Quechua and Achuara Jívaros are maintained by marriage. Intermarriage with the Jívaro proper, "Untsuri Shuara," also exists. This pattern of marriage with otherwise warring Jívaro groups seems to have at least a 200-years time depth. Also, on the Curaray, Corrientes, and Pindo rivers, Záparo–Quechua bilingualism and biculturalism exists — here people in the river bank settlements are "Quechua," but many "become Záparo" in the forest. In the latter capacity not only is Záparoan spoken, but aggressive raids against Huarani Auca households have reputedly been made in the recent past. Some Záparo–Quechua bilingualism still exists on the Rio Bobonaza. Finally, more profound influences on Quechua life in the southern areas have come from the extension of the trade network (for furs, gold, medicines, and cinnamon) and from the rubber boom of the late nineteenth century to early twentieth century than from the establishment of haciendas as in the northern case.

From this point on, my paper deals with the southern dialect, with the Quechua of the Bobonaza drainage — the "Canelos Quechua."

The people in this southern area *refer* to themselves in Quechua as *runa*

---

[3] For example, shamans from the Canelos Quechua are regarded as the most powerful in the world by the Jívaro (see Harner 1972), and highland Indians from near Ríobamba regularly visit Canelos Quechua shamans. But, other highland Indians such as the Salasaca and the Otavaleños generally avoid Canelos Quechua shamans and go directly to shamans and curers in Tena and Ahuano.

[indigenous person]. They also use the term *Alama*, "friend" or "mythic brother,"[4] among themselves to *address* those who come from the Bobonaza or Curaray drainages and are southern Lowland Quechua speakers. In Spanish they use the term *gente* [people] as a reference for themselves. (When speaking Spanish all Jungle Quechuas use *gente* in contrast with *blanco*.) There is no term other than *Alama* used to differentiate the people of the Bobonaza drainage from other Quechua speakers in highland and lowland Ecuador. In speaking Spanish, though, the Jungle Quechua of this zone use *gente* for themselves, and from that point distinguish themselves as people from both *runa llacta* (literally, "indigenous land" — which is used as though it were Spanish, when speaking Spanish) and *blancos* (literally "whites" — including Negroes). Jívaros and some colonists who have been in the area for a generation or more designate the Bobonaza Jungle Quechua as *Alama* (and in Jívaro sometimes as *Aram Shuara*), but this is regarded as mildly pejorative by the Indians when used contrastively by any but southern-dialect Jungle Quechua speakers. Very few Indians north of Santa Clara on the Puyo–Napo road even know the term *Alama*, and no one knows its meaning.

When speaking Quechua, the division of ethnic categories and territories is quite clear. The Indians themselves seldom refer to their own referent dialect group, except by implicit contrast, when making the following distinctions. In the west — the Andes — there are two "lands": *runa llacta* and *ahua llacta*. The former is "indigenous land" but is used in the area under study only to refer to highland Indian territory — regarded

---

[4]   The derivation of the term *Alama* comes from a myth segment, dealing, in various ways, with older brother/younger brother authority and tension. In brief, an older and younger brother were on a huge stone in the middle of a great river, having been placed there by a giant condor. The older brother called a great cayman which came to the rock to help the brothers across, but the younger brother jumped down first, crossed, and by the time the cayman made the return trip for the older brother the younger had disappeared. Walking through the forest, lost, and searching not only for the brother, but also for a lost homeland, the older brother reached out to break off a piece of tree mushroom (*ala*) and as he pinched it the mushroom cried out "ouch, my mythic brother, don't pinch me, real brother" (*aiai alajma ama tiushi huaichu huauqui: aiai* [ouch], *ala* [mushroom, mythic brother], *j* possessive, *ma* emphasis, *ama* [no], *tiushi* [pinch], *hua* [to me], *i* command, *chu* negative complement to *ama, huauqui* [real brother]). On saying this the tree mushroom transformed into the younger brother who rejoined his sibling and they went on to more adventures.

There is more to the *ala* complex than this, for ancient peoples had the ability to send their souls (*aya*) into special rocks and logs when their bodies died, from whence a mushroom would emerge to await a wandering *runa* who, in hunger, would pinch the mushroom and awaken the ancient *runa*. In this way, older and younger statuses can fluctuate, because, although the younger brother was lost, rediscovery of him through this process indicates abilities of soul transformation suggestive of ancient, older status. The term *ala* is used in direct address by all acknowledged male participants in Canelos Quechua culture and is, thereby, a crucial ethnic marker. On being called *ala* or *alaj* one must immediately reciprocate the same term, acknowledging mythic brotherhood, or he must reciprocate a pejorative, negative, ethnic term such as *auca* [heathen], or *mashca pupu* [barley gut, Ecuadorian intruder].

as all of the Andes. The latter term, *ahua llacta*, is literally "highland" but refers politely to all non-Indian Ecuadorians. The *ahua llacta* term in Jungle Quechua is used as a synonym for the Spanish *blanco*. Neither the designation *gente* in Spanish, nor the designation *runa* in Quechua, is used for the Ecuadorian highland *blanco-mestizo*.

To the north there are two territories of Quechua which correspond to the two dialect areas, called respectively *Alchirona Llacta* and *Napo Llacta* (representing the northwest and northeastern dialect divisions). (Sometimes *Ansuj Llacta* is added to indicate Quechua settlements southwest of the Napo river, on a feeder river to the Jatun Yacu river.) To the north and south lies *Auca Llacta* [heathen lands]. In the north this includes the Cushmas (Cofán, Tetéte, Secoya, and Siona), who are but dimly known by reputation, and the hostile Huarani (called *Llushti Auca* [naked heathens] and *Tahuashiri* [ridge people] in Quechua). On the Curaray river, and recently along the Bobonaza as well, distinctions are made between the Huarani or "true" *Llushti Auca* to the west, now clustered on the Curaray above the mouth of the Villano and the Nushiño rivers, and the *Awishiri (Tahuashiri) Aucas* to the east, who now live between the Cononaco and Tivacuna rivers. The legendary (in Quechua legend) *Puca Chaqui Auca* [red leg heathens] of the Tiputini drainage are said to constitute a third division, and the Canelos Quechua insist that these unknown people speak another language and use bows and arrows. Oil company observations seem to confirm Canelos Quechua insistence on a *Puca Chaqui Auca* group. Also belonging to *Auca Llacta* in the north are Záparo speakers, most of whom are bilingual in Jungle Quechua, and many of whom are trilingual in Spanish as well. Northern Achuara from the Corrientes and Conambo river systems are also part of *Auca Llacta*. Tessman (1930), Steward (1948), and Steward and Métraux (1948) give historical data supporting these divisions made by the southern dialect group of Quechua-speakers.

Due east of *Alama* land, in Peru, live *Andoa Runa* in the most eastern territory of the culture area of the Canelos Quechua. Other *Auca Llacta* are said to exist there, especially the Candochi Jívaroans on the Pastaza, Záparoans from the Marañon river, and Cocama on the Tigre River. Within their own territory the Jungle Quechua identify one another by the administrative center closest to their settlement, unless they actually come from that area, in which case identity is by clan segment and actual residence. From west to east the major identifying settlements are the *Puyo Runa* (sometimes *Pinduj Runa*), which include all people from the Pinduj river south to the Pastaza river, north on either side of the Napo road for a few kilometers, and northeast to Cabecera de Bobonaza. *Canelos Runa* includes people from east of Cabecera de Bobonaza to Canelos and from Canelos north to the headwaters of the Villano and Curaray rivers, east to Chambira, and south to the headwaters of the

Copotaza river. *Paca Yacu Runa* includes those around the settlement of Paca Yacu north to Villano, and *Sara Yacu Runa* includes all people there south to the Capahuari river, north to the Conambo river, and east on the Bobonaza river to Teresa Mama. *Montalvo Runa* includes the territory north to the Conambo river, east to Peru, and south to the Capahuari. Each *runa* territory is divided into *llactas*, which have recognized living or dead founders and consist of intermarried segments of clans which trek (*purina*) periodically to identified zones, where they encounter other people from other *runa* territories similarly engaged. Sara Yacu-Canelos is seen as the cultural hearth of contemporary Canelos Quechua culture, but the greatest population concentration is between the Pinduj and Pastaza rivers. The people themselves see their origin area as somewhere around contemporary Yurimaguas, in Peru.

Because of the designation of Canelos as the stereotypic center of southern Quechua culture, because the people of this zone have so frequently been designated as the "Canelos tribe" in the literature, and because the designation "Canelos Quechua" is becoming increasingly accepted in Ecuador, I shall hereafter refer to the people of the southern Lowland Quechua dialect as "Canelos Quechua." The reader is warned however that in the Dominican and administrative site of Canelos proper there exists *more intrusion* from Quijos Quechua and Highland Quechua than with any other area of Canelos Quechua territory, including Puyo. Figure 1 indicates the major geographic and ethnic divisions made by the Canelos Quechua in contrastively defining their position vis-à-vis other nonwhite ethnic categories in the Ecuadorian Oriente.

Marriage between the Canelos Quechua and both cultural groups of Jívaro has taken place for at least two hundred years. The Canelos Quechua have virtually absorbed the Záparo speakers in the last fifty years, and marriages with highland Indians, occasionally highland whites, and Indians from both northern dialects today take place. For the Canelos Quechua, *Indígena* [Indian] or preferably *nativo* [native] is synonymous with their way of life, and they aggressively insist that the appropriate synonym in Spanish for *Indígena* is *gente*. Incorporation of Jívaros, usually classed as *Auca*, will be discussed below when presenting some aspects of the Canelos Quechua kinship system.

Although the Canelos Quechua are not homogeneous in their ethnic makeup, they are nonetheless a self-identifying, if highly individualistic, indigenous aggregate with clear cultural markers; and as an aggregate they are not merging into *blanco–mestizo* culture. We must understand the expansion of Lowland Quechua ethnicity as a rational response to expanding opportunities in the money economy under the continuance of internal colonialism in Ecuador.

Economically, the staple of lowland life is *yuca* [manioc]. *Chacras* [cleared fields] cover from one to three hectares. Land is cleared with ax

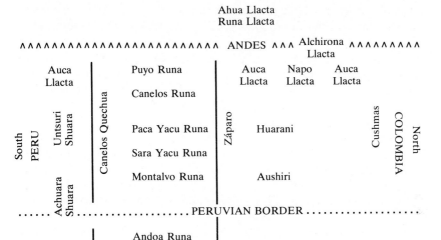

Figure 1. Ethnicity and territory as seen by the "Canelos Quechua"

and machete by a man, his sons, and sons-in-law, more often than not
without help of kinsmen or friends, although *mingas* [reciprocal labor
exchange] may take place. Men plant plantains, bananas, corn, and
naranjilla. The same men carry the manioc stems to the clearing; then
women do the actual planting, keep the *chacra* clean, harvest the *yuca*,
carry it to the house, prepare it, and serve it. Sweet potatoes and some
yautía are also grown on the *chacra*, and these are also the responsibility
of women. Palm shoots, *chontaduros*, *yautía*, a variety of fruits, peppers,
tomatoes, and herbs are grown in kitchen gardens in back of the house as
well as on the *chacra*. Near Puyo the naranjilla (*Solanum quitoense* and
several other species) is grown as a cash crop; otherwise, the Canelos
Quechua have few crops of cash value, though they are ringed on their
western and northern flanks by sugar and tea plantations.

Manioc beer (chicha or *asua*) of very low alcoholic content (more of a
gruel) is a staple of life, and the making and serving of chicha constitutes a
focal point of symbolic interaction within the household. The masticated

yuca is stored in large pottery jars (*tinajas* or *asua churana manga*) and served in thin, finely decorated bowls (*mucahuas*). All pottery is made by coiling. Women make their own *tinajas* and *mucahuas* and guard small secrets pertaining to color, design, and ways to get the thinnest possible sides and rims. Knowledge and techniques are passed from mother to daughter or from mother to son's wife. The pottery is fired without a kiln. This is the finest pottery made today in the Ecuadorian Oriente, and most, if not all, pottery sold in the highlands as "Jívaro pottery" comes from the Canelos Quechua. Indeed, some Jívaros marry Quechua women and bring them to their own houses in order to have better pottery than the Jívaro women can provide.[5] Black pottery cooking pots (*yanuna manga*) and eating dishes (*callana*) are also made, sometimes with thumbnail decorations (*sarpa manga*).

Fine decorated pottery for intrahousehold use is not disappearing with the introduction of metal pots and pans, but the black pottery is rapidly dwindling. People buy the new goods, or trade other things to obtain them, but they maintain at least one or two *tinajas* for chicha storage and at least one *mucahua* for serving.

Several fish poisons, such as barbasco, are grown in the *chacra* to be used during relatively dry times of the year, when the rivers run quite low and clear. Hallucinogens such as *ayahuasca* (three *Banisteriopsis* species) and *huanduj* (several *Datura* species) are grown, together with *huayusa*, tobacco, and a large variety of medicinal and magical herbs. Men fish with spears, traps, weirs, lines, and nets, and hunt with traps and blowguns. Although many Quechua men make curare poison, using some forty or more plant and other substances, more powerful curare for the blowgun darts comes along trade networks originating in the east. Peruvian Achuara bring poison to Conambo, Montalvo, Copotaza, and Sara Yacu, and Copotaza Achuara or Conambo Achuara carry it on westward. Muzzle-loading shotguns are also used for small game, and cartridge guns are becoming available. Long treks (*purina*) to gather turtle eggs, to hunt for large quantities of meat, to catch and dry large fish, to keep a distant *chacra*, and to buy the appropriate black, red, and white clays for pottery decoration are made by a family once or twice a year, sometimes alone and sometimes with a larger kinship or settlement group.

Travel is frequent among the Canelos Quechua, and it is usually by foot. The rivers are too rapid and untrustworthy as far as depth goes (sometimes flooded, sometimes quite low) to provide stable avenues for

[5]   A crucial aspect of Canelos Quechua cultural perpetuity is bound up with the transmission of knowledge and secrets in pottery making. Three souls go to make up each storage jar and drinking bowl: the clay giver soul, the woman's own created body soul, and the household soul. These souls and the knowledge behind each are transmitted generation by generation through women, just as special knowledge of the clan souls acquired through psychedelic experiences are transmitted generation by generation through males. In my future ethnography I will devote considerable time to analysis of such cultural continuity.

transportation on the Pastaza east to Ayuy or on the Bobonaza east to Canelos. The Curaray itself meanders so much that it is about as efficient to travel on foot from one point to another as to make one oxbow turn after another by canoe. Nevertheless, canoes are used when cargo is to be moved, and the Canelos Quechuas are excellent canoe makers and superior boatmen.

The nuclear family is a very tightly knit unit with man and woman sharing equally in decision making, spatial mobility, and in upward socioeconomic mobility in some cases. Residence is ideally matri-patrilocal but generally bilocal. There is no term for this unit except the Quechua term *huasi* [house], and the Spanish terms *familia* and *casa* are used synonymously for *huasi*.

The maximal kinship grouping, and segments of this grouping, are referred to as *ayllu*. The *ayllu*, as the maximal clan, is a stipulated descent system from a common animal ancestor, often a variety of puma or jaguar. Each *ayllu* is today identified with a set of surnames and extends through much of Canelos Quechua territory and on into other culture areas, as well. For people in any clan segment, extended clan (also called *ayllu*) reckoning is from father or father's father back to his father's wife. Within the extended clan there are tightly knit stem kindreds, reckoning from an old, founding shaman. These kindreds are also called *ayllu*, but because of the intertwining of *ayllu* membership through marriage with other *ayllu* segments within a territory, the resulting intermarried segments often refer to themselves by the territorial term, *llacta*.

Each *ayllu* (maximal and extended) maintains its special culture, transmitted to intimate residential in-laws. In this transmission special concentrations of knowledge, or culture, concatenate into the territorial *runa*, which expands and contracts with the *purina* system and fissions across *ayllu* lines in the *llacta* system. In this way shared knowledge embedded in the dispersed *ayllu* of antiquity is transferred repeatedly across *ayllu* boundaries and maintained through conflict and competition in the *llacta* system. *Ayllu* members maintain their *ayllu* ideology, how-ever, through visionary experience, through mythology, and through actual travel. They can reactivate the maximal *ayllu* concept after many generations through the system of shared descent from a common animal ancestor and through shared possession of the souls of the deceased.

In ascending order of kin and neighbor units, a child is born into a *huasi* [household] unit, in which the woman's cultural maintenance through pottery tradition and the man's maintenance through *aya* [soul] acquisi-tion assures each newborn of a place in a maximal clan extending back into mythic time. The *huasi* itself exists within a *llacta*, a defensible territory, which was established by a founder in alliance with other founders of *ayllu* segments. These minimal *ayllu* segments within a *llacta* are stem kindreds. Beyond the stem kindred is the extended clan, which includes localized and dispersed kinsmen within and beyond a *runa* territory. And beyond the extended clan is the maximal clan, the everlasting system of stipulated descent into mythic time and structure. The ancient relationships among founders of maximal clans, during the time when all animals were human and humans crawled on the ground like babies, are repeated today as myths and are thought to provide the basis for integration of the Canelos Quechua, long before humans came to dominate their sector of the biosphere.

A developmental sequence exists which ties male *huasi*, *ayllu*, and *llacta* founders to the knowledge of mythic times. On marriage a male must, by taking *huanduj* [*Datura*] converse with the soul-master, *Amasanga*, and have the soul-master cure him of magical darts (*supai biruti*) sent by jealous suitors of his wife. Also, the bride must visit the wife of the *Amasanga*, the *chacra mama* or *Nunghuí mama*, to get her sacred stones and knowledge to make the manioc grow. If a man wishes to head a stem kindred then he must, through a long period of time, acquire the status of *yachaj* [shaman], becoming both curer and potential mystical killer; and when, if ever, he seeks to found a *llacta* he must have made pacts with the various spirits (*supai*) and souls (*aya*) of the territory, in which process he becomes a potential *bancu* [seat] for the souls and spirits. He usually does not serve as *bancu*, however, because retaliation for the evil done by the spirits and souls through the *bancu* leads many people to attempt to eliminate the *bancu*'s social capital — his family, neighbors, and friends — by witchcraft and assassination.

As the process of soul acquisition and making pacts with spirits goes on, something else also occurs due to the constant outward movement of affinally-related clan segments: *a maximal clan evolves within a territory*. This maximal clan is often named after a given area. Terms such as Puyo Runa, Canelos Runa, Sara Yacu Runa, etc. then take on another meaning, for not only do the territories exist as interrelated clan segments, but certain clans come to dominate, and knowledge of the *runa* territory suggests the dominating clan. The territorial clans represent a process of "social circumscription" (Carneiro 1970) overlaid with territorial circumscription. Segments of extended clans do cut through these territorial boundaries, however, as do alliances formed through intermarriage. Such cross-cutting of the circumscribed territorial clans suggests an evolution toward an incipient, as yet acephalous, ethnic state of southern Jungle Quechua.

All maximal clans of the Canelos Quechua include Achuara Jívaros as members of Quechua extended clans. Also, in many of the maximal clans there is one Achuara or even Untsuri Shuara local group (*caserío*) which insures intraindigenous ethnic contrast (Quechua versus Jívaro) *within* the maximal clan itself. This ethnic contrast between two very different indigenous peoples, together with the countervailing complementarity through cross-cutting intermarriages, is an essential element in the definition of Canelos Quechua ethnicity and social structure and is a key to continuity of indigenous identity during times of rapid change.

The term *ayllu* may refer to the *caserío* when this local group consists of only one segment of the extended clan; otherwise it refers to the speaker's own descent group within the *llacta*, or *caserío*. If the speaker has no descent group members in the *caserío* he will use *ayllu* to mean members of the descent group of his wife, or deceased wife. *Ayllu* is regularly used to denote extended clan and, when involved in territorial disputes with Jívaros or with colonists, *ayllu* as maximal clan is invoked. In this latter sense indigenous ethnicity is stressed over intraindigenous divisions, and the concept of common, *indigenous descent*, together with the acknowledgement of extensive networks resulting from stipulated clan intermarriage, is used vis-à-vis outsiders. Such a process of assertion of common descent of otherwise contrastive Indian ethnic identities is well under way in several parts of the Oriente, one of which is the Comuna de San Jacinto, near Puyo.

The Jungle Quechua call themselves Christians, and so distinguish themselves as opposed to all other Indians, except the Highland Quechua. Practices such as genuflecting and kissing the hand of priests and nuns are ubiquitous. There are few churches in the *caseríos*, and where these exist a priest (or evangelist) may visit a few times a year, on the occasion of special fiestas. More generally, the central church for the Lowland Quechua is in a major town, or outlying post (Puyo, Canelos, Sara Yacu, Montalvo, Jesús Pitishca). Everywhere, though, other worlds associated with the sky and an inner earth, and other spirits, creatures and souls associated with the tropical forest and treacherous stretches of rivers, are talked about and visited with the aid of hallucinogens.

THE COMUNA DE SAN JACINTO DEL PINDO

The Comuna de San Jacinto del Pindo (Map 1) was established by executive decree in 1947 by the then national president, Dr. José María Velasco Ibarra. This decree was necessary due to the extreme conflict between colonists and Indians in and around the town of Puyo. Puyo is only nine kilometers east of Shell Mera, the town founded by the Shell oil company in its explorations beginning in 1937. Indians were inhabiting the area around Puyo (along the Pinduj — now Pindo-Puyo — river) and at the mouth of the Pindo where it joins the Pastaza long before 1899, when a priest (Alvaro Valladares) and some Indians (Jívaro and Quechua) arrived from Canelos. Long a trading site for furs, gold, cinnamon, and wood, Puyo began to expand rapidly as a national frontier town when the Shell company completed the Baños–Shell Mera road in the mid-1930's.

There followed about fifteen years of highland colonist settlement in Puyo, which meant squeezing out the Indians, who were apparently vociferous in making their land claims known as more and more settlers moved into their *chacra* plots and began to raise sugarcane for the production of *aguardiente* [rum]. The 1947 presidential decree supposedly was made not only due to Indian–highlander conflict, but also due to growing national attention to the Indian plight in this area, stemming from explorers' accounts. One of the most important guides to the Oriente lived near Puyo, and Velasco Ibarra himself was supposedly respectful of this guide and the others of his extended clan (including one of the many powerful shamans of the area — see Eichler 1970:109). This guide presumably had enough important contacts among prominent Ecuadorians to force some attention to Indian problems among colonists and traders. Also, it seems, many highlanders seeking to exploit the Oriente were sorely in need of Indian guides and labor, and they turned to the Puyo Runa for such help. It benefited all to have a permanent Indian aggregate with marginal dependence on Puyo's money economy but able to subsist on its own when labor was not needed.

Whatever the specific historical causes, the *comuna* was established just south of Puyo. Its 16,000-hectare territory is bordered on the east by the Puyo river, just after its junction with the Pindo-Puyo, and on the west and south by the Pastaza river. The northern pinnacle begins at the Caserío San Jacinto (the oldest official *caserío* on the *comuna*) and runs southwest to where a bridge now crosses the Chinimbimi, a branch of the Pastaza. Today, eleven official *caseríos* of from 25 to 120 people and at least two other dispersed *llactas* ring the *comuna*, and throughout the *comuna* people also live separately, on particular *chacras*, but with identity claimed to one or two *llactas*. The estimated population of the Comuna de San Jacinto during 1973 is 1,600.

The *comuna* is ringed by sugar and tea plantations on all but the eastern flank, and one road cuts the *comuna* en route to the tea plantation south of the Pastaza. This road cuts through a rocky, fertile alluvial plain called La Isla [the island] because the Chinimbimi fork and Pastaza river enclose it. Here, along the road, there are more than 150 colonists illegally settled, almost all in conflict with the *comuna* members generally, while many form cooperative dyadic relationships with particular individuals from all of the *caseríos*. At the terminus of the road (Puerto Santa Ana) there is an all-colonist (*colono*) settlement at the base of a hill, with an all-Untsuri Shara Jívaro settlement on top of the hill.

In spite of cash cropping around the *comuna*, the *comuneros* only recourse to cash is the naranjilla and sale of forest products (including medicines, wood, furs, and a variety of off-and-on products bringing little

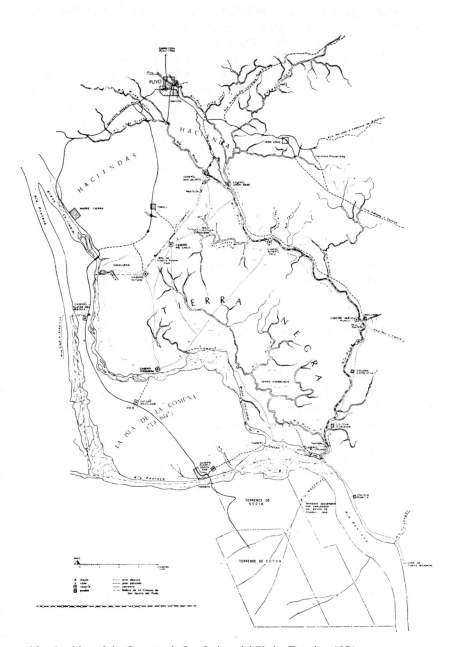

Map 1.   Map of the Comuna de San Jacinto del Pindo, Ecuador, 1971

cash, such as pottery, tourist lances, beads, and live animals). Basically, the *comuneros* farm their manioc and plaintain *chacras* and supplement their diet with poultry, wild birds, fish, and small game. The major change in this has been the impact of cattle during the past eight years.

The *comuna* is loosely governed by a cabildo, with elected president, vice-president, secretary, treasurer, *síndico* [lawyer], and a *vocal* [spokesman] from each of the *caseríos*. The election is held annually, and thus far has resulted in officials who are bilingual and bicultural, but who are the children of prominent or high-ranking extended clans, or the male affines attached to prominent, high-ranking clans. Deals made by the cabildos with prominent *colonos*, including the governor of the province, have improved their financial standing; a stratified system of high-ranking cabildos, having differential access to money through public officials in need of *comuna* land and/or labor, has occurred. However, the intra-*comuna* prestige game involves conspicuous giving (Erasmus 1961), with rank accruing to the giver. Ranking on the *comuna* leads, usually, to uneven access by the cabildos, which in turn places them in a position of economic betterment vis-à-vis most other *comuneros*; but the need for conspicuous giving within the *comuna* tempers this class sytem, and suggests one of ranking evolving into stratification (see Fried 1967). Thus far there is no whole clan of Quechuas on the *comuna* with differential access, though individuals from high-ranked clans do manage to place themselves in a position of differential access to local power domains channeling national resources.

Every single *comunero* is concerned with male fertility and female fecundity. Families are generally very large — ranging upward from one or two children when the parents are eighteen or nineteen to a dozen or so by the time the parents reach their forties. Some fathers continue to sire children into their seventies or eighties. This rational serious concern with exploding the population of the Puyo Runa is tied directly to the political economy. The *comuneros* want to populate their territory and other territories totally, knowing full well that this plan depends on gaining increased access to the money economy.

The strategy adopted is to build new *caseríos* only on the border of the *comuna*, as territorial holding units, while at the same time entering into contractual arrangements with colonists who are attempting to gain a foothold on the island. By "renting" land to *colonos*, and using the money to buy cattle off the *comuna*, the people of this area are trying to build capital resources (cattle, marketable land areas) while acquiring new land and at the same time protecting their *comuna* holdings.

In order to do the latter, constant protests are lodged against colonists renting *comuna* lands. This must be done in Quito, at the Ministerio de Previsión Social, for this is the governmental department established to administer the *comuna* system. Since there is no local agent of the ministerio it is also necessary to depend on local officials, the governor and political heads (*teniente político*, *jefe político*) of the adjacent administrative units. In dealing on the national level the *comuneros* enter one power domain (Adams 1970), where only conflict with *colonos* is stressed and where superior power and support is sought. In dealing with the local or regional level of the same domain, conflict *and* cooperation with officials and colonists must be stressed; economic support and expansion of promised facilities (e.g. a road in another part of the *comuna*) are requested *often with the result of loss of ground on original grievances*.

More will be said about power domains (national and local) in an ensuing section. Suffice it to say at this point that pro tem transfers of authority from the Ministerio de Previsión Social to the IERAC (Instituto Ecuatoriano de Reforma Agraria y Colonización) are sometimes made in order to bring a local-level competitive domain to the Indians. When this is done, though, *the Indians lose their strategic duality of national–regional domain manipulation*. They then must cope through a unified national–regional domain — one that has as its charge furtherance of *colonist expansion* and, hence, *Indian disenfranchisement and territorial encapsulation*.

The expansion of *caseríos* on the *comuna* is taking place rapidly, and is accompanied by local-level clamor by the Indians for national facilities on the larger *caseríos*. For example, there is a Catholic church at San Jacinto and a Protestant one at Puyo Pungo. There are now schools at Unión Base, Rosario Yacu, Río Chico, Chinimbimi, Puyo Pungo, Amazonas, and Playas del Pastaza. Children are taught or preached to in Spanish. In the schools, teachers are recruited from various parts of the nation. They live in the schoolhouse, and teach there for about eight months of the year. The sixth grade is the highest, from which some children go on to school in Puyo, this being paid for by their families.

The experience of the Comuna de San Jacinto del Pindo is being copied by a number of other people in definable *runa* territories that are becoming bounded by colonizing non-*runa* from the highlands. East of the Puyo–Napo road there are two other *comunas* (San Ramón and Arajuno), and still more are talked about. The *comuna* at Canelos has now become quasi-official by executive decree, and there is talk all down the Bobonaza of establishing *comunas* at the sites of the various administrative towns. In fact, the term *comunero* is being increasingly applied to all Indians, whether or not they live on the *comuna*, and many, if not most, *blanco-mestizos* knowing anything at all about the residence of Indians think that *comuna* means *caserío* and are surprised, or even bewildered, to find that *comuna* refers to the grouping of maximal clan segments in a given area. The Indians always explain their social-territorial structure to non-Indians in kinship terms, noting the intersection of extended clans in

240 NORMAN E. WHITTEN, JR.

the past. When pushed, for example, by curious *blancos* in Puyo as to why there are many families from different backgrounds and with different origins, the reply is that such families were previously related in grand-parental generations through marriage, so that *all present* comuneros *are descended from a common, ethnically diverse, breeding population.* By invoking this rule of stipulated ethnic descent the *comuneros* become, in their own eyes, a distinctive race — different from all *blanco-mestizos* and generally related to, but nontheless distinct from, all other Indians.

I will say more about the Comuna de San Jacinto after setting forth more of the relevant social environment of the Jungle Quechua by reference to internal colonialism, expanding infrastructure, colonization, and the relationships between power domains in this frontier cultural ecological setting.

INTERNAL COLONIALISM

Internal colonialism refers to situations ". . . where an independent country has, within its own boundaries, given special legal status to groups that differ culturally from the dominant group, and created a distinct adminis-trative machinery to handle such groups" (Colby and van den Berghe 1969:3). The plural nature of Ecuadorian society has been documented repeatedly (see Jaramillo Alvarado 1936; Whitten 1965; Burgos 1970). What is usually assumed, though, is that expanded economic oppor-tunities will result in the breakdown of plural segments and the estab-lishment of a "mixed" or "mestizo" national ethnic category. Pareja Diezcanseco sums up a prevalent intellectual view on contemporary Ecuador:

Ecuador is not a country inhabited by white folk, for as an ethnic minority they only add up to scarcely one-tenth of the total population. Neither is it a country of Indians, for in that case its history would be one of regression, or else, of stratification . . . the nation is *Mestizo* . . . Once the Indians enter civilized life . . . *the Mestizo part of the population will be more homogeneous* (1970:88, emphasis added).

The swelling of the "Mestizo part" of the country is seen by many, within and outside of Ecuador, as part of a growth of ethnic homogenization and a basis for the cultural and social revolution that will do away with a caste system where political and economic control rests with the very few *blancos*. But a large percentage of the nation is Indian, and a small, but concentrated, percentage is black (not mulatto). The national concept of mestizo contains a denial of *blanco* [white] supremacy and affirms roots to Indian and (sometimes) Negro, or at least Moorish–mulatto, ancestry. Such an *ideology of mixture* allows for considerable *exclusion of the nonmixed*, including highland and lowland Indians, and ethnically distinct black communities in northwest, north, and southwestern districts. Furthermore, economic and political integration of Ecuador is taking place through internal colonization, particularly through an expansion of highland mestizos to lowland areas inhabited primarily by Indians in the east and blacks in the northwest (see Whitten 1965, 1968, 1969a, 1969b, 1974).

Casagrande et al. (1964:281–325) and Gillette (1970) give preliminary analyses of colonization in Ecuador. The former state:

The theoretical interest in studying colonization lies both in the processes whereby an already established sociocultural system is extended, replicated or reintegrated, and in colonization as a *creative process*, since colonists frequently must accommodate themselves to a new ecological situation, and to novel sociopolitical and economic arrangements (Casagrande et al. 1964:282).

In an earlier work (Whitten 1965), I also took this approach to the predominantly black population of San Lorenzo, a northwest coastal rain-forest town. I gave primary attention to the internal social and political structure of black *costeños* and thought of colonists as having to adapt to the new, local scene. But, in the view taken here, another important creative process must be stressed. This is the process of colonization from the high Andes to tropical lowlands. The process is characterized by a transposition of *blanco* ethnic values, reinforced through demographic shifts, causing local peoples classed as *negro* or *indio* to face a socioeconomic environment with an effective, continuing, ideational blockage to strategic resources exploited within their territories.

As highland mestizos descend the Andes they enter zones which lack members in the contrasting, upper-class, *blanco* category, and, it seems, in the absence of such *blancos* they assume membership in the *blanco* category themselves. As a consequence, those who would be cholo or mestizo in the sierra become *blanco* on the coast and eastern slopes. "*Blanco*-ness" is reinforced by generalizing the non-*blanco* ethnic contrast — lumping black *costeños* into one pejorative category and lowland Indians into another. In eastern Ecuador, Indians have again and again had their residences forced completely out of the commercial and administrative towns, while economic dependence on these towns continued to increase.

It seems to me that the process of breaking up specific Indian linguistic-ethnic units ("tribes") is leading not to increased assimilation of Indians to "mestizo ways" but rather to an expanding generalized category "Indian" (*Indio*) to which *mestizos contrast themselves for virtually all purposes, when new opportunities in the money economy arise.* National and labor policies designed to speed up change in the mestizo sector, then, increasingly retard opportunities for those classed as *Indio*.

The crucial environmental factor for the contemporary Lowland Quechua is the expanding, contrastive ethnic category *blanco*, which includes the mestizo in the absence of upper-class *blanco* culture bearers. *Blanco–mestizo* ethnicity forces Quechua ethnicity to intensify, and the strategies played in the arena of expanding and generalizing ethnicity have powerful economic consequences for both ethnic categories, *particularly when one ethnic category (the Jungle Quechua) is encapsulated by national policies of "Indian protection" while the other* (blanco–mestizo) *is given wide powers through the national policy of colonization.*

By "ethnicity" I mean *patterns of human interaction which form the basis for categorical social relations with observable, or projected economic consequences.* Categorical social relationships are characterized by stereotypic criteria, as distinct from structural relations which are characterized by group membership or network relationships which are characterized by extant exchange patterns between interacting individuals (see Southall 1961:1–46; Mitchell 1966:52–53; Banton 1967; Whitten and Szwed 1970:43–48; Whitten and Wolfe 1973). Land access is intimately tied to the economic consequences of ethnic status.

In Ecuador today, Indian lands can only be legally protected from invasion by colonists with the formation of *comunas indígenas* [native communes]. The formation of *comunas* is Indian-initiated but depends for administration on the Ministerio de Previsión Social; special laws pertain to the actions of Indians (and colonists) on the *comunas* (see Peñaherrera de Costales and Costales Samaniego 1962). The Instituto Ecuatoriano de Reforma Agraria y Colonización (IERAC), by contrast, is established not only to do away with latifundia holdings in the highlands, but also to encourage as rapid a penetration as possible of colonists into the Oriente, particularly in the zones where oil exploration is under way and where the pipeline and access roads are being built. Colonists are by definition *blanco* in the Oriente in contrast to all people classed as *Indio*.

All Oriente people classed as Indio *or* Indígena *fall into a national power domain which is essentially static. It must await Indian protest before it will even investigate infiltration and invasion of legitimate Indian land. All people classed as* colono (blanco) *in the Oriente fall under a domain of national expansion and dynamic bureaucratic manipulation aimed at opening new land claims for non-Indians.* More will be said about the domains in the ensuing section.

In terms of oil exploration, Indians are generally regarded as "hunters" of the interfluvial zones and so are hired primarily to set up camps, to stay in the forests, and to work only "on the line" for the oil companies. *Blancos*, by contrast, are seen as new potential agriculturists, are employed near camps and near towns, and are regarded as the proper spokesmen for all workers (including the Indians).

Quechua has long been the national trade and work language for communicating with all lowland Indians, while Spanish has been used primarily for the *blancos*. Today special bilingual line bosses (mostly recruited from the Summer Institute of Linguistics schoolteachers) are hired to deal with real and potential "Indian problems," while problems of labor organization, minimal wage, etc., are regarded nationally as a strictly *blanco–mestizo* concern.

EXPANDING INFRASTRUCTURE AND POLITICAL ECONOMY

An infrastructure is the network of transportation facilities enabling economic expansion, together with the administrative and educational apparatus, which establishes a bureaucratic information system facilitating the expansion based on transportation networks. Hegen (1966) provides a good base for the study of infrastructure expansion in the upper Amazon up to the mid-1960's. In his study Hegen makes a dramatic, if unrealistic, statement related to colonists (pioneers), which draws our attention to the nation as a whole:

Pioneering creates sociocultural demands and establishes a tax source which in turn will supply funds to satisfy these demands. It will stimulate the establishment and growth of trade, manufacturing and service industries, and the general exchange of goods, based upon a money economy. It will lead to regional specialization, fulfilling thereby the requirements of the demand-supply complex. Above all . . . pioneering will revolutionize the static social and political life of the people by integrating them into the responsible, decision-making processes of a modern democracy (1966:36).

Although apparently writing his conclusion prior to the events themselves and making enormously overgeneralized statements about a political economy which is now in the hands of foreign companies and a national military dictatorship, Hegen does direct attention to the expanding infrastructure itself and its importance in opening previous frontier zones to national bureaucratic controls. The official, national expanding infrastructure "follows" the *blanco* settlements, which mark the first results of the colonization programs. Pioneer settlements are not distributed willy-nilly around the jungle, nor are they necessarily first established in the best river-bank agricultural zones. They tend to cluster in areas where resources of value to international commerce exist, at a given time, as well as in the areas already targeted for national development. Not surprisingly, the two areas — those designated for development and those of special interest to foreign concerns for resource extraction — often coincide.

244 NORMAN E. WHITTEN, JR.

Regardless of the strategic importance of *colono* settlement to national planning, however, one inescapable need must be met — the colonists must find a stable food supply. And they are usually totally ignorant of tropical agriculture. Where Indian settlements exist, the *colono* food supply becomes the native *chacra*. To understand the informal aspect of an expanding infrastructure, we must put native peoples of the Oriente into the picture and carefully note the cycle whereby new lands are "opened" by *blanco* pioneers muscling into Indian *chacras*. By the time an official agent of a responsible bureaucracy arrives via plane or helicopter to an area to investigate alleged irregularities, the colonists are in control of major manioc plots, planted by Indians but claimed by colonists, and the stereotype of Indians as hunters is used to force the natives away from their own productive agricultural lands. This forces the Indians to open new territories to be later exploited in the same manner, unless effective counterstrategies are concurrently enacted. The Lowland Quechua seem remarkably effective in devising counterstrategies that are peace-producing and accommodating in terms of warding off destruction of their population.

Good land for growing crops within any given *runa* territory is limited, and the Jungle Quechua often opt to remain near enough to the national infrastructure tentacles to press early claims during times of invasion. This gives them more opportunity for social network maintenance within a known geographic zone than is characteristic of other Indian groups. The Lowland Quechua are particularly effective in losing one thing to gain something else vis-à-vis colonists and in maintaining strength vis-à-vis various quasi-sympathetic and relatively helpful brokerage agencies (Catholic and Protestant missions, military bases, powerful *hacendados*, land speculators, and even some Peace Corps volunteers). This allows them not only to survive in such a situation of replacive colonization, but actually to expand under such an impress. But the price of their expansion is often peonage, in one form or another, to one of the patronage "helpers."

If we were dealing with nineteenth-century and early twentieth-century exploitation of natural resources (as we are when dealing with the history of the Jungle Quechua), we might by now be able to construct an adequate model of Indian–*blanco* relationships. Steward (1948:507–512) did just this, though the many new data turned up will demand a reexamination of his model sequences. But the penetration in the last five years of foreign oil companies (Texaco-Gulf in the north, Anglo and Amoco in the central Oriente, together with subsidiary exploration companies and subcontracting companies), and their new technologies, make it clear that the frontier itself falls within an expanding technological sphere superior to, and guided by, agencies more powerful than Ecuador's political economy. *Blancos* and Quechua alike fall into power domains of national bureaucracies and, also, supranational domains reflecting new levels of politico-economic integration (Wolfe 1963). These latter domains are most productively considered as competitive to national interests.

Richard N. Adams (1970) presents us with an exhaustive and highly productive model and methodology for the study of dynamic structure of power in contemporary nations. He defines "power domain" as

... any arrangement of units wherein two or more units have unequal control over each other's environment. Wherever there is a distinctive difference in the relative power exercised by two units with respect to each other, there is a domain, and the two units pertain to different levels of articulation. Units in confrontation at one level will usually pertain to distinct domains. (Adams 1970:56).

Regarding the expanding infrastructure itself, a bit more needs to be said. The Puyo–Napo–Tena road has moved to Cotundo east of Tena, and the Papallacta–Baeza road (from the sierra toward the Oriente) opened in 1971. The Baeza–Cotundo section is under way. The oil pipeline constructed by Texaco-Gulf in late spring, 1972, runs from just south of Esmeraldas up the western cordillera and moves from just south of Quito to Papallacta and follows the Papallacta–Baeza road. It swings north from Baeza following the Quijos river and Coca river northeast to the Agua Rico river and then due east to Santa Cecilia and south to Coca. The Coca–Santa Cecilia section is completed with access road, and oil is now being pumped for foreign consumption. The construction of this roadway virtually obliterated the Cofán, Secoya, and Siona Indians in this area (see Robinson 1971).

REFUGE, STRATEGY, AND ETHNIC DISENFRANCHISEMENT

In the area around Puyo the infrastructure expansion is taking place in large part by foot and by plane. From a small airport at Shell Mera, which used to see a maximum of two flights a week, there were over 100 per day until around February 1973. Most of these fly cargo to the oil camps, but many flights fly colonists and food for colonists. Neither the Jívaro nor the Quechua of this zone intend to let *blancos* invade their territory or take over their land. But they are perfectly willing to exchange usufructory rights to land on a temporary basis for cash that will allow them to expand their own territories. Quechua and Jívaro, as well as *colonos*, want to be near the loci of national interaction — the airports, the proposed roadways, and the basic walking trails. Because the terrain along the Pastaza and Bobonaza is very rugged, it is not clear that there will be roadways in the foreseeable future, though many are on the planning boards. This means that the Indians have a temporary refuge area from Puyo due east, even though the Puyo area is itself the most developed in the current Oriente.

But this refuge area will not last for long. Recently an airport has been opened at Canelos, and Montalvo appears to be the central Oriente analog to Santa Cecilia in the north. The Canelos Quechua are increasingly hemmed in, and maximal clan segments and *purina* treks are cut in their fringe areas by *blanco* penetration settlements. Their rational, firm desire, to participate in the expanding Ecuadorian economy results in dynamic adaptive strategies which are contingent on national acceptance for success. Practically, I think, they must be "allowed" to continue their legal *comuna* formation, while at the same time fully participating in *colono* expansion.

This mixed strategy, which insists on both boundary establishment and land acquisition, also demands a duality of ethnicity — Indian and bicultural. The former stresses communal ownership of property and the latter individualism. Such a mixing of survival requirements and their strategic presentation to representatives of different national bureaucracies may seem paradoxical, but from the Quechua perspective it is the only way to avoid being further hemmed in and bounded by "protective" measures which establish rigid *comuna* boundaries. The national concept of *comuna Indígena* suggests a reservation complex governed from afar as a total institution. It is supposed to be locally maintained by internal primitive democracy through total agreement by all indigenous members, themselves ideally living in blissful, childlike, ignorance of their treacherous external social environment. Since, of course, no such group of Indians exists on or off any *comuna*, it is easy for developers and those seeking patronage roles to decide that the Indians are too disorganized to maintain "their" *comuna* structure and to use such a rationale to take an even heavier hand in rigidifying Indian territorial boundaries.[6]

The national concept might even now be transformed to reflect the Lowland Quechua notion of *comuna* as a corporate *holding company*. By this perspective the corporation allows for the carrying out of united extended clans' subsistence pursuits, while at the same time allowing people to variously employ their individually and familistically held land and social "stock" to give backbone to expansionist, colonizing functions of their own, eventually increasing the assets of the *comuna* holding corporation. I frankly doubt that Ecuadorian non-Indians will allow this

---

[6]   One floundering United States Peace Corps project recently gave "motivational training" to a valiant group of *comuneros* fighting for their very lives to hold their territorial boundaries against a massive onslaught of territory-hungry land-grabbers. At the same time, the Peace Corps saviors helped land-grabbers from the highlands to formalize their land claims on institutionalized Indian territory and even offered courses in new agricultural skills to the exploiters. The rationale behind the motivational training was that the Indians had not yet learned to live "communally" on their *comuna*!

to happen. They will probably continually seek to contain indigenous expansion. Indians themselves will probably continue to attempt to use the *comuna* corporation established through *blanco* containment strategies to break out, economically, politically, socially, and symbolically, unless all their energies are taken up in simply protecting their *comunas* from very real *blanco* invasion.

The well-known international process of Indian disenfranchisement and exploitation, as a complement to ethnic annihilation, rushes on in the Ecuadorian Oriente. The fixing of blame on the disenfranchished by the invocation of an "Indian problem" exacerbates Lowland Quechua territorial consolidation and leads to heightened ethnic awareness, to *blanco* discrimination against Indians, and to *blanco* patronage of those people who are socially and politically disenfranchised.

A pamphlet on Ecuadorian ethnocide (Robinson 1971) is receiving some justifiable attention in Latin America. The very real annihilation of surviving native groups in countries such as Ecuador cannot pass without such attention, concern, and hopefully remedial action. The focus here of my own preliminary report on Jungle Quechua ethnicity seeks to anticipate the complementary problem of total disenfranchisement and structural confinement of the survivors of national ethnocide.

POSTSCRIPT, AUGUST 1973

From the work over the past year, I see the following as unfolding. As the pressures from the militaristic Ecuadorian government, Gobierno Nacionalista Revolucionario del Ecuador, working with the ideology of a "political culture" (*cultura politica*), increase on the Canelos Quechua, these valiant people seek more and more ways to adapt their ways of life to new exigencies in their environment. At one level, they enter a domain of rapid change, but at another they intensify traditional beliefs and practices which give the only meaning possible in a biosphere experiencing chaotic stimuli. As national planners observe the rapid change they assume that the Canelos Quechua are plunging toward mestizo-ship in the political culture. But the Indians are increasingly expanding their self-identification system at one level, and becoming more and more "Indian-conscious" at another level.

It is apparent to any Ecuadorian or foreign planner, evaluator, or administrator that the Canelos Quechua have a dynamic set of "lifeways" which is puzzlingly nonnational. But because these people have fewer and fewer overt signs of stereotypic Indianness (they wear clothes, eschew face painting and feather wearing in the presence of mestizos, and speak a language which many Ecuadorians understand), differences are attributed not to cultural continuity but to disorganization resulting from rapid change. Our posit that people who survive, expand their population, and consolidate their social system in the face of chaos have a clear, nonanarchistic, social structure is generally dismissed, perhaps because it is too destructive of national and international ideology aimed at simplistic models of how the poor should behave.

I think the following two complementary positions regarding jungle peoples are the only allowable ones in Ecuador today: (1) we must mourn their passing, make great noises about ethnocide, condemning those who destroy indigenous peoples, and do much self-searching to see if, somehow, we are all guilty of the destruction of native life; and (2) we must respect the mestizo all the more, for he is the last living embodiment of nativeness; the native has become a national with civilized *blanco* values, and in the new *blanco–mestizo* "lifeway" lies both the future and the past of national consolidation.

Again, the complementarity of ethnocide mourning, plus heightened *blanco–mestizo*-ness, establishes a basis for considering the contemporary Jungle Quechua as a flagrant contradiction to national ideology. Perhaps this is why so much contempt is heaped upon these people, even by those nationals and nonnationals who cry loudly for Indian rights. I suspect that all over the world there is a complementarity in the expansion of ethnic culture and its denigration by those who seek to mourn the passing of other traditional cultures and to "help" the expanding ethnic cultures reach a new, "nondifferent," position within the nation. The problem with such help, given the rationale sketched above, is that it is probably a force equally as destructive as planned ethnocide, for it grows from the same source and serves the same national purpose.

REFERENCES

ADAMS, RICHARD N.
  1970   *Crucifixion by power: essays on Guatemalan national social structure, 1944–1966*. Austin: University of Texas Press.
BANTON, MICHAEL
  1967   *Race relations*. New York: Basic Books.
BROMLEY, RAYMOND J.
  1972   Agricultural colonization in the upper Amazon basin: the impact of oil discoveries. *Tijdschrift voor Economische en Sociale Geografie* 63(4):278–294.
BURBANO MARTÍNEZ, H., L. ANTONIO RIVADENEIRA, J. MONTALVO MONTENEGRO
  1964   "El problema de las poblaciones Indígenas selváticas del Ecuador." Paper presented at the Fifth Congreso Indigenista Interamericano, Quito, October.
BURGOS, HUGO
  1970   *Relaciones interétnicas en Ríobamba*. Instituto Indigenista Interamericano Ediciones Especiales 55. Mexico.

CARNEIRO, ROBERT L.
 1970 A theory of the origin of the state. *Science* 169(3947): 733–738.
CASAGRANDE, JOSEPH B., STEPHEN I, THOMPSON, PHILIP D. YOUNG
 1964 "Colonization as a research frontier: the Ecuadorian case," in *Process and pattern in culture: essays in honor of Julian Steward*, 281–325. Chicago: Aldine.
COLBY, BENJAMIN N., PIERRE L. VAN DEN BERGHE
 1969 *Ixil country: a plural society in highland Guatemala*. Berkeley: University of California Press.
EICHLER, ARTURO
 1970 *Snow peaks and jungle*. New York: Crowell. (Originally published 1955.)
ERASMUS, CHARLES J.
 1961 *Man takes control: cultural development and American aid*. Minneapolis: University of Minnesota Press.
FERDON, EDWIN, N., JR.
 1950 *Studies in Ecuadorian geography*. Monographs of the School of American Research 15. Los Angeles: University of Southern California.
FRIED, MORTON
 1967 *The evolution of political society: an essay in political anthropology*. New York: Random House.
GILLETTE, CYNTHIA
 1970 "Problems of colonization in the Ecuadorian Oriente." Unpublished master's thesis, Washington University, St. Louis.
HARNER, MICHAEL J.
 1972 *The Jívaro: people of the sacred waterfalls*. Garden City, New York: Doubleday.
HEGEN, EDMUND E.
 1966 *Highways into the upper Amazon basin: pioneer lands in southern Colombia, Ecuador, and northern Peru*. Center for Latin American Studies Monographs 2. Gainesville: University of Florida Press.
JARAMILLO ALVARADO, PIO
 1936 *Tierras del Oriente*. Quito: Imprenta Nacionales.
MITCHELL, J. CLYDE
 1966 "Theoretical orientations in African urban studies," in *The social anthropology of complex societies*. Edited by Michael Banton, 37–68. New York: Praeger.
OBEREM, UDO
 1971 *Los Quijos*. Memorias de Departamento de Antropología y Etnología de América. Madrid.
ORR, CAROLYN, BETSY WRISLEY
 1965 *Vocabulario Quichua del Oriente del Ecuador*. Mexico: Instituto Lingüístico de Verano.
PAREJA DIEZCANSECO, ALFREDÔ
 1970 "Introduction," in *Snow peaks and jungles*. By Arturo Eichler. New York: Crowell.
PEÑAHERRERA DE COSTALES, PIEDAD, ALFREDO COSTALES SAMANIEGO
 1961 Llacta runa. *Llacta* 12. Quito.
 1962 Comunas juridicamente organizadas. *Llacta* 15. Quito.
PEÑAHERRERA DE COSTALES, PIEDAD, ALFREDO COSTALES SAMANIEGO, *et al.*
 1969 *Los Quichuas del Coca y el Napo*. Escuela de Sociología de la Universidad Central, Serie de Documentos y Estudios Sociales 1. Quito.

250 NORMAN E. WHITTEN, JR.

PORRAS, G., P. PEDRO I.
1961 Contribución al estudio de la arqueología e historia de los valles Quijos y Misaguallí (Alto Napo) en la región oriental del Ecuador, S. A. Quito: Fenix.
ROBINSON, SCOTT S.
1971 El etnocidio Ecuatoriano. Mexico: Universidad Iberoamericana.
ROBINSON, SCOTT, S., MICHAEL SCOTT
1971 Sky Chief. Thirty-minute color documentary film.
SCHEFFLER, HAROLD W., FLOYD G. LOUNSBURY
1971 A study in structural semantics: the Siriono kinship system. Englewood Cliffs, New Jersey: Prentice-Hall.
SOUTHALL, AIDAN
1961 "Introductory summary," in Social change in modern Africa. Edited by Aidan Southall, 1–82. London: Oxford University Press.
STEWARD, JULIAN H.
1948 "Tribes of the montaña: an introduction," in Handbook of South American Indians, volume three: The tropical forest tribes. Edited by Julian H. Steward, 507–534. Bureau of American Ethnology Bulletin 143. Washington, D.C.: Smithsonian Institution.
STEWARD, JULIAN H., ALFRED MÉTRAUX
1948 "Tribes of the Peruvian and Ecuadorian montaña" (sections entitled "The Jívaro," "Záparoan Tribes," and "The Quijo"), in Handbook of South American Indians, volume three: The tropical forest tribes. Edited by Julian H. Steward, 617–656. Bureau of American Ethnology Bulletin 143. Washington, D.C.: Smithsonian Institution.
TESSMANN, GÜNTER
1930 Die Indianer Nordost-Perus: grundlegende Forschungen für eine systematische Kulturkunde. Hamburg: Friederichsen, de Gruyter.
WHITTEN, NORMAN E., JR.
1965 Class, kinship, and power in an Ecuadorian town: the Negroes of San Lorenzo. Stanford, California: Stanford University Press.
1968 Personal networks and musical contexts in the Pacific lowlands of Ecuador and Colombia. Man 3(1):50–63.
1969a Strategies of adaptive mobility in the Colombian-Ecuadorian littoral. American Anthropologist 71(2):228–242.
1969b The ecology of race relations in northwest Ecuador. Journal de la Société des Américanistes 54:223–235.
1974 Black frontiersmen: a South American case. Cambridge, Massachusetts: Schenkman.
WHITTEN, NORMAN E., JR., JOHN F. SZWED, editors
1970 Afro-American anthropology: contemporary perspectives. New York: Free Press.
WHITTEN, NORMAN E., JR., ALVIN W. WOLFE
1973 "Network analysis," in Handbook of social and cultural anthropology. Edited by John J. Honigmann, 717–746. Chicago: Rand McNally.
WOLFE, ALVIN W.
1963 The African mineral industry: evolution of a supranational level of integration. Social problems 11(2):153–163.

SECTION B:
THE ANDEAN HIGHLANDS

Introduction

The indigenous cultures of the lowland and montaña regions had, until this century, comparatively limited contact with Spanish colonial and national governments. In contrast, indigenous societies in the Andean highlands have a long history of struggle, incorporation, and domination within the institutional arrangements established after the conquest. The independence of the South American republics altered some aspects of social relationships between the ruling elite and the Indians but the patterning of culture and social structure reveal a high degree of continuity of Hispanic ideology and social hierarchy. The papers in this section deal partially with the historical struggles of the indigenous survivors of the conquest, but are primarily concerned with describing and analyzing the contemporary situation. A major theme throughout the papers is the way in which the different sociocultural groups strive to obtain selected benefits of their modernizing nations while simultaneously struggling to maintain their ethnic and social identity.

Van den Berghe outlines the major analytical distinctions between ethnicity and class in highland Peru, and stresses the need for empirical investigation in order to understand the objective and subjective aspects of relationships between class and ethnicity. He describes the boundaries of various ethnic groups in Peru and discusses the nature of social hierarchy in a variety of contexts. In addition, he documents the dynamics of social mobility within a stratified and culturally heterogeneous community, and shows how class status is, and is not, related to ethnicity.

Albó expands on some of the issues introduced by van den Berghe. He focuses on the role of Indian languages (Aymara and Quechua) as social classifiers and how languages function to maintain group boundaries. He discusses how the pattern of "double monolingualism" (e.g. groups speaking either an Indian language or Spanish) is related to a "dual society" and the oppression of the indigenous group by those who use only Spanish. In conclusion, Albó outlines the argument for the extinction of Indian languages and presents an alternative view in favor of their revitalization.

Schwarz analyzes the way in which an Indian group in the Colombian Andes has been able to maintain its ethnic identity after almost 450 years of continual contact and subordination to Hispanic and Colombian institutions. He shows the relationship of various strategies of opposition and accommodation to specific historical contexts and details the problems presently facing the Guambiano Indians.

Nash traces the struggles surrounding worker participation in the mining industry in Bolivia. She discusses the organizational problems related to worker participation in running the mines, and analyzes the failure of nationalization to bring about substantive changes in the workers' control over the products of their labor.

Ethnicity and Class in Highland Peru

PIERRE L. VAN DEN BERGHE

Throughout the world, the practical import of ethnicity is intimately linked with the unequal distribution of power and wealth. Put in different terms, the relationship between ethnicity and class constitutes the key to an understanding of ethnic conflicts. The rather embarrassing lack of success of social scientists in grappling with problems of ethnicity at the theoretical and, even less, at the practical level, may be explained in part by our intellectual heritage.

Until recently, anthropologists tended to study ethnic groups in isolation from each other, and hence to neglect the field of ethnic *relations*. In sociology, ethnic relations have long been studied, but the functionalist mainstream in the United States largely failed to put ethnic relations in their political and economic context, and thus failed to understand the nature of ethnic ethnicity, except as a policy problem.

Happily, in the last ten to fifteen years an increasing number of sociologists and anthropologists have studied group relations in the colonial or postcolonial societies of Africa, America, and Asia (Aguirre Beltrán 1957; Balandier 1955; Barth 1969; Benedict 1965; Colby and van den Berghe 1969; Despres 1967; Hoetink 1966; Kuper 1967; Kuper and Smith 1971; Mayer 1961; Smith 1965; van den Berghe 1967b, 1971). The comparative treatment of ethnicity has greatly increased in sophistication, as witnessed by a spate of recent textbooks on the subject (Banton 1967; Mason 1970; Schermerhorn 1970; Shibutani and Kwan 1965; van den Berghe 1967a). The emergence or resurgence of micro-nationalisms, especially in Europe and Africa, and the bitter conflicts to which they led have challenged social scientists to deal with what a number of us have called plural societies.

Before turning to the specific case of highland Peru, let me summarize what I consider to be fairly well-established parameters of ethnic relations:

1. Ethnicity and class are interrelated but *analytically distinct* phenomena.[1] The fact that different social classes most commonly show subcultural differences and, conversely, that ethnic groups living under a common government are more often than not ordered in a hierarchy of power, wealth, and status does not make class reducible to ethnicity, or ethnicity to class.

2. The specific relationship between class and ethnicity and the relative importance of each are empirical questions to be answered in every particular case. One must, therefore, be wary of any schemes which, from an *a priori* theoretical position, attribute a paramount role to either.

3. Ethnicity is both an objective and a subjective phenomenon, the interrelation between these two aspects being, once again, an empirical question. Any conception of ethnicity which reduces either the objective or the subjective side of it to an insignificant role distorts reality. (Currently, extreme subjectivist views of ethnicity have supplanted the older objectivist standpoint.) Ethnic groups are defined *both* by the objective cultural modalities of their behavior (including most importantly their linguistic behavior) and by their subjective views of themselves and each other.

4. Ethnic conflicts, like class conflicts, result from the unequal distribution of, and competition for, scarce resources. Class and ethnic conflicts are frequently found simultaneously in the same society, but the lines of ethnic and class cleavages are often not the same.

Turning now specifically to the Peruvian case,[2] several conclusions seem to be consensually accepted among Peruvians and foreign social scientists:

1. Peru is both class-stratified and ethnically diverse.

2. There are great regional and even local variations in patterns of ethnic relations.

3. Physical criteria of group membership, while not totally absent, are clearly secondary to sociocultural criteria.

4. Ethnic boundaries between *mestizos* and Indians are fluid, with considerable intergenerational movement into the *mestizo* group.

---

[1]   Here, so as not to burden the text with arguments already stated elsewhere, I am not considering the distinction between social race and ethnicity. While many authors have recently advocated lumping the two under the single label of ethnicity, and treating race as a special case of ethnicity, I have argued in favor of retaining the distinction, on both theoretical and empirical grounds. As phenotypic criteria of group membership are of such secondary significance in Andean Peru, there is no need to elaborate this point here.

[2]   I am doing so with considerable trepidation, as the present paper is being written during the initial stages of a period of fieldwork in the department of Cuzco. Fortunately, the extensive and excellent literature on Peruvian ethnic relations helped me fill the gaps in my knowledge. In addition to the works cited here, I am also indebted to a number of Peruvian colleagues with whom I discussed these problems orally, and among whom I should like to mention Jorge Capriata, Julio Cotler, Jorge Flores Ochoa, Fernando Fuenzalida, José Matos Mar, and Oscar Nuñez del Prado.

5. Objective indices of ethnic membership are extremely variable from region to region and from situation to situation and, even in combination, can lead only to loose probabilistic statements. Even language is weakly diacritic, due to the extensive degree of bilingualism in the highlands of both *mestizos* and Indians.

6. Ethnic boundaries to a considerable extent are defined subjectively, relatively, and situationally, rather than objectively and absolutely. Even at the local level, there is seldom consensual agreement as to who belongs to what ethnic group. The same terms can be used with a wide variety of meanings and of referents. There are, in most cases, no easily identifiable ethnic groups.

7. There is such a considerable degree of overlap between class and ethnic status that frequently it is difficult to disentangle the effect of each; but it is also clear that neither class nor ethnicity can be discounted, and that ethnic and class-based disabilities tend to be cumulative.

Perhaps the most sophisticated attempt to account for the complex interplay of class and ethnicity in Peru is found in the "sociology of dependence" approach to the problem, and more specifically in Fuenzalida's concept of *cadena arborescente*[3] (Bourricaud et al. 1971; Delgado 1971; Fuenzalida 1970; Fuenzalida et al. 1970; Matos Mar et al. 1969a, 1969b, 1971; Quijano 1971). The approach interprets Peruvian social structure in terms of multiple and interrelated chains of dependence between persons or groups of unequal power, wealth, and status. These chains of dependence converge at the apex into the national and, beyond it, the international ruling oligarchy, as the structure of control is extremely centralized. Peruvian social structure is conceived as a multitude of binary relations of dependence and domination based on half a dozen or so interrelated dimensions.

In geographic terms, the countryside is dominated by the town, the town by the regional metropolis, the regional metropolis by the capital city, and the capital city by the great centers of world trade, power, and culture. In class terms, the peasants are dominated by the small-town bureaucracy and petty mercantile class, the small-town bourgeoisie by the elite of the provincial capital, the provincial elite by the Limeño oligarchy, and the Limeño oligarchy by the world cosmopolitan elite. Ethnically, the *mestizos* dominate the *cholos* who in turn dominate the Indians. Linguistically, the Quechua or Aymara monolingual is in a position of inferiority vis-à-vis the Limeño cosmopolite who speaks Spanish, English, and French. Educationally, the illiterate, the primary-school graduate, the secondary-school graduate, and the university graduate form a hierarchy of prestige and power. Administratively, the district is subordinate to the province, the province to the department, the depart-

---

[3] "Branched-out chain" would probably be the most nearly adequate translation of this mixed metaphor.

ment to the central government in Lima, and ultimately, Peru to the world powers. Like the famous automobile race, "Caminos del Inca," everything of any consequence in Peru begins and ends in Lima.[4]

Besides centralization and inequality, these relations of dependence and domination are characterized by the fact that the closer one approaches the bottom of the pyramid, the more atomized and marginalized people are to national life, and, conversely, as one approaches the apex, the better interconnected and integrated the organs of domination.

Basically, the sociology of dependence framework constitutes the extension of a Marxian binary-conflict model of analysis to a variety of lines of cleavage, including the ethnic one. "Indianness" in Peru, according to this scheme, can be defined as the low end of a dependency chain on nearly all dimensions of unequal relations: the most Indian person is the illiterate, monolingual, rural peasant. This view of ethnicity comes close to reducing ethnicity to class, or at least to one special aspect of class. It conceptualizes ethnicity, not as a matter of a person being *either mestizo or* Indian, but as being *more* or *less* Indian or *mestizo*. The absence of clear-cut objective criteria which enable one to draw consensually agreed-upon ethnic lines leads Fuenzalida, for example, to reject for Peru the concept of plural society, which, to him, implies fairly well-drawn ethnic boundaries.

This sociology of dependence approach to ethnicity has at least four major strengths. First, it anchors the study of ethnicity squarely in the matrix of relations of power and relations of production, outside which ethnic relations can scarcely be understood. Second, it reacts healthily against the naive cultural determinist approach that the Indians are the heirs to the pre-Columbian civilizations, and the *mestizos* the carriers of Spanish culture. Even the most isolated Indian communities have undergone enough cultural change to make it misleading to consider them linear descendants of pre-Columbian cultures. Especially in the highlands where cultural syncretism is greatest, the two traditions have sufficiently blended to make any clear-cut objective differentiation of culture traits between Indians and *mestizos* an impossible task. It is sometimes even impossible to determine which is the "native" tongue of a bilingual person. Many highland people grow up with both Spanish and Quechua spoken at home from early infancy.

Third, the concept of dependence, by relating ethnicity to class, allows for a flexible description of a fluid and complex situation. It stresses the impossibility of dissociating ethnicity from class status and emphasizes

---

[4]   To mention a few trivial but illustrative examples from personal experience, I have had to send to Lima from Cuzco to obtain duplicate Volkswagen keys, to get a minor camera repair done, to develop films, and to find missing screws for a refrigerator door. In no other country in the world, including proverbially centralized France, have I felt so utterly dependent on the telephone and the local airline as lifelines to the capital city.

their relativity to the persons interacting and, indeed, to the specific situation at hand. Fourth, this approach to ethnicity avoids the trap of extreme subjectivism, which reduces ethnicity almost purely to the mutual perceptions and definitions of the situation by members of the groups present.[5] The dependence approach links ethnicity to objective relations of power and of production.

The one main shortcoming of the dependence approach, however, is that it tends to submerge ethnicity too much under class, and to understate the causal impact of culture, especially language, as factors *distinct from* class. To speak of Indians without reference to their position as oppressed peasants is obviously absurd. But to think that one can substitute *campesino* for *indígena* (as the present reformist government with its knack for euphemisms has made fashionable),[6] and thereby gain a satisfactory understanding of the structure of domination in Peru is also untenable.

Once military conquest establishes a situation of gross inequality amongst ethnic groups, cultural differences, and especially language, serve to perpetuate, accentuate, and reinforce the inequalities between victor and vanquished. The inequalities of class and ethnicity become *cumulative*, and the system of domination becomes doubly oppressive and exploitative. Access to government, to education, and to wealth is impeded by the double barrier of class and ethnicity. It is further incapacitating to be a peasant who cannot understand the language in which he is governed.

The impact of the so-called revolution which has taken place in Peru since the Velasco regime illustrates this point. To be sure, the various reforms introduced by the Revolutionary Government of the Armed Forces did substantially undermine the power of the oligarchy, and agrarian reform did appreciably alter patterns of land tenure. Thus the Velasco regime did, to a limited but not insignificant degree, affect *class* relations in Peru, but the impact of the change has been most significant at the top of the class order which, in the nature of the case, is non-Indian.

For the Mancha India (the heavily Indian southern departments) of Peru it may, I think, be said that the *reforma agraria* did not appreciably affect the position of dependence and exploitation of the Indians vis-à-vis *mestizos*. Apart from the relative slowness with which agrarian reform is being implemented and the overwhelming technical problems faced by any political revolution trying to improve living conditions with a system

---

[5] Barth's conception of ethnic boundaries, while usefully reacting against the naive ethnographic "objectivism" of defining ethnicity in terms of culture traits, goes too far, in my view, in the direction of subjective reductionism (Barth 1969). Ethnicity is always a blend of objective and subjective factors.
[6] Much as the government seems to delude itself that it solved the "Indian problem" by calling Indians "peasants," it eliminated the *barriadas* on paper by renaming these slums *pueblos jovenes*.

of production that is not only exploitative but *archaic*, land reform in the highlands can be said to have failed partly because of the ethnic barriers between the "revolution's" active agents and its supposed beneficiaries.

For ideological and practical reasons the government wants to transform the *haciendas* into cooperatives. Ideologically, cooperatives fit into the romanticized indigenist conception of Inca communalism and into the progressivist-technocratic mentality of the military rulers. Practically, cooperatives are an alternative to distribution of land into supposedly uneconomic *minifundias*. (In a real sense, the whole Andean agriculture and livestock breeding is archaic and low in productivity, whether run on a large or a small scale; and the case for economies of scale at the foot-plow level of technology has yet to be made.) The peasants, on the other hand, with a sound understanding of their class interests prefer, by and large, personal land ownership.

With typical bureaucratic arrogance and paternalism, the government through numerous reformist agencies (most notably SINAMOS) tells the people, and especially the Indians, what is good for them. The *salon* radicalism of the young university graduates hired by these agencies is compatible with a profound contempt for the peasants' alleged ignorance and backwardness. The peasants have exchanged their feudal *mestizo* overlords for a multitude of *mestizo* bureaucrats and technocrats. The cooperative *empleados*, as a junta of petty tyrants, have replaced the former grand tyranny of the *hacendado*. In the words of one peasant, "Before, we had one master; now we have ten." From the peasant's viewpoint the main difference between the *hacienda* and the cooperative is that, in the latter, there is more room for corruption and inefficiency and perhaps a little less for personal abuse of power. Exploitation and domination are more impersonal, collectivized, and bureaucratized.[7]

This kind of "democratic centralism" is, of course, extremely common in regimes with socialist or populist inclinations, but, where there is an ethnic as well as a class difference between exploiters and exploited, the system of domination is all the more difficult to shake. Language, illiteracy, culture, geography, and other factors insulate the Andean Indian from the outside world, and, in the last analysis, it is the outside world that

---

[7]   The best evidence for the failures of agrarian reform can be found in official speeches by government officials seeking to refute the attacks of the "enemies of the revolution" of "one extreme or the other." For example, the speech of the Minister of Agriculture reported in *El Comercio* of Lima on October 16, 1972, rejects charges of "presumed abuses in the application of the law on the part of responsible officials"; denies that there is any reason for "lack of confidence toward those who belong to the ruling bodies of the cooperatives"; denounces those who provoke "confrontations with the technicians whose contribution is indispensable for the success of the enterprises"; and denies "rumours to the effect that the government intends to nationalize rural enterprises and that the beneficiaries of the Agrarian Reform would thus be converted into mere wage earners." There could scarcely be a better summary of the main reasons for peasant discontent with agrarian reform and of the causes for the serious drop in agricultural production in the highlands.

counts. His options are either to leave his community, and in effect cease to be an Indian, or to stay and be dependent on *mestizo* or *cholo* intermediaries for his relations with the outside. Under a radical guise the university student politician, the government technocrats, and the Maoist schoolteachers are a new, emerging class of power brokers manipulating peasant masses to pursue their political and career ambitions. Radicalism is a technique of *arribismo* for the intellectual.[8] The fact that some of them are of Indian origin is of little consequence. In order to achieve power and wealth, they have to cease *being* Indians and peasants, but they must continue *dominating* the peasant masses in one form or another. Their former "Indianness" becomes a useful legitimation for their political ambition, and their knowledge of Quechua becomes an instrument of manipulation.

In an attempt to formalize the relationship between class and ethnicity, we may suggest three types of situations depending on two main factors. The first factor is the degree of inequality between ethnic groups. The second is the degree of resistance to "passing" from one ethnic group into another.

The first and rather uncommon situation type exists when the ethnic groups within a society are of relatively equal class status. Such a situation prevails where, as in Switzerland or in recent years in Belgium, the ethnic groups are nearly proportionately represented at all levels of the class hierarchy and in the major educational, business, state, and other institutions. Though conflict and competition between ethnic groups may be intense in such a situation, the ethnic composition of the population remains relatively stable, irrespective of whether there is resistance to "passing" from one group into the other. Some passing may occur through intermarriage or from other causes, but a major incentive for passing, namely improvement in one's social status, is lacking if the ethnic groups are of approximately equal status.

The two other situations of inequality between ethnic groups are far more common. The second type of society, characterized for example by South Africa, Rhodesia, and many former European colonial regimes in Africa, exists when the constituent ethnic groups are unequally represented at the various class levels, and where the dominant group erects caste or quasi-caste barriers to prevent access into it by members of subordinate groups. Such societies are frequently racist, as physical features are an easy criterion for excluding the "lower orders." Such societies obviously have a rigid social order, though considerable *cultural* assimilation may take place. Thus in both the first and the second type of society ethnic boundaries tend to be relatively stable, albeit for greatly different reasons. In the first type the incentives for change in ethnic

---

[8] *Arribismo* means literally the desire to be on top. It could be translated as "careerist ambition."

group membership are few; in the second type the incentives are great, but ethnic membership change is prevented by force.

The third type of situation is most commonly found in Spanish America, particularly Peru. The ethnic groups are clearly hierarchical, but the culturally dominant group is relatively open to members of other ethnic groups, who become culturally assimilated. Assimilation into the *mestizo* group may and often does take one or two generations, but, by and large throughout Spanish America, an Indian who learns to speak fluent Spanish and who acquires what is regarded as the local variant of *mestizo* or *criollo* culture ceases to be regarded as an Indian. The result is a relatively fluid ethnic situation in which the subordinate group steadily decreases in proportion.

Let us return to the Peruvian case and more specifically to the southern Andean region of Peru where the Indian population is still most heavily concentrated. To students of societies where ethnic boundaries are more sharply drawn, the fluidity and indeterminacy of the Peruvian situation is at first disconcerting. There is often little consensus, even at the local level, as to who is Indian and who is not. Physical appearance is of marginal significance. To be sure, a small percentage of foreigners and Peruvians of predominantly European descent are identified as *blancos* or *gringos*, but they barely account for one percent of the population in the highlands and perhaps three to five percent on the coast. Between the overwhelming majority of Indians and *mestizos*, physical appearance is not diacritic.

Language, which is in many parts of Spanish America, for example in Mexico or Guatemala, the best single indicator of ethnic status, is not a clear-cut criterion in highland Peru where Quechua-Spanish bilingualism is extremely widespread among *mestizos* and fairly widespread among Indians. Enough people are equally fluent in the two languages from infancy to make language an imperfect index of ethnicity. Other culture traits, such as dress, diet, the use of coca, and so on, are equally unreliable in the broad center of the ethnic spectrum. Perhaps one quarter of the population is consensually defined as Indian and a tenth as *mestizo*, but the majority in between will be variably classified, depending on a wide variety of factors.

More than any other word, the term *cholo* is symptomatic of this indeterminate state of affairs. That term has generated an abundant literature in Peruvian sociology and anthropology, and, broadly, social scientists have given the word *cholo* three kinds of usages. Some scholars have used the word to designate a group of people intermediate in status between Indians and *mestizos*. Some of those would concede that it would be difficult to define a *cholo group*, but think that they can objectively identify individuals as *cholos*. In a few ethnographies of local communities social scientists have even claimed to identify more than three ethnic groups, differentiating between *cholos* and *mozos* or between *mestizos* and *mistis*.

Other sociologists and anthropologists have preferred to use the term *cholo*, or rather *cholificacion*, to designate a process of movement from "Indianness" to "*mestizo*-ness"; or a process of syncretism between the two cultures (Bourricaud 1967). Finally, some social scientists have claimed, in my view quite rightly, that the term *cholo* does not correspond to any objective reality at all, but rather that it is used up and down the social scale as a term of derogation toward one's social inferiors. In other words, who is *cholo* is determined not by any objective characteristics a person may possess but by the social distance between the person so designated and the one who does the name-calling.

If relativity and subjectivity of definition characterize the use of the term *cholo*, do they not also apply to the terms Indian and *mestizo*? I would be inclined to say yes, but to a lesser degree. Philip Mason (1970) cites cases of town registries where ethnic classifications fluctuate widely according to the inclinations of successive town clerks, so there is obviously a considerable element of subjectivity in defining who is Indian or who is *mestizo*. However, it is clear that this element of subjectivity decreases steeply at both the upper and lower end of the status spectrum.

Let me illustrate the situation with the community of San Jerónimo, some ten kilometers away from Cuzco, which I have just begun studying. The term *cholo* is scarcely used locally, except in derogation, yet, to an outsider, it might seem most appropriate to designate the entire community as *cholo*. A periurban district of some 10,000 inhabitants, San Jerónimo is not "obviously" Indian as is, say, Pisac or Chinchero, nor is it big and cosmopolitan enough to be clearly urban and *mestizo*. From the perspective of the middle-class urbanite from Cuzco, at most 10 percent of the population of San Jerónimo could be unequivocally classified as *mestizos*. Yet, if by Indian one means a coca-chewing peasant, who is a native speaker of Quechua, who dresses in homespun clothes, and so on, an even smaller proportion of the population would fit the description.

What are the objective parameters of the local situation? Quechua is the dominant language of San Jerónimo in the sense that practically everybody (with the exception of the author and his family) speaks it fluently, and most people speak it at home in preference to Spanish. Yet, the use of Spanish is also widespread: perhaps one-fourth of the population speak it with facility (though not necessarily flawlessly); one-half speak sufficient Spanish for limited everyday discourse; and the remaining fourth, principally women, speak little or no Spanish. Anywhere between 70 and 80 percent of the population has achieved minimal literacy, and complete primary education is the rule for the younger generation. Secondary education is spreading fast, and quite a few San Jerónimo youths are students or graduates of the University of Cuzco.

Economically, the town is better off than most in the department of Cuzco. San Jerónimo is a reasonably prosperous market town, providing a wide range of goods and services to Cuzco. It is located on the main Cuzco–Puno road, boasts several bus lines, has a famous weekly meat market, and is the site of the University of Cuzco experimental farm. Though its cobblestoned streets are both rustic and odorous, the town has long had electricity and potable running water. Nearly all houses are built of adobe and tiles, but most have no toilet facilities, indoors or out. The town boasts a good municipal swimming pool, a stadium, one secondary school for boys and one for girls, a fairly modern town hall, a large church with richly decorated altars, a new police station, and a large departmental penitentiary under construction (by far the most modern and best-built edifice in San Jerónimo).

Though extremes in wealth are lacking, San Jerónimo is clearly stratified by class. Few people are destitute, but the great majority live quite modestly in small two- or three-room houses with little patios where they keep small livestock. A great many people own or cultivate small plots of land in or around town, and so combine part-time farming with petty trade or artisan occupations such as tailoring, stonemasonry, carpentry, shoemaking, and the like. The large *haciendas* are all in the process of being expropriated under the land-reform program, but a score or so of families are distinctly better off than the rest of the population. They live in larger, better-built houses, own more land, and are better educated; they frequently earn fixed salaries as teachers or employees, or run sizable businesses such as restaurants. A few people own television sets and older-model private automobiles. Usually referred to as *la crema*, this local elite is clearly *mestizo* (but fluent in Quechua). By Cuzco standards, they are middle class rather than upper class, and might be referred to as *cholos* by upper-class Cuzqueños.

Below that class level, however, ethnic boundaries are much more ill-defined, and consensus as to who is Indian or *mestizo* disappears. At one extreme is an informant, who, although himself highly educated and completely fluent in Spanish, is the son of illiterate, monolingual Quechua peasants from a remote district. He described all the people of San Jerónimo as *mestizos*, arguing that, because they live in a town, dress in store-bought clothes and have a life-style different from that of peasants, they could not be described as *indígenas*. At the other end of the definitional spectrum is a high-status municipal official who classified some 90 percent of the San Jerónimo population as Indian, basing his judgement on a combination of linguistic, economic, and dress-style criteria. Both Indians and *mestizos* who have the necessary economic means assume religious cargos, and do so for much the same mixture of religious and prestige reasons. There are three organized *comunidades campesinas* in town, but these communities are not Indian by any conventional definition. They are made up of small landowners, who, for the most part, live in town, but who own or cultivate plots located in an arbitrarily defined geographical sector of San Jerónimo District. Ethnicity is not a criterion of membership. There are no political authorities, such as *varayoq*, which could be defined as Indian. Educationally, some sons of Indian peasant families are university students, and, conversely, some poorer persons usually described as *mestizo* have only primary education and may be barely literate. Many well-to-do artisans and owners of stores or trucks may be native speakers of Quechua, though they would also be fluent in Spanish. The general consensus is that ethnicity is less important as a distinguishing characteristic than it once was, and that today *"el dinero es que manda."* The economic criterion of status, which is, of course, far from being the only important one, is perhaps the most visible. It finds its symbolic expression in the assumption of religious cargos: the four main *mayordomos* who sponsor *novenas* in honor of the patron saint incur expenses of $1,200 or more (in a country with a per capita income of some $360 a year). This lavish spending at *fiestas* takes the publicly visible and audible form of fireworks, music, food, and drink, and is highly competitive.

From the above account it would be easy to conclude that class is all-important and that ethnicity is not, or has ceased to be. Yet the fact remains that Quechua and Spanish as languages are in a clear hierarchy of prestige, power, and wealth, and thus that the degree of fluency in each determines to a considerable extent the status of its speakers. Even locally, where the average level of competence is higher in Quechua than in Spanish, it is a far greater disadvantage to be monolingual in Quechua than in Spanish. Anyone who matters socially, economically, or politically speaks fluent Spanish. Except for the parish priest and the anthropologist it is scarcely a handicap not to know Quechua, but for anyone who seeks class mobility through education, politics, or business, knowledge of Spanish is a prerequisite. There are many people who, though fluent in Quechua, are said to be ashamed to speak it and to prefer struggling through in their limited Spanish.

Of course, San Jerónimo is in no sense "typical" of Peru, or even of the sierra. Given the wide range of ethnic situations found in Peru, no town could ever be regarded as a microcosm of the country. Within the single department of Cuzco, a whole continuum can be found. At one extreme are solidly Indian areas like Ocongate, Ccatca, or Chinchero, where the bulk of the population is still monolingual Quechua, where the ethnic line between Indians and *mestizos* is sharply drawn, and where the socioeconomic structure corresponds rather closely to that ethnic cleavage. A small bilingual *mestizo* minority controls the political and economic resources as landowners, civil servants, policemen, shopkeepers, labor recruiters, or, more recently, as SINAMOS bureaucrats and technicians. The Indians form the bulk of the peasantry and of the agricultural wage earners. At the other end of the spectrum are urban or periurban areas like Cuzco or San Jerónimo, where ethnic lines are blurred and much more complexly interwoven with class, where consensus as to who is Indian or *mestizo* is almost entirely lacking.

The one extreme approaches the ideal type of the plural society, with sharply drawn lines of cultural cleavage that closely correspond to the politico-economic hierarchy. At the other end of the continuum, ethnic lines are so intertwined with class lines that the two phenomena tend to merge empirically into each other. In neither case, however, is ethnicity simply *reducible* to class. Though ethnicity and language correlate with and partly determine class position, class is also determined by a number of nonethnic factors. Conversely, there are many aspects of ethnicity that are independent of the relations of power and production which constitute the class order.

Analytically, then, it is equally as important to understand the specific relationship between class and ethnicity as it is to keep the two phenomena clearly distinct.

The complex dynamics of cultural and linguistic change can only be understood in relation to class and, particularly, to social mobility. Social mobility in Peru and indeed in much of Latin America is also ethnic passing. Paradoxical though the situation may seem, ethnicity accentuates stratification, but, at the same time, the very inequality of ethnic groups creates a dynamism of social and cultural change. Ignorance of Spanish shuts the Indian population off from participation in the "national" society much more completely than class barriers could. Even the unemployed *lumpenproletariat* of Lima is a more active participant in the mainstream of Peruvian life than the sierra peasant or shepherd. Yet, the obvious advantage of learning the dominant language and culture generates a continuing process of Hispanization (or, more precisely, in the sierra, a continuing extension of bilingualism). Clearly Hispanization is much more than a process of cultural change. It is intimately linked with a process of *social* and *geographical* mobility. The monolingual, illiterate sierra peasant becomes a bilingual, literate, urban proletarian. Through a multifaceted process of ethnic, class, and geographical mobility which typically takes a substantial part of an individual's lifetime, tens of thousands of Indians annually enter the *mestizo* class order.

Much controversy has surrounded the nature of the "open-class" system characteristic of industrial societies. By comparison, *class* differences in Peru and other Latin American countries are much larger and more clearly marked. On the other hand, Peru and other Spanish American countries lack the rigid ethnic (and racial) boundaries encountered in a number of highly industrialized countries. Peru might be said to have both a highly stratified class system with many remnants of a preindustrial, agrarian order and an "open-ethnicity" system allowing considerable mobility from the subordinate ethnic group to the lower-class echelons of the dominant ethnic group

REFERENCES

AGUIRRE BELTRÁN, GONZALO
 1957 *El proceso de aculturación.* México: Universidad Naciónal Autónoma de México.
 1967 *Regiones de refugio.* Mexico: Instituto Indígenista Interamericano.
BALANDIER, GEORGES
 1955 *Sociologie actuelle de l'Afrique noire.* Paris: Presses Universitaires de France.
BANTON, MICHAEL
 1967 *Race relations.* London: Tavistock.
BARTH, FREDRIK
 1969 *Ethnic groups and boundaries.* Boston: Little, Brown.
BENEDICT, BURTON
 1965 *Mauritius: problems of a plural society.* London: Pall Mall.
BOURRICAUD, FRANÇOIS
 1967 *Cambios en puno.* Mexico: Instituto Indígenista Interamericano.
BOURRICAUD, FRANÇOIS, *et al.*
 1971 *La oligarquia en el Peru.* Lima: Instituto de Estudios Peruanos.
CASTILLO ARDILES, HERNÁN
 1970 *Pisac.* Mexico: Instituto Indígenista Interamericano.
COLBY, BENJAMIN N., PIERRE L. VAN DEN BERGHE
 1969 *Ixil country; a plural society in highland Guatemala.* Berkeley: University of California Press.
DE LA FUENTE, JULIO
 1965 *Relaciones interétnicas.* Mexico: Instituto Naciónal Indígenista.
DELGADO, CARLOS
 1971 *Problemas sociales en El Peru contemporaneo.* Lima: Instituto de Estudios Peruanos.
DESPRES, LEO
 1967 *Cultural pluralism and nationalist politics in British Guiana.* Chicago: Rand McNally.
DOBYNS, HENRY F.
 1964 *The social matrix of Peruvian indigenous communities.* Cornell Peru Project Monographs. Ithaca, New York: Cornell University.
FUENZALIDA, FERNANDO
 1970 *La matriz colonial de la communidad de indígenas Peruana.* Lima.
FUENZALIDA, FERNANDO, *et al.*
 1970 *El Indo y el poder.* Lima: Instituto de Estudios Peruanos.
HOETINK, H.
 1966 *The two variants in Caribbean race relations.* New York: Oxford University Press.
KEITH, ROBERT G., *et al.*
 1970 *La hacienda, la comunidad, y el campesino en El Peru.* Lima: Instituto de Estudios Peruanos.

KUPER, LEO
1967   *An African bourgeoisie.* New Haven, Connecticut: Yale University Press.
KUPER, LEO, M. G. SMITH, *editors*
1971   *Pluralism in Africa.* Berkeley: University of California Press.
MASON, PHILIP
1970   *Patterns of dominance.* London: Oxford University Press.
MATOS MAR, JOSÉ, *et al.*
1969a   *Peru problema.* Lima: Instituto de Estudios Peruanos.
1969b   *Dominación y cambios en el Perú rural.* Lima: Instituto de Estudios Peruanos.
1971   *Peru hoy.* Mexico: Siglo XXI.
MAYER, PHILIP
1961   *Townsmen or tribesmen.* Cape Town: Oxford University Press.
QUIJANO, ANIBAL
1971   Nationalism and capitalism in Peru. *Monthly Review* 23(3):1–122.
SARFATTI LARSON, MAGALI, ARLENE EISEN BERGMAN
1969   *Social stratification in Peru.* Berkeley: University of California, Institute of International Studies.
SCHERMERHORN, RICHARD A.
1970   *Comparative ethnic relations.* New York: Random House.
SHIBUTANI, TAMOTSU, KIAN M. KWAN
1965   *Ethnic stratification.* New York: Macmillan.
SMITH, M. G.
1965   *The plural society in the British West Indies.* Berkeley: University of California Press.
VAN DEN BERGHE, PIERRE L.
1967a   *Race and racism.* New York: John Wiley and Sons.
1967b   *South Africa, a study in conflict.* Berkeley: University of California Press.
1971   *Race and ethnicity.* New York: Basic Books.

The Future of Oppressed Languages in the Andes

XAVIER ALBÓ

This work refers directly to the problem of Quechua and Aymara, independent languages in Peru and Bolivia, both major languages, but of little official importance.[1] Only those zones in which the independent and official languages coexist are considered directly. These areas include the greater part of the central and southern range of Peru, and the entire altiplano and almost all the valleys of Bolivia. Primarily Spanish zones, such as the tropics and the coast, are only indirectly concerned, as in many of their centers the national official language is used, but they are considered as recipients of Quechua and Aymara migrations. The situation has its parallel in various provinces of Ecuador, especially

The present work has benefited much from the collaboration of Gamaniel Arroyo of the Peruvian Ministry of Education and of Doctors Cerron and Parker of the Plan for Linguistic Support of the University of San Marcos in Lima and of the discussions held in Bolivia with the personnel of the National Department of Adult Education of the Ministry of Education, of the National Institute of Cultural Investigation for Popular Education (INDICEP), Oruro, the Centre of Investigation and Promotion of Rural Affairs (CIPCA), and with the historiographer Dr. Barnadas.

[1] According to the latest available census the population of Bolivia was distributed in 1950 (Dirección General de Estadística 1955), according to mother tongue, into Spaniards (34 percent), Quechuas (35 percent), and Aymaras, totalling three million (in 1972 the estimate of the total is close to five million). In Peru the census of 1961 (Dirección Nacional de Estadística y Census 1966) distributes its ten million (estimated fifteen in 1972) inhabitants into monolingual Spaniards (60 percent); Quechuas (35 percent), of which two thirds speak the Ayacuchano and Cuzqueno dialects, and the other third central dialects unintelligible to the former; and Aymara (4 percent). In Bolivia the problem is more extensive but also simpler. In the south of Peru the problem presents the same characteristics. In 1958 Schaedel estimated that in the eight provinces of the south of Peru, with a total population of 2.8 million, there were 12 percent monolingual Spaniards and 54 percent monolingual Quechua or Aymaras, the rest being bilingual, generally of native origin (Schaedel 1967). On the national level the problem is less extensive and more complex, as the fragmentation of the Quechua dialects is great up to the point of obstructing mutual intelligibility. This aspect has been treated by Torero (1964, 1970, 1972); Parker (1963, 1972a); and Escobar (1972b).

from Imbabura to Chimborazo, with the difference that there Quechua has an even lower prestige than in Peru or Bolivia. But, because of the lack of sufficient data, I will here have to omit Ecuador. Although the empirical illustrations come only from the Andes region, the problem is up to a certain point parallel with that of other places in which similar dual structures exist, with dominating minority groups and other dominated majorities of different cultures.[2]

The situation of other ethnic groups, of the jungle and in a few enclaves of the high plateau, such as the Uru of Bolivia and the Jaqaru of Peru, is not considered in this work as they have very different problems. The greater part of these miniscule groups are rapidly becoming extinct, and it is very clear that, due to the great inequality of forces, they are condemned to assimilate themselves to other majorities, however much perhaps there be efforts in favor of their survival made by missionaries, academic groups, and others.

THE CONCEPT OF OPPRESSED LANGUAGES

The languages to which we are referring are usually termed native, autochthonous, vernacular, indigenous, and so on. But these adjectives do not sufficiently express the social dimensions which mold their peculiarities.[3] Besides, Greek is the "indigenous" language of Greece. Moreover, in traditionally Spanish zones of the Andes Spanish is the "native" tongue, while Quechua is the foreign tongue of the immigrant groups. Or, if we do not accept this criterion, we should also not accept that Quechua be called native in so many regions of Argentina, Bolivia, Ecuador, and also Peru where it was introduced either by the Incas only a few years before the colonization or perhaps even by the missionaries when the area was already in full domination by Spain.

Another group of concepts elaborated by sociolinguistics, such as that of languages of "little prestige," "unofficial," "substandard," "with a low functional specialization," and so on, brings us closer to the problem of languages such as Quechua and Aymara. But these concepts are still limited to the phenomenological sphere. They simply describe some social qualities of those languages, as opposed to those of others ("of

---

[2]   But only up to a certain point. For example, within the continent, Paraguay offers quite a few similarities but the Guarani are less oppressed (Rubin 1968), thanks especially to the fact that during colonization, besides the situations such as we describe in this work, there was an unusual case of the Jesuit reductions where the Guarani did not undergo the same social oppression (Meliá 1969, 1971). In Guatemala and in several Mexican states the situation is more complicated than in the Andes because of the great number of native languages.

[3]   In spite of the fact that UNESCO (1953) defines the vernacular tongue in terms of social and political domination.

greater prestige," and so on) which coexist within the same social structure. But they do not establish a causal explanation which claims to get to the root of these peculiarities. For this reason I suggest here that they be characterized as oppressed languages.

In sociology, especially in the Third World where social contradictions are more violent, it is common to organize the analysis of society on the basis of a division between a dominating class or group and the dominated, and also between an oppressor group and an oppressed group, concepts inspired more or less remotely by Marxism. From this have also arisen concepts derived from other disciplines, such as the "pedagogy of the oppressed" (Freire 1970). By analogy, and in line with that which has already been suggested by Meliá (1971) for the Guarani, the use of the term "oppressed language" may help us to understand better the peculiarities of many languages which are ordinarily characterized by such purely historical concepts as "indigenous," or more superficially as "of low prestige."

Thanks to particular historical circumstances, human groups of certain languages and cultures have been dominated by groups of various other languages and cultures. These historical circumstances may be brought about by migrations, as has happened with so many ethnic groups in the United States, or by the arbitrary way in which state boundaries are drawn, as has been seen in many new African states, but the clearest cases are those of conquests, wherein the paradox arises that the oppressed groups are at the same time the more established in the country, whereby they become major sectors of it. This is the case of the populations of the Andes.

Subsequent to a conquest, the gradual result is that the culture of the conquered groups, while conserving its independence in many respects, loses its fundamental autonomy, especially on the political level, and little by little loses many other elements. Its economic, social, religious, expressive, and axiological structures, in spite of their manifest peculiarities, become reinterpreted in the new situation of domination in which they find themselves. For example, the symbolism of programmed festivities may reinforce the system of oppression, marking within a festive atmosphere the reaffirmation of authority in a village of mestizos. A dual asymmetrical structure arises, characterized not only by the cultural dichotomy between the dominating minority and the dominated majority, but also and primarily by the mutual and unequal interdependence between the two groups. The culture of the dominated group becomes attenuated and in reality is reduced to a subculture. However it continues to have many autonomizing compensations, which, echoing Lewis (1959, 1966), allow us to speak legitimately of a "native subculture of poverty" and which give it a certain continuity which is often indirectly fostered at the same time by the dominating group. But the inequality of power which characterizes this situation impoverishes the subculture more and more and slowly paralyzes its creative dynamism. This is what Ribeiro (1970) calls "deculturalization." In most cases the subculture develops its reactive and conservative mechanisms of defense; and at certain times native revitalizing movements would arise with the more expressive elements recovering their effectiveness. But on the whole, particularly with the coming of industrialization in the dominating sector, and unless the composition of forces in the basic dual structure changes, the destiny of the impoverished native subculture is to become increasingly atrophied, is to continue impoverishing itself or functioning in relation to the dominating structure, and finally to be reduced to a simple characterization of the lowest social class within a "more modern" national society. Because of this process Greaves (1972; cf. Stavenhagen 1965) has cast doubt on the validity of the model of dual culture as it is applied in the Andes region, suggesting as an alternative the utilization of a model of classes. It is debatable whether we have already arrived at this point of the process, particularly in the areas under consideration, but without doubt this is the outcome which will result from this process. It seems adequate for the moment to speak of an oppressed subculture and of a pressure which, throughout the ages, not only establishes, but preserves, such that the composition of the forces in the matrix structure does not change. Obviously there are limits to this process in the so-called "refuge zones" (Aguirre Beltrán 1967) where sociocultural independence is better maintained and the dominating minority group is less culturally remote from the dominated majority class. But these counter examples are not comparable in frequency, nor do they exhibit such processes as are indicated here. Cases such as that of the Greeks' cultural integration with the Roman dominators are not encountered in these latitudes.

Within this wider context, the cultural element of language undergoes a similar process, but with peculiarities worthy of note. Thanks to its high level of internal structure, the language maintains its independence at a level higher than that of other cultural elements. There is no room here to speak of its reduction to a "sublanguage" or "dialect" of the dominant language. Quechua and Aymara continue to be languages in the full sense of the word, but the impoverishment and internal degeneration process also has its place here. The dynamics of the linguistic changes, occurring within the context of an oppressing dependence, acquire a clear directional extralinguistic aspect: linguistic change is no longer ruled so much by internal linguistic laws (although this element is still present), but more by the necessity of yielding more and more to the language of the dominating group and gradually acquiring new elements of its structures, first on the level of vocabulary, and later also on that of phonology and grammar. This situation may be prolonged for centuries, thus the languages may remain living in large sectors of the population, but with a diminished vitality. They are oppressed languages. In some cases, after a phase of bilingualism, in which the dominated group acquires as a second language that of the dominating group, the oppressed native language may be completely lost, leaving its mark only in dialectical variants of Spanish reflecting the native substratum. Here again one can encounter some pockets of greater resistance: in refuge zones, and in the more dense nuclei — centers of cultural tradition such as Cuzco; one may also speak of rapprochements between the dominating language and the dominated in some instances. But again, these cases are infrequent, and their consequences are somewhat different.

We have intimated that in an indirect manner the dominating social group can foster the partial independence and subsequent continuity of the impoverished native subculture. This may occur because of the dominant culture's interest in maintaining the status quo and the privileges guaranteed it by the existent dual structure. At this level again the peculiarities of language as a cultural factor play an important role, thanks to their greater independence. In an extreme situation of rigid dualism the bilingual society would consist in reality of a double monolingualism: on the one hand, the dominating minority speaking only Spanish, and on the other, the dominated majority which speaking only its native language (various ones the length of the Andes), with intermediaries proficient in both languages being relatively scarce. In this ideal model the double monolingualism accomplishes the optimum function of social distinguisher and maintainer of the system. The language becomes an identifier, and, in certain cases, a very effective social discriminator, which, like a calling card, ensures the communication of an individual's social classification whatever the circumstances: language cannot be changed so easily as dress, and "accent" even less so. Furthermore language acts not only as a social identifier, but also as a block to eliminate the possibility of social transition, cutting communication between those of different language groups and obliging those of the same sociocultural (language) category to communicate only verbally among themselves. This reduces intergroup contact to a few stereotyped situations, thereby assuring the rigidity and permanence of the system. Social oppression in the dual society produces double monolingualism and this in turn guarantees the persistence of the dual society. The oppressed language becomes in turn oppressive.

DIMENSIONS OF LANGUAGE OPPRESSION IN THE ANDES

The area under consideration exhibits, in some regions more than in others, a double monolingualism even more pronounced than that characterized — a result of the dual asymmetrical oppressing structure.

At the same time the increase in the numbers of bilingual speakers, particularly those of Quechua and Aymara origin who learn Spanish, on the one hand, shows a greater flexibility in what previously was rigid dualism, but on the other hand, may foreshadow the step toward the "modern society" of classes in which, as the end result of the process, the oppressed cultures and languages would have to yield to the developing impetus of the dominating culture.

Let us begin with the historical dimension, which here we can only sketch. Examining the official language policies of Spain during colonial times, there appears at first sight to be a surprising contradiction, but which ultimately confirms the outline presented in the previous paragraphs. As Ricard (1961) has effectively documented, the policy of Spain in America was always one of reserving public life for the Spanish class and Spain decreed repeatedly that the Indians must be Hispanicized once and for all. Nevertheless, in general, this policy always proved ineffective and the Indians continued being monolingual in their own languages. I would add that the policy necessarily had to prove ineffective, because the inherent dualism of the asymmetrical structure which the Spanish-Creole elite basically never wanted to touch demanded it. Thus a systematic divorce between word and reality was produced — an inconsistency analogous to the one which always existed between the laws and the practice regarding the Indians. Independence did not change things; rather it worsened the contradictions, particularly in the past century during which the latifundia system has dominated. Enthusiasm for "modernizing" (Hispanicizing) the Indian in the press or in parliament redoubled, while at the same time neolatifundismo robbery transformed aboriginal communities into estates, reinforcing the dual structure, and thereby making it impossible for these enthusiasms to be effective. Only in the last decades have changes in the social structure been observed, changes which carry with them an increase in bilingualism, of the Hispanicizing process, and at the same time, a limited uplift in the prestige of Quechua and Aymara. These changes are primarily the result of the presence of new factors such as agrarian reform and, on the coast, the industrializing process. These factors will be discussed later.

At the present, the oppressive situation and the processes of change evidence themselves in the unequal distribution of functions for each language in the various spheres of activity.[4] These unequal distributions are represented diagrammatically in Figure 1, which refers only to the regions in which there is a Quechua or Aymara majority. But even here there is clear functional discrimination: if there were no language oppres-

---

[4]   For a broader discussion of this point is Cochabamba see Albó (1969, 1970). Here I limit myself to preserving a synthetic, macrosocial vision based especially on Bolivia. What I here call spheres of activity are similar, without being identical, to what Fishman (1968) calls *domains*.

Spheres of activity

Technico-professional world

Official world

Institutions of mutual relations:

Socialization in schools

Written means of communication

Oral means of communication

Politics

Commercial networks

Expressive world (religious, artistic, folklore)

Traditional rural world

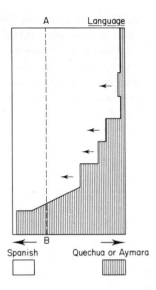

Figure 1.   Functional distribution of languages in the bilingual zones of the Andes (estimate)

sion in these areas the usage line would coincide in any sphere of activity with the line AB, because in such regions approximately seventy percent of the population is Quechua or Aymara. But it is not so, for among monolingual and bilingual speakers it is understood that, outside the sphere of rural tradition, Spanish is prevalent. And in the case of the technico-professional world and of the official world it is assumed that Quechua and Aymara should be almost completely excluded.

The apparent exception, or rather ambiguity, in that which I have called the expressive world, in reality confirms what has already been said. Turner (1969) has already pointed out that, if we want to emphasize the emotive communitarian (gemeinschaft) pole, as opposed to the structural (gesellschaft) pole, it is easier to choose symbols derived from the more oppressed or marginal sector of society, a fact which I can confirm from the study of sociolinguistics in the valleys of Cochabamba (Albó 1970).

Within this keynote, the recent advances of the oppressed languages in the sphere of institutions for mutual relations are significant. A few years ago the use of Spanish in radio or in the political world was as imperative as it still is today in the technico-professional world. Only in scholastic institutions, and correlatively in the world of the press, are the oppressed languages still almost completely absent, although the new plan of bilingual education in Peru and several timid attempts at Quechua and

Aymara by the press in Bolivia[5] promise some change in the near future. Until now, however, these recent developments have only smoothed over the situation without changing it.

In the light of this near absence of Quechua and Aymara in certain functional sectors we can better understand the concrete form in which these languages have become atrophied. In the first place their very idiomatic internal structures have become degenerated, the main symptom being the growing impoverishment of vocabulary,[6] particulary in semantic areas related to the spheres in which Quechua and Aymara are excluded. The impoverishment may be followed by the disappearance of ancient vocals (e.g. the terminology of relationship), or by the absence of neologisms in the face of new technical advances (e.g. *radio*), or often by the formation of roots in which one term is of native origin and connotes the traditional semantic area and the other term is a borrowing from Spanish which means the modern semantic area, which is generally more socially prestigious. For example, in Quechua, a traditional kitchen would be *q'uncha*, but a modern one would be *cocina*; and in Aymara the paternal father-in-law would be *awkchi*, while a maternal one would be *suegro*. Independent numerals are maintained to count the flock, but Spanish borrowings may be used for the time or for dates. To quantify this lexical impoverishment one need only examine the Chuquisaca work of Stark (1972), wherein a third of the vocabulary are Spanish borrowings, and Lastra's work (1968) in Cochabamba, where more than half are borrowings. If, instead of using vocabulary lists, we base our studies on the frequency with which the borrowings are repeated in the text, we have figures collected in a sample of twenty Quechua-speakers of a graduated social scale in rural Cochabamba (Albó 1970:359). The frequency of Spanish borrowings grows according to the topic: fear of spirits (11 percent), production of chicha (12 percent), agriculture (24 percent), other rural experiences (33 percent), politics (41 percent), modern medicine (48 percent). This impoverishment may reach a point in which

---

[5] There is presently a monthly Quechua-Spanish periodical in Cochabamba and an Aymara-Spanish one in La Paz, both oriented toward the education of the peasant. The latter has an edition of 5,000 copies. In a daily Cochabamba newspaper I have also seen some advertisements in Quechua.

[6] There is also a certain amount of atrophy in the phonological and grammatical spheres. For example, in the Quechua of Cochabamba the phonological series of the glottal and aspirate occlusive, typical of Bolivian Quechua but absent in Spanish, occupies the lowest place in Lastra's list of frequency of phonemes (1965), and there is evidence that traits such as these, and other grammatical points such as the object-verb order or the density of modal verb suffixes, lessen in frequency of use as the social level of the speaker rises (Albó 1970:228–253, 309–376). But in general in these spheres it is not so much a question of impoverishment. The native structures of phonological and grammatical order are not so easily lost, but rather they alternate with those acquired from the dominating Spanish language. Likewise, for new speakers of Spanish what are most characteristic of their substandard Spanish dialects are the phonology and grammatical constructions inherited from the mother or substratum tongue.

the use of the independent language becomes almost impossible for certain topics, such as the explanation of the functioning of a tractor, or for the typical abstract conceptualizations of the academic world. Because of this we tend to treat primitive languages as being only of use for dealing with the very concrete. It is evidently not true that such languages lack the mechanisms to form abstract terms or neologisms adapted to new technological advances: they could form them as did the Germans in the time of Luther or as Indonesian is doing at present. It is simply that the present configuration of the social structure does not give them a chance to develop these internal potentials.

One related aspect of the atrophy of the oppressed languages is the neglect or abandonment of attempts at rendering them to a uniform writing. In the popular conception there are many who think that it is a question of "dialects" so primitive that they are not even suitable to be written. In general, chaos reigns. Parker (1972b) has even said that there are perhaps more alphabets than authors, since several use various ones. The invading oppression of Spanish has required of the more accepted alphabets, up to now, and almost irrevocably, that they minimize the very contrastive systems of Quechua and Aymara phonology in order to adapt them, incongruously, to the contrasts and inconsistencies of the dominant Spanish alphabet. Several linguists who write not for their colleagues but for the public have had to yield to the force of the extralinguistic factors, leaving the most logical in order to come close to the Spanish.[7] If these languages were not excluded in the schools, and thus from the written and academic world, it would be easier to suggest that it is necessary, little by little, to create a uniform written form. Whether it succeeded or not would become relatively secondary under the linguistically distorting but socially integrating tutelage of the Spanish system.

Already, on an extralinguistic level, the atrophy brings about apprehension in the Quechua or Aymara speaker in the use of his own language — one of the clearer windows of the personality — thanks to its symbolic power which identifies it with less prestigious members of society. The school is one of the principal instruments for fostering this atrophy. On the one hand, with its constant discouragement of the vernacular in the class or in public acts before the community, it is instrumental in creating the feeling of shame and public loss of prestige in using a native tongue. And on the other hand it is inaffective in forming a coordinated bilingualism which might succeed in helping people use with equal skill the mother tongue and the official Spanish language. In the

---

[7]   Such is the case of the biblical societies which have left us a phonemic alphabet suggested by Pike as a similarity to the Spanish alphabet, especially in the publications of the Center of Alphabetization and Aymara Literature (CALA) in La Paz. The sociolinguistic complexity of the problem of the alphabet and its relations with Spanish has been treated by Albó (1970:150–159).

majority of cases the school system only creates subordinate bilingualism which hastily defends itself in a substandard Spanish dialect of as low a prestige as the native tongue. In this way the oppressed continue to need their mother tongue as an expressive medium of their personality, while in the eyes of the public world they are diminished if not totally disregarded. Those who place themselves in the perspective of the established order would say that the reason for this frustration is "because they do not know Spanish well." Those who place themselves in the subversive platform would say that the cause is "because the established order does now want to accept our language."

COUNTERCURRENTS AND RECENT STRUCTURAL CHANGES

As a counterpoint to all that has been said up to now we should point out the groups which have attempted to assert a place for Quechua and Aymara and the factors which have reduced or altered the rigidity of the traditional structure. For the first we will be guided by the documented bibliography of Rivet and Crequi-Montfort (1951–1956).

The pioneers are the missionaries: in the first decades of colonization many missionaries in Peru proclaimed the evangelization of the Indian in Spanish and also in Latin, either through indolence or to avoid heretical formulations of the holy doctrine. But at the end of the sixteenth and at the beginning of the seventeenth centuries a noticeable flowering of religious and linguistic works in Quechua and Aymara occurred (Albó 1966:402–404). But we must turn to the nineteenth century to find followers to this precursor. There is a pause of almost two centuries with only sporadic works, many of them new editions, appearing in Quechua or Aymara. These were dedicated almost exclusively to the religious topic and to two subsidiary fields: practical linguistics, to train new missionaries, and, on a much smaller scale, drama, also with evangelizing ends.[8] The pragmatic character of this movement is marked by the topics treated, and also by the growing concentration on the "general," or common,

---

[8]   It becomes difficult to reduce the facts in Rivet and Crequi-Montfort's bibliography (1951–1956) to statistics because of its lack of dates and of the great amount of material, including many works with only linguistic allusions. Limiting ourselves to the religious and linguistic material with many fragments in Quechua or Aymara, we have the following approximate figures for groups of years: 1532–1580 — 2 religious (1 Quechua, 1 Aymara) and 2 linguistic (both Quechua); 1581–1650 — 38 religious (24 Quechua, 14 Aymara) and 23 linguistic (17 Quechua, 6 Aymara); 1651–1800 — 32 religious (24 Quechua, 8 Aymara) and 23 linguistic (17 Quechua, 6 Aymara). The last period, in spite of being more than twice as long, has less production than the second. In concrete terms, there are only six works which can be attributed with certainty to the period 1651–1750. In Ecuador the entire process is dephased, the first productions coming in the second half of the eighteenth century.

languages, particularly Quechua and to a lesser extent Aymara.[9] Little by little, partly because of a certain missionary policy, the innumerable local languages which teemed at the beginning of colonization were yielding before the Quechua, which even extended to new regions beyond the old frontiers. With this subunifying process through the diffusion of a common language of low prestige, the double monolingualism of the dual structure became more evident.

The second recovering surge comes in the nineteenth century, above all in relation to romanticism. The bulk of production continued to be of a religious character, with contributions from the biblical societies augmenting the output, or of a linguistic character, already secularized. But the novelty is that in this century poetry, songs, and tales began to be published in Quechua and Aymara. Also at the beginning of the same century arose the extensive propositions and counterpropositions of the literati, and, on a commercial level, innumerable trilingual pamphlets with the "most usual tongues." Within the romantic impact should be placed the first educational and political writings in the native language. It is notable that, in spite of its asserting an independent tone, the pan-Andean rebellion of Tupac Amaru has not left any mark on the Rivet and Crequi-Montfort bibliography (1951–1956), except that we know of a link between this leader and the curate Valdés, gathered for the famous Quechua tragedy, *Ollantay*, presented before Tupac Amaru in his general quarters (Lewin 1967:238, 513–514). In contrast, and in spite of the Hispanicizing impetus of the independence, some of the independence proclamations were the first political documents translated into Quechua. Nevertheless, in these and later translations of political documents into Quechua or Aymara, it is rather a question of dealing with individuals who want their wit to shine without claiming seriously the politicization of the Indians. More realistic·were the efforts of such educators as the curate Beltrán in Oruro, or Dr. Juliaca Nuñez Butrón, editor of the periodical *Runa Soncco*, but such cases were rare.

A third surge, coming after the publication of the Rivet and Crequi-Montfort bibliography (1951–1956), can be attributed directly to the international linguistic community, and more indirectly, to the increase in the numbers of programs of national or international aid to the field, together with the socioeconomic rise of the peasant. From all this, in the last few years the quantity of studies in these languages has sharply increased and their quality has improved; techniques of teaching them, in specialized institutions of good quality, have advanced,[10] and new pro-

[9]   In the first decades it was possible to speak of a third "general" language, Puquina.
[10]   Such as the Plan of Linguistic Support of the San Marcos University in Lima and the Maryknoll Institute of Languages in Cochabamba. There are more than twenty centers in Peru and Bolivia where Quechua and, to a lesser extent, Aymara, are taught. Outside South America, Aymara is taught at one university and Quechua at more than a dozen, many of

jects of bilingual promotion[11] and the circulation of literature in the native language[12] have been initiated.

Partly as a result of the academic surge and partly as a result of political changes, lately new trends in educational politics have taken place, with the oppressed languages being taken more into account. Up to this moment action had not gone beyond preliminaries in Peru, and, in Bolivia, not even beyond the goodwill of some secondary offices of the Ministry of Education and some private institutions. Thanks perhaps to a major governmental decision and to the greater support from academic institutions, the plans which are being formulated in Peru are gaining in precision, although there are still some important ambiguities. For example, on the one hand, drastic changes such as the obligation of teaching a native language as a second language in high schools are announced, and the oppressed groups are encouraged to demonstrate creativity in their own language. But on the other hand, the plans seem to be oriented toward Hispanicization, with the help of the mother tongue only in the first stages,[13] and even here educational aspects, such as the production of texts and the preparation of teachers which would permit more revolutionary teaching changes, are neglected.[14]

These have been the main countercurrents, but they have been at the level of personal enthusiasm and initiation of decisions. On the level of effectiveness the main impacts toward a new situation have come rather

them having prepared fine teaching materials. For more details see the *Andean Linguistics Newsletter*, published since 1969 by Louisa Stark, of the University of Wisconsin, Madison, and Gary Parker, of the Universidad Nacional Mayor de San Marcos de Lima.

[11]   Particularly the Ayacucho project (Burns 1968, 1970) and others more recent, born in the shadow of the summer linguistics institutes. Aside from the forest groups, in 1970 the effort reached five provinces, 39 teachers, and 1,500 Ayacucho students. In Bolivia it has reached up to now 3,000 literate Aymaras in a variable number of schools of two provinces and a considerably smaller number of Quechua children in Cochabamba. Between 1967 and 1973 23,000 certificates in Aymara were given out, and in Cochabamba, 1000 in Quechua (facts provided by the Summer Linguistics Institute of La Paz).

[12]   Particularly the Center of Alphabetization and Aymara Literature (CALA) in La Paz, affiliated with the Summer Linguistics Institute, which has published more than fifty pamphlets, particularly of a religious kind. Among these a hymnal and a bilingual pamphlet have reached sales of 30,000 copies a year. Two other religious Catholic Aymara publications have in two years reached the sum of 50,000 and 80,000 copies, very high figures in the Bolivian context. But production is small outside the religious context.

[13]   Moreover, we are passing from the bilingual plan (teaching pupils to write in the mother tongue and then in Spanish together with teaching of spoken Spanish) to the oral plan (teaching of spoken Spanish with the mother tongue as a medium of instruction, followed by teaching written Spanish), under which the native will continue being incapable of writing in his own language. See the criticism of Pozzi-Escot (1972) of the bilingual method.

[14]   The most basic documents on Peruvian linguistic policy are those of the Ministerio de Educación (1972) and those in *Educación* (1972), a monograph on bilingual education. See also Parker's résumé (1972a). In this atmosphere were born also other studies such as those of Escobar (1972a, 1972b). For the more timid efforts of Bolivia, see INDICEP (1971) and Centro Pedagogico Portales (1972).

from changes in the socioeconomic factors such as those suggested above. The industrialization in the cities and in the mines and the mechanization in the plantations have stimulated migration, above all to Lima and the Peruvian coast, and with it, Hispanicization.[15] But other processes are stimulating at the same time a greater Hispanicization and greater prestige for the oppressed languages. Some of these processes, such as the colonization of the tropics, are also expanding the frontiers of the languages. The two most influential factors have been perhaps agrarian reform, particularly the Bolivian, where it occurred much earlier than in Peru, and the coming of the transistor radio. As a result of agrarian reform the rigid dualist plan has been broken to a large extent. The reform has transformed the social, economic, and political status of the peasant; has increased social as well as geographical mobility; has made the commercial rural network more dense; and has placed schools throughout the countryside.[16] As a result of all this, the rural population has discovered the possibility and functionality of bilingualism, and, at the same time, it no longer feels such shame in using its language in a new context. As for the transistor radio, its popularization in the last decades has brought it to the most distant dwelling, originating another process, also with a contrasting effect. On the one hand, Spanish is now heard everywhere daily, and on the other, the developing agencies, the curates, the politicians, merchants, artists, and so on, have realized that through radio they have the entire countryside at hand, and have begun to diffuse their messages in Quechua and Aymara, contributing thus indirectly to the reevaluation of the languages.[17]

The present linguistic situation, as a result of these recent changes, cannot even be vaguely estimated. In Bolivia the only information we have is from the census of 1950, which was before the agrarian reform (Dirección General de Estadística 1955).[18] In Peru we can count the comparative figures of the censuses of 1940 and 1961 which already reflect something of the migration to the coast. These show, for the whole

---

[15]   It would be interesting to start a study which would establish what socioeconomic factors have triggered so effectively the Hispanicization of the Peruvian coast, with special attention being given to the industrializing and migration process of today.

[16]   In Peru the proliferation of rural teaching partly preceded the agrarian reform. In Bolivia the great push came a little after the reform. Before this in Bolivia there were only isolated efforts, primarily in the border zone with Peru, around the nuclei of Waritaza, in the department of La Paz, and Vacas and Ucureña in Cochabamba. In all these cases Hispanicization above all was the aim.

[17]   In La Paz in 1972 there are twenty radio stations, of which the majority broadcast sometimes in Aymara, and the stronger ones also in Quechua. Four of them, of which three are commercial and almost completely urban, transmit almost all day exclusively in Aymara.

[18]   Between 1967 and 1972 there were local censuses in the main cities as a preparation for the national census, abandoned several times and eventually carried out in 1976. In these local censuses all question of language was eliminated. The results of the Peruvian census of 1972 are not yet known.

country, an increase from 47 to 60 percent of monolingual Spaniards, a relatively stable figure of bilinguals (from 17 to 19 percent), and a clear reduction in the percentage of monolingual natives (35 to 20 percent). But if we limit ourselves to the mountain regions, which have the greater indigenous concentrations, particularly in the south of the country, there were no great changes. According to the census of 1961, Quechua or Aymara would continue being the mother tongue of the great majority of the population in several provinces, such as Ayacucho (93 percent), Apurímac (95 percent), Cuzco (89 percent), and Puno (94 percent). It is a question therefore of changes which have taken place primarily on the coast, the great focus of industralization and immigration.

THE DILEMMA AND THE PLANNING OF THE FUTURE

The panorama of light and shadow presented here up till now does not allow us to foresee with any precision the course which the future will take. The changes in more industrialized sectors, particularly on the Peruvian coast, seem to predict that, as industrialization advances, the Andes will be Hispanicized. But this advance seems still very distant in many regions, and in others, such as the Aymara milieu around La Paz, in spite of the close influence of the city, movements reevaluating the native are arising.

To all this is added the existence of a double radical option with relation to the oppressed languages: accelerate their extinction or revitalize them. In principle, the question of whether one learns Spanish or not should be marginal to this dilemma, but more often Hispanicization coincides with accelerating the process of extinction. Those who advocate a Hispanicization and extinction believe that their opponents are engaging in romanticism and that they would maintain the status quo, even unwillingly, which would impede progress. At the same time those who want to reevaluate the native languages believe the first to be conservative in imposing their dominant ethnocentrism, and that they are, in this way, perpetuating the oppressive situation in which the native populations find themselves.

To progress in the midst of these dialectics, it is convenient to present sketchily the main arguments which are usually wielded in favor of one or the other alternative and weigh the value of each one to arrive at a formulation which is perhaps complex, but more balanced and attainable. In the discussions on the topic, emotional facts usually abound; the complete argument is never fully explained, by which we may easily suppose that the one option completely excludes the other. Thus it is necessary to make a careful and calm distinction if we wish to advance.

The main arguments which favor at least the partial extinction of the oppressed languages (or Hispanicization) are:

1. Given the established order, it is always easier to maintain it than to change it. The proposals should then arise from the stability of the present.

2. Economically the cost of a radical transformation of the system would be excessive. Concretely, the development of the vernacular tongues and the preparation of material in three (or more) languages in place of one implies a multiplication of effort which does not justify the possible advantages therefrom (cf. Bowers 1968).

3. National and Latin American integration demands a common language of communication. On the national level, in Bolivia, as well as in all Peru, only Spanish can fulfill this function, thanks to the growing number of Spanish monolinguals and the multiplicity of native languages and dialects, whose speakers can be incomprehensible to one another. On the continental level this fact is even more evident. Moreover, the vehicle language of integration should count on a vast written production, multifaceted and on every level.

4. With the maintenance, and even more with the promotion, of the native languages in the face of Spanish, national divisions (vertical) are favored, and, if there are a number of languages, they stimulate unnecessary and counterproductive cultural (horizontal) conflicts among groups which, because they are weak, should be more united.

5. With the maintenance of the primitive or atrophied native languages, in the final analysis a certain harm is done to those that we claim to favor, as their full entrance into the modern national system is blocked or at least delayed.

6. Peasants passing into the national culture are often the first to want to forget their language and use Spanish, or to desire this step at least for their children, so that they will not have to suffer just as they did.

The main arguments which favor at least the partial revitalization of the oppressed languages are:

7. The present situation clearly embodies an injustice in denying the native population its full right to the use of their own language without socially discriminatory effects.

8. It is indispensable for the self-development of the native groups that they first become themselves, find their group identity and self-confidence. Only then will they become self-dynamic and be in a situation to participate actively in the progress of the country. Otherwise, at the most they will *be* developed, but they will remain mere passive recipients and not participants. If at the moment some of them think only of Hispanicization, it is precisely because the present structure has made them lose their identity and only permits them social achievement through their own alienation.

9. To communicate a message effectively we must use the language and signs of those who are to receive it. At the same time, this same criterion

of methodology should be used for the integration of present native populations into the life of the country, at either educational, political, commercial, or other levels.

10. The roots of Andean identity are in Quechua and Aymara. The national symbology should be inspired from this source, and one of the most powerful Andean symbols is the language.

11. In fact, the country is constituted of various cultural groups which could be called nationalities (Ovando 1961). Given this fact, integration is only valid if harmonic respect exists between these groups. Only then is it possible to establish the foundations for a Bolivian, Peruvian, or continental unity. But if the language is not included in this process, the doors are closed from the beginning, as the loss of the language is the death of the village.

12. The native languages are as mature and as capable as the modern ones. Their outlawing is based on the false belief that they are incapable of being vehicles of progress. The premise being false, the conclusion is also.

Not all the arguments deduced by one or the other side have the same force and implications. Moreover, according to the individual's underlying conceptions, some would attribute subjectively more importance to certain reasons, attaching little to others. Concretely speaking, there are arguments which are counterbalanced by others. For example, 4 and 6 against 8 and 11; 1 against 7; 12 against 5. Argument 4, on the production of divisions, may be strong in its vertical dimension to one who has a harmonic functionalist vision (although argument 11 of the opposite side may have some force). But to a Marxist, the vertical division would also appear convenient in pointing out the fundamental contradiction which can put into operation the dialectic of the struggle between classes. Nevertheless, this same Marxist will accept the force of the same argument 4 in its horizontal dimension, because for him these cultural divisions among the exploited obscure the fundamental contradiction and underline others in a counterproductive manner.[19] Again, arguments 10 and 11 will seem strong to those who are familiar with their premises and have lived with the problem of the ethnic minorities of so many European countries. Arguments such as these have been used since the nineteenth century by the Irish, the Czechs, the Flemish, and the Catalans. In my opinion, there is a basis of truth in them, especially in argument 11, and they reflect emotive forces which can be very influential at times. Nevertheless, if they become absolute they do not sufficiently consider the dynamic and changing character of the cultures, and, within them, of the languages. Synchronically, the cultural model is necessary for the survival of the individual and of the group, but diachronically, the ele-

---

[19]   It is interesting from a critical viewpoint that a young Marxist of Indian extraction (Reinaga 1972) has established a Marxist theory of the Andes by his dogmatic elimination of the Indian culture elements in his proposals copied from industrial Europe.

ments of these cultures change constantly, particularly with the coexistence of other factors such as migrations, contact and interchange between cultures, and new technical conditioning, which invalidate the previously manifest solutions in a culture. In spite of its strong cohesive value, language, just like religion, is not free from the effects of this agitation and it would be premature to say that it is untouchable. Taking all things into consideration, it is clear that there are sufficiently weighty reasons for each side to make. It is impossible to contemplate a simple solution consisting of choosing either extreme and rejecting the other.

Granted that each has his own underlying conceptions, one cannot place oneself in the absolutely neutral situation of the passive observer. To maintain the pretense of a scientific nirvana is unscientific, as beneath the illusion of neutrality the conditionings which doubtless exist in such an ivory tower are not expressed. A way of pointing out these conditioning conceptions is to present a plan for the future.

In a plan it should be clear what is the ultimate goal and what steps are necessary so that this may be effectively achieved. In the final analysis what is sought is not so much the perpetuation or the isolation of particular cultural or linguistic forms, but rather that those individuals and groups who presently live and express themselves in an atrophied form, because of the structural oppression, be able to live and express their internal potentialities in a fully adequate manner. That is to say, the goal is the person and the group of persons, rather than the culture or the language.[20] Whether the achievement of this goal comes through the efforts of the dominated native element or of the dominating foreign element depends partly on the conception which one has of development and promotion. As for myself, I believe that the achievement of this goal is more probable if from the beginning one stimulates the development of the supposed internal potentialities of the presently oppressed groups. But the choice of one road or the other also depends irremediably on the means at hand. To propose an objective and be determined to achieve it by utopic or inadequate means is the same as not seriously wanting the objective, with all the practical and ethical implications which such a rejection may have.

In the light of these premises and arguments, which are, in my opinion, no more relevant to one or the other option, the following opposed criteria arise: as for the goal of full personal realization among the oppressed groups, neither argument 8 (for revitalization) nor argument 3 (for Hispanicization) can be ignored. As for the effective means to attain

---

[20] Sometimes I have the impression that some of the anthropologists who speak against ethnocide and opt for the maintenance of cultures in isolation do not do it so much because of an absolute cultural relativism or for humanism, but rather because deep inside they are afraid of being without "subjects" to study in their field. An ethnologist with these characteristics might be characterized as an entomologist.

the goal, again, neither argument 9, on the necessity of communicating to each on his own terms, nor argument 2, on the economic limitations to multilingual intentions on a grand scale, can be ignored. In summing up what has been said, it seems that the implementation of the goal demands two general principles:

A. The language (and the other cultural elements) of the major oppressed sector should be recognized and promoted to assure the initial effectiveness of the message and to create self-confidence and group consciousness, thus awakening the creative action and the active participation of this sector in the global society.

B. The Spanish language should also be encouraged in the oppressed sector to the extent that its members are able to manage the language completely, because, given the immobility of social and economic conditions, this is the only way presently possible for the said sector to acquire the technical and academic capacity necessary for a dialogue on an equal basis with the dominant group and no longer to be marginal and oppressed in the innumerable processes of national and continental integration.

The second principle has, without doubt, a taste of fatalism and of impotence before the inevitable, and if we consider the historical perspective we should have to accept the enslaving preeminence of such integrating movements. Nevertheless, I neither affirm nor negate the fact that the final result will be the extinction of the oppressed native language with full Hispanicization of the groups which speak it today. This depends on the level to which the means here suggested succeed in attaining the balance of powers. If they do not succeed, industrialization will probably sooner or later implicate the languages' extinction; but if a certain balance is achieved and if, moreover, the interested groups decide it, it is possible that the evaluation of the native languages will lead to a pluralism which will be comparable to a certain point with certain European countries.

At the beginning of the use of principle A there are difficulties other than those imposed by the social and, particularly, the economic, limitations to which I have already alluded. For example, in the beginning, the production of literature, and particularly expressive literature, in native languages should not be excluded, nor should the teaching of those languages with second-language method in the secondary schools and universities. But limitations exist. As for the level of execution, priority of funds should be given to the most economically advantageous means, but in the implementation of B there is a difficulty. The Hispanicizing policy has already been adopted by all the important organs, including the pioneers of bilingual education and the educational planners of the Peruvian government.[21] Also on this level, there is considerable ground

---

[21] I have already mentioned the ambiguities of the bilingual educational plan of Peru. The Summer Linguistics Institute and its filial institutions for bilingual education and publica-

to cover to achieve more effective techniques of teaching a well-assimilated standard Spanish. For this, the actual grammatical perspective must be put aside and we must insist more on oral and written practice. But the most imminent risk is that the effort made on behalf of principle B will drown any initiative made to implement A. To help avert this conflict the oppressed languages should no longer be outlawed in education, but should rather, within reason, be encouraged. And, in general, to attain the equilibrium of powers, the accent should be more on principle A.

To conclude, I will limit myself to underlining a point which I consider very important and profitable, but on which the existing renovating projects insist very little. It is a question of a more systematic use of the oppressed languages in the means of social communication, especially radio, not so much to "give advice" from top to bottom, but rather so that these media be converted into a vehicle of expression for the Quechuas and Aymaras in their own language thereby overcoming the obstacle of illiteracy. Probably by this path, together with parallel efforts on educational levels and on a more basic level, in the economic spheres, there will be an acceleration of a stronger sort toward the reevaluation of the oppressed languages and it will be possible to encourage the creativity, now in a state of lethargy, of its speakers. Problems such as the production of literature or the unification of the alphabet, which sometimes cut off or sterilize progress, will be resolved more easily if this previous basis exists.

REFERENCES

AGUIRRE BELTRÁN, GONZALO
    1967   *Regiones de refugio*. Mexico: Institute Indígenista Interamericano.
ALBÓ, XAVIER
    1966   Jesuitas y cultural indígenas, Perú 1568–1606. *América Indígena*
            26:249–308, 395–445.
    1969   "Sociolingüística de los valles de Cochabamba, Bolivia." Paper read at
            the fifth symposium of PILEI, São Paulo.
    1970   *Social restraints on Cochabamba Quechua*. Latin American Studies
            Program Dissertation Series 19. Ithaca, New York: Cornell University.

---

tions have not seriously considered the problem discussed here of producing the identity and the participating creativity of the native oppressed groups. At the most they will say that "in the Hispanicization of Quechua-speakers one should not claim to transfer in a rapid step that which is basically intransferable in its essence" (Burns 1970). The team of INDICEP in Bolivia is the one which has gone the farthest in its revitalizing plans. We may also remember that its founder is French-Canadian. But, in spite of the evident evolution, his formulations do not sufficiently consider the global socioeconomic context nor the dynamic aspects of the culture, particularly in a situation of cultural contact and dependence.

BOWERS, JOHN
  1968   "Language problems and literacy," in *Language problems in developing nations.* Edited by Joshua A. Fishman et al., 381–401. New York: John Wiley and Sons.
BURNS, DONALD
  1968   "Bilingual education in the Andes of Peru," in *Language problems in developing nations.* Edited by Joshua A. Fishman et al., 403–414. New York: John Wiley and Sons.
  1970   "La Castellanización de la población no Hispano-hablante en el Perú: meta y metodología." Paper presented to the Thirty-ninth International Congress of Americanists, Lima.
CENTRO PEDAGOGICO PORTALES
  1972   Bulletins presented to the first congress of national languages, Cochabamba, February.
DIRECCIÓN GENERAL DE ESTADÍSTICA
  1955   *Censo de 1950.* La Paz: Argote.
DIRECCIÓN NACIONAL DE ESTADÍSTICA Y CENSOS
  1966   *VI censo nacional de población.* Lima: Dirección Nacional de Estadística y Censos.
Educación
  1972   *Educación* 7. Lima: Ministerio de Educación.
ESCOBAR, ALBERTO
  1972a *Lenguaje y discriminación social en América Latina.* Lima: Milla Batres.
  1972b *El reto de multilingüísmo en el Perú.* Lima: Institute de Estudios Peruanos.
FISHMAN, JOSHUA A.
  1968   "The relationship between micro- and macro- socio-linguistics in the study of who speaks what language to whom and when," in *Bilingualism in the barrio.* Edited by Joshua A. Fishman et al., 100–128. Washington D.C.: Office of Education.
FREIRE, PAULO
  1970   *The pedagogy of the oppressed.* Translated by Myra B. Ramos. New York: Seabury.
GREAVES, THOMAS C.
  1972   Pursuing cultural pluralism in the Andes. *Plural Societies* (Summer) 33–49.
INDICEP
  1971   Conclusions of the seminar on the planning of adult education for 1972. Lima.
LASTRA, YOLANDA
  1965   Segmented phonemes of Quechua of Cochabamba: thesaurus. *Boletín del Institute Caro y Cuervo* 20:48–62.
  1968   *Cochabamba Quechua syntax.* Janua Linguarum: Series Practica 40. The Hague: Mouton.
LEWIN, BOLESLAO
  1967   *La rebelión de Túpac Amaru y los orígenes de la independencia de Hispanoamérica.* Buenos Aires: SELA.
LEWIS, OSCAR
  1959   *Five families: Mexican case studies in the culture of poverty.* New York: Basic Books.
  1966   *La Vida: a Puerto Rican family in the culture of poverty.* New York: Random House.

MELIÁ, B.
1969 *La création d'un langage chrétien dans les réductions des Guaraní au Paraguay*, two volumes. Strasbourg.
1971 El Guaraní dominante y dominado. *Acción: Revista Paraguaya de Reflexion y Dialogo* 11:21–26.

MINISTERIO DE EDUCACIÓN
1972 Bulletins and policy statements from the Primer Seminario de Educación Bilingüe. Lima.

OVANDO, JORGE
1961 *Sobre el problema nacional y colonial de Bolivia.* Cochabamba: Canelas.

PARKER, GARY J.
1963 La clasificación genética de los dialectos Quechuas. *Revista del Museo Nacional* 32:241–252. Lima.
1972a "Notes on the linguistic situation and language planning in Peru." Paper presented to the Twenty-third Georgetown Round Table on Language and Linguistics, Georgetown, Guyana.
1972b *Sugerencias para un alfabeto general del Quechua.* Center of Investigation of Applied Linguistics Document 15. Lima: Universidad Nacional Mayor de San Marcos de Lima.

POZZI-ESCOT, INES
1972 "El uso de la lengua vernacula en la educación," in *Primer Seminario Nacional de Educación Bilingüe.* Edited by the Ministerio de Educación, 43–54. Lima: Ministerio de Educación. (Also published in *Educación* 7.)

REINAGA, RAMIRO
1972 *Ideología y raza en América Latina.* Mexico: Ramiro Reinaga.

RIBEIRO, DARCY
1970 The culture-historical configurations of the American peoples. *Current Anthropology* 11:403–434.

RICARD, R.
1961 Le problème de l'enseignement du castillan aux Indiens d'Amérique durant la période coloniale. *Bulletin de la Faculté des Lettres de Strasbourg* 39:281–296.

RIVET, PAUL, GEORGES CREQUI-MONTFORT
1951–1956 *Bibliographie des langues aymará et kičua*, four volumes. Paris: Institut d'Ethnologie.

RUBIN, JOAN
1968 *National bilingualism in Paraguay.* Janua Linguarum: Series Practica 60. The Hague: Mouton.

SCHAEDEL, RICHARD P.
1967 *La demografía y los recursos humanos del sur del Perú.* Mexico: Institute Indígenista Interamericano.

STARK, LOUISA
1972 *Sucre Quechua.* Madison: University of Wisconsin Press.

STAVENHAGEN, RODOLFO
1965 Siete tesis equivocados sobre América Latina. *Política Exterior Independiente* 1. Rio de Janeiro.

TORERO, ALFREDO
1964 Los dialectos Quechuas. *Anales Científicas de la Universidad Nacional Agraria* 2:446–478.
1970 Lingüística y historia de la sociedad Andina. *Anales Científicas de la Universidad Nacional Agraria* 8:231–264.

1972   "Grupos lingüísticos y variaciónes dialectales," in *Primer Seminario Nacional de Educación Bilingüe*. Edited by the Ministerio de Educación, 3–12. Lima: Ministerio de Educación.

TURNER, VICTOR
1969   *The ritual process: structure and antistructure*. Chicago: Aldine.

UNESCO
1953   *El uso de las lenguas vernáculas en la educación*. Paris: UNESCO.

Continuity and Change in Guambiano Society, 1535–1973

RONALD A. SCHWARZ

Guambía is an Indian community in the southwestern Andean region of Colombia. It is part of the municipality of Silvia in the department of Cauca. The reservation territory begins at the 2,600-meter level and reaches to almost 4,000 meters in the eastern section. To the north and east Guambía is bounded by reservations of Paez-speaking peoples, and in the west are several large haciendas and the town of Silvia. The northwest and southern frontiers separate Guambía from the reservations of Quizgó and Totoró in which languages related to that of the Guambiano were spoken, but whose inhabitants today speak Spanish in preference to their native tongue. The primary characteristics distinguishing the Guambianos from other groups in the region are their language, an Indian style of dress and adornment, and their physical features.[1]

In contrast to the deculturation experienced by other indigenous groups in the area, the Guambianos have maintained much of their tribal culture and social structure while incorporating new features and adapting to the complex demands of colonial, and later national, institutions. This paper deals with the effect of outside forces on Guambiano society and the ways in which they have adjusted to the shifting sociocultural contexts. I consider the events which relate to the decline and growth of the population and focus on the relationship of the latter to economic and political developments in this century.

---

[1] Ethnographic material on the Guambianos is found in Douay (1890), Hernandez de Alba (1944, 1946, 1948), Osorio (1966–1969, 1969), Otero (1952), Reyes (1945), Rowe (1954), and Schwarz (1973). Linguistic information can be found in Rivet (1946) and Matteson et. al. (1972).

THE POPAYÁN VALLEY AT THE TIME OF THE CONQUEST

When the Spanish arrived in Colombia the valley of Popayán (referred to by the Indians as Pubenza) and the surrounding mountains were densely populated.

This city of Popayán has many large villages within the boundaries of its juris-diction. Towards the east it has the *populous province of Guambia*, and others called Guanza, Maluasá, Polindara, Palacé, Tembio, and Colaza, all thickly peopled. The Indians of these districts have much gold . . . of which they make ornaments, . . . They are warlike . . . (de Cieza de León 1864:114–115; emphasis added).

Population estimates for the region range from 100,000 to 500,000, with the former figure being probably the more accurate (Lehmann 1946:973). Most groups in the region shared a common cultural-linguistic base referred to as Guambiano-Coconuco (1946:969). At the time of the conquest the relatively autonomous tribes and *provincias* were loosely organized in a military confederation, the seat of which was in Popayán (de Cieza de Leon, 1864:126). According to de Cieza de León (1864:118):

The Province of Popayán was one of the most populous in South America and, had it been conquered by the Incas, would have been one of the best and richest of all.

Communities in the central Andes generally averaged more than 3,000 inhabitants, while the figure cited for the northern Andes is between 500 and 3,000 (Steward and Faron 1959:57). In the Popayán valley only the "city" appears to have had a population over 3,000. The land was fertile, rich in game and foodstuffs, and there was sufficient virgin land in which villages could be established as the population expanded. Among the practices of the region which had an effect on population one can cite the following: infanticide (of the first male child), polygyny, and intertribal warfare in which the women as well as the men participated (de Andagoya 1865, 1892; de Castellanos 1881; de Mosquera 1855; Hernandez de Alba 1946).

THE EFFECT OF THE CONQUEST AND
COLONIAL INSTITUTIONS

The early attempts of the Spanish to gain control over the tribes in the Popayán region were met with fierce resistence. After several unsuccess-ful moves to capture the city of Popayán, Sebastián de Belalcázar went north to recruit additional forces. Belalcázar, a rather vicious soldier, had not been pleased by the events which prevented him from achieving rapid victory and he proceeded to destroy villages along the route to Cali (referred to as Lile). Human slaughter and the burning of homes became his policy. Whole populations were eliminated or reduced to a small fraction of their original size. Pascual de Andagoya, who served briefly as adelantado of the province of Popayán, described what he encountered on his first visit to the area:

> On the ten leagues of road towards Popayán [from Cali] there are many villages with five hundred to eight hundred houses; of which, when I arrived, no memory remained, except the ashes; for all had been destroyed, and the inhabitants killed by Belalcázar . . . The whole is a very beautiful land, with plains, rivers full of fish, and abundant hunting of deers and rabbits. This land, now laid waste, was a most populous and fertile country . . . When I arrived it was so laid waste that there was not a duck fit to breed, . . . and where there were over one hundred thousand houses in the space of these thirty leagues, I did not find ten thousand men (1865:64–65).

Reinforced by warriors from local tribes, Belalcázar returned south to assault the city and on December 24, 1536 he "founded" Popayán.

The Spaniards' difficulties with the native population did not, however, end with the victory in Popayán. Initially, the local tribes supplied food and participated in battles against surrounding hostile groups which were their traditional enemies. The conquerors' need for women, food, and services increased as their rule in the area was consolidated, and they used force when their demands were not met. Some Indians fled to the more inaccessible parts of the territory. Others refused to plant and cultivate their crops. The use of this tactic, however, contributed significantly to the decline in population in the region:

> In Popayán, the Christians never sowed during the whole time they were there, having the crops of the Indians to live on . . . [to resist the Spanish] the Indians determined not to sow, and there was no maize for eight months, which caused so great a famine that many ate each other, and others died (de Andagoya 1865:66).

De Cieza de León observed that the natives' refusal to sow was not just a protest, but part of their strategy of opposition to the conquerors.

> . . . they preferred to die rather than be subjected, such was their hardihood and they believed that the want of provisions would force the Spanish to leave the country (1864:115).

But the Spanish, impressed by the climate and natural resources of the region, were determined to stay. Popayán became an important political and religious center during the colonial period, and the capital of an *intendencia* with boundaries stretching from Ecuador to the Caribbean.

Relative peace was established in the Popayán valley and nearby mountainsides by the middle of the sixteenth century. Once their position of dominance was secure, the Spanish subjected the remaining Indians to a variety of economic, religious, and political institutions which affected, but did not always destroy, native community life.

In some areas the clergy began its work immediately. Among the earliest New World Indians converted to Catholicism were members of the Guambiano-Coconuco tribes, including a Guambiano chieftainess. Their acceptance of Christianity was facilitated by the lack of a formal "confederation-wide" religion and the curates' concessions to the lesser gods, sacred objects, magic, and so on, which were dismissed as "superstition."

Economic Exploitation and Population Decline

In 1542 following Belalcázar's installation as adelantado of Popayán, Charles I, influenced by Bartolomé de Las Casas, promulgated a revised set of laws for the colonies. These laws declared the American natives free persons, vassals of the crown of Castile, and prohibited anyone from using them against their will (Haring 1947:44–54). Shortly thereafter, from 1545–1550, the colonists imported African slaves to New Granada. Many were brought to the Popayán region to work in the mines. The blacks replaced the Indians as the lowest and most exploited group on the social ladder and made possible some enforcement of the laws prohibiting Indian slavery. Nevertheless, abuse was common, and the Indians had few civil liberties and minimal economic freedom. On encomiendas and haciendas they were almost totally subject to the rule of the colonial landlords.

Colombia during most of the colonial period was a poverty-stricken disease-ridden part of the Spanish empire, and much less important to it than Peru and Mexico. Diseases were widely prevalent, and the Indians had no immunity to many of them. Most severe were leprosy, smallpox, typhoid fever, and paratyphoid. Epidemics in the sixteenth, seventeeth, and eighteenth centuries led to the decimation of the Indian population in the Popayán valley.

During the late seventeenth century, the crown passed additional laws protecting the Indians from the widespread abuse of their persons and usurpation of their lands. A system of communal land holdings, *resguardos* and *parcialidades*, was instituted and took into account the territorial claims and leadership structure of the natives. On the reservations, rights to the land belonged to the group as a unit. The territorial integrity of the reservation was protected by law and the sale and rental of land was prohibited. Non-Indians were prohibited from residing within the reservation. The distribution of land to the Indians was made to the native cacique in his capacity as representative of a social group. As the Indians increased in numbers and integrated economically into the larger society, communal lands were gradually assigned to individuals demanding usufruct privileges.

The same legislation established a system of native government, the cabildo. Although there was some local variation, the Indian government generally consisted of a governor, a first and second magistrate (*alcalde mayor* and *alcalde segundo*), a trustee (*sindico* or *fiscal*), and constables or deputies (*alguacils*). The governor and the alcaldes shared the decision-making authority. The job of the alguacils was to transmit orders from the higher authorities and administer punishments such as whipping and imprisonment in stocks. Elections for these offices were to be held annually.

In Guambía and other neighboring reservations the office of captain (*capitán*) was added to the cabildo. This official was not responsible to civilian authorities and had life tenure and greater power than the elected officers: "The captain was, therefore, like the original hereditary cacique, the chief of each aboriginal group" (Hernandez de Alba 1946:926–927). These actions, though forcing some changes in the native way of life, had the general effect of preserving the social and cultural integrity of the tribal and subtribal units.

The reservation of Guambía and the neighboring ones of Quizgó, Pitayó, and Quichaya (the last two inhabited by Paez-speaking groups) were established in 1700. In that year the Real Audiencia de Quito, in the name and by order of "His Majesty King Philip V gave to the Indian pueblos of Pitayó, Quichaya, Guambía and Quizgó, . . . represented in the person of cacique Juan Tama, the rights to the lands which later constituted the Indian reservations of the same names" (Ministerio de Agricultura 1960).

Although the reservation lands were initially given over to Juan Tama, by 1731 the cacique of each of the four reservations was recognized by the authorities and responsible for collecting tributes. (Archivo Central del Cauca 1731a). Tributes paid by the Guambianos were the highest in the region, which suggests that then, as today, their agricultrual output was superior to that of the neighboring Indian groups.

Population Growth in Guambía During the Colonial Period

The population of the four *parcialidades* located in the territory of Guambía was very small during the colonial period; census lists are rare, and though the names of the caciques of each are listed, the name of the reservation (or *parcialidad*) is not. This reflects the persistence of the preconquest pattern of referring to places by the name of the cacique or *capitán.* Table 1 is the most complete census list available in the archives in Popayán for the territory of Guambía during the colonial period. It is not possible to tell from this which of the caciques was the chief authority in what is today Guambía. Since the population figure of 278 is extremely small it requires some explanation: first, it may reflect the severe effect of colonial policy and the diseases of the previous centuries — many Indians fled to inaccessible regions, and those in contact with the whites contracted the fatal illnesses; second, it is likely that the census figures provided by the local leaders were below the actual numbers of inhabitants; and finally, much of the Guambiano population continued to live on neighboring haciendas even after the *parcialidad* was established.

From 1731 the population of the *parcialidad* increased to approximately 444 in 1780 and to 663 in 1808.

Table 1.   Social organization in Guambía, 1731

Cacique	Husbands*	Wives*	Children	Totals
Juan Calambás	17	22	58	97
Luis Cantero	18	21	43	82
Gonzalo Paz	–	–	–	32
Cayetano Tombe	–	–	–	67
Total				278

Source: Archivo Central del Cauca (1731b).
*   Widowers and widows are listed as "husbands" and "wives." Bachelors are listed as "children." All men married or over eighteen years of age, however, would have had to pay tribute.

FROM INDEPENDENCE TO 1890

Reservation Policy: Dissolution and Integration

Developments following the establishment of the Republic of New Granada, comprising Colombia, Venezuela, and Ecuador, in 1821–1822 worked against the interests of the Indians. During the colonial period the church and Spanish administrators had often intervened on their behalf and represented their interests against those who wanted to control the Indians' land and services. After the revolution, the Indians lost the support of the crown, and the political influence of the church decreased.

Immediately following consolidation of the republic, laws were passed correcting some of the abuses suffered by the Indians during the colonial period (Decreto de 1820, articles 1, 3, 8, 9, 14; Ley de 1821, article 1). These included return of lands illegally obtained, full citizenship and the right to education, protection against exploitation by church officials, and the elimination of tributes and forced labor (Balcazar-Pardo 1954:5–11). The laws had little effect, however, in preventing the exploitation of the indigenous population.

The main thrust of the new legislation was the gradual dissolution of the reservation system. The new criollo aristocracy wanted to abolish reservations and allow local landlords to increase their holdings. They also wanted to foster the development of a class of small landholders. In addition, the reservations were viewed as institutions which contributed to the maintenance of Indian culture and therefore as barriers to the development of a national cultural identity. The destruction of the reservation system was part of the overall policy of "civilizing" the Indians and integrating them more fully into emerging political, economic, and religious institutions.

The undermining of the reservation system began as early as 1820. Simón Bolívar, then president of Colombia, declared that upon return of the land which rightfully belonged to the Indians, each family should be allocated as much land as its members could cultivate. Land not distributed was to be rented to the highest bidder (Balcazar-Pardo 1954:5–6 — Decreto de 1820, July 5, articles 1, 3, 4). Twelve years later details of the distribution process were specified and included safeguards prohibiting the sale of parceled land for a period of ten years (Balcazar-Pardo 1954:35–36 — Ley de 1832, March 6). When the new regulations were implemented and land divided among the native inhabitants, breakup of the indigenous communities quickly followed. Fals Borda describes the sequence of events in a community north of Bogotá:

The Saucites . . . lost their communal title to the land; each individual became responsible for his own plots and for the subsistence of himself and his family. This land distribution was, indeed, a democratic measure, but it proved to be unrealistic. . . . Unable to use their landlord apprenticeship to good advantage, Saucites . . . sold plots to local *hacendados* and sundry speculators at less than the assessed value of the property; misery asphyxiated many peasants . . . (1955:20).

Implementation of national policy, especially in the department of Cauca, was slow and subject to modification by local authorities.

Federal Decentralization and Conservatism in Cauca

In 1853 a constitution was promulgated which decentralized much of the governmental structure. Under the presidency of a conservative, Mariano Ospina Rodríguez (1857–1861), the decentralization of powers increased, and in 1858 New Granada became the Granadine Federation, made up of six nearly sovereign states. The liberal constitution of 1863 increased the fragmentation of power and its dispersal into the hands of state and local officials, while extending, in theory at least, the liberal principles of equal human rights (Helguera 1969:227–228).

While most of the country was responding to concepts of equality and democracy prevalent in European intellectual circles, the department of Cauca in the middle of the nineteenth century was the bastion of conservative forces. According to the liberal governor of Cali at the time, Cauca

presented such a picture of Spanishness and colonialism that an impartial observer would not have found much difference between its civilization and that of fourteenth-century Spain — the Spain of the military orders, holy miracles and infernal spirits, privileges for the few, oppression of the majority, and the fatal rule of the nobles and the friars (Mercado 1853).

Ironically, the colonial structure and medieval world view of the Caucanos were beneficial to many indigenous groups in the region. In most of the nation the policy of division resulted in deculturation and increased poverty of the indigenous population. In Cauca, the conservative legislature, under the laws of the Granadine Federation, nullified the provisions of the 1850 law. They declared that until further notice purchases of reservation land made under that law were void and they were to continue functioning as communal entities (Balcazar-Pardo 1954:61 — Ley 90 de 1859, articles 10, 11). One of the consequences of the conservative Indian policies pursued by the Cauca legislature is that the *departamento* [state] now has fifty-four reservations, more than any in the nation.

The Usurpation of Guambiano Land

The actions of the Cauca legislature, while protecting the reservation from the national policy of dissolution, did not prevent white encroachment on lands belonging to the Guambianos. Several large haciendas were organized in territory which had originally been part of Guambía. The story of the loss of this land to the whites continues to circulate in Guambía. Below is a version obtained from one of the old political leaders.

THE STORY OF THE THEFT OF GUAMBIANO LAND BY WHITE MEN IN THE NINETEENTH CENTURY. Long ago all the land south of the Piendamó river [from Peñas Negras?] to the stream called Rio Molino [Mill River, later changed to Quebrada de Fajardo] formed part of the reservation of Guambía. The stream is called Rio Molino because long ago a stone mill was established there, and with that begins the story of the fight. I do not know why they built a mill since at that time there was little wheat cultivated here. Nevertheless, it was built, and used by many who came from various parts of the province of Popayán to have their wheat ground. These people had to ask permission from the Guambiano cabildo to pasture their pack animals on reservation land. Such requests were always granted. Under this pretext they kept asking for additional land and soon began to cultivate some of it. In this fashion the whites began to gain possession of the land. The cabildo, noticing what was happening, refused to rent any more land. And the fight began.

The cabildo of the reservation, realizing that the whites would not return land to the community once they had rented it, initiated litigation to recover the area usurped by the whites. The papers went to Popayán, to Bogotá, and the Indians attending to this matter had to make many trips and return trips. This was because the white authorities did not attend to Indians quickly and because the Indians at the time were very ignorant. The authorities deceived them with stories and made them make many useless visits. The only white man to help them was a man named José Edubije Sánchez.

The aforementioned papers went from office to office and were delayed for a long time. Finally, they heard that in Bogotá there had been a decision in favor of the Indians. Upon hearing the news they were going to get their land returned, the Guambianos were very happy. When the word got out that the papers were in the mail from Bogotá — which in those days was carried by horseback on mountain trails — the whites left Silvia to meet the courier and stole the papers from him. Shortly afterwards, the whites produced a document showing that they had won the case and that the Indians had lost the land.

Since the cost of all the trips by the Indians was expensive, they had to sell even more of their land to the whites who had forced them to make the trips in the first place. These lands were sold from one hacienda owner to another and form part of the present-day borders of Guambía.

It is said that the titles to the land granted by the king are to be found in the archives in Quito, but some say that these too have been removed by the whites.

The Indians' struggle to maintain their territorial integrity became an important feature of their political life during the years following independence, but it was not until 1966 that full title to the land was obtained.

Stability and Change in Guambiano Society from the Conquest to 1890

Three-and-a-half centuries of alien rule had a substantial impact on Guambiano society. At the time of the conquest the province of Guambía was one of the most populous in the region with more than sufficient natural resources. Warfare, the destruction of villages, and disease resulted in the exodus or elimination of between eighty and ninety percent of the indigenous population. Those remaining were forced into a network of economic, political, and religious institutions which were controlled by individuals indifferent to their needs and hostile to their interests. Much of their land was taken from them and they were located on encomiendas and later haciendas and reservations. The reservation population increased rapidly in the nineteenth century and by 1890 was about 1200.

Early in the colonial period the Spanish introduced new foodstuffs and animals. Wheat, onions, garlic, cattle, sheep, goats, pigs, and chickens provided new sources of food and material for clothing. Metal-tipped tools were introduced but the verticality of much of the terrain prevented the use of draft animals in farming. The traditional slash-and-burn system continued as the principal method of soil preparation, as did the practice of reciprocal labor exchange and communal labor (*mingas*). Horses were adopted for personal use and for the transportation of goods. Clothing styles were modified at the insistence of local authorities but the Guambianos maintained a distinct costume.

The preconquest settlement pattern of small clusters of homes dispersed throughout the reservation remained unchanged in spite of various attempts by local authorities to organize villages. The aboriginal two-room, wattle-and-daub, straw-roofed house, and the circular one for menstruating women, continued to be used.

The Guambianos adopted Christianity and actively participated in many Catholic religious festivals. The priests' practice of adjusting the church's cycle of religious activities to native patterns, incorporating native concepts into Catholic doctrine, and their indifference to many aspects of the native religious system, facilitated the development of a syncretic pattern and the preservation of many indigenous beliefs and practices. The Indians' understanding of Catholic doctrine was severely limited because few of them had more than a rudimentary knowledge of Spanish. The compadrazgo system was introduced by the clergy and used for baptisms, marriages, and other ritual events.

Other important changes resulted from the elimination of intertribal warfare, which had been an integral part of their society. Warfare had been an important factor related to intercommunity ties, tribal leadership, and social mobility. By preventing these activities from occurring, the Spanish undermined the traditional basis of support for social inequalities of power, prestige, and privilege. It also closed off the customary path for social mobility — military prowess.

The decrease in the numbers of Indians, through conquest and disease, their lack of spatial mobility in the reservations, the power of the leaders, and church restrictions on polygynous marriages, undermined traditional supports for the indigenous system of social stratification. In preconquest times, marriages, at least among the ruling class, followed a pattern of class endogamy. By the latter part of the nineteenth century the sanctions for this marriage rule were either substantially reduced or nonexistent, and persons with a "noble" heritage began to marry individuals of a "lower" class. As Douay (1890:761–762) notes, the violation of the endogamous marriage rule led to an even greater loss in the prestige of the upper class. Thus, as a consequence of 350 years of exploitation and rule by outsiders, the degree and kind of social inequality within Guambiano society decreased. This tendency, although dominant, was by no means the only one reinforced by Hispanic rule.

The colonial and Colombian governments introduced a cabildo system within the reservation which in structure and organization was similar to

the preconquest political system. The national government, by supporting the cabildo and allowing the lifetime leaders, the caciques, to function
in the traditional manner, partially mitigated the potentially disruptive
effects of the elimination of warfare. Nevertheless, the system imposed
by the Spanish was devoid of the supernatural supports of the preconquest indigenous system and restricted the authority of the political
officials. The role of this institution was increasingly important in the
twentieth century as the population grew and land became scarce. In
Guambía, the ability of the cabildo to adjust to the demands of an expanding community and complex network of external relations was
a major factor in enabling them to maintain territorial and cultural integrity.

POPULATION GROWTH AND SOCIAL ORGANIZATION IN
THE TWENTIETH CENTURY

In 1890 the Guambianos were an exploited Indian tribe with a primitive
technology and a surplus of land; they were marginal to a cash economy,
monolingual, and with little awareness of events outside the region.
Today [1973], Guambianos control much of their own marketing, use
chemical fertilizers and gas-generated threshing machines, and are linked
to the nation and world by buses and transistor radios. They own stores,
buses, typewriters, and coffee farms; they borrow from banks, teach in
local schools, work as government extension agents, send their children
to high school and college, and are represented in the municipal council.
Two Guambianos have been to New York, and one has studied in Israel.
Almost everyone is bilingual.

    These developments are a consequence of an interrelated complex of
internal and external events among which causal factors are difficult
to isolate. The most important are the rapid growth of the reservation
population to more than 7,500 in 1973, and the transformation of
Colombia from an essentially rural-agricultural society to a modernizing urban-industrial nation. The developments led to new pressures,
goals, and conflicts. At the same time reservation land was becoming
scarce; the needs of the urban centers for agricultural products were
increasing. To meet the new demands, adjustments in the traditional
technology and economic organization were necessary and a new balance
between man and land had to be achieved.

    The demand for farm products in urban areas increased their value
and agricultural extension programs were established in Guambía.
Roads to Silvia and the reservation were built, and these, together
with the introduction of the telegraph, the telephone, and transistor
radios, improved communication between the rural and urban sectors.

An increase in educational opportunities on the reservation provided many Guambianos with the linguistic skills and cultural background to deal with the outside world. Improved health services and the availability of antibiotic drugs decreased mortality rates and contributed to the population explosion. The ecological, technological, and demographic changes have transformed Guambiano society, yet they resist full social and cultural assimilation. Although they are bilingual, Guambiano is still the preferred language. They continue to wear expensive native-style clothing and strive to maintain other aspects of their culture and territorial integrity.

In the following sections I discuss in detail some of the events of this century, their impact on Guambiano society, and the way in which traditional institutions have adapted to the new sociocultural context.

Ecological and Social Change

Before 1890 the only permanent land a person had was his home and surrounding garden. The rest belonged to the community. Usufruct rights were allocated by local caciques for a two-year period and there was sufficient land to permit an individual to cultivate as much as he desired. In this context, economic status was dependent mostly on a person's ability and good fortune.

By 1970 this pattern was radically altered. The major factor causing the change was the growth of population from 1,500 in 1900 to approximately 7,030 in 1970. Taking the maximum estimate for land suitable for cultivation at 3,000 hectares, the hectare-per-person average declined from 2.00 in 1900 to 0.43 in 1970 (Table 2). Land, which during the early part of the century was available to those willing to clear it, was by 1940 controlled by individuals and redistributed among their heirs. Property values increased at an alarming rate and competition for this scarce resource resulted in frequent and serious conflict.

Government policy after 1890 also contributed to the change in the man/land relationship. The main thrust of Indian legislation was to establish a basis for eventual abolition of reservations; prohibiting the sale, rental, and mortgaging of reservation land among Indians was a secondary concern. A white secretary from town was appointed to the cabildo by municipal officials in 1913 to encourage Indians to obtain adjudications for their holdings. A document of adjudication gives the holder the right to maintain permanent control of his land and transmit it to his heirs. The government wanted to have land registered as individual holdings in order to lay the foundation for private ownership.

Although the government in Cauca did not follow through on the policy of abolishing the reservation, obtaining adjudications became a

Table 2. Changes in the man-to-land ratio in Guambía

Year	1900	1913	1930	1940	1950	1960	1970
Population	1,500	2,100	3,100	3,830	4,700	5,750	7,030
Average number of hectares per person	2.00	1.43	0.97	0.78	0.64	0.52	0.43

Figures are based on an estimated size of the reservation at 6,000 hectares, of which a maximum of fifty percent is suitable for cultivation. The actual figure is closer to forty percent and the ten percent is added as a corrective factor to account for inaccuracies in the map used to estimate area and difficulties in calculations because of the uneven topography.

permanent feature of Guambiano economic and political life. Since the statute prohibiting the sale of land within the reservation was never effectively enforced, some individuals, most of them ex-governors and ex-alcaldes, acquired substantial holdings. Conflict over land became a regular feature of social life and outside authorities were frequently involved in bringing about a settlement. These authorities, mayors, judges, and Indian Affairs officials, tend to support litigants who have legal title to the land in question, and in general this practice applies even in those cases where the land was acquired illegally (e.g. by purchase).

Table 3 shows the distribution of registered parcels to which individuals have permanent rights. They represent about half of the territory and close to seventy-five percent of the good farm land. The unequal pattern of land holdings became the basis for a class system that has emerged in Guambía over the last sixty years. Almost all the families (more than ninety-nine percent) own a home and produce enough to meet subsistence needs. However, an increasing number of individuals now supplement their farm income through wage and contract labor both on and off the reservation. The more prosperous Guambianos frequently employ poorer neighbors in agricultural work and a modified form of "patron–client" tie has emerged in established residential areas. In Guambía, however, the "patrons" normally work in the fields with the "clients" they hire. In addition, the cultural gap between "rich" and "poor" usually found in a patron–client relationship is not characteristic of the situation

Table 3. The distribution of registered parcels of land to which individuals have permanent rights: adjudications from 1903 to January 1964

Number of lots	1	2	3	4	5	6	7	8	9	10+
Number of persons with each	1,383	702	330	175	75	102	28	16	27	14

Source: Robalino (1964:32).

in Guambía and there are many land-poor individuals who are relatively well-educated.

Some of the potentially disruptive effects of land scarcity have been mitigated by other developments of recent decades. Technical assistance in agriculture and animal husbandry have helped increase farm output and prices for these products continually improve. Wage labor in the agricultural sector, with the government, and through the sale of craft work to tourist shops in town have provided additional sources of income. No single development, however, has had more impact on the economic system than the recent construction of all-weather roads on the reservation. The roads, begun in 1963, and which continue to be extended today, have accelerated the rate of change and have fostered new social and economic patterns within the community and between the reservation and the outside world. Guambianos previously sold most of their produce to, and made many purchases from, white and mestizo traders (*negociantes*) who came to Guambía almost daily. These middlemen made substantial profits in their transactions with the Indians, sometimes as high as two hundred percent, though between fifty and a hundred percent was closer to the average markup. Today, Indians sell their goods directly in rural and urban markets throughout the region and receive a more equitable price for their produce. In addition, some of the buses they travel on are owned by Guambianos, and when they sell their produce to a middleman, that person is likely to be another Guambiano rather than a non-Indian.

This outward commercial extension has been complemented by the setting up of stores (*tiendas*) by Indians on the reservation. These supply such basic needs as salt, coffee, rice, flour, and flashlight batteries, and often do a brisk business in beer and aguardiente, an anise-flavored liquor. Store ownership has made it possible for some Guambianos with small land holdings to improve their economic position.

The improved transportation system has also stimulated the purchase of small farms (*fincas*) off the reservation. More than 150 Guambiano families have bought coffee *fincas* in neighboring municipalities and some are buying land on nearby Paez reservations. Once a family establishes itself in one of these communities others tend to follow, and there are now several areas with ten to twenty Guambiano households. Residence on these farms is generally seasonal and most families spend the larger part of the year in Guambía. The tendency for some persons to remain in these regions is, however, increasing.

POLITICAL ASPECTS OF POPULATION GROWTH IN THE TWENTIETH CENTURY

The organization of political affairs of the reservation has changed in this century although the cabildo structure has remained essentially intact. During previous centuries and the early part of this one, the lifetime caciques directed political activities, including the allocation of usufruct rights and selection of cabildo officers. Most critical matters dealt with by political leaders had to do with moral offenses, the organization of community projects (e.g. bridge building), and protecting the reservation from encroaching whites. As the elder caciques died off during the early decades they were not replaced and the position was gradually eliminated. Political activities were directed by an active and growing cabildo, and an influential group of ex-cabildo officers. The major role of the cabildo became the allocation and registration of land holdings, and the transmission of these rights to heirs. During the past thirty years much of the cabildo's work involved settling disputes arising out of conflicting claims to a parcel of land.

Today, the cabildo in Guambía consists of thirty-four members: a governor, four alcaldes (regional mayors), twenty-seven alguacils, and two secretaries. The secretaries serve indefinitely but all other offices are held for one year. The governor and the alcaldes are elected, and the other positions are filled through appointment. The cabildo has very limited jurisdiction and is responsible to the mayor of Silvia and other government officials.

Neighborhood Units

The territorial group which has a political and administrative character is the *vereda* [neighborhood]. The distribution of most cabildo positions is done according to *vereda* composition, and many community activities are organized within this unit. *Veredas* are territorial units recognized by the Colombian and Indian governments. Each has a name, and within the municipality a Guambiano generally identifies himself as a resident of Pueblito, Cacique, La Campana, and so on. *Vereda* boundaries are normally defined, ending at a river or the edge of a string of mountains.

Each of the nineteen *veredas* in Guambía in 1970 was represented in the cabildo by at least one alguacil who communicated messages to the residents about workdays, meetings, and other special events. Some of the larger *veredas* have local Virgins for which annual fiestas are held; most have at least one store (*tienda*), and five have primary schools. The *veredas* range in size from 14 to 232 households, most having between 25 and 90.

Stability and Change in the Vereda *System, 1900–1970*

This section deals with two aspects of the political response to population change: the establishment of new *veredas* and the addition of low-level positions in the cabildo (alguacils). Developments indicate areas of stability in certain aspects of Guambiano social organization and reveal a strategy of adaptation which facilitated the maintenance of tribal unity. The process of *vereda* growth seems also to be related to a need for identity at a level beyond that of the family or network of kin, yet within which relationships are primarily of a personal rather than bureaucratic nature. In addition, new *veredas* provide a setting in which new and younger leaders emerge.

During the early part of the twentieth century the settlement pattern in Guambía consisted of isolated households, usually with several nuclear families and small clusters of households widely separated from one another, two to five hundred meters apart. There were only five *veredas*, each of which encompassed large sections of the reservation. For example, the region referred to as Piendamó during the early decades of this century was a single *vereda* stretching for almost five kilometers on both sides of the Piendamó river. Between thirty and fifty households were dispersed throughout the area and serviced by a single alguacil. It took him from four to six hours to visit these homes. Today the same territory is divided into nine *veredas*, contains more than three hundred households, and is represented in the cabildo by twelve alguacils.

The growth of *veredas* and increase in the number of alguacils reflect elements of stability as well as change and are related to the major themes or principles operative in Guambiano society: equalilty and accompaniment. Table 4 shows there is a clear pattern of growth in the number of *veredas* and number of alguacils which roughly follows the increase in Guambiano population. While the figures cited reveal a pattern of growth, the two lower lines, which present averages of persons per *vereda* and persons per alguacil, show relative stability. On the one hand, there is a tendency which is incremental and linear, and on the other, a sequence of numbers which suggest that organizational aspects of the society involve flexibility, stability of social units, and political continuity.

Guambiano population has more than quadrupled during the twentieth century. The number of *vereda* units and political positions have undergone a roughly proportional increase. The stability reflected in the ratios presented is more than just a statistical accident or the result of the application of formal rules of social organization to increasing numbers of inhabitants. There are *no explicit rules governing either* the formation of *veredas or* the numbers of persons an alguacil should represent. Each case is worked out in terms of itself and takes into account the special circumstances and needs of those involved in making the demands. In the case of

Table 4. Political aspects of population growth

	1913	1930	1940	1950	1960	1970
Number of *veredas*	5	7	9	13	16	19
Population	2,100	3,100	3,830	4,700	5,750	7,030
Number of alguacils	6	14	15	16	22	27
Average number of persons per *vereda*	420	443	425	361	359	370
Average number of persons per alguacil	350	221	255	294	261	260

the alguacil the process works from either the top or the bottom. In some instances the alguacil indicates to his alcalde that there are too many houses and people for him to cover efficiently, whereupon the alcalde may appoint an additional one. In other cases the alcalde takes the initiative in adding an alguacil.

This informal and pragmatic approach to *vereda* and cabildo growth reflects one of the key features of Guambiano social organization, its flexibility. Guambianos take into account the needs of groups and individuals, and adjust the system to meet changing circumstances. It is the flexibility of the system which has been among the more constant elements of their society during this century.

The tendency for stability in the size of social units and systems of representation may also be related to the question of sentiments and social mobility or the desire for prestige. Except for the largest *vereda*, Cacique (which is actually divided into localized groups), *veredas* are "little communities." Bonds of kinship, affinity, compadrazgo, and those established through working together and participating in ceremonial events, link members of a *vereda* together in a multiplex network. The inhabitants know one another primarily as individuals, human beings with idiosyncratic qualities. Leadership and prestige within this group is a function of performance. Within the *vereda* a person's skill as a political leader or religious specialist is tested and evaluated. Command over material resources gives a person an initial advantage insofar as it reflects the results of his labor, but wealth is neither a necessary nor a sufficient condition for prestige and power. These are reserved for those who work with and for others and who participate in political activities.

GUAMBÍA IN 1973: CONFLICTS AND PROSPECTS

Events during the twentieth century have transformed Guambiano society from a "little community," with a surplus of natural resources, and marginal to the larger society, to a larger, more mobile and heterogeneous group, faced with a scarcity of natural resources, and well integrated into the regional economic system. All aspects of the culture, from methods of cultivation to health practices, contain elements of traditional and modern systems. The Guambianos, though generally conservative, maintain a pragmatic view toward technological innovation and have a social organization flexible enough to adjust to the shifting demands of a rapidly growing population. They are a unique example of an indigenous group enjoying the benefits of technological progress and striving actively to maintain their social institutions and cultural heritage. Events discussed in earlier sections have also, however, increased some forms of social conflict, and problems exist today which threaten their ability to maintain themselves as a viable sociocultural unit.

The major problem is the shortage of land and how to accommodate the growing population economically within the present reservation boundaries. Another serious problem is the competition between territorial sections for resources made available to the community for development projects. In regard to the latter, one may point to a conflict that occurred during the early stages of the road construction program. Leaders in one section feared the building of the roads was a move toward opening the reservation to white settlers. Others supported the project, and while this problem was eventually solved the conflicts it generated laid the foundation for a schism which resulted in an attempt to divide the reservation in 1971.

The groups which crystallized during the conflict over the road project are, in 1973, opposed with regard to the issue of land reform. They all agree it is urgent but disagree about how it should be done. One faction is working actively with the national agrarian reform agency (INCORA), while a large majority of the leaders, including the present cabildo governor and most ex-governors, prefer to work out a private arrangement with hacienda owners. Much of the blame for the internal conflict belongs to the politically idealistic and naïve extension agents of INCORA. They have supported leaders with no prestige in the community and have failed to deliver on promises of land titles to those Indians working with them on a farm cooperative. Part of the problem is the lack of action by the national government to expropriate haciendas adjacent to Guambía, but the invasions led by a few have alienated most potential supporters who are not disposed to using violence to accomplish their goals. On the other hand, it is possible that the invasions will motivate the government to move more quickly.

Looking at the prospects for the Guambianos continuing as a cultural minority integrated into the economic and political institutions of Colombia, there are grounds for optimism. Greater contact with the rural peasant subculture which occurs in those regions to which the Guambianos migrate has already accelerated shifts in cultural and social patterns away from the traditional way of life. But, as Guambianos group together in these regions there is a strong likelihood that the rate of deculturation will be markedly reduced. Most significant, however, is the fact that the vast majority of Guambianos maintain their homes on the reservation and prefer to stay there even though they have the cultural and technical skills to be successful elsewhere. They are proud of their Indian identity, but not arrogant in displaying their pride. They have experience of the world outside of Guambía but choose to stay where they are. They are facing a major crisis because of the lack of farmland on the reservation but they are patient, persistant, and pragmatic, and it is likely that this problem too will be overcome.

REFERENCES

ARCHIVO CENTRAL DEL CAUCA
1731a Sig. 32:10 (Collection II, 7t). Unpublished document.
1731b Sig. 34:68 (Collection CII, 7t). Unpublished document.
1807   Sig. 67:13 (Collection CII, 19t). Unpublished document.
ARROYO, JAIME
1907   *Historia de la governación de Popayán*, . . . Popayán.
BALCAZAR-PARDO, MARINO
1954   *Indígenas, baldíos y estados antisociales.* Popayán.
DE ANDAGOYA, PASCUAL
1865   *Narrative of the proceedings of Pedrarias Davila in the provinces of Tierra Firme or Castilla del Oro,* . . . Translated and edited by C. R. Markham. London: Hakluyt Society.
1892   "Replación de los sucesos de Pedrarias Dávila en la tierra firme de los descubrimientos en el mar del sur," in *Colección de documentos* 1553 as *Parte primera de la chronica del Peru* . . . . Seville: M. de Mon- York: C. W. Bennett.
DE CASTELLANOS, JUAN
1881   *Historia general de las conquistas del Nuevo Reino de Granada.* Bogotá.
DE CIEZA DE LEÓN, PEDRO
1864   *The travels of P. de Cieza de León* . . . , part one. Translated and edited by C. R. Markham. London: Hakluyt Society. (Originally published 1553 as *Parte primera de la chronica del Peru* . . . . Seville: M. de Montesdoca.
DE MOSQUERA, TOMÁS CIPRIANO
1855   *Memoria sobre la geografía física y política de la Nueva Granada.* New York: C. W. Bennett.
DOUAY, LEON
1890   "Contribution a l'américanisme de Cauca (Colombie)," in *Congrès International des Américanistes: compte-rendu de la septième session*, 753–786. Berlin.
FALS BORDA, ORLANDO
1955   *Peasant society in the Colombian Andes: a sociological study of Saucio.* Gainesville: University of Florida Press.

HARING, C. H.
1947 *The Spanish empire in America.* New York: Harcourt Brace.

HELGUERA, J. LEON
1969 "The problem of liberalism versus conservatism in Colombia: 1849–1885," in *Latin American history: select problems.* Edited by Frederick B. Pike, 223–258. New York: Harcourt, Brace and World.

HERNANDEZ DE ALBA, GREGORIO
1944 Etnología de los Andes del sur de Colombia. *Revista de la Universidad del Cauca* 5:141–226. Popayán.

1946 "The highland tribes of southern Colombia," in *Handbook of South American Indians*, volume two. Edited by Julian H. Steward, 915–960. Bureau of American Ethnology Bulletin 143. Washington D.C.: Smithsonian Institution.

1948 "Sub-Andean tribes of the Cauca valley," in *Handbook of South American Indians*, volume four. Edited by Julian H. Steward, 297–315. Bureau of American Ethnology Bulletin 143. Washington D.C.: Smithsonian Institution.

LEHMANN, HENRI
1946 "The Moguex-Coconuco," in *Handbook of South American Indians*, volume two. Edited by Julian H. Steward, 969–974. Bureau of American Ethnology Bulletin 143. Washington D.C.: Smithsonian Institution.

MATTESON, ESTHER, *et al.*
1972 *Comparative studies in Amerindian languages.* The Hague: Mouton.

MERCADO, RAMON
1853 *Memorias sobre los acontecimientos del sur de la Nueva Granada durante la administración del 7 de Marzo de 1849.* Bogotá: Imprenta Imparcial.

MINISTERIO DE AGRICULTURA
1960 "Informe anual." Unpublished report. Silvia, Colombia.

OSORIO, OSCAR
1966–1969 La institución del compadrazgo entre los Indios Guambianos. *Revista Colombiana de Folclor* 4(10):136–151.

1969 "El sistema del parentesco entre los Indios Guambianos, una tribu del suroeste de Colombia." Degree dissertation. Bogotá. Universidad de Los Andes.

OTERO, JESUS MARÍA
1952 *Etnología Caucana.* Popayán.

REYES, ANGEL
1945 Sobre los Indios Guambianos. *Boletín Indigenista* 5(3):220–225.

RIVET, PAUL
1946 Le groupe Kokonuko. *Journal de la Société des Americanistes* 33:1–61.

ROBALINO, ELOY A.
1964 "Agencias de desarrollo y proceso de cambio socio-cultural." Unpublished manuscript, Universidad Nacional, Bogotá.

ROWE, JOHN H.
1954 An ethnographic sketch of Guambía, Colombia. *Journal for Ethnology and Its Related Sciences of the Linden Museum* 415:129–156.

SCHWARZ, RONALD A.
  1973   "Guambía: an ethnography of change and stability." Unpublished doctoral thesis, Michigan State University, East Lansing.
STEWARD, JULIAN H., LOUIS C. FARON
  1959   *Native peoples of South America.* New York: McGraw-Hill.

Workers Participation in the Nationalized Mines of Bolivia, 1952–1972

JUNE NASH

Worker participation in industry has been, historically, a management innovation to gain worker cooperation in times of labor–management tension. One of the first experiments was promoted in Canada when, after the strike of 1913 in the Colorado Fuel and Iron Company, John D. Rockefeller and W. L. Mackenzie, the Minister of Work, signed the contract for a short-lived plan for worker participation in the management. During World War I, a few Italian industries introduced worker councils as a means of increasing productivity. After the war, Antonio Gramsci promoted the councils in Turin after the failure of a general strike in May 1920. Gramsci (1957:23) viewed worker councils as a kind of territorial base for promoting workers' self-government. He envisioned the role of the factory council as follows:

In the Factory Councils, the worker, because of his very nature, plays the role of producer as a result of his position and function in society, in the same way as the citizen plays a role in the democratic parliamentary state. In the Party and trade unions, the worker plays his role "voluntarily" participating in a contract which he can tear up at any moment. The Party and the trade unions, because of this "voluntary" character, because of their "contractual" nature, are not to be confused with the councils which are representative institutions and do not develop mathematically but morphologically, and in their higher forms tend to give a proletarian meaning to the apparatus, created by the capitalist for the purpose of extracting profit, of production and exchange (1957:25).

This was the first concerted attempt by the Left to transform factory councils, which were set up by managers to accelerate production, into a defense of workers' interests for the purpose of "preparing the working classes organizationally, politically, and culturally for the task of managing industrial enterprises" (Gramsci 1957:13).

The reality of worker participation in industry has been more closely approximated in Yugoslavia than in any other industrial nation. Vanek (1974), using his knowledge of the movement in Yugoslavia and contrast- ing that movement with experiences in the Soviet Union and the United States, defines the ideal nature of a participatory democracy:

1. Firms controlled and managed by workers with management by all on the basis of equality, to be carried out by a workers' council, an executive board and a director of the firm.
2. Income sharing based on an income-distribution schedule that is equitable.
3. Worker usufruct of capital assets.
4. Market economy with fully decentralized management, no direct interference from outside except in fixing of maximum and minimum prices.
5. Freedom of employment with firms free to hire and fire, and individuals free to come and go.

The judgement of the effectiveness of the new organizations, designed to increase worker participation, has to shift from a straight evaluation based on gross national product to an assessment of self-fulfillment of people. The motivation to work and the greater social aims of production are an immediate concern of firms organized under such a plan. The Marxist adage about capitalism — that it is designed to create more useful products for more useless people — might be reordered to consider a social design that will create more useful people concerned with producing for more socially gainful ends.

Vanek's model has been widely disseminated in Latin America, and the Peruvian edition of his book (Vanek 1971) has influenced the formation of industrial communities there. I shall assess Bolivia's experience in worker participation in the tin-mining industry from the point of view of the two conditions Vanek uses in his model of equilibrium analysis: degree of efficiency and degree of self-determination. I should point out several problems in data analysis that make such an analysis nearly impossible. First of all, efficiency in tin mining cannot be measured by simple productivity ratios either per capita, per man-hour, or per enterprise because of the constantly dwindling resource base. The figures of fine tons produced are misleading because of the lowering levels of metal content — it takes continuously more work to get out the same amounts of mineral. Metric tons are a better index of sheer human productivity, but the comparative indices are hard to get because they do not enter into international trade.

The second condition of equilibrium proposed by Vanek, "self-determination," is hard to measure because it is contingent on the level of worker consciousness, not only of their exploitation as a class but of their potential to be prime movers in history. This consciousness is dependent on ideological inputs as well as concrete experiences that reinforce the willingness of workers to sacrifice themselves for an end. Bolivia's trade union movement has relied in the post-1952 period more on the former and less on the latter. The rhetoric of revolution was honed to a fine point in the annual succession of coups from September 26, 1969, when Ovando seized power from Barriento's Vice-President Siles, to October 8, 1970, when Torres caught the presidential ball as it was flipped from one to another military pretender in the "Week of the Generals," to the August 19 takeover by Colonel Hugo Banzer, who moved up through the American stronghold in Santa Cruz, where Gulf Oil had its holdings, to seize the presidency after only three days of sporadic fighting. Action on the part of the workers in these sorties into and out of power by various military representatives was limited to imploring the real power holders for guns. Technology had outmoded political persuasion. Without an active role in decision making in industry, the workers' ability to enter into decision making in politics was limited.

The first stage of worker participation in industry began with the nationalization of the tin mines on October 31, 1952. Anayo (1952) traces nationalization back to 1949 when the Left Revolutionary Party (PIR) called upon the legislature to nationalize mines without indemnization and with a strong worker control. Bedregal (1963), on the occasion of the tenth anniversary of the nationalization decree, claims that this act, along with the agrarian reform, formed the nucleus of the National Revolutionary Movement (MNR). Lora (1972) traces it to the Thesis of Pulacayo which he, as leader of the Revolutionary Party of Workers (POR), helped to draft in 1946. These claims to paternity prove one thing: the bastard form of nationalized mines was a popular creation, and all political parties that had a stake in labor claimed to have fathered it.

Those who moved toward nationalization of the mines pointed out that the mines under the tin barons were more exploitive of the labor force than during the colonial period (Anayo 1952). Certainly the production was more intense: during three centuries of colonial rule, 105,454 tons of minerals were extracted from the Cerro Rico of Potosi, while during the Republic, the same amount was exported in three years. In the period from 1935 to 1949 alone, over one million tons were extracted (Anayo 1952:42).

Assessing the damage of unrestricted mineral exploitation during the first half of the twentieth century, Canelas (1966:20) asserts that the tin barons succeeded in (1) maintaining a permanent national budget deficit such that the government lacked even the minimum impulse to economic growth, (2) extracting an extraordinary amount of natural resources with low taxes, (3) constantly increasing the external debts to cover deficits in costs for imports to care for public services that directly or indirectly serviced the mines, and (4) contributing to growing inefficiency in the recuperation of minerals by failing to invest in modern machinery for concentration work within the country. The profligate waste of human resources is summarized in Anayo's statement (1952:105) that "Capitalism . . . signifies the destruction of one man for every four that enters work."

Despite severe exploitation and the high risk of their work, miners have always been poorly paid in Bolivia. The level of living in mining communities as described by Bloomfield, sanitary engineer of the Institute of Inter-American Affairs (cited in Anayo 1952:101 ff), was lower than that described by Marx for the Lancashire workers in the eighteenth century. Several families lived in a single habitation, with up to fifteen persons living in eight square meters. People took turns to cook, even to sleep in the few beds. He noted that:

Problems related to morals result in the dissolution of many marriage ties . . . The absolute impossibility of rest for workers is because those occupying the same quarters work in different shifts, and on returning from a hard day's works, find others engaged in activities.

The hope of nationalization was summarized by Anayo (1952:143) in the following litany:

To liquidate the fifty years of backwardness, of exploitation, of extermination imposed by the great mining companies, we must nationalize the mines.

To destroy the reactionary forces that block progress we must nationalize the mines.

To make possible the economic, social and cultural transformation of the welfare and of the liberty of the Bolivian people we must nationalize the mines.

Nationalization became a reality at a sunrise ceremony at Siglo XX-Catavi six months after the revolution — time enough for the former owners to return shiploads of capital goods destined for the mines to the country of origin and to cut off further explorations and to exploit to the maximum existing shafts. A worker relates the meaning of nationalization for underground workers:

On the 31st of October they signed the act of nationalization in Siglo XX in the field of Maria Barzola. They declared a day of festivities. All the works were paralyzed, neither factories, nor masonries, nor those who worked in the constructions in the city of Oruro worked that day. We workers of all the mines gathered together for this act in Siglo XX where there was a huge concentration. They set off some dynamite as if they were in a ferocious combat, a war

When we worked in the companies of the ex-barons of tin, there were no drilling machines nor automatic shovels for the majority of us in Santa Fé. They had compressed air only where there were no drills, and this was in only a very few areas. After nationalization they put in pipes in all parts, even into the most oppressive areas where the heat was so intense you could hardly stand it. Before, a worker had to swing a wet burlap in all directions to drive out the heat into the tunnels or the shafts when they were driving a shaft down to another level. After the revolution they had pipes set up for ventilation.

Before the nationalization of the mines, many workers could not secure a contract. They had to work two years as a peon of the house at the behest of any *cuadrilla* [work group], earning no more than the base wage without a contract. For example, in my case, when the month of May came I should have been let on the job after I was fired serving as a peon for two years. Instead when I came back to work the engineer told me. "Listen, Rocha, you cannot continue as a *pirkin*; you have to work as a driller." I was afraid when he said this because never in my life had I worked with a machine, nor did I know anything about the sickness of the miners and how one contracted it. It just scared me to hear, "You are going to work with the drilling machine."

Nationalization of the mines was a grandstand play for the peasants and workers who had brought Paz Estenssero to power. Leaders of the labor movement tried to promote a greater participation by workers through *Control Obrero* [Worker Control]. The revitalized Federation of Mine Workers Unions of Bolivia (FSTMB), along with the newly organized Bolivian Workers' Control (COB), drafted the decree for worker participation that was passed for the mines on December 15, 1953. This same worker summarizes the effect of the decree on workers from his perspective:

After the Central Obrero Boliviana [COB] was organized, the secretary general of the federation declared that the administrators of the nationalized mines were taking advantage of their position in the cashier's office, the head office of personnel, the supply office, with the heads of the encampment and of welfare. In the personnel office there was a list of workers called *maquipuras* [irregular, non-supervised workers] who were not people who worked, but only appeared as names on the pay ledger and the chief received their pay.

As a result of these abnormalities, the secretary generals in the nationalized mines asked that COMIBOL organize a directive which would serve as a base to control each company. They wanted to form a Worker Control with the right of veto. The government of Victor Paz Estenssero prevented the organization of this group. With great effort, the miners organized it but without the right to a veto. Without this, nothing had any worth. The workers of Siglo XX took a stronger position than the other mines. They wanted to enter into a strike, the first threat during the time of Victor Paz Estenssero. Paz Estenssero did not want any problem in this period of office and he gave in to their demand. After that they did not have these kinds of arbitrary acts that were happening in the nationalized mines. They had more earnings than ever because every receipt had the signature of the men in charge of Control Obrero. No one had the right to dispatch any drug, any work material in any part, no matter how urgent it was, without passing through the Control Obrero.

In Santa Fé we did not know what the Control Obrero was and for what it served since our company wasn't nationalized in the year 1953. We only knew that the Control Obrero had to interfere in all kinds of arbitrary acts that existed in the company. In the year 1954 our company was nationalized as well as Japo. Immediately we organized the Control Obrero with the right to veto. The first secretary general was Victor Carrasco who was secretary of the union organization in the federation of miners. He apprehended various employees who had taken advantage of the earnings of the company. For example, Señor Manuel

Cano had made a good house in Oruro with materials from the company. He came in person to Oruro to collect materials for the shops in Santa Fé saying that he needed pipes, wood, all kinds of fixings for the construction of housing. They discovered it when the Control Obrero looked over a mountain of receipts from the year 1952. He was changed to another post. Also they discovered a Señor Minaya, chief of the offices. He was a Paraguayan who had taken advantage of 30,000 bolivianos. Another chief of the offices, a Chilean, had taken 25,000 bolivianos to his country, but they couldn't get it back. The Control Obrero is the one which put a quota on everything and made things more rational.

The decree called for worker control to intervene in production planning, organization of work, decision making in investments, vigilance over expenditures, and disciplining of personnel (Ruiz Gonzales 1965:279). However, the main concentration of worker control in fact was an attack on the administration which took for granted that the managers were the owners of the house and the workers were the outsiders. The very function of being a watchdog was at odds with the other administrative functions contained in the decree. The aggressive stance taken by miners in the worker control minimized one of the common weaknesses of the system: the assimilation of workers' outlook to that of administrators. But it severely limited their managerial functions.[1]

The limitation of functions exercised by worker control had a structural base in the failure to take a position independent of the union. Even after such councils are formed and operating smoothly, it is important to retain a strong union organization that operates in the capacity of watchdog over both managerial and worker representatives and that oversees the problems of salary and welfare in which worker control councils often get bogged down. In the case of Bolivian mine workers, there never developed a clear-cut separation of functions. The FSTMB controlled the selection of worker control representatives and dominated in the selection of issues. Frequently the secretary general of the union was the director of worker control. The ever-present fear of the rank and file that their representatives were becoming an elite corps as they entered into managerial functions was exacerbated.

Another structural weakness was the fact that there was only one worker representative in the worker control. As Ruiz Gonzales (1965:272ff) said, "Only one such representative who carries out functions of control and effective intervention in complex administrative tasks as required by the decree is in the same situation as the shipwrecked sailor hanging from a log on the high seas."

[1]   Selsef (1970) has spelled out the major problems encountered in the Argentine experience as follows: (1) difficulties in the exchange of information with the base, (2) workers dedicate more energy to salary and welfare than to management of enterprise, and (3) workers assimilate to the point of view of managers. These problems point to the need for continued surveillance of trade unions independent of the worker control group operating outside the particular enterprise.

As a result of these functional ambiguities and structural inadequacies in defining lines of jurisdiction between worker control and the union, workers failed to gain a sense of participation and this increased their sense of frustration.

The experience with worker control was one part of a larger contradiction that existed in popular participation in the MNR government from 1952 to 1964. The working class held positions in the senate, in up to four ministries, and their foremost leader, Juan Lechín Oquenda, occupied at one time the post of minister of mines and petroleum and the vicepresidency in Paz's final term, at the same time continuing as president of the COB and of the FSTMB. The contradiction between these roles became particularly sharp as labor's discontent with the government, particularly over the issue of the economic stabilization that put a freeze on wages and prices in 1957, sharpened. The same replication of functions was found at lower levels of the union and political hierarchy.

As a result of the elite positions union leaders occupied in a nonlabor government, the rank and file workers felt more and more disinherited by the revolution they had made a reality in 1952. In a postmortem on the MNR period made by a rank-and-file worker at the San José mine in April 1970, this lack of confidence is underscored:

During cogovernment we had many workers as senators and congressmen, and what did they do for the workers' movement? Nothing. But we can indicate clearly that they had a great opportunity to traffic with syndicalism because they are the new rich. Many of the worker ministers live very comfortably; they have automobiles, houses not only in Coban, but in Cochabamba, and they don't even belong to the working class because they do not know the mineshaft while we, of the working class, continue living in the mineshafts.

He concluded his attack on the old leaders with a call for the independence of the working class. Of the many such attacks that I heard in the months following the regeneration of the labor movement in the April 1970 congress of the FSTMB, the phrase that seemed to sum it up best was that of a rank-and-file member of the San José mines who said at a union meeting, "This kind of petty-bourgeoisie politics broke the skull (*descalabró*) of the working class." Lechín himself admitted in an address to union delegates to the COB meetings in May 1970:

We have to recognize that the experience of cogovernment caused the compromise to the working class and the entrance into power by governments of this period. This experience and the attitude assumed by different political parties undermines our union independence of political parties.

But he concludes with this ambiguous statement: "However, we must recognize that we cannot remain simply a spectator because that is a peril to the working class."

The reversal of nationalization began with vigor in the 1960's and was accelerated by the Triangular Plan signed in August 1961. The plan called for the recapitalization of the mines with a loan of US$ 37,750,000 from the Bank for Inter-American Development (BID), West Germany, and the United States, to be used for exploration of new mineral deposits, metallurgical work to increase recovery rates, replacement of needed material, equipment to rehabilitate mines, and commissary supplies (Zondag 1966:232). The loan was contingent on the "rationalization" of the labor force. It was this provision that split the ranks of labor, and worker control was the scene on which the battle was fought. Federico Escobar, leader of the Siglo XX-Catavi mine union and head of worker control there attacked the plan as an imperialist design to gain control over the mines. Lechin defended it in the publication called *Control Obrero* (1961:4) stating:

Since when can something die before being born? The Triangular Plan has not yet been born in this country; perhaps it will be born today in accord with the information of the press. The comrades have begun blaming the Triangular Plan for all the evils of the working class and their social problems. But the means adopted are prior to and not a consequence of the plan but of other things (quoted in Canelas 1966:106–107).

Because of the resistance of the workers, the plan did not bring about a reorganization of the work force until 1965. There was in fact an increase in the number of above-ground workers from 1962, when there were 16,813, to 18,819 in 1965. The increase in above-ground workers was due in part to an overinflated bureaucracy expanding in accordance with Parkinson's law, but also to a policy of absorbing men too sick to work underground in supernumerary posts above ground. The "rationalization" of the work force did not begin until 1965 when General René Barrientos, who had seized power after the November 4, 1964 rebellion when Paz was unseated by the combined action of workers and students, sent troops into the mines in May.

The decade of the sixties was a time for the attack on the nationalized mines from managerial and government leaders as well as from workers. From the time of nationalization to 1965, the mines had lost $106,000,000, a figure partly inflated by fiscal manipulation but accurate enough to demoralize the operation of the mines (Arce 1965:17). Labor costs had gone up from US$0.70 a pound in 1952 to US$1.29 in 1960. United States critics such as Stokes (1963) and Zondag (1966) blame worker inefficiency for the increase of costs. In defense of workers, Canelas (1966:43) pointed to the Ford, Bacon, and Davis, Inc. report (1956), which showed that, despite reduction in overall figures for refined exported tin, there was an increase of 30 percent of gross mineral extracted in the first five years of nationalization. He pointed out that men in Catavi, who had turned out 1.22 tons per *mita* [work shift] in 1950, were turning out 1.31 tons per *mita* in 1955, and there was an overall production increase of 1,052,405 tons of crude ore in 1950 to 1,459,389 tons in 1955. The declining production noted by Stokes, who used figures on refined mineral to prove his case, was due to the fact that it required ten meters of advance to extract a ton in 1960, in comparison with one meter in 1950. The failure to explore new tunnels and declining administrative efficiency were blamed for this.

Federico Escobar, the secretary general of Siglo XX-Catavi's union and head of worker control, attacked the administration for having benefited Patiño, one of the former owners, more than the workers in the course of nationalization. Bedregal, then president of COMIBOL, countered the attack by claiming that COMIBOL was crippled by world market prices which had dropped severely in the post-Korean war period. The United States had taken advantage of the nationalization of mines to break its contracts with the former companies which were pegged at the high wartime price of US$1.83 per pound of refined tin and reset their price at US$0.90. He tried to enlist the support of labor with his statement that:

Nationalization of the mines does not have as an object only the betterment of the conditions of work and of the life of the miner, but also the entire transformation· of the economic and social conditions of the Bolivian nation (Bedregal 1959:14).

His appeal to nationalism in an attempt to overcome the developing class antagonisms in the mine is summed up in the position that:

In the natural order of political priorities, first is the country and then unionism; first is the national liberation and then the liberation of the working classes. If one insists on altering this nationalist order of priorities, believing that the union can earn when the nation is losing, we have confronted the interest of the workers to the interests of the nation as a community weak and irresponsible; that is, we have added the new forces of the proletariat to the old forces of the counterrevolution.

Labor did not buy this position and advised the management of their discontent by calling a strike. Later, Bedregal tried a frontal attack on labor with the report of a national investigation commission's summary of the damage caused by the union. The report (Comisión Investigadora Nacional 1965) arrived at a sum of US$45,076,718.29 with the following items included:

Cost of *Control Obrero* and directors	$5,604,725.29
Loss of production by directors of unions failing to attend jobs	8,333,063.40
Loss for excess workers on surface	15,813,723.19
Cost of strikes	13,187,942.32
Cost for activities during disputes	47,944.19
Debts of FSTMB	350,552.58

Debts of union leaders	$295,113.38
Debts of workers	1,315,618.00
Debts of clubs	128,036.03

Assessing this balance sheet, one can see that labor was charged for all the damages caused by the failure of the industry to settle labor disputes. In addition, one can clearly see the dependency that trade unions had fallen into, relying on income from the administration to maintain them in power.

While both sides in the attack on COMIBOL used the Ford, Bacon, and Davis, Inc. report (1956) to bolster their claims, the conclusions censure both low worker productivity and technicians' failure, but with the target being managerial inefficiency in overcoming these pitfalls. Arce, an engineer in Patiño mines, pointed to the nub of the technological problem in nationalized mines stating (1965:15) that "a fiscal administration cannot carry out risks of long-range exploration" since they are constantly subjected to criticism and review, oftentimes by men who had little or no knowledge of mining. The resulting policy in the mines was one of intensive exploitation of existing reserves, a point most of the workers made to me on the basis of their immediate experience. Arce's recommendation was that there should be holding companies of *Sociedades Anonimas* which were decentralized, with directorates including workers to "create a spirit of belonging between workers and employers that would reinforce efficiency and production by both healthy and constructive competition."

Despite the attack from both management and labor on the policies of COMIBOL, both sides were dedicated to vindicating the process of nationalization and preventing the mines from falling back into private hands. In part this was due to self-interest. The union leadership had benefited in the 1952 populist period, when unions had a greater recognition and opportunity to benefit financially under nationalized restraints which were more subject to populist pressures and more willing to invest in cooptation funds. Management benefited in the very position they occupied in replacing previous foreign incumbents at technical and managerial levels. These vested interests made nationalization an irreversible process. Neither the government nor the military attacked COMIBOL because they were using it as their own private purse, as one miner said in the congress at Siglo XX-Catavi in 1970.

The problem was to overcome the lack of confidence of the workers in nationalization. The thesis worked out by the political commission at Siglo XX-Catavi pointed to the fact that COMIBOL "as inheritor of the *rosca* [oligarchy of tin barons] has constituted a true superstate over the blood of the workers, limiting the role of the workers to produce and obey." But it attributed this failure to a false nationalization in which the middle class maintained control of the decision-making apparatus and continued as subservients of the international private capitalists. The union "line" became one of splitting the economic and political consequences of nationalization. This was expressed by an aspiring candidate for union office at the San José union meeting:

I believe that nationalization of mines and of Gulf is a positive step for the Bolivian people and for the liberation of Latin American countries, but it is a negative step economically because the world market is controlled now by imperialism . . . Who fixes the prices? It is no more than the imperialists who are the great monopolists. . . . Nationalizations are positive from a political point of view, but from an economic point of view we do not control the world market.

One of the theoreticians from the Universidad Mayor de San Andrés who was called upon to give a course in the union of San José gave a Marxist class analysis of nationalization and its failure:

COMIBOL does not benefit the worker because it is not in the hands of the workers. The passage of property from private hands to the state only means that the same internal relations continue. State capitalism produces a bureaucracy in conformity with administrators, superintendents who belong to the bourgeois class. This bourgeoisie has a self-interest in the company. The bourgeoisie is antinational.

He went on to point out that the bourgeoisie is not a great homogeneous block but has internal contradictions that the working class must learn to take advantage of. While nationalization benefits one sector of the bourgeoisie by giving them more possibilities of work and earning money, it disfavors another group, the commercial sector, because many *gringos* leave, and they lose many dollars in the sale of whisky, good clothing, and other luxuries.

   In analyzing the failure of nationalization in the brief period of revitalization of the union movement from the XIVth Congress of Miners in April 1970 until the Banzer coup of August 1971, union leaders pointed to the error of letting COMIBOL fall into the hands of "the politicians of turn, the bourgeois bureaucrats, and the military" and the necessity of regaining worker control to ensure the gains made by the revolution. During this period, the union started an all-out drive to reestablish wages at the pre-Barrientos level and cut down bureaucratic expenditures in order to finance labor's demands. They pointed out that COMIBOL personnel in the La Paz central office increased from 265 in 1954 to 475 in 1970, with administrative employees earning up to one hundred times as much as interior workers. Expenditures for the central office were US$2,750,000 per year, without counting funds for purchases that never arrived in the mines. Lechin summarized the case in a report to the delegates on September 29, 1972: "There is no possibility for a worker to enter in the mine to produce and leave his lungs there, but there is to increase the bureaucracy. For this there is no limit. There we have to get rid of the parasites" (tape recording). He called for the workers to manage the funds they contributed to the social security and the reinstatement of worker control with the right of veto.

A week later, and only twelve days after the first anniversary of his September 26, 1969 coup, Ovando had to yield the presidency to Torres after Miranda made a bid for power that failed. One of his first moves to coalesce the waning labor support of his predecessor was to increase wages. Contract workers were still dissatisfied, but Torres promised to give more support to the unions, and so the miners rallied around him when Banzer made the first of his abortive moves to unseat him in January 1971.

In a move to gain greater worker contribution to production, Torres proposed a plan for coparticipation in nationalized industries. In theory, coparticipation was to mean a "substitution of exclusive authority of the employer by the collective authority of all those who take part in production." However, the degree of entry by workers was not explicitly stated (Andrade 1971). The Bolivian Petroleum Company (YPFB) and the National Housing Cooperative (CONAVI) accepted the proposal as presented immediately. The FSTMB made it a central point for discussion in the popular assembly that opened on May 1, 1971. The proposal was designed to gain greater cooperation from the workers in raising production; but since they lacked a veto power, the miners considered it a company ploy.

The assembly included representatives of most of the organized segments of labor except for the peasants, whose representatives were considered either too much subject to government control or too far left,[2] and for party representatives from the Workers' Party of Bolivia (POR), the Communist Party of Bolivia (PCB–Moscow line), the Left National Revolutionary Party (PRIN), and the National Revolutionary Movement (MNR), as well as some student representatives of the Left Revolutionary Movement (MIR) and the Christian Revolutionary Democrats (DCR), In the discussions, the union representatives of the FSTMB dominated proceedings. They differentiated coparticipation from worker control in that they proposed to work "from below to above rather than the reverse," as had occurred in the early years of nationalization when only top leaders entered the councils. They demanded that a majority of the representation in the council of workers and managers should be labor, and they demanded that the president of COMIBOL should be chosen by the directors of COMIBOL from a list drawn up by the

[2]   The Union of Poor Campesinos (UCAPO) was refused a seat in the Popular Assembly along with some unions of *campesinos* considered to be dominated by the government.

directorate. COMIBOL rejected these two proposals and called for the president to be named by the executive power in a council of ministers from a list presented by COMIBOL. The ultimate aim of coparticipation as envisioned in the assembly was "the social property of the means of production" (Andrade 1971).

The duties drawn up by the FSTMB and presented to the popular assembly were more specific than those included in the 1953 decree for worker control:

1. Attend with voice and vote in the directors' meetings;

2. Inform themselves of all aspects relating to activities of the company, such as plans, projects for exploitation of minerals, reforms of administrative structures, costs, accounting, commercialization, financing, evaluation, and control of growth of these plans and works without any limitation;

3. Take into account contracts of purchases, local contracts, transportations and to prove to themselves that the prices, qualities, and conditions are the most favorable that can be obtained;

4. Control the distribution of articles in the *pulperia* and shop in the interests of avoiding favoritism;

5. Interview for the hiring and firing of workers;

6. Control and intervene in the increases and modifications of day work of personnel and transfer of workers and employees.

The FSTMB combined its presentation of demands with an attack on the administration of COMIBOL by generals. They pointed out that before the Barrientos regime began, when the president of the company was civilian, the bureaucracy cost US$40,000, and after that the costs rose to US$400,000 as the presidency became occupied by the military. They asked that the administration seek a new market for minerals in the socialist countries. Lora (1972:84) summed up the contrast between worker control and coparticipation, stating that while the first was individual and bureaucratic, coparticipation was collective and exercised by the working class itself. The contradiction in function between that of vigilance over the operation of management and participation in the administration as coequals that I pointed to above remained implicit in the new plan.

The Left was divided on the importance of the assembly and its major proposal for coparticipation. While some called it "a symphony of the Left" (*Presencia* 1971) others accused it of being reformist in orientation and self-seeking (Lora 1972:16).

The Banzer coup makes any speculation as to how coparticipation would have worked out an academic issue. However, the reaction of the rank and file in the period when the plan was still being discussed in July of 1971 revealed a lack of confidence in the labor leadership and a fear of their resurgence of the elitism that characterized the labor movement in the cogovernment period. Rank-and-file leaders in San José mine broke up a meeting scheduled for a discussion of the plan when I visited that center in July 1971. They resented the fact that Juan Lechín, who was scheduled to appear and explain the new measure, had not come; and many expressed suspicion of both local and national leaders and their motivation for implementing the plan before many of the concrete problems of contract prices and incentives had been ironed out. The heritage of corruption from the period of cooptation had born its harvest of mistrust.

Bolivia's experience with worker participation reveals the contradictions implicit in any compromise form of entry into management short of a socialist reorganization of the aims and structures of industrial enterprises. However, this should not imply that such movements should not be undertaken. Many of the worker control representatives rose to the occasion and gained enough entry into the administrative process to shake up the bureaucratic process thoroughly and to threaten its usurpation of control over the lives of thousands of workers. Worker control succeeded in establishing some of the minimal conditions for living and working in mining encampments that had, under the old management, reduced workers to bestial levels. For the first time they questioned the premise of production geared to meeting external demands and lacking even minimal interest in the lives and welfare of the men and women who produced the wealth. In the early years of nationalization, miners did produce more ores, although these yielded less refined metal than before. Poor administration and ineffective technical control were probably as much, or more, responsible for declining productivity in later years as lack of discipline in labor.

As for the criterion of self-determination for judging Bolivia's experience with participation in the tin-mining industry, I felt that, in the accounts miners gave and in the reports I have read on the experience in the fifties and sixties, there was a growing awareness of the need for further exploration and capitalization; but these demands were never channeled through the worker control representatives. Many workers have told me of the failure of the administration to open new shafts. They respected the ability of some of the old foreign technicians and felt that the demagoguery of nationalist leaders inhibited the efficient exploitation of the mines. Their growing alienation from the administration of COMIBOL caused them to resist yielding information about veins they knew existed. However, these demands for opening up new shafts and providing the equipment to work effectively were not publicly aired. Their watchdog function was simply a reversal of the Robin Hood role; the administration was still the owner, they were still the underdog, although they patrolled the streets of the managerial elite instead of stealing from them.

One could probably make a good case for decline in efficiency in the nationalized mines. In the old *pirkin* system of exploitation favored in the time of the *rosca*, the worker was paid for the mineral content of what he produced. He was highly motivated to use all his ingenuity and senses to work the veins. Miners develop an eye and a taste for where the veins are. Some even explore the face of a newly blasted area with their tongues to sense the location of the vein. Under the private companies, some could get fairly high returns, and they exploited their bodies and souls, which they sold to the devil,[3] in the desire to find the metal. After nationalization they were paid in relation to brute loads, a fairer system from an overall perspective, but one that failed to mobilize the total involvement of the miners as the old system had done. In the *pirkin* system, self-exploitation was greater, but workers reported a greater sense of adventure. They followed the veins of metal without too much concern for organizing tunnels and channels of entry and exit, and they profited in terms of the value of the ore.

Worker participation cannot be conceived of as a solution for the class struggle or as the achievement of socialist aims. It is only a prelude to such victories that at best can provide an arena where workers can gain the experience necessary to gain full control over their destiny in the future. Trade union movements too often bog down in bread-and-butter questions. Even worse, they generate alienation not only against the owners of industry but against the work itself. This serves to minimize the sense of social participation in productivity that would provide the basis for a socialist economy. With a division of labor between trade unions and worker councils, the former could retain the function of preventing the exploitation of workers and attending to their economic concerns, while the latter could enter into the transformation of administration into a concern with the wider interest of the community. The failure to maintain this division of functions minimized the effectiveness of both worker activities during the populist period of nationalization.

Vanek envisions a democratic form of socialist enterprise achieved through a modified market controlled system to avoid the bureaucratic apparatus of the Soviet state. He does not, however, go into the contradictions that still exist in a production system part free market and part planned. These contradictions are just now rising to the surface as inflation, unemployment, and inadequate incomes for most workers in Yugoslavia are stirring up worker resentment; and this is exacerbated by the high life-style of some management representatives who have profited from the enterprises (*New York Times* 1972). Latin American countries must work out their own model for worker participation in administration whether prior to or after a revolutionary transformation of structures.

---

[3]   I have summarized rituals and beliefs concerning the devil, or Supay, a pre-Conquest hill spirit, in "Devils, witches and sudden death" (Nash 1972).

Worker participation shifts the workers' perspectives from a concern with the class struggle to an interest in the division of labor. It makes postrevolutionary decisions a priority before the revolution. For the Bolivian rank and file during the revival of interest in the issue when the popular assembly was convening in June and July 1972, it seemed to indicate a concern with the division of spoils rather than a reconstruction of their role in industrial production. Without careful planning and preparation for this phase, the experience can end in the frustration that would defeat ultimate aims.

REFERENCES

ANAYO, RICARDO
  1952   *Nacionalización de las minas de Bolivia*. Cochabamba: Imprenta Universal.
ANDRADE, CARLOS
  1971   Article in *Presencia*. August 8, 1971.
ARCE, ROBERTO
  1965   *Recomendaciónes para la rehabilitación de la industria minera*. La Paz.
BEDREGAL, GUILLERMO
  1959   *Nacionalización y la responsibilidad del sindicato*. La Paz.
  1963   *COMIBOL: una verdad*. La Paz: Departamento de Relaciones Pública.
CANELAS, AMADO
  1963   *Nacionalización de las minas de Bolivia: historia de una frustración*. La Paz: Altiplano.
  1966   *Mito y realidad de la Corporación Minera de Bolivia, COMIBOL*. La Paz: Los Amigos del Libro.
COMISIÓN INVESTIGADORA NACIONAL
  1965   *Daño y costos del sindicalismo a COMIBOL*. Informe 4. La Paz.
Control Obrero
  1961   *Control Obrero* 8. August.
FORD, BACON, AND DAVIS, INCORPORATED
  1956   *Report on the mining industry of Bolivia*, nine volumes. Volume one: *Summary*; volume two: *Significant aspects of the Bolivian Mining Industry*. La Paz: Ministry of Mines and Petroleum.
GRAMSCI, ANTONIO
  1957   *The modern prince and other writings*. New York: International.
LORA, GUILLERMO
  1972   *Bolivia: de la Asamblea Popular al Golpe del 21 de agosto*. Santiago, Chile.
NASH, JUNE
  1972   Devils, witches and sudden death. *Natural History Magazine* 81(3): 52–58.
New York Times
  1972   Article in *New York Times*. November 18.
Presencia
  1971   Article in *Presencia*. August 8.
RUIZ GONZALES, RENÉ
  1965   *La administración empirica de las minas naciónalizadas*. La Paz.

SELSEF, JORGE
   1970   *Participación de los trabajadores en la gestión ecónomica.* Buenos Aires: Ediciones Librero.
STOKES, WM. S.
   1963   "The *contraproducente* consequences of the foreign aid program on Bolivia," in *The new argument in economics: the public vs. the private sector.* Edited by H. Schoeck and J. Wiggin. New York: Van Nostrand.
VANEK, JAROSLAV
   1971   *La economia de participación: hipótesis evolucionista y estrategia para el desarrollo.* Lima: Instituto de Estudios Peruanos.
   1974   *The participatory economy: an evolutionary hypothesis and a strategy for development.* Ithaca: Cornell University Press.
ZONDAG, CORNELIUS
   1966   *The Bolivian economy 1952–65: the revolution and its aftermath.* New York: Praeger.

PART FOUR

*Population, Migration,
and Urbanization*

Social Demography and the Anthropologist

WILLIAM E. BERTRAND

Editors' Note: Important new directions have been taken in studies of human demography in Latin America. We asked Dr. Bertrand to write a review article; his paper serves as an introduction to the others included here.

In recent academic and social history the term *population* has been closely related to the term *problem*. The United Nations, in choosing population as the organizing theme for its deliberations on world problems in 1973, underscored its importance in the global enterprise. It would be an understatement to say that population trends are an important and very active topic in the world today.

The timeliness of the topic has led to heavy investment on the part of United States foundations and academic institutions in an effort to stimulate research and training in related areas. As a result of this financial impetus, or, to be fair, because other scholars had suddenly become aware of the potential impact of the processes of mortality, natality, and migration in human systems, the number of interested scholars suddenly increased. What had been the domain of the relatively few formal demographers expanded to include sociologists, economists, social psychologists, and a few anthropologists.

To be sure, the conflict about the relative importance and ultimate direct of population trends is far from over. On the one hand we have the dire empirical models (Meadows, Meadows et al. 1972) predicting ecodisaster in spite of whatever modern man can accomplish. In response to this kind of argument some social scientists from less-developed countries have suggested alternative models with somewhat less calamitous consequences, and some possible solutions (Kaplan 1974). Whatever the outcome of this series of debates at the scientific political level it is certain that population studies, in one form or another, will be with us for some time.

POPULATION AND THE ANDEAN COUNTRIES

Latin America, with its high crude birth rate, changing patterns of morbidity and mortality, and increasing levels of both internal and external migration, has been a special concern of students of demography. As a special case, the peoples that inhabit a few northern Andean countries present the scholar with a wide range of population-related problems. The great cultural and geographic diversity found in these countries is a major reason for their interest to the student of demography. From the isolated Indian groups in the Andean highlands, where overcropped and eroded land makes subsistence a problem for the increasing numbers of inhabitants, to the hyperurban masses of Caracas, Quito, and Bogotá the full range of population questions is in evidence. Answers to questions such as high birth rates, exploding central cities, and resultant socioeconomic pressures on resources are of primary interest to governments in the region.

   The diversity of problems, combined with the necessity for immediate solutions and availability of funds, has had the effect of making population an important area of research throughout South America. Scholars trained in the fields of demography and sociology are noticed in increasing numbers in the continent and increasing amounts of valuable demographic information are being produced. There is, however, a lack of understanding, within social science and at the political level, of how the demographic equation can be translated into useful information for developmental purposes. What does a high crude birth rate mean in the campo, in the *tugurio*, in the factory?

ENTER THE ANTHROPOLOGIST

I have noted that until very recently the study of populations has been confined to the formal demographer, the people statistician, and the sociologist. They regard the anthropologist as somewhat lost in his Indian tribes and the case-study method. The interdisciplinary barrier is such that in two comprehensive reviews of social science and population topics no reference is made to the field of anthropology (Elizaga 1972; Macisco 1972). At the same time the authors point out one of the shortcomings of the field of demography in Latin America as being a "lack of a comprehensive theory or systematic reference framework for the orientation, organization, and evaluation of investigations" (Elizaga 1972:122).

   The formal demographer, using as his primary data material from censuses, and the sociologist, working from survey information, have been inundated with quantities of statistical information. My interpretation of their concern with a lack of comprehensive theoretical frameworks within which much of the statistical information could be ordered is that qualitative cultural-based information is lacking. The "systematic reference framework" referred to by Elizaga is essentially a series of premises which can stand across cultures and geographic boundaries. It is precisely in this part of the social system that the anthropologist can provide a contribution to the study of populations.

What do the various death and birth rates mean in social terms? How can migration be realistically interpreted in a manner which indicates to policy makers the dynamics behind the decision to change life-styles and residential patterns? Such questions confronting the social scientist are often best answered, or at least investigated in depth, by the anthropologist.

If we conceptualize the study of demography as covering the vital processes of mortality, natality, and migration, and look at the sources of information which in effect define the different social sciences the domain of the anthropologist becomes clearer. Below is a formal representation of the traditional discipline matrix expressed in terms of research methods and unit of observation utilized.

Formal demography: Census data
Sociology: Survey data
Anthropology: Case and community studies
Psychology: Individual observation

From the quantities of data generated by sociologists, demographers, and other collectors of various kinds of statistics the anthropologist should take his clues. The variations in birth or migration rates provide strong hints as to where cultural factors may be affecting life processes. Once these areas have been identified the anthropologist-demographer can focus on relevant sociocultural factors. It should be noted, however, that to do an adequate job in these subject areas the anthropologist must extend his methodological abilities so as to become familiar with the techniques and methods of the demographer and sociologist. This crossing of disciplinary lines, while always difficult in the halls of tradition-bound academia, is a necessity if the anthropologist is to make a useful contribution to the study of population. Without the ability to understand and properly utilize more-quantitative methods, anthropology must remain content to produce interesting monographs of dubious impact or importance. The qualitative information must be integrated with the quantitative to understand the importance and relevance of its impact at the national or regional level.

It should also be noted that this field of endeavor falls clearly in the realm of applied anthropology and the scholar who does not wish to taint himself with problems of the real world should settle for a more traditional approach to research. Particularly for citizens of the involved countries the action-research or "applied" label means that their relationship to degree-granting institutions in the United States may become strained. For the United States researcher the "applied" label can result in a kind of disciplinary isolation with resultant difficulties in achieving the academic rewards so well socialized into the aspiring graduate student. Since professional training at the graduate level is extremely limited in institutions in the northern Andean countries, the researcher who wishes to remain a legitimate "academic" should consider these potential difficulties. It should be mentioned however that there appears to be a significant shift in the attitude of major United States and European degree-granting institutions toward more applied training, especially in the area of population problems.

The anthropologist who chooses to be the innovator and move into a new problem area must also run the risk of all who produce information with potential value for decision makers. He must accept responsibility for his findings and view their potential for disrupting the social fabric on which he is reporting. For the anthropologist, who has a traditional commitment and closeness to the people he studies, the question of "value freedom" and ultimate impact of published information is a serious one. Extra care should be exercised in reporting only the most salient and valid of observations and the researcher should avoid speculation or unsupported generalizations. As a final threat the anthropologist who enters into the realm of social demography should expect sharp criticism from his colleagues, the demographer and sociologist. They will show a marked reluctance to admit the case study to the world of X^2 and life tables.

For the brave soul who does enter into the subject area of population the potential for useful discovery is a field of recognized importance with a demonstrated need for anthropological methods. The availability of relatively sophisticated census and survey data makes the generalization of findings, the leap from community to society, a possibility. Real improvement in methods and techniques is one of the promises that population studies hold out for the anthropologist.

The countries of South America provide a fascinating opportunity for the social anthropologist interested in demographic questions to do important and potentially useful work. The variety of cultural, racial, geographic, and economic conditions present in the area affords the researcher with virtually unlimited combinations for cross-cultural and comparative study. The examples of such studies collected in this volume are representative of several important topics and different research styles. They represent a sound base for arguing the value of contributions from anthropology in the development of a science of population.

Scrimshaw's paper is a superb combination of traditional anthropological techniques and methods from demography and sociology. García and Blumberg deal with the utility of sound sociocultural data in planning and demonstrate how the lack of it can short-circuit even the most prudent and well-prepared efforts. Finally, the value of viewing a cultural system as a complete entity in trying to interpret specific demographic features or observed reactions of different populations to economic and cultural stimuli is established in Richardson's paper.

THE PAPERS

Scrimshaw, with her complete and ambitious study of migration to Guayaquil, Ecuador, touches on two themes of importance, fertility and migration. By combining survey sampling techniques with intensive fieldwork she is able to offer definitive, well-documented answers to three research questions with specific implications for population policy. First she documents the lack of difference between the recent migrant's fertility and that of his urban counterpart. This phenomenon appears to be caused by the rapid assimilation of urban values by the young childless migrants. Scrimshaw establishes a motivating factor behind the move from country to city as being a desire for more education for the migrants' offspring. While these and other findings in Scrimshaw's paper provide useful data to the student of migration, it is her sound methodological presentation that makes her paper a significant step in legitimizing the anthropologist as an important contributor to social demography.

In their study of the unplanned consequences of sociocultural and ecological factors in a new city in Venezuela, García and Blumberg make a strong case for the utility of the research anthropologist in dealing with planned population changes. Their excellent summary of the contemporary positions of social scientists regarding squatter settlements can be translated into an indictment of planners and social scientists who have not done their sociocultural homework. The emergent view of the squatter slum migrant as an individual who is capable of making sound decisions in terms of optimizing his own position can be expanded to cover most urban areas in Latin America. This extremely well-documented work provides us with an example of how complete ethnographic and sociocultural information may be useful in preventing waste in investments specifically designed to meet the needs of changing population pressures.

Richardson, in analyzing the socioeconomic base of a seemingly divergent system of residential pattern and horizontal mobility, shows how cultural and historical perspectives can be used to explain this pattern. Again we see the utility of anthropological methodology in putting into focus a migration case which does not fit the classical pattern of migratory movements. By demonstrating the continuity of these movements with past economic patterns he offers considerable insight into how ethnohistorical factors can be used to explain current residential and migratory patterns.

While these papers represent an excellent cross-section of anthropological work directed toward questions of population it is important to cite others who have made important contributions to the field in the countries with which we are concerned. One of the first topics of interest to the anthropologist which had implications for the study of population was the urban *tugurio*. William Mangin, one of the pioneers of the study of *tugurios*, began what has been a continuing contribution to the anthropological literature in the early 1960's (Mangin 1963, 1967, 1970). Lisa Peattie (1968, 1971), in Venezuela, and Flinn (1968) and Cardona (1970), in Bogotá, added more information to the social anthropological perspective of the lower-class barrio. In Colombia the exemplary work of Virginia Gutiérrez de Pineda (1973) offered a sound base of information about the family. Ramiro Cardona (1970), from a slightly different perspective, had been extremely productive in wedding qualitative data with more statistical census-type information. These are just a few examples of the impressive beginnings of an anthropological base for population studies in the northern Andean countries.

The papers presented in the following section are another firm step toward establishing the utility of the anthropological perspective in contributing to the solution of man's problems. It is only with work such as this from all of the disciplines in the social sciences that a unified explanation of human behavior can be developed.

REFERENCES

CARDONA, RAMIRO, *editor*
  1970 *Migración y desarrollo urbano*. Bogotá: Asociación Colombiana de Facultades de Medicina (ASCOFAME).
ELIZAGA, J. C.
  1972 Internal migration: an overview. *International Migration Review* 6(2): 121–146.
FLINN, W. L.
  1968 The process of migration to a shantytown in Bogotá, Colombia. *Inter-American Economic Affairs* 22:77–88.
GUTIÉRREZ DE PINEDA, VIRGINIA
  1973 *Tradicionalismo y familia*. Bogotá: Asociación Colombiana de Facultades de Medicina (ASCOFAME).
KAPLAN, MARIOS
  1974 Hacia un modelo mundial alternativo. *Desarrollo* 8:27–39.

MACISCO, JOHN J., JR.
1972   Some directions for further research on internal migration in Latin America. *International Migration Review* 6(2):216–223.
MANGIN, WILLIAM
1963   Urbanization case in Peru. *Architectural Design* 33(8): 366–370.
1967   Latin American squatter settlements: a problem and a solution. *Latin American Research Review* 2(3):65–98.
1970   *Peasants in cities.* Boston: Houghton Mifflin.
MEADOWS, D. H., MEADOWS, D. L. *et al.*
1972   *The limits to growth: a report for the Club of Rome's project on the predicament of mankind.* New York: Universe.
PEATTIE, LISA
1968   *The view from the barrio.* Ann Arbor: University of Michigan Press.
1971   "The structural parameters of emerging life styles in Venezuela," in *The culture of poverty: a critique.* Edited by Eleanor B. Leacock, 285–298. New York: Simon and Schuster.

Families to the City: A Study of Changing Values, Fertility, and Socioeconomic Status Among Urban In-migrants

SUSAN C. SCRIMSHAW

> Since urbanization is traditionally considered a prime force leading toward lower fertility, it is of theoretical interest to study closely the prospect of fertility decline among recent migrants in the developing nations.
> J. J. MACISCO, JR., R. H. WELLER and L. F. BOUVIER[1]

The explosive growth in the rate of rural-urban migration in Latin America in the years since World War II has stimulated questions about the effects of urbanization on the fertility behavior of migrants (Kiser 1971:381; Stycos 1965:255). Urban in-migrants swell the cities as they pour in, but do they also contribute proportionately more children to the next generation than their urban-born neighbors? While the validity of the widely accepted belief that rural fertility generally is higher than urban fertility has been questioned (Robinson 1963:292), many researchers present strong cases for the existence of such a differential under most conditions (Carleton 1965:27; Davis and Casis 1946:199; United Nations 1961:91; Micklin 1969:481; Weller and Macisco 1970:3; Pool 1969:1; Mertens and Miro 1969:7).

This paper is based on a study supported by USAID (Contract Number 0113-26332-00, AID/csd-2479 Task Order Number 3B) and by the Ford Foundation. The research and findings are fully described in a report by Susan C. Scrimshaw entitled *Migration, urban living and the family: a study among residents in the* suburbios *and* tugurios *of Guayaquil, Ecuador* prepared for Division of Social and Administrative Sciences, International Institute for the Study of Human Reproduction, Columbia University.

While many people participated in the project, I would particularly like to acknowledge the contributions made by my colleagues at the Institute, most notably Dr. Samuel M. Wishik, Dr. Mario Jaramillo Gómez, and Dr. Moni Nag.

[1] In *The family in transition* (1969:285).

Given a rural-urban fertility differential, do rural immigrants to cities reproduce at higher "rural" rates, or do they adopt some or all of the urban attitudes and behavior which are related to the relatively lower urban fertility patterns? If the exposure to the urbanization process does affect the fertility or urban in-migrants, how soon after immigration is fertility behavior modified? Both Hawley (1969:25) and Goldberg (1959:214) indicate that while no precise knowledge is available, lowered fertility as a result of acculturation to the urban milieu occurs after about two generations.

Zarate (1967:1), however, found that fertility does not always correlate with length of urban residence. Speare, Speare, and Lin found the same situation in Taiwan after controlling for education (1972:10). For Thailand, Goldstein (1971:45) reports no "substantial difference in fertility levels between the migrant and non-migrant segments of the Thai population." Macisco, Weller, and Bouvier (1969:287) report that in Puerto Rico, migrants have *lower* fertility than nonmigrants. They state "following available evidence, there is no clear-cut answer to this question of possible fertility differentials between migrants and nonmigrants."

In a 1970 article, Weller and Macisco suggest that selective migration may provide an explanation for the relatively low fertility of urban in-migrants in some countries: "Perhaps migration itself is selective of low fertility." Similarly, Goldstein writes ". . . urban places either attract those with much lower fertility levels, or migrants fairly rapidly assimilate the general patterns of fertility behavior in the place of destination" (1971:35).

It is obvious that there is no answer applicable to all migrants to cities everywhere. It also is clear that research on the subject has barely begun. We need to understand a great deal more about the factors affecting fertility in rural and urban areas. Some apparent contradictions, such as evidence that some migrants have lower fertility than long-term urban dwellers, may be understood by looking at the values held by migrants and the values associated with low fertility. In the following pages we will summarize the findings of a study of urban in-migration and urban living in Guayaquil, Ecuador, which examined the questions raised in the preceding paragraphs:
1.   What values are involved in the relatively lower urban fertility as compared with the relatively higher rural fertility?
2.   What is the process of acquiring these values?
3.   How long does it take migrants to Guayaquil to acquire them?

METHODOLOGY

The data presented here were collected by a combination of methods:

intensive anthropological research followed by a randomly sampled survey of two thousand households in the squatter settlements (called *suburbios*) and central-city slums (called *tugurios*) of Guayaquil. In each household, all women between the ages of fifteen and forty-five and all men currently in a sexual union with women in that age range were interviewed on such subjects as housing; job histories; economic factors; union and fertility histories; knowledge, attitudes, and practice of contraception; and migration (if migrants). One hundred households in each of two rural villages (one coastal and one in the Ecuadorian Andes) also were interviewed.

This intensive–extensive methodology was designed to help the anthropologist cope with some of the problems of studying a large city, which cannot be approached in the same way as a small village, where every individual can become an acquaintance of the researcher. At the same time, it was believed that the usefulness and accuracy of survey research could be increased by designing and testing questions during the anthropological phase and combining the findings from both phases for a breadth and depth of understanding not available through either method alone.[2]

MIGRATION AND ADAPTATION TO THE CITY

Migrants[3] to Guayaquil come from the sierra (the Ecuadorian Andes) and the coast, and from cities over 10,000 and tiny villages (see Table 1). They are young (see Figure 1) and tend to be positively selected. Most men (65 percent) are single when they migrate, as are nearly half the women (48 percent). About a third of the women (36 percent) bring children with them, but most of those who do bring only one or two. They are motivated primarily by what are called "pull" factors: the perceived opportunities in the city for jobs, education, and "a better life." Significantly more men are motivated by jobs and the opportunity to advance, while women seek education and a better life ($P < 0.01$).

Beyond these obvious reasons emerging from the survey data, the migrants I knew, and especially the men, had a deep concern with making a better life for their children. Because schools in the rural areas may not even go through the primary grades, migrating to the city has definite advantages. Women who migrated alone often were motivated by boredom and restriction on their activities in the villages, and the complemen-

---

[2] See the Appendix for a more detailed description of the methodology.
[3] For the purposes of the study of adaptation of migrants only individuals who were fifteen or older at the time of migration were interviewed. There were 381 men and 850 women who fitted into this category.

tary attractions of independence and excitement in the city. Both men and women expected better health care in the cities.

Table 1.   Size of place of birth for migrants

	Men						Women						Row totals	
	Sierra		Coast		Oriente		Sierra		Coast		Oriente			
	Number	Percent	Number	Percent	Number	Percent	Number	Percent	Number	Percent	Number	Percent	Number	Percent
Cites over 10,000	77	20	70	18	–	–	115	14	230	27	–	–	492	40
Towns under 10,000	26	7	49	13	7	2	39	5	136	16	8	1	265	22
Rural	47	12	104	27	–	–	66	8	254	30	–	–	471	38
Column totals	150	39	223	59	7	2	220	26	620	73	8	1	1,228	100

Total   Men — 380 — 100 percent   Women — 848 — 100 percent

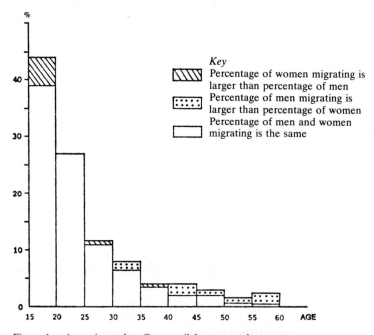

Figure 1.   Age migrated to Guayaquil for men and women

Migration in Latin America sometimes involves several steps, where migrants move first to a town or small nearby city before moving to a major city (Macisco n.d.:3). In the current study, 46 percent of the men and 32 percent of the women who came to Guayaquil had lived in a town or city other than their birthplace before migrating. Thus, less than half of all migrants had participated in step migration. This does not mean necessarily that most migrants came straight from their birthplace to reside in Guayaquil, with no previous experience beyond their home town. More than half of the men and women (69 and 56 percent respectively) had visited Guayaquil before migrating there. This finding bears out an impression gained during the intensive study that a great deal of visiting goes on between relatives in the city and the country.

These relatives also provided vital help for migrants during the adaptation process. Three-fourths (76 percent) of the men and two-thirds (66 percent) of the women knew someone in Guayaquil before migrating, and over half stayed with friends or relatives after arrival. This type of help appears to have produced a different migration pattern for some migrants to Guayaquil. In the classic pattern migrants usually move first to the central-city slums and only later to the squatter settlements, where they can build a home and hope eventually to own the land (Mangin 1967:68). While more than half of the migrants now living in the *suburbios* originally came by way of the *tugurios*, staying there from a few days to over eight years, as many as a third migrated directly to the *suburbios*, their adaptation facilitated by friends and relatives there to welcome them.

Adaptation to the city seemed rapid. New migrants were defined as having arrived during the past year or so and were pointed at because they "went out" less often. Before too long, however, they would demonstrate greater familiarity with the city life and move about more freely. The "country bumpkin" was a well-developed concept and no one liked to remain one for long.

The real evidence of adaptation lies in the comparison of migrants with long-term urban dwellers. Male migrants and long-term urban dwellers were similar in many characteristics related to economic status. There was no statistically significant difference between the types of jobs held by the two groups, nor for most of the variables used in constructing a socioeconomic scale. The three exceptions were related to housing. Significantly more migrants than nonmigrants had poorer housing (usually bamboo), slightly more living space, and no electricity ($P < 0.05$, $P < 0.01$, $P < 0.05$). Also fewer migrants had television sets than did nonmigrants.

The likely explanation for these differences is that significantly more migrants live in the recently settled areas of the *suburbios* ($P < 0.05$), where most of the houses are still bamboo, and electricity has not yet reached all homes. However, there is more space per family because the squatters have established as much space as possible for themselves. Thus, the recently built house of cheap materials (which later will be replaced by a better one) is correlated with more living space. The difference in television-set ownership could be due to the scarcity of electricity rather than to economic factors, as migrants and nonmigrants do not differ significantly in their overall economic situation. The newly settled *suburbio* areas may lack some amenities, but they usually represent a step up for those who move there because they have a chance to claim a piece of the swamp and build their own homes.

While there are few economic differences between migrants and nonmigrants, the two hundred rural dwellers were not as well off. The people in the coastal village appeared to be better off economically than the people in the sierra village, but both villages ranked below all the urban sample areas in terms of the variables used to estimate economic status. Nor did the migrants feel they had all come from the top economic strata in their villages or towns. A third felt they had been better off than their neighbors, 24 percent felt they had been "worse off," while the remainder felt their situation had been about average.

Migrants appear to be positively selected in terms of education. While the rural school system is reportedly far less complete and extensive than the urban (Erickson 1966:157), there is no statistically significant difference between the years of schooling for migrant and nonmigrant males ($P > 0.05$).

The data on education from the two rural villages support the idea that migrants, especially male migrants, as a group are more highly educated than the rural residents left behind. In both rural villages, 9 percent of the adults had received no formal schooling as compared with 5 percent of long-term urban dwellers and 7 percent of urban in-migrants. Ninety-seven percent of the sierra village residents and 98 percent of the coastal village residents had stopped their education after six grades or less, as compared with 67 percent of long-term urban dwellers and 91 percent of urban in-migrants. Because migrant and nonmigrant urban men showed no statistically significant difference, the figures on adult migrants are strongly influenced by the relatively lower educational status of migrant women. Three percent of the sierra village adults and 2 percent of the coastal village adults continued beyond the six primary grades, while 33 percent of urban nonmigrants and 9 percent of urban in-migrants continued their education. Less than one percent in both villages completed secondary school, while 6 percent of urban nonmigrants and 3 percent of migrants did. It is worth noting that a third of the migrants who entered seconday school completed it while only about a fifth of urban nonmigrants completed secondary school. Thus migrants clearly have more education than the rural norm.

There is a significant difference in reported educational levels for migrant and nonmigrant females ($P < 0.01$). This is not surprising in view of the relatively greater differences between male and female roles in the urban areas. The differences in educational levels of migrant males and females are statistically significant ($P < 0.02$), but the same is true for urban men and women ($P < 0.05$). This means that women in both the rural and urban settings have different (usually lower) educational levels than men, but that urban women have received significantly more education than migrant women, while men in both groups are roughly on a par. Given the low levels of education in rural areas, male migrants probably come from the more educated portion of the rural population. While some individuals acquire additional education after migrating (mostly on the secondary school level), comparisons with their reported years of schooling at time of migration reveal that most did not. However, of those who pursue further education in the city, proportionately more migrants persevere than among their long-term urban dweller counterparts.

Migrant and nonmigrant men's feelings about their current situation were also very similar. The majority of both groups described their current situation as "so-so," while 25 percent said it was "bad" and 13 percent said it was "good." Roughly two-thirds of both groups focused on the same reason for their "bad" or "so-so" current situations: "no money." Most, however, were optimists. Sixty-eight percent of both groups combined felt their situation would improve in the future. Most of the remainder felt things would remain the same (15 percent). A few felt things would get worse and the rest did not know.

The two groups of men also showed similar distribution in their assessment of what "a better life" meant. To most it was "everything one needs." To 14 percent it was "money," and to another 14 percent it was "having a job."

Male migrants and nonmigrants did have different answers to the question: "What is the problem which preoccupies you most at the moment?" ($P < 0.02$). While portions of both groups were concerned about their economic situations, proportionately more of the migrants were concerned with debts, while more of the nonmigrants had "family" problems.

There were no statistically significant differences between migrant men and urban nonmigrant men for the variables probably related to aspiration such as desire for change in their own lives and hopes for children.

As rural aspirations are similar to those held by migrant and nonmigrant men in the city, it appears that all the men studied had aspirations in common. However, the migrant men were probably in a better position to have a chance at attaining their aspirations than were rural men. By migrating, they had done something concrete to improve their lives.

It is, of course, difficult to predict the eventual success of migrants in attaining the upward mobility they desire. Looking retrospectively, the very fact that they do not differ economically from their nonmigrant urban neighbors means they have attained some degree of success. Both the data and the people themselves indicate that life is better in the city than in rural areas. The success of the migrants is evident by their rapid assimilation.

However, the nonmigrant urban dwellers to whom in-migrants are compared are themselves at or near the bottom, with little mobility. While the migrants have moved up on the socioeconomic scale simply by moving to the city, it is difficult to predict their success beyond that initial move upward. It may be that, in studying the slums of Guayaquil, we have caught them during one stage in their progress toward a higher socioeconomic status than their nonmigrant counterparts will attain — but it would take another large study to find out. Nevertheless, my feeling after a year of living and working in Ecuador is that the migrants will be more upwardly mobile than their nonmigrant neighbors in the *tugurios* and *suburbios*.

FERTILITY

Sexual Unions

Types of sexual union in Ecuador fall primarily into two categories: those formalized by both church and state (formal marriages) and *compromisos*, sexual unions recognized by family and neighbors in which a man is expected to take responsibility for his partner and their children. In a *compromiso* as in a formal marriage, the family unit is known by a composite name composed of the last names of both partners. Partners in a *compromiso* do not always live together. If the man already has another union he will divide his time (not always equally) between the two households. Where he can, he will set up each woman in a separate household. If that is impossible (usually for financial reasons) there are nearly always relatives for one of the women to live with.

In addition to *compromisos*, there are more casual alliances or affairs which may or may not later become *compromisos*. As almost anywhere in the world, there are also "one-night stands" and prostitution.

Women begin to enter sexual unions as early as ages twelve and thirteen. Nonmigrant women are significantly younger when they first enter a union than are migrant women ($P < 0.01$). The mean age at first union is 18.4 for nonmigrants and 19.6 for migrants. Since around half of the migrant women were single at migration, the process of migrating probably delayed their first union.

Men have early sexual experience but start unions at later ages than women.[4] While over half the men had had sexual experience by age

---

[4]   It must be kept in mind that the sample consisted of all women between the ages of fifteen and forty-five but was limited to men currently in unions with women in those ages. Thus the two groups are only roughly comparable when union patterns are examined.

fourteen, most were in their late teens or in their twenties when they began their first union.

One third of all first unions had ended by the time the woman was interviewed. Nearly half of all first unions were legal marriages, but most of those that ended (83 percent), ended in separation rather than divorce or widowhood. Over two-thirds of women whose first union had ended went on to form a second union. A smaller proportion (23 percent) of these second unions also ended, again mainly through separation.

Forty-one percent of those women ending their second union initiated another one. Forty-three percent of these unions ended, with separation once more the principal reason. Over half of these women went on to a fourth union, but the number is very small at that point, so that out of 2,522 women who had sexual unions, only 14 (0.6 percent) had as many as four. Of the total number of women between the ages of fifteen and forty-five studied, 18.6 percent had never entered a union.

Another way to look at union histories is to compare women by the length of time since the start of the first union. Fertility behavior among women with different lengths of time since the first union then can be compared. However, this measure does not take into account interruptions in unions. For example, if two women start their first unions at the same time, and one is later divorced but initiates a new union after two more years, then she will have been exposed to pregnancy two years less than the other woman who started her first union at the same time.

Dr. Samuel Wishik and three staff members of the International Institute for the Study of Human Reproduction have developed some alternate ways of analyzing union histories for polygynous men which can also be applied to women (Wishik et al. 1972). We call the measure of years since the start of the first union to the present the *alliance span*. To deal with the problem of separations during the alliance span we developed a measure called *years in alliance*. Years in alliance is defined as: "The number of years . . . engaged in any alliance . . . alliance span minus the total time periods spent in no alliance at all" (Wishik et al. 1972:12). Figure 2 shows years in alliance and alliance span for the women studied. It is clear that years in alliance is a more accurate measure of exposure to pregnancy, greatly facilitating comparisons of groups of women.

Years in alliance does differ for migrant and nonmigrant women. The mean for migrants is 11.31 years in alliance and for nonmigrants it is 10.08 years. Thus, while migrant women married later than nonmigrant women, they are also older. The mean age for migrant women is 31.6, while the mean for nonmigrant women is 27.3. The difference is statistically significant ($P < 0.01$).

The male sample cannot be treated in precisely the same manner as the female sample because only men who were in unions with women between the ages of fifteen and forty-five were interviewed in the first place.

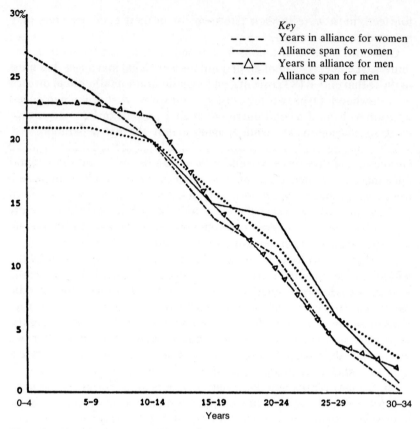

Figure 2.   Years in alliance and alliance span for men and women surveyed in Guayaquil

This was done in order to concentrate the effort on the study of fertility. Thus, men who never started unions or were not currently in unions were not interviewed. Of the men who were studied, 29 percent had ended their first union, primarly through separation. More men began a second union than had ended their first one. Obviously, some of these men were polygynous. As can be seen in Figure 2, years in alliance is a more accurate measure of years during which responsibility for pregnancy was possible for men, just as for women (at least within formal unions). However, in order to take polygyny into account, another measure is necessary, which we have called *alliance years*. Alliance years is defined as the: "Sum of woman-years of relationships a man has spent in all his alliances separately or concurrently. A man who maintains two wives concurrently for ten years would have twenty alliance years at the end of the tenth year" (Wishik et al. 1972:12). This is clearly a more accurate measure of potential "child-producing" time for men in societies where polygyny occurs.

When the union histories of men and women are compared, it is evident that men have more unions than women. When ever-married women (in order to make the two groups roughly comparable because only men who were currently in unions were interviewed) are compared with the men, only 24 percent of the women have had two unions, compared to 31 percent of the men. Proportionately fewer women have had three unions — 2 percent as compared with 8 percent for men. Only 1 percent of the women had had four unions, compared to 2 percent of the men. No women had had more than four unions, while a few men (1 percent) had.

Family Size and Fertility

Table 2 reports the incidence and outcome of first and subsequent pregnancies for the women studied in Guayaquil. For first pregnancies, admitted induced and spontaneous abortions are relatively low, as are stillbirths. Total pregnancy wastage is only 103 per 1000 live births. It is possible that some pregnancies were missed. As the data were collected with great care, it is doubtful, however, that more could have been obtained retrospectively, i.e. some women had forgotten completely one or more pregnancies. The only concealment I suspect is of some induced abortions. It is likely that some of the "spontaneous" abortions were actually induced. About 89 percent of all firstborn survived at time of interview. Subsequent pregnancies show a rise in the proportions of both admitted induced abortions and spontaneous abortions, while stillbirths and infant and child deaths remain fairly constant. It is clear that with each succeeding pregnancy, the chance that another child will not be a welcome addition to the family increases. The rising proportions of admitted induced and spontaneous abortions probably reflect this. After about the tenth pregnancy, the numbers become too small to permit reliable interpretation.

Table 3 is a summary table of mean pregnancies and mean living children by age for migrants and nonmigrants. It would appear at first that migrants have higher fertility than nonmigrants. While the mean pregnancies and living children for both groups as a whole differ by about one child (3.4 pregnancies and 2.6 living children for nonmigrants as opposed to 4.2 pregnancies and 3.6 living children for migrants), when the means are compared age group by age group the differences are slight. The apparent difference in overall fertility is thus created by the significant difference in the age-group distributions of the two groups of women discussed previously. The larger proportion of older migrants thus weights the means for pregnancies and living children when age is not considered. When analysis of covariance is performed with age at

Table 2.   Frequency and outcome of first and subsequent pregnancies for urban women

Pregnancy number	Total Number	Percent[a]	Induced abortion Number	Percent[b]	Spontaneous abortion Number	Percent[b]	Stillbirth Number	Percent[b]	Live birth Number	Percent[b]	Children dead since birth Number	Percent[c]
1	2,268	20.7	6	0.3	169	7.4	26	1.1	2,067	91.1	225	10.9
2	1,978	18.1	19	0.9	197	9.9	31	1.5	1,731	87.5	194	11.2
3	1,649	15.0	26	1.5	180	10.9	21	1.2	1,422	86.2	154	11.8
4	1,322	12.1	19	1.4	146	11.0	12	0.9	1,145	86.6	125	10.9
5	1,034	9.4	27	2.6	117	11.3	10	0.9	880	85.1	83	9.4
6	794	7.2	21	2.6	83	10.4	10	1.2	680	85.6	61	8.9
7	594	5.4	23	3.8	94	15.8	11	1.8	466	78.5	48	10.3
8	429	3.9	17	3.9	58	13.5	5	1.1	349	81.4	33	9.5
9	302	2.7	19	6.2	52	17.2	4	1.3	227	75.2	28	12.3
10	207	1.8	12	5.7	35	16.9	5	2.4	155	74.9	24	15.4
11	136	1.2	6	4.4	24	17.6	3	2.2	103	75.7	11	10.7
12	86	0.7	4	4.6	12	13.9	0	0.0	70	81.4	10	14.3
13	56	0.5	3	5.3	12	21.4	1	1.7	40	71.4	8	20.0
14	32	0.2	2	6.2	4	12.5	1	3.1	25	78.1	3	12.0
15	19	0.1	2	10.5	7	36.8	0	0.0	10	52.6	1	10.0
16	8	<0.1	1	12.5	3	37.5	1	12.5	3	37.5	0	0.0
17	5	<0.1	0	0.0	2	40.0	0	0.0	3	60.0	0	0.0
18	3	<0.1	1	33.3	2	66.6	0	0.0	0	0.0	0	0.0
19	3	<0.1	1	33.3	1	33.3	0	0.0	1	33.3	0	0.0
Total	10,925		209		1,198		141		9,377		1,008	
Percent[a]		99.8		1.9		10.9		1.2		85.8		10.7
Mean (N = 2,936)	3.7									3.2		

[a] = Percentage of total pregnancies.
[b] = Percentage of row total (i.e. percentage of 1st pregnancy, etc.).
[c] = Percentage of live births.

Table 3.   Mean number of pregnancies and of living children for migrant and nonmigrant women by age

Age	Nonmigrant Mean pregnancy	Mean living children	Migrant Mean pregnancy	Mean living children
Lowest–19	0.4	0.3	0.5	0.5
20–24	1.7	1.4	1.9	1.6
25–29	3.7	2.9	3.6	2.8
30–34	5.2	3.9	4.6	3.7
35–39	6.5	4.8	6.6	4.9
40+	6.9	5.1	7.1	5.4
Total	3.4	2.6	4.2	3.6

marriage and current age held constant, there is no statistically significant difference between migrants and nonmigrants in either the number of pregnancies or the current family size. While migrants marry slightly later, they average more years in alliance because they tend to be older. Again, when years in alliance are held constant, no significant differences in the numbers of pregnancies or family size are apparent.

Completed fertility for the population studied was about seven pregnancies, with about five children still alive. This turns out to be about two children more than the expressed ideal family size, discussed further on.

Table 4 summarizes number of "children ever fathered" reported by men, by alliance years and by age. The mean number of children ever fathered is slightly lower than the mean pregnancies for women in each age group. However, comparisons are difficult because it is doubtful that men can provide the details on pregnancy wastage and dead children that women can supply. In fact, the means for men more closely resemble the mean number of living children for women than they do the mean number of pregnancies.

Table 4. Children ever fathered by age of men and alliance years

Age	0–4	5–9	10–14	15–19	20–24	25–29	30–34	35–39	40–44	Total
–19	0.53	–	–	–	–	–	–	–	–	0.53
20–24	1.30	2.23	–	–	–	–	–	–	–	1.47
25–29	1.53	3.04	4.79	–	–	–	–	–	–	2.59
30–34	2.03	3.54	4.93	6.18	7.00	10.25	–	–	–	4.20
35–39	1.33	3.84	5.52	5.98	11.88	9.00	–	–	–	5.77
40–44	2.60	4.93	5.24	6.65	7.27	10.43	8.00	–	11.50	6.51
45–49	2.00	5.00	5.78	6.67	8.00	8.95	8.25	15.00	15.00	7.72
50–54	–	6.00	7.67	6.50	7.14	9.70	8.82	13.00	–	8.49
55–59	–	4.00	6.00	6.00	9.20	10.14	11.25	–	–	9.70
Total	1.46	3.37	5.26	6.34	8.24	9.56	9.50	13.67	12.67	4.76

Women's fertility has a definite age limit, while men's does not. Men go on to produce children so that men between the ages of fifty-five and fifty-nine have an average of 9.7 children (the few cases of men over fifty-nine were dropped). Thus, men apparently have more children on the average than do women. Statistically, this can happen only if some men never marry, and if other men have more than one spouse (simultaneously or sequentially). This is indeed the case in the population studied.

The fertility behavior of migrant and nonmigrant women has been discussed, but in a study of adaptation to urban values, the migrant or nonmigrant origin of the spouse is also potentially of significance.

In order to explore this further, the men and women interviewed were matched with their respective spouses and four types of couples designated: migrant men married to migrant women, migrant men married to nonmigrant women, nonmigrant men married to migrant women, and nonmigrant men married to nonmigrant women. After establishing that there were no significant differences in the number of pregnancies and living children among families in the various sample areas ($P > 0.05$), multiple stepwise regression[5] was performed, using the combined data from all sample areas for the four types of couples. The number of pregnancies and the number of living children in the *current* union were considered the dependent variables (each in a separate run). The independent variables included the four marriage types already described: the duration of the current union; economic status; aspirations; education; and knowledge, attitudes and use of contraception. Except for a very slight negative correlation between economic status and the dependent variables (0.037), none of the variables affected pregnancies or living children except the duration of the current union. This varied among the four marriage types (see Table 5). Migrants married to migrants had current unions about two years longer than the other three marriage types, which resembled each other very closely. They also had about one more child than the other three groups.

Table 5.   Table of adjusted means and standard errors for analysis of covariance using pregnancies in current union as the dependent variable

Treatment group[a]	Mean duration of union	Treatment mean[b]	Adjusted mean	Standard error adjusted
1	11.96	5.2086	4.5540	0.1899
2	9.92	4.1094	4.1279	0.1970
3	9.59	4.0814	4.2087	0.1700
4	9.69	4.0766	4.1730	0.0848

[a] 1 = Migrants "married" to migrants.
    2 = Migrant men "married" to nonmigrant women.
    3 = Nonmigrant men "married" to migrant women.
    4 = Nonmigrants "married" to nonmigrants.
[b] Mean number of pregnancies.

Analyses of covariance were performed to see if the differences in the number of pregnancies were significant when the duration of the current union was controlled for. In one case, the dependent variable was the number of pregnancies; in the second run, it was the number of living children. The covariates were duration of current union. As Table 5 shows, controlling for the duration of union eliminates any significant

[5]   All multivariate analyses were run by using the computer programs available in the Statistical Package for the Social Sciences (SPSS) and by the Biomedical Division of University of California at Los Angeles (BMD).

difference in the number of pregnancies among the four groups. The same held true when number of living children was considered.

Migrants "married" to migrants have probably been in their unions longer because three-fourths of them started their unions before migration. Migration evidently delayed the age of first union for those who migrated single. What is so surprising is that even those migrants who married while in their villages show no significant differences ($P > 0.05$) in fertility from the other three groups including long-term urban dwellers when the differences in length of union are adjusted for. That is very fast adaptation indeed, particularly because the data from the rural villages shows a mean family size of several children more than the urban family-size mean.

Similar analyses also were performed on the women alone, looking at their complete fertility histories. The regressions on the data for the women showed the same result as those for the couples: only duration (in this case years in alliance) had any effect on fertility.

The analysis of covariance again told the same story. Alternately using the number of pregnancies and the number of living children as dependent variables, and years in alliance as the covariate, no significant fertility differences between migrant and nonmigrant women existed. Aware that the age of onset of first union and the current ages varied for the two groups, we also ran the analysis using those variables as covariates. Again, there were no significant differences in the number of pregnancies or in family size.

SUMMARY AND CONCLUSIONS

Migrants from rural areas to Guayaquil in Ecuador appear to be a highly selected group. Most are young, and migrate single or before starting their families. They accommodate rapidly to the city, assisted by friends and relatives, so that as a group statistically they resemble long-term urban dwellers. For many accommodation appears to be a matter of a few years rather than a generation.

Their fertility is statistically equal to that of long-term urban dwellers when age and duration of union are held constant. This may be influenced by the intermarriage of migrants and nonmigrants, but as migrants married to each other show the same pattern it is doubtful. It appears more likely that migrants are an aspiring group who see the potential for the realization of some of their aspirations in urban values as probably related to comparatively low fertility.[6] The foremost such value men-

---

[6]   Urban fertility in Guayaquil is not low, at a complete fertility of about seven pregnancies with an average of five living children. However, rural fertility is at least two pregnancies higher, so that urban immigrants have altered their fertility behavior.

tioned in this study was aspiration for children's education. People felt their own lives would not change very much, but that their children had a chance for improvement through education. They also made a direct connection between the number of children they had and the extent to which they could educate them; fewer children could be sent farther through school. The economic advantages of fewer children were also perceived.

In the two rural villages studied, aspiration levels were high, but economic and educational levels were low, and possibilities for improving the situation were poor. Also low were the levels of knowledge of ways to prevent the occurrence of pregnancy within a union and acceptance of the concept of pregnancy prevention.

In the city, the available means of improving their situation were quickly perceived and utilized by migrants. Not only was this true for employment and educational opportunities, but migrants did not differ significantly from nonmigrants in their knowledge and use of contraception. Overall knowledge and use levels were relatively high (44 percent of the women used some form of contraception at some time, and 22 percent of the women are current users). Unfortunately, many of the methods used are fairly ineffective (such as rhythm and withdrawal), and the demand for acceptable means of preventing pregnancy is high (three-fourths of the women interviewed want no additional children). Nevertheless, urban dwellers manage to have fewer pregnancies than their rural counterparts.

On the basis of the evidence presented here, some answers to the questions posed in the beginning of this paper emerge. Some of the values leading to lower fertility are aspirations for children and improved economic status of the family. The city provides at least the hope of realizing these aspirations, as well as the means to limit fertility. Migrants adapt to the city rapidly, and have fertility patterns similar to the urban ones within the same generation.

APPENDIX: METHODOLOGY

Guayaquil is a tropical port city of approximately one million people located where the Daule and Babahoyo rivers meet to form the Guayas river, which empties into the Pacific Ocean 100 miles downstream.

The two areas that receive most of the migrants are shown on Map 1. The *tugurios*, or central-city slums, are in the heart of the business district, which extends westward from the river. There is a small transitional zone to the west of the *tugurios* containing some slum dwellings, and then the vast *suburbio* begins, crawling visibly further into the swamps and estuaries each year. The area in downtown Guayaquil between the *tugurios* and *suburbio* is mostly middle and lower upper-class housing. The very wealthy live in suburbs to the north.

The intensive phase of the project focused on the *suburbios.* I located a house in an area which is solid ground in the dry season, but within walking distance of the swamps still being settled. It was intermediate between the best and worst dwellings in the area.

In this setting, I conducted traditional ethnographic research through participant observation, interviews, and conversation. Many questions were tested for possible use in the survey. A total of sixty-five households were studied in January through May 1971.

On the basis of the intensive work, five questionnaires were designed and pretested:

1. Household: Basic questions on houshold composition, ages, occupations and education of household members, house type and ownership, household inventory, and exposure to mass media.

2. Migration (urban questionnaire): Administered to any individual who had arrived in Guayaquil at or after age fifteen. It included questions on situation at place of origin, reasons for, and circumstances of migration, expectation of changes the city would bring to his or her life, accommodation to the city, and current expectations and aspirations.

3. Male: Administered to males involved in a sexual union with a woman (or women) in the fifteen to forty-five-year age group. Questions were asked on job history, working hours, aspirations for self and for children, knowledge, attitudes and practice of contraception, fertility and sexual union histories, attitudes toward induced abortion, ideal family size, and feelings about children and *machismo*.

4. Female: For women between the ages of fifteen and forty-five. If, however, there was a girl under fifteen in a sexual union she also was interviewed. This questionnaire elicited information on nutrition and beliefs about food; food-buying habits; employment history; sexual union history; a detailed fertility history; knowledge, attitudes and practice of contraception; knowledge, attitudes, and use of family-planning clinics; female sterilization; induced abortion; and ideal family size.

5. Migration (rural questionnaire): Administered to household heads and teenagers in the villages in order to learn the extent of knowledge about Guayaquil, and to measure the feelings about migrating there.

The sample was drawn by Professor Albino Bocaz of Centro Latino Americano de Demografía (CELADE), Santiago, Chile, with the assistance of Ernesto Pinto Rojas. It did not involve the entire city of Guayaquil, as the upper and upper-middle classes were not part of the study population. The upper classes live mainly in a few exclusive neighborhoods, which were eliminated. The sample then was drawn in four areas:

1. The central-city slums (*tugurios*),
2. The *suburbios* settled at the time of the 1962 census,
3. The *suburbios* settled since the 1962 census, and
4. An intermediate zone between the *tugurios* and *suburbios*, which contained a few *tugurio*-type buildings.

The sixty-five families studied intensively also were interviewed as a special sample in order to see how they compared to a random sample and to compare what they would tell an interviewer with what I already knew about them. They "fit" well when compared to the large sample. The report on which this paper is based contains a comparison of data obtained intensively and extensively.

The number interviewed in each area was in proportion to the estimated population of the area. Households were revisited twice if eligible individuals were not at home when the first visit was made. The refusal rate for households was a low 1.65 percent. In all, 2,294 families were interviewed in the city. Slightly under a hundred families, also selected randomly, were interviewed in each village.

Interviewing began on September 13, 1971. There were six teams of five girls each, three full-time teams and three part-time teams. All of the blocks selected for the survey had been canvassed by November 14. Coding, key-punching, and verifying were completed by December 15.

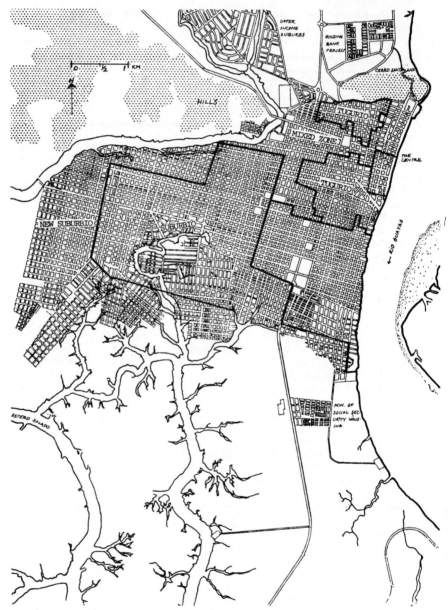

Map 1.   Plan of Guayaquil and sample zones for survey

REFERENCES

CARLETON, R. O.
1965 Fertility trends and differentials in Latin America. *Milbank Memorial Fund Quarterly* 43:27–29.
DAVIS, K., A. CASIS
1946 Urbanization in Latin America. *Milbank Memorial Fund Quarterly* 24(3):186–207.
ERICKSON, E. E.
1966 *Area handbook for Ecuador.* Washington, D.C.: U.S. Superintendent of Documents.
GOLDBERG, D.
1959 The fertility of two-generation urbanites. *Population Studies* 12(3):214–222.
GOLDSTEIN, S.
1971 *Interrelations between migration and fertility in population redistribution in Thailand.* Institute of Population Studies Research Report 5. Bangkok: Chulanlongkorn University.
HAWLEY, A. H.
1969 "Population growth and urbanization in developing countries." Paper presented at the National Academy of Sciences Woods Hole Conference, July 27–August 8.
KISER, C. V.
1971 Unresolved issues in research on fertility in Latin America. *Milbank Memorial Fund Quarterly* 49(3, part 1):379–388.
MACISCO, J. J., JR.
n.d. "Some thoughts on an analytical framework for rural to urban migration." Paper prepared for Centro Latino Americano de Demografia (CELADE), Santiago, Chile.
MACISCO, J. J. JR., R. H. WELLER, L. F. BOUVIER
1969 "Some general considerations on migration, urbanization, and fertility in Latin America," in *The family in transition: a round table conference sponsored by the John E. Fogarty International Center for Advanced Study in the Health Sciences, National Institutes of Health, Bethesda, Maryland, November 3–6. Forgarty International Center Proceedings* 3:285–297.
MANGIN, W.
1967 Latin American squatter settlements: a problem and a solution. *Latin American Research Review* 2(3):65–98.
MERTENS, W., C. A. MIRO
1969 *Influencia de algunas variables intermedias en el vivel y en las diferenciales de fecundidad urbana y rural de America Latina.* Santiago, Chile: Centro Latino Americano de Demografia (CELADE).
MICKLIN, M.
1969 Urban life and differential fertility: specification of an aspect of the theory of the demographic transition. *Sociological Quarterly* 10(4):480–500.
POOL, D. I.
1969 "The rural-urban fertility differential in Ghana." Paper presented at the General Conference of the International Union for the Scientific Study of Population, London, September.

ROBINSON, W. C.
  1963   Urbanization and fertility: the non-Western experience. *Milbank Memorial Fund Quarterly* 41:291–308.
SPEARE, A., JR., M. C. SPEARE, H.-S. LIN
  1972   "Urbanization, nonfamilial work, and fertility in Taiwan." Paper presented at the Annual Meeting of the Population Association of America, Toronto, April.
STYCOS, J. M.
  1965   Needed research in Latin American fertility: urbanization and fertility. *Milbank Memorial Fund Quarterly* 43(2):255–273.
UNITED NATIONS
  1961   "Demographic aspects of urbanization in Latin Amerca," in *Urbanization in Latin America.* Edited by P. Hauser, 91–115. Population Branch, United Nations. New York: International Documents Service.
WELLER, R. H., J. J. MACISCO, JR.
  1970   *Migration, aspirations for social mobility, and fertility in developing countries: suggestions for further research.* Providence, Rhode Island: Population Research and Training Center, Department of Sociology, Brown University.
WISHIK, S. M., K. H. CHEN, S. KLEIN, S. SCRIMSHAW
  1972   "The definition and measurement of male fertility." Paper presented at the Annual Meeting of the Population Association of America, Toronto, April.
ZARATE, A. O.
  1967   "Community of origin, migration and completed marital fertility in metropolitan Monterrey." Paper presented at the Annual Meeting of the Population Association of America, Cincinnati, April.

The Unplanned Ecology of a Planned Industrial City: The Case of Ciudad Guayana, Venezuela

MARÍA-PILAR GARCÍA and RAE LESSER BLUMBERG

Since 1961, a planned industrial city has been rising in a remote resource frontier region of Venezuela, hundreds of miles from the nearest large city. While its planners' efforts have been, relatively, highly successful concerning industrial development, in another aspect their plans have gone awry: Ciudad Guayana (Map 1) is growing in precisely the opposite compass direction than planned, and the distribution of its people in physical and social space bears little relationship to the master plan.

We are not attempting an indictment here of what may well be the best example of integrated urban and industrial planning in the Third World, but rather we are trying to understand why Ciudad Guayana is growing in the opposite compass direction to the one planned, and what the underlying factors of generalized importance are for urban planning anywhere in Latin America.

Basically, we shall argue that the planners did not appear to anticipate or affect the actual distribution of the city's lower-income population — its majority — because their models failed adequately to consider salient sociological, legal, and ecological factors — or the implications of their own policies for the spatial distribution of the poor. Based almost exclusively on easily quantifiable physical, industrial, and economic variables, the planners' models did not address such less precise factors as:

1. *Structural factors and social class.* Despite a thriving economic base, less than a third of the population has stable industrial employment.[1]

The authors express their appreciation to William L. Leeds for his constructive and helpful criticisms.
[1] Approximately 26 percent of the total economically active population and 30 percent of the employed economically active population worked in manufacturing in 1970, according to the July *Encuesta de hogares* (Ministerio de Fomento 1970).

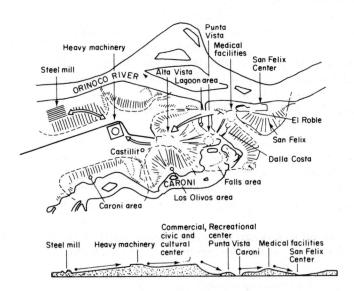

Map 1. Ciudad Guayana (reprinted from *Planning urban growth and regional development* [Rodwin et al. 1969], by permission of the M.I.T. Press, Cambridge, Massachusetts)

Moreover, structural unemployment is relatively high: in slack times it may rise to 15 or 20 percent.[2] Not surprisingly, at least half of the population of Ciudad Guayana must be classed as lower income.[3]

2. *Life-style and social relations.* As a consequence of structural instability and poverty, it would appear that the low-income people need housing without a fixed payment, stores that sell in small quantities and on credit, and access to the people who constitute their major source of economic opportunities — their fellow poor.

The first two factors involving a structurally marginal lower class are common to virtually any Third World city today — planned or unplanned. However, there are additional factors involved in the Ciudad Guayana situation which may be unique — just as there are sure to be in any other example. Nevertheless, these "unique" factors may contain generalizable elements, and are thus no less important to a broad understanding of the process of urban settlement. Here we shall discuss three.

3. *Legal factors.* (a) First and most important is the *Ley del Trabajo* [Law of Work] for the unionized industrial workers which compensates them for the time and transportation cost of their journey to work if the site of their employment is more than 1.25 miles from a populated center. (The steel mill and other industries providing the main employment are located considerably farther away, we may add.)[4] This law clearly reduces the need for industrial workers to live near their jobs. (b) A second law affecting settlement patterns is the *Ley de Bienhechurías* [Law of Home Improvements]. This law provides compensation to the owner of an expropriated property for any improvement he or she may have made. It means that if a person's shack is expropriated, one may come out with a

[2] The July 1970 *Encuesta de hogares* shows that 13.9 percent of Ciudad Guayana's economically active population was unemployed. However, this figure oscillated during the previous twelve months between 13.9 and 15.9 percent (Ministerio de Fomento 1970).
[3] We follow a frequent usage in Venezuela and consider Bolívares 1,000 ($235) as the upper limit to define "lower-income." The study *Mercavi 70* (Banco Nacional de Ahorro y Préstamo 1970) found that 54.2 percent of the families of Ciudad Guayana have a monthly income of Bolívares 1,000 or less. However, we should mention that the low-income groups may be considerably larger because the average figure tends to hide the following facts: (1) that the average family in Ciudad Guayana consisted of 5.5 persons and (2) that the data are for employed persons only. Unemployment in Ciudad Guayana averages around 15 percent of the economically active population but has risen to 20 percent in slack times. By considering these factors, Caminos, Turner, and Steffian (1969) presume that perhaps more than 80 percent of the population of Ciudad Guayana could be considered as lower class.
[4] The approximate distance from SIDOR-ALCASA (two of the main industries) to the farthest shacktowns on the eastern side is over eighteen miles. The average distance from SIDOR, the steel mill, to downtown San Félix is approximately fourteen miles.

large cash settlement. This makes expropriation more expensive and more rare than otherwise would be the case. Below, other legal factors will be discussed as well.

4. *Ecology*. The climate is so favorable that the most casually constructed shack suffices in the year-round mild, warm weather. Thus, with a minimum of effort and expense, squatters may build a shelter on invaded land. Furthermore, since the terrain is flat and the shape of the city long and narrow, large numbers of these "jerry-built" shacks might be expected to be highly visible. (In contrast, the planners were quite cognizant of ecological factors such as prevalent winds, terrain, and impact of the rivers which are of greater importance for the economic base.)

5. *Planners' housing policies*. Viewing the shacks (*ranchos*) as social cancers, and unsightly ones as well, Corporación Venezolana de Guayana (CVG), the public agency developing the city, virtually from the beginning *prohibited* their construction in the western half of the city where the *future* planned growth was targeted. In contrast, the small amounts of housing made available by the planners for the poor often proved unsuited to the life-style and housing needs of this structurally marginal group.[5]

The natural result of the above, we propose, has been to facilitate the city's growth to the east, in the direction opposite to its industrial base. In addition to a more detailed description and explanation of this result, we shall attempt also to identify a series of variables that we propose must be taken into account in future theories and policies of urban development wherever a large structurally marginal population may exist.

Correspondingly, this paper will be organized in three sections. The first part answers the questions "What and where is Ciudad Guayana and what are the planners trying to do?" The second part describes and attempts to explain the pattern of urban growth in opposition to the planners' models. The third summarizes the three main recent approaches toward urban development and housing for the poor in Latin America. Then, it focuses on the additional variables that, we propose, must be included if planning models are to influence successfully the pattern of settlement — and the chances of success — of a Third World urban population.

[5]   Other variables which may be of crucial importance in specific instances include: the local or national political situation, the nature of any local conflicts (e.g. ethnic, interinstitutional, etc.), the kind of planning model being used, and in general the kind of policies of the planning and government institutions and their willingness and ability to make them known to the people.

1. WHAT AND WHERE IS CIUDAD GUAYANA AND WHAT ARE THE PLANNERS TRYING TO DO?

A planned industrial city is being created out of the tropical forest and savanna of Venezuela's resource-rich Guayana region.[6] Ciudad Guayana is located at the confluence of the Orinoco and Caroní rivers. The Orinoco serves as the means of transportation of the industrial products to foreign markets, and the Caroní provides the hydroelectric potential necessary for the industrial plants. The city is 698 kilometers — about 420 miles — by road from Caracas, the capital city, and roughly 250 miles south of the metropolitan region of Barcelona-Puerto La Cruz, which is not only the largest urban complex in the eastern part of the country, but also the major port, trade, and service center for the entire area. The site was chosen to maximize the resource base for building an industrial city. The region of Guayana has extraordinary natural resources, such as rich, high-grade iron ore, hydroelectric potential, petroleum, natural gas, and a great variety of other mineral resources. With such abundance of resources and with good roads and the great Orinoco "highway" to the sea, Ciudad Guayana is admirably equipped to be a center for industry. As recently as 1950, the population of the future Ciudad Guayana was only 4,000. However, by the year 1961, when the planning of the city began, the population had reached 42,000 and by 1965 it had risen to 73,000. By 1970, its population was estimated as 142,000 and by 1972 it had risen to an estimated 175,000.[7]

On December 29, 1960, the administration of President Betancourt created a public corporation to develop the region of Guayana and to plan the physical, economic, and social development of the city of Ciudad Guayana. When the Corporación Venezolana de Guayana (CVG), in collaboration with planners from the Joint Center for Urban Studies of the Massachusetts Institute of Technology and Harvard University, initiated the planning of the city, there was already a series of separate settlements along an eighteen-mile corridor with an approximate population of over 40,000 people. At the western end of the site chosen for the new city there was a steel mill, still under construction, and at the eastern end, an old provincial community called San Félix with about 75 percent of the total population. Between them were a mining-company town

---

[6] This largely unexploited region includes all the national area of Venezuela south of the Orinoco river that extends over nearly half the country's land area. The region of Guayana lies within the tropics. The eighth parallel, together with the great Orinoco river, defines its northern boundary; in the south it reaches into the equatorial belt.

[7] For the years 1950 and 1961 see Ministerio de Fomento (1950, 1965); for the year 1965 see the survey published by the Banco Central de Venezuela (1966) for the Corporación Venezolana de Guayana (CVG); and for 1970 and 1972 see the Corporación Venezolana de Guayana's *Inventario de edificaciones* (1971) and *Informe anual* (1970, 1971, 1972).

called Puerto Ordaz with approximately 25 percent of the population, another mining settlement called Palúa, and various smaller developments. The Caroní river, running north–south, cut the area into eastern and western halves. A bridge was already under construction, but, as we shall show, the eastern and western halves have not been fully bridged socially.

One of the objectives of the 1961–1963 plan of urban development was to achieve a balanced physical growth and a unified city (see *Informe anual* 1963). Because the planned site for Ciudad Guayana consisted of a set of separate centers, the problem was to tie them all together; in particular, to connect the largest and easternmost existing settlement, San Félix, with the planned new city center to the west. Within this strategy, the goals for Ciudad Guayana, as outlined in the 1963 CVG report, included: (1) the concentration of heavy industries to the west, close to the steel mill, and their future expansion toward the residential areas in the east; (2) the development of residential areas close to the existing ones with their progressive expansion toward the west, or the steel mill. Due to the abovementioned laws of work regarding transportation, the gradual reduction of the distance between the residential areas in the east and the industrial places of work in the west was considered of primary importance.

In figures, the aim of the CVG was to reverse the 1961 pattern of population distribution, with 25 percent of the people on the west side and 75 percent on the east, to one with 75 percent on the west by 1970.

2a. URBAN GROWTH TRENDS IN OPPOSITION TO THE PLANNERS' MODELS

After twelve years of planning, as the CVG's annual reports indicate, the planners have not been successful in achieving the projected spatial residential distribution and the urban growth westwards. For example, by 1970, only 29 percent of the population was living in the western sector — versus 25 percent in 1961 — instead of the 75 percent projected in 1963 (see *Informe anual* 1963, 1970). The CVG report for 1970 stated its inability to achieve the desired goals of population distribution and projected a revised and less ambitious set of goals for the west.[8] At the

[8]   On the one hand, Anthony Downs (1969:212) stated in 1964 the new goals of getting 60 percent of the population to the west side by 1970. On the other hand, the 1970 *Informe anual* stated both an optimistic and a pessimistic alternative. Under the pessimistic alternative, only by 1995, when the population approaches 500,000 inhabitants, will the west sector begin to have a larger population than the east. Under the optimistic alternative, by the time the population approaches 500,000, the west sector will have two-thirds of the total. To achieve the optimistic alternative, the policies outlined in the 1970 *Informe anual* were: (1) to limit the growth of the east side by postponing investment in services and infrastructure (bridges, highways); (2) to prohibit the invasion of land and the building of shacks in the east; and (3) to build lower-income housing units in the west.

same time the CVG's policies did not include opening the west to the kinds of planned squatter developments which could have had a significant impact in turning the tide.

When one analyzes the discrepancies between the goals and what is actually happening it appears that the main problem is that the residents, especially lower-income people and recently arrived migrants, have been constructing their own squatter shacks in the east. They are doing so, at least in part, because of bureaucratic delays and the strict allocation of housing lots or facilities in the "self-help" as well as the more conventional planned housing programs.[9] (Other reasons for this will be discussed below.) This is hardly surprising when we look at CVG policies with respect to lower-income housing. As noted, the problem is that San Félix is spatially farther than Puerto Ordaz from the industrial places of work, and from the planned commercial and business centers of the new (Alta Vista) sector of Ciudad Guayana. These centers remain undeveloped and therefore empty (except for the CVG building and a drive-in cinema) while unplanned, small, credit businesses flourish close to the lower-income settlements in and around San Félix.[10]

2b. FACTORS THAT EXPLAIN THE DISCREPANCIES BETWEEN THE URBAN GROWTH TRENDS AND THE PLANNERS' MODELS

1. *Structural Factors and Social Class*

At the beginning, the planners of Ciudad Guayana recognized the need for information about the projected rate of population growth, the type of migrants to the city, and the income levels of the population.[11] Even

---

[9] Quoting Rafael Corrada: "The program of settlement communities for squatters became entangled in bureaucratic procedures. Families were carefully screened to make sure that the poorest or most 'deserving' ones got the available lot first and that no speculation could develop. As a result, it took nearly a year to allocate 434 lots in one settlement community. Even more disappointing was the effective screening of 'antisocial' families by social workers interested in developing 'uncorrupted communities'" (1969:246).
    "Administrative procedures slowed down the settlement program to about half of the rate of incoming squatters. During 1962–1965, squatters built shacks at a rate of about 85 a month. Only 37 of these were built in settlement communities. In the same period the total number of ranchos increased by approximately 2,500. Thus the program allowed around 1,500 ranchos to be located at random outside the settlement communities" (1969: 247).
[10] The middle class has its shopping center in Puerto Ordaz, also relatively little used by the people of the shacktowns.
[11] Among the most relevant studies are: (a) the *Migration survey* (1965) carried out by the CVG and the Banco Central de Venezuela; (b) the *Survey of family living conditions in Santo Tomé de Guayana* (Banco Central de Venezuela 1962) and the study about *Family income in Santo Tomé de Guayana* (Banco Central de Venezuela 1965); (c) "Preliminary studies for the building of low-income housing in Ciudad Guayana" (Banco Obrero n.d.); (d) the Venezuelan censuses of 1950 and 1961 (Ministerio de Fomento 1950, 1965); (e) any of

though some of these data were ultimately collected, they seem seldom to have been used by those who should have been doing what we may call the social planning. Instead, the planning concentrated — successfully we may add — on the industrial base and on the provision of services and physical amenities for the middle and upper classes to bring them and keep them in remote Ciudad Guayana. Meanwhile, a great number of people with very low incomes were arriving,[12] and, while the planners were planning their economic models and the location of civic centers and shopping complexes, these people were building their houses.

The planners' concern to eliminate the *ranchos* built by the people, strongly supported by the middle and upper-class residents of Ciudad Guayana, led the CVG to *prohibit the construction of these* ranchos *in the western part of the city.* The obvious result was that the city continued to grow toward the east. Given the fact that most of the people of Ciudad Guayana were poor and in general able to live only where they could build their shacks, the result could not have been otherwise; yet the planners did not seem aware of this. Even such a relatively realistic planner as Downs, in 1964, made the unrealistic projection that by 1970, 60 percent of the people would be located on the west side (Downs 1969). However, no corresponding plans to permit large-scale shacktown developments or other alternatives on the west were made. More understandably absent from the developers' plans were the unsightly bars and petty-commerce kiosks that form a ubiquitous part of the lower-class life and sources of employment. Nevertheless, the economic and social importance of these bars and petty businesses has been shown by Morse (1965), Lewis (1960, 1966a, 1966b, 1968), Mangin (1967), Peattie (1968), and Talton (1969), writing about the shacktowns of Puerto Rico, Mexico, Peru, and Venezuela.

Another important factor influencing the spatial distribution of lower-income population is the marginal nature of much of their employment. In Ciudad Guayana, Peattie (1968) has shown that in the *barrio* she studied, La Laja, only one out of six was steadily employed; the others lived off the sixth. Marginality strikes both sexes. Lower-income females, largely unskilled, have little choice but casual and service employment. Typical jobs include laundress, servant, and the like; and some work as part or full-time prostitutes. Moreover, over a fifth of the households are female-headed and cannot count on a male potential wage earner in the

---

the household surveys (*Encuesta de hogares*) published three times a year by the Ministerio de Fomento; (f) studies made by the MIT-Harvard team: Peattie (1968), Porter (1969), Appleyard (1969), Corrada (1966, 1969), and other studies included in Rodwin (1969).
[12]   As we have already mentioned at least 54.2 percent of the incoming population to Ciudad Guayana could be classified as lower-income.

house.[13] Also, many males have low potential as wage earners. Although some males work in industries,[14] many are unemployed or work in the service jobs, petty commerce, or in construction. This last occupation, construction worker, also has been found to be very important among the lower classes of Peru, Puerto Rico, Brazil, and Venezuela, as reported by Turner (1966b, 1967, 1968a), Mangin (1967), Peattie (1968), and Talton (1969). Since these kinds of jobs, constituting the real economic prospects of the low-income men and women, are mainly located on the east side of Ciudad Guayana, it is little wonder that the projections of even the relatively more realistic planners, such as Downs, were not met.

2a. *Life-style*

Because the planners apparently did not understand the life-style and housing needs of the lower classes, imposed by their structural economic marginality, they constructed a relatively limited number of housing units, most of them too expensive for such a population. These units required a down payment plus fixed installments.[15] However, had the planners asked for the advice of social scientists at this period (early and mid-1960's), they probably would have followed the same policies. At that time, as we shall see below, the prevailing social science orthodoxy viewed shacktowns as a kind of cancer on the body of the city. Instead of being worked with, they were to be eradicated.[16] In Brasilia, for example, they are completely banned from most of the developed areas, and, as a result, they sprang up so far from town that Brasilia has been experiencing a very strange growth pattern.

In addition to considering the shacks as a form of social pathology, the social science wisdom in those days believed that those fixed monthly installments — the obligation of paying for a home — would stabilize people by providing them with a sense of responsibililty. Moreover, the benefits of home ownership were alleged to include holding families

[13]   The studies by Safa (1964) in Puerto Rico; Peattie (1968) in Ciudad Guayana; García (1971) in Caracas; and the *Mercavi* study (Banco Nacional de Ahorro y Préstamo 1970) in different cities of Venezuela have shown that approximately 25 percent of the lower-income households have a female as the head of the family.

[14]   Approximately 31 percent of economically active males worked in manufacturing, as against 48 percent in commercial, construction, and service activities, according to the July 1970 *Encuesta de hogares* (Ministerio de Fomento 1970). Furthermore, only 14.5 percent of the economically active women work in manufacturing, as against 62 percent in services and 17 percent in commerce.

[15]   According to Rafael Corrada (1969:241) the down payment required for this income group (less than Bolívares 1,000) was usually 0–10 percent, with an amortization period of 15–20 years and an interest rate of 4–6 percent.

[16]   Some of the proponents of this approach include Coronado (1955), Berckholtz (1963), Patch (1961), Sanabria (1966), Silveira (1963), Schulman (1966), Lleras-Restrepo (1955), and Ospina-Pérez (1948).

together and solving most of the problems of social disorganization. Structural underemployment, and its consequences for life-style and housing needs, were just not considered. Similarly the planners, taking this approach with respect to Ciudad Guayana (Davis and McGinn 1969a, 1969b; MacDonald 1969, among others) did not mention that much of the population of the city did not have steady or regular incomes. Thus, rather than forcing responsibility on them, fixed monthly payments for a home would have forced an impossibility on them because their own incomes were sporadic and their employment opportunites marginal. Furthermore, even though industrial jobs were being created faster in Ciudad Guayana than perhaps in any other comparable planned city, there were not enough to take care of the economic needs of the in-migrants who came. And it must be remembered that they did not come as fast as the planners had originally expected.[17]

The low-income people had to devise their own solutions, but these solutions generally were not viewed as such by the planners. Instead, they were seen as a problem. As we have noted, the plans for Ciudad Guayana called for expansion to the west, but the city was growing to the east — and the planners did not seem to see any relationship between their plans and its logical results, namely, that given the prohibition of *ranchos* in the west, the people continued to build them in the east.

Nevertheless, despite the ban, there was one note of greater realism in Ciudad Guayana that did not exist in many of these other planned cities, particularly Brasilia. The planners faced the fact that squatting was inevitable. Therefore, they permitted, and in fact, even encouraged, self-help construction projects, i.e. "planned slums" and reception areas for newly arrived migrants.[18] This did not come at the beginning, but a bit later, when the planners realized that the people not only were building their own shacks, but that they were building them on land that the planners would have liked to reserve for other uses. Realizing that it was impossible to build sufficient low-cost housing fast enough, and wanting to reserve for other purposes the area where people were squatting, the developers moved to create model programs for self-help housing in the form of "planned slums" and of reception areas in the east. Unfortunately, these programs, according to Corrada (1969:246) soon bogged down in bureaucracy: people were rigidly selected and they had to wait

---

[17]   Corrada (1969:245) notes that in 1965 it became clear that the total population was about 20,000 less than expected.

[18]   The CVG considered squatting unavoidable and therefore formulated a settlement strategy according to which the key to controlling slums in Ciudad Guayana lies in the ability to control lot sizes and the arrangement pattern for the placement of shacks. There were designated settlement areas inside the city (in the east) where families could squat with security of land tenure: the "reception areas" and the "planned" slums. The self-help construction projects involve assisting lower-income people in building their own permanent houses as their time and income permit.

for months. Indeed, the planners wanted to wait still longer, until more socioeconomic and demographic studies could be completed. Meanwhile, the people continued to build.

By the time planners started the self-help housing programs, new studies started to appear in the literature on housing in Latin America. These were critical of the view that shacktowns were a cancer to be eradicated. We shall discuss this further below, but let us mention two of these "revisionist" authors: Mangin (1963, 1967) and Turner (1963, 1966b, 1967). First of all, they are noteworthy in that they actually provided data to supersede the myths about the *barrios*. They actually went into the lower-class areas, lived among the people, observed them, and found out what their needs were with respect to housing — rather than attempting to impose a moralistic solution. What they found out was that people coming to the city for economic opportunities really did not care about off-street play areas for their children and other such physical amenities. Instead, they learned, many of the amenities provided in these so-called low-cost housing programs priced the poor out of the market or caused disasters when — with depressing frequency — they lost their jobs. Abrams (1964), Peattie (1968; 1969b), Talton (1969), Wagner et al. (1966), and Caminos, Turner, and Steffian (1969) make a similar point with respect to Venezuela, Brazil, Colombia, and Peru.

Turner, writing about the situation in Lima, Peru, posits that housing needs differ greatly by socioeconomic levels or stages. At the first level he suggests, when they are newly arrived in the city, what the poor need most is easy access to the kind of jobs that they can get — basically service jobs. Turner, who was peripherally involved in the planning of Ciudad Guayana (he is also from MIT), saw that at the first level, the immediate needs of the lowest-income people lay not in having pretty housing but in having their basic needs provided. Generally speaking, with their low levels of skills and inadequate income, such people have to live where they can walk to their work place. To judge from the experience of Ciudad Guayana, economic opportunity for most of the people was initially less likely to be in industry than in marginal service tasks. Therefore, lower-class people have to be near that part of the population from whom they can gain income for performing services.

Turner next posits a second level or stage: once people begin to climb out of the minimum subsistence level and are already earning money, they can afford to travel to work on public transportation. At this second stage, what people need most, then, is security in their housing tenure — particularly freedom from the burden of paying rent — Flinn (1968) and Peattie (1968, 1969b) make similar remarks for Colombia and Venezuela. At this stage, their employment situation remains highly unstable. Therefore, if they have to stop paying for a house when unemployment strikes, they will be forced back to level one.

2b. *Social Relations*

Another sociological variable that relates to the prevalent distribution of the low-income people in the east is their pattern of social relations. It has been found by Bryce-Laporte (1970) and Safa (1964) in Puerto Rico, and Peattie (1968) and Talton (1969) in Venezuela, that unemployed men tend to spend a great deal of their time socializing in the neighborhood bars because it is highly functional for them. Studies on how lower-class people gain employment emphasize the importance of this informal context. As we have noted, for most lower-class people, the most likely source of income is from providing services and being involved in petty commercial activities, rather than from suddenly landing a highly-paid industrial job. Thus, the informal setting provides the equivalent of country club business deals for the middle and upper-middle classes. Also, socializing in bars or in the *barrio* is a kind of "social investment" that may materialize in economic help when the person is out of a job for long periods of time. The poor male worker will need the help of friends, *compadres*, and neighbors, when unemployed, and those who usually will help him are people of the same *barrio*. This is one more reason why lower-income people in Ciudad Guayana tend to live in the east.

Numerous studies in Latin America — Morse (1965), Browning and Feindt (1971), Flinn (1968), Matos Mar (1961), Germani (1961) and Peattie (1968) — have shown the influence of kin on migration. And in Ciudad Guayana, the incoming migrant would be most likely to have a relative or *compadre* already living in the east who could help in finding a place to live and a job. If such a migrant were to go to a CVG planned reception area or lower-income housing development, he or she might be isolated both physically and socially from possible sources of help. This is because, as Stinchcombe (1969), Porter (1969), Corrada (1969), and Peattie (1969c) have emphasized, the unplanned shacktowns are much less segregated by socioeconomic status than the planned housing of the CVG. Similarly, other studies in Latin America — Mangin (1967) in Peru, Lewis (1966a) and Safa (1964) in Puerto Rico, and Flinn (1968) in Colombia — have encountered the same problem of social class segregation in the public housing programs.

Up until now we have discussed the factors stemming from economic marginality, the common fate of vast proportions of the population of any Third World city. Our discussion, we believe, is thus applicable to virtually any Latin American planning effort. In addition, however, each urban development is bound to be affected by certain specific variables. In the case of Ciudad Guayana, we shall consider three sets of factors unique to the situation: several Venezuelan laws, the local climate, and the CVG planners' specific housing programs. In other situations, legal, ecological, and political factors may prove equally important, although in different detail. Conversely, they may not, and factors absent in Ciudad Guayana, such as racial stratification, may loom as crucial. The important point here is that no urban planning effort will reach maximum success if no search is made for the unexpected and unique factors that may enter into the equation.

3. Legal Factors

Some peculiar developments related to the legal system in Venezuela ought to be mentioned because we think these laws have had strong influence in the spatial distribution of the shacktowns in Ciudad Guayana. We refer to three laws: (a) the *Ley del Trabajo* [Law of Work]; (b) the *Ley de Bienhechurías* [Law of Home Improvements]; and (c) the *Ley de Despidos, Retiros y Aguinaldos* [Law of Job Dismissals and Bonuses].

a. LEY DEL TRABAJO. As we mentioned above, in Ciudad Guayana there is a work law that states that companies have to pay for the trip if the distance to work is over 1.25 miles from a center of population. Also unionized workers receive half-time pay in Ciudad Guayana for the distance travelled over 1.25 miles. This law means that it is more convenient for the low-income people to be located in the east, close to their relatives and friends, than to be located in the west, close to the main industries. We must remember that workers are related by bonds of kinship and/or friendship to the population which is economically dependent on them and which is living on service activities supported by them. Moreover, as the industrial workers have their travel time compensated, and their relatives have to live near the other poor people in order to make a living, it makes great sense for the poor majority to live where the poor people are. Thus, this law contributes to the fact that the shacktowns of Ciudad Guayana tend to be located farther from industrial jobs than might be the case in other cities, such as Lima, the site of Turner's study.

b. LEY DE BIENHECHURÍAS. This Venezuelan Law of Home Improvements means that if expropriated, people who have built shacks must be paid for the improvements put into them.[19] Often, it makes the cost of expropriation too high, leading to a de facto solution of letting the people them-

---

[19]   Corrada states: "Ranchos have been expropriated in Ciudad Guayana at an average cost of $310 in two-year-old sites and $890 in ten-year-old areas. These figures indicate an average appreciation rate of $75 per year, mainly as a result of the squatters' improvements. These expropriation costs are much higher than the $47 for a lot and $324 for a lot with minimum public services (water taps, paved street, and electricity), which were the development costs in the settlement communities" (1969:239).

selves improve their housing, as the CVG can no longer pay to expropriate the housing of the poor. Also it means that it is a good investment for
the low-income people to improve their shacks, because if they are
expropriated they will make a profit. The statistics cited by Corrada
(1969:239) show how the squatters' investments in home improvements
have skyrocketed the cost of expropriating any but the newest, roughest
shacks.

c. LEY DE DESPIDOS, RETIROS Y AGUINALDOS. One other law that should be
mentioned dictates that in Venezuela when a long-time worker is dis-
charged he or she is required to receive from fifteen days' to a month's
salary for every year worked. If the person works for a big company and
has several years of employment, this is a considerable amount of capital.
The studies of Peattie (1968) and Talton (1969) show that this capital is
often translated into small enterprises. When people receive the money
for expropriation from previous shacks, or receive severance pay or some
other lump-sum payment (such as the special Christmas bonus, the
aguinaldo) which Venezuelan law has provided in good number, they are
often able to capitalize on this. This is done by opening a small service
business, or perhaps building a house that they can rent, or maybe adding
a room to their present house and getting some income from it by converting it into a small commercial venture, such as a tiny food store or bar.

The three laws described above are certainly, if not unique to Venezuela, very unusual. Nothing comparable is mentioned in the works of
Mangin and Turner because the countries where they did their studies are
much poorer than Venezuela, with its petroleum-based economy.
Indeed, it is unlikely that these governments could have enforced any law
compensating workers for travel time to work. Therefore, Venezuela's
peculiar position of being one of the richest of the developing Latin
American countries may have created legal factors that contributed to the
growth of the city of Ciudad Guayana to the east.

4. *Ecology*

An ecological factor, the year-round mild, warm climate of Ciudad
Guayana, also contributes to the fact that despite possible home
improvements, the housing of many of the poor remains basically crude
shacks. In such a warm climate, almost any material can be used by the
poor to build their house: cardboard, zinc, aluminium sheets, etc. Therefore, in Ciudad Guayana the lower-income people would be less concerned with the type of structure and the materials needed to build the
house than in other, colder cities. They presumably would be prepared to

live in unfinished houses and low-standard shacks if by doing this they could achieve the second-level goals suggested by Turner: residential stability, home ownership, and the economic security of not having to pay a monthly rent or mortgage — and, we might add, of not worrying about paying for the land because it was acquired by invasion.

5. *Urban and Housing Policies of the CVG*

In contrast to its urban development policies which followed what Peattie (1969c:461) has termed the "centralized incremental" model of relatively rigid top-down planning, CVG's housing programs for the lower class have been characterized by somewhat greater — albeit still insufficient — proclivities to adapt solutions to the actions of those below. This greater responsiveness to the action of those below she has termed the "evolutionary incremental" model. However, even in housing, the model most frequently used in Ciudad Guayana was the top-down "centralized incremental" one. In this model the values most likely to be implemented are those of the planners and high government officials. These, as we have shown, are very different from the lower-class values. The prohibition of shacks in the western part of the city was perhaps largely due to the fact that the middle and upper classes, the planners, and the government officials tend to dislike them. This is undoubtedly one of the principal reasons that lower-class people had to devise their own "evolutionary incremental" model to implement their values and needs in their unplanned housing developments, services, and commercial activities.

A further and more general obstacle to the official policies was that they were not known by the population to whom they were addressed. Appleyard's study of Ciudad Guayana (1969) revealed that half of the people in the sample did not know what the CVG was; and of those who did hear about it, half of them did not know what the CVG's proper functions were. Therefore, since the population did not know, much less understand, what was happening in Ciudad Guayana and what the future plans for the city were, they could not possibly act according to the CVG's policy and plans. In fact, they have been acting against those plans as we noted.

It is a truism in the philosophy of science that the variables included in one's research are dictated by one's underlying theory or approach. Therefore, below we shall discuss three social science orientations toward the social reality of the shacktowns, because each one leads to different policy implications with respect to housing. In the case of the first two — those used explicitly or implicitly by the planners of Ciudad Guayana — we argue that important structural variables (e.g. degree of employment, instability) were precluded from consideration by the conceptual bias of the approach. We conclude this section with a preliminary delineation of the factors that we propose must be included.

3a. THREE APPROACHES TOWARD URBAN DEVELOPMENT AND HOUSING

1. *Prevailing Orthodoxy: The Social Cancer Approach*

The first and most popular view about shacktowns in Latin America, from World War II through the mid-1960's, considered them as a "social cancer" in the body of the city that is caused by the "vices" and "pathologies" of lower-income people. Laziness, family disorganization, "voluntary" unemployment, lack of formal education, irresponsibility, and delinquency have been mentioned among the causes for the existence and persistence of the shacktowns (see note 16 for the proponents of this approach). This "cancer," say proponents of this view, must be cured by eradication of the shacktown either by sending the people back to the farms — from which they are often incorrectly assumed to have just come — or by moving them into housing projects and planned satellite cities.

At the beginning of the planning of Ciudad Guayana, large and influential sectors of government officials, planners, and middle and upper classes, and even social scientists in both North and South America shared this approach. The prevalent orthodoxy held that transforming the housing of the poor would transform the people from shiftless squatters to solid citizens.[20,21] Paying a fixed monthly amount for a house, planners believed, would bring social mobility and civic responsibility to the lower class. We think, however, that the planned housing developments of Ciudad Guayana represented mobility only for those who had already begun to rise. These are predominantly the people who either had special skills or had arrived earlier and acquired a toehold in the industrial sector before job and educational qualifications for such employment rose steeply. In contrast, the planned "low-income" housing — characterized by the virtual absence of little credit groceries and bars and the difficulty of access to the marginal service-employment opportunities — was clearly unsuited to the needs of the nonindustrially employed and

---

[20]   MacDonald believes that: "The persistence of high unemployment among the settled population may be reduced by shifting more of the shanty dwellers into modest housing developments. Presumably voluntary unemployment will decrease as family stability and responsibilities increase. This stability could be promoted by better housing and the long-term responsibilities of paying it off" (1969:121).
[21]   Laun (1973) cites a quote of former Colombian president Lleras-Restrepo (1955) as typical: "The transformation of housing and of social habits represent an educative and civilizing work [as well as] an effective increase in labor's productivity."

unemployed poor who are more numerous than those in the stable industrial jobs.

2. *The Culture of Poverty Approach*

In the 1960's a revisionist movement appeared that stressed the positive aspects of the shacktowns, implicitly or explicitly using the concept of the "culture of poverty" Lewis (1960, 1966a, 1966b, 1968).[22] In Latin America, a somewhat parallel conceptual orientation emerged, using a concept of "marginality" in which marginality was a characteristic of the poor as individuals, not of their relation to the economic structure (Mattelart and Garretón 1965; Vekemans and Venegas 1966a, 1966b). However, even though this approach stresses the ingenuity of the poor under unfavorable structural conditions, it also seems to imply that the culture of poverty — and the shacktowns — may be permanent and self-perpetuating due to personality and value-orientation factors of the people involved.[23]

There is a "laissez-faire" or "self-help equilibrium" approach epitomized by Turner, which may be considered an intermediate case between the second and third (structural) approaches. Turner notes that shacktown dwellers are most in need of rent-free housing close to their sources of employment and that they gradually expand and improve their dwelling as their finances and employment status permit. A viable solution, then, would be not to move the lower-income people to public housing, which requires a fixed monthly payment they cannot always meet and which may be located too far from their sources of employment. Instead, Turner argues, one must encourage this natural process of shacktown evolution and let the inhabitants work out their own solutions to their housing problems.

It may be argued that the planners of Ciudad Guayana implicitly followed this approach in the development of reception areas, "planned slums," and self-help housing programs for the people who could not afford to pay for a house. As we have indicated, their success seems quite limited, as great numbers of low-income people built their houses outside of these planned developments. We have already mentioned the strict

---

[22] Oscar Lewis (1966b) formulated the concept of "the culture of poverty" as "a label for a specific conceptual model that describes in positive terms a sub-culture of Western society with its own structure and rationale, a way of life handed on from generation to generation along family lines."

[23] Although the concept of the "culture of poverty" is much more sophisticated than the one of social disorganization or "cancer," Lewis has been severely criticized over the last years for stressing *internal personality and value orientations* which allegedly make the culture of poverty self-perpetuating. According to his critics, Lewis blames the victims while underemphasizing external economic factors.

selection of people who were to live in them and the bureaucratic delays that further constrained the programs. Perhaps a more important reason for this limited success was that planners did not take into account many of the needs of the lowest-income people stemming from their precarious structural position in the economy. Thus, lots, houses, and credit were still more expensive, and the developments more rigidly segregated by social class than in the unplanned shacktowns favored by the poor. Therefore, these programs of the CVG failed in part to accomplish all their targeted goals because they failed to "bend" far enough to accommodate the structural situation of the lowest-income groups.

3. Structural Approach

The third approach to the shacktowns of Latin America differs from the first two in stressing that the shacktowns owe their existence to external and socioeconomic structural factors. This approach also emerged in the 1960's. All those associated with this view (most importantly, Quijano 1966, 1968, 1971; Cardoso and Faletto 1969; Lessa 1970 and Travieso 1971, all in Latin America; and Mangin 1970 in the United States) would agree that: (1) the nature, size, and rate of growth of the economic base of a given Latin American city or country are inadequate to provide stable and abundant subsistence opportunities for a large percentage of the labor force; and (2) as stressed by Turner and the advocates of the second approach, the shacktowns represent an ingenious, adaptive solution to surviving on the unstable economic margins of society.

This third approach seems to be best typified by Mangin, who says that self-help efforts of the shacktown residents within the confines of their shacktown are not enough, since their problems stem from the disequilibria of an economic structure that fails to provide them sufficient economic opportunity. This approach thus denies Turner's notion that the individual, by his or her own labor, can manufacture the resources needed to participate fully in all the advantages society has to offer. Mangin (1970) says that it is not, in most cases, "the fault" of the lower-class people that they do not often attain economic and social progress. Rather, it is the existing socioeconomic structure that denies them opportunities for improvement in such areas as education, employment, and housing.

In our opinion, of the three approaches to the shacktowns, the structural one offers the best explanation of their existence, nature, and continual expansion. In addition, we propose that it helps to explain the pattern of location and growth of the shacktowns of Latin America in general, and of Ciudad Guayana in particular. It does not appear that this approach was ever emphasized by the planners of Ciudad Guayana. However, had they considered the structural variables, they might have predicted, and therefore successfully intervened in, the distribution of shacktowns in the city because it is primarily structural constraints that create and perpetuate them.

3b. PRELIMINARY DELINEATION OF STRUCTURAL FACTORS IMPORTANT FOR INTEGRATING LOW-INCOME POPULATION INTO URBAN AND HOUSING DEVELOPMENT PROGRAMS

1. The first structural factor that must be taken into account is: *what* percentage of the urban population may be expected to be *economically marginal*, and *why*.

The "why" is easier to answer: no Latin American urban economy has managed to create stable jobs as fast as the increase in available labor force. In Venezuela, in recent years, for example, the creation of jobs of any description has run about one percent a year behind the increase in the aspiring labor force.[24]

The question of what percentage of the population may be expected to be economically marginal is more complicated. As we have seen, many service-sector jobs are forms of symbiosis (at best) which permit the otherwise unemployable to live off the earnings of their more fortunate, stably employed counterparts. In fact, a good deal of the petty service-sector activities in Ciudad Guayana — as in Third World cities in general — must be considered as much a form of *involution* as the "agricultural involution" discussed by Geertz (1966) in Java — where, under population pressure, agriculture intensified to the point where people were virtually harvesting single grains of paddy rice with razor blades. Similarly, the subsistence activities of the service sector have involuted to an analogous degree and for roughly the same reasons of population pressure on an insufficiently dynamic and absorptive economy.

The case of Ciudad Guayana shows that such an economy may be very dynamic in some sectors and in total growth figures, while still insufficiently absorptive for the types of people who come. Indeed, Peattie (1969a:406) cites this as a problem common to Venezuelan growth in general: it is taking place on a capital-intensive, high-technology base, requiring few and relatively highly skilled workers; whereas Venezuelan workers are many and relatively unskilled. The result of this structural disequilibrium is the high rate of unemployment, underemployment, and what we may term "involuted" employment.

2. The next element to be considered in the marginality equation is the *types of people* — as compared to the *types and quantities of jobs*.

[24] Victor Childers, in his "Human resource development in Venezuela" (n.d.), uses primarily CORDIPLAN statistics to arrive at the gap between labor force and new jobs.

With respect to the types of people, we must first consider their *demographic profile*: What percentage are in the economically productive years, versus dependents? What is the sex ratio? We learn that in Ciudad Guayana the demographic profile is surprisingly normal for such a young pioneer city;[25] there are many more women with children here than one might expect on the frontier. The children mean a higher dependency ratio — we note that the rate of Ciudad Guayana population growth is so explosive that more than half the population has yet to celebrate its fifteenth birthday (see MacDonald 1969:110–111). The mothers of these children, as we shall point out, face marginality from two sources: familial and economic.

3.   On the one hand, marginality springs from a *prevalent family structure* where unions are impermanent alliances easily broken by the economic instability of the male partner. Studies show that approximately 25 percent of the low-income households have a female as the head of the family. Such findings have been noted by Safa (1964) in Puerto Rico; Peattie (1968) in Ciudad Guayana; García (1971) in Caracas; and the *Mercavi* study (Banco Nacional de Ahorro y Préstamo 1970) in various cities of Venezuela. On the other hand, the Ciudad Guayana industrial *economic base* has virtually no secure niches for the unskilled females with little education.

4.   *The level of education*, then, is perhaps the next salient characteristic of the population. In Venezuela, education was not widely available in rural areas when the present adult population of Ciudad Guayana (mostly migrants from eastern Venezuela) was growing up. Thus for both sexes, the average level is much less than completed primary school. In fact, Davis and McGinn (1969b:277) note that 80 percent of the population in their Ciudad Guayana study were rural or small-town educated, and that, barring the imported professionals, the average level was under three years of primary school.

Ironically, as Ciudad Guayana has evolved, the larger companies (e.g. the steel and aluminum mills) generally have raised the minimum educational requirements for most stable jobs to a primary-school graduation certificate. This illustrates neatly the convenience of *"credendialitis"* as a sorting device for employment in a market of surplus labor. But "blame the victim" theories are hard to sustain here: one cannot be accused of being a lazy, shiftless dropout if there was no primary school offering education beyond the third grade anywhere within miles when one was growing up. In general, the willingness of companies to offer on-the-job training to applicants without "appropriate" credentials varies directly

[25]   See Banco Central de Venezuela (1966: table 12, page 16). Also reprinted in MacDonald (1969:110–111).

with labor scarcity. And in Ciudad Guayana, this ends the discussion of level of education.

Type of education is another problem. Even when outside agencies give training courses to the unskilled, they might not inculcate a level of skills high enough, or run a placement service active enough, to make their graduates much more attractive to the increasingly selective modern-sector employers. Davis and McGinn (1969b) mention these problems with respect to training programs for construction workers that apparently did not lead to the expected better jobs.

5. And what are the expected better jobs? *Stability* is the next (and perhaps most crucial) factor. If a worker is hired for a good job after months of unemployment only to be laid off after a few months, scarcely a ripple has been made in his or her level of marginality. The factors associated with stability of employment tend to be tied to both the economic structure and the Venezuelan work law and are complex. For example, in some industries with high technology (e.g. modern textile manufacturing), workers can be trained for their jobs in a negligible amount of time. Venezuelan work laws start giving most employees expensive fringe benefits such as vacation, severance pay, and bonus rights after four to eight months on the job. Accordingly, it is little wonder that one source estimates the average duration of employment for unskilled workers in such industries to be just below the "magic number" (see CEVEPOF-CISOR 1973:48).

In Ciudad Guayana, the industrial jobs by contrast tend to be stable, highly paid, unionized, and to require a relatively high level of skills. The problem, of course, is landing such a job in the first place. But once employed, the worker is protected by the investment the companies would have to make to train a replacement and the power of the unions. Thus two distinct strata of job stability exist in glaring contrast: an unusually stable industrial sector and a residue of frequently unstable service, commercial, and construction jobs for which the remaining two-thirds of the economically active population competes.

6. In short, *economic indexes for planners* should include the average duration of the job, and the average number of hours of employment it provides on a year-round basis, cross-tabulated by type of industry or economic activity. Even if the planners may not be able radically to change the economic structure, they should be able to formulate more realistic and ameliorative policies if they know to what extent a city's economic base is lopsided with unstable industrial jobs and marginal commercial enterprises.

7. Less obvious but also important information for planners concerns

the *work and housing laws*. We have shown how three of these laws affected population distribution in Ciudad Guayana. In addition, we have suggested that the content of a government's work laws may affect the policies of employers concerning duration (and other conditions) of employment.

8. Also stemming from the argument presented in this paper is the suggestion that planners examine the *social implications* of local *ecology*. Thus a warm, benign climate can reduce the need for elaborately constructed shelter. Similarly, a toll bridge or ferry connecting two halves of a river-bisected city can increase the access of the poor to economic opportunities located on the other side. The planner must remain sensitive to possible unanticipated social consequences of ecology.

9. *Labor force entry factors.* What causes the contrast between those who have already found a toehold in the island of stable industrial employment and those still struggling in the vast surrounding sea of marginality? The cause, in Ciudad Guayana, apparently does not lie in superior moral qualities, attitudes toward modernization, or labor-force commitment. Instead, Peattie (1969a:406) indicates (and we agree) that it seems a function of either (a) having been among the first to arrive or (b) having arrived with a higher level of skills than one's fellow migrants — or both. Moreover, she sees forces at work tending further to separate those with a toehold on stability from the still-marginal: (1) the capital-intensive technology of Ciudad Guayana requiring a relatively small number of workers with relatively high levels of skills and (2) the growing need for formal education as part of the entry requirements for many industrial jobs, which correlates with the ending of the first pioneering phase of establishing a labor force and economic base simultaneously.

10. Peattie's notion of a growing gap between those beginning to make it and their still-struggling counterparts leads us to two more factors having ramifications for housing policy: (a) *migration* and (b) *mobility*.
Both the rates and nature of migration and mobility should be studied to determine probable population size and composition, and quality and size of housing needed by the residents. A main advantage of the shack is its easy *expandability*. Under the impetus of added family members, including in-migrating adult kin, or good fortune, people may strive for expanded quarters. A housing policy that freezes people into units that are difficult either to upgrade or expand may be shutting the door on the evolutionary potential of low-income housing as manifested in the shacktowns.

11. Furthermore, aside from instability of income, an obvious problem

exists with *level of income* for the economically marginal. The combination of these factors is devastating with respect to any housing program based on middle-class notions of convenient monthly payments.

With respect to income level, we note that the percentage of wages needed for food is inversely related to wealth. Thus, even a hypothetical "model" subsidized housing program, aimed at charging only 10 percent of monthly income of the very poor, and providing a moratorium during periods of unemployment, may cause real hardship. Consumer studies of United States working and middle classes may find that 20 percent of net (or 25 percent of gross) income is "reasonable" for rent. But for people facing the option of living rent-free in a squatter's shack or cutting their food budget and living in a tiny planned housing unit, the former seems the "reasonable" choice.

12.   Another desirable type of information for planners is a consumption budget study by level, stability, and frequency of receipt of income for the population in question. Among the poor, such a study would probably reveal that, because of their economic situation, expenditures for food — in addition to being a high percentage of income — tend to be made for minute quantities purchased on a daily basis and often for credit (see Lewis 1960, 1966a for typical data supporting this). Accordingly, such information could make it clear that these life-style requirements of the poor are not served by large "cash-and-carry" supermarkets alone.

Above, we have suggested that planners collect information on the "mix" of jobs available in the *local economy*, emphasizing the percentages which are stable and the percentage of each wage level for each of the major economic activities. Now we are calling for two types of information collected from the *individual household*: (a) economic activities data, and (b) consumption budgets. The combination of these data could provide realistic information as to how much — if anything — different segments of the lower-income groups could pay for housing without great inconvenience.

13.   The list of studies we have been proposing requires one crucial addition: a survey in which the planners *ask the poor people* about what they want and need in housing. This could touch on cost, size, expandability, access to kin, primary schools, credit groceries (and even bars), public transportation, desired municipal services, and architectural features — such as adapting the building materials and ventilation to the tropical climate.

14.   *Political considerations* — including the relative power of the housing and mortgage lobby — may lead to adoption of plans for low-income housing that effectively freeze out or result in disservice to the over-

whelming majority of the intended clientele. The power of the housing and credit groups may mean that "financial" criteria are used to determine the nature and cost of low-income housing units.[26] By these "financial" criteria, housing for the very poor is a bad risk.

Other political factors are the *power* of the planning institution versus other institutions, and versus organized subgroups of the local population. In the case of Ciudad Guayana, the power potential of the CVG is quite high, although it is not always realized, for reasons having to do with national political policy — an area beyond the scope of this paper.

SUMMARY AND CONCLUSIONS

We have not intended this report as a mere explanation of why the city of Ciudad Guyana is growing in the opposite direction of the planners' models, although we feel that our explanation of the reasons for the city's growth to the east are clear and adequate. Instead, we have sought to highlight the structural conditions that generate the economically marginal people, who have flocked to the east, and the life-style and housing adaptations forced upon them by their structural conditions. Neither the structural marginality nor the resultant life-style and housing needs have entered much into urban development and housing policies — in Ciudad Guayana or anywhere else. Thus, in a final section, we have attempted a preliminary delineation of the factors — primarily structural — that we argue must be taken into account in urban and housing development if a low-income population is involved.

What would be the result in Ciudad Guayana if none of the factors we have stressed is now taken into account and the city continued to grow under existing conditions? We may speculate about a long list of possible consequences, but let us mention just four points:

1. The city will continue to grow vigorously toward the east.

2. Because of the work law reimbursing commuting time and costs, the expenses to the large industries in the west will continue to rise with increasing average commuting distance and number of workers.

3. It would appear that the eastern and western halves of Ciudad Guayana will grow increasingly segregated by socioeconomic class and economic activity.

---

[26]   Laun (1973), in an unpublished University of Wisconsin paper about low-cost urban housing in Colombia, stresses the extent to which these programs utilized terms and criteria of cost and resident selection parallel to those used by commercial lending institutions. This cut off the really poor and reduced to a "trickle" the truly low-cost housing units constructed. For example, Laun discusses late 1940's lending laws aimed at providing more low-cost housing for the poor which nevertheless required "a first mortgage collateral and adequate income prospects to assure mortgage payments."

4. As a result, political conflict between the eastern and western parts of Ciudad Guayana might be expected to increase (see Stinchcombe 1969, who made a similar prediction) due to the increasingly divergent interests of the two halves.

Our final point must be that even if the real housing needs of the poor become known by means of social science research incorporating the factors outlined in the preceding section, this does not mean that housing policies will automatically begin to reflect the structural conditions and needs of the intended residents. For housing policies generally reflect the power distribution in a society, and power is something which for the poor is usually in short supply.

REFERENCES

ABOUHAMAD, JEANETTE
1959   *Estudio de El Pedregal.* Caracas: Universidad Central de Venezuela.
ABRAMS, CHARLES
1964   *Man's struggle for shelter in an urbanizing world.* Cambridge, Massachusetts: M.I.T. Press.
APPLEYARD, DONALD
1969   "City designers and the pluralistic city," in *Planning urban growth and regional development.* Edited by L. Rodwin et al., 422–452. Cambridge, Massachusetts: M.I.T. Press.
BANCO CENTRAL DE VENEZUELA
1962   *Survey of family living conditions in Santo Tomé de Guayana.* Caracas: Corporación Venezolana de Guayana (CVG).
1965   *Family income in Santo Tomé de Guayana.* Caracas: Corporación Venezolana de Guayana (CVG).
1966   *Encuesta sobre características demográficas, ingresos familiares, características de la vivienda, tipo de transporte utilizado de las familias de Santo Tomé de Guayana, febrero 1965.* Caracas: Corporación Venezolana de Guayana (CVG).
BANCO NACIONAL DE AHORRO Y PRÉSTAMO
1970   *Mercavi 70.* Caracas.
BANCO OBRERO
1959   *Proyecto de evaluación de los superbloques.* Caracas: Tipografía Vargas.
n.d.   "Preliminary studies for the building of low-income housing in Ciudad Guayana." Internal report, Banco Obrero, Caracas.
BERCKHOLTZ, PABLO
1963   *Barrios marginales: aberración social.* Lima.
BEYER, GLENN
1967   *The urban explosion in Latin America.* Ithaca, New York: Cornell University Press.
BONILLA, FRANK
1971   "Rio's favelas: the rural slums within the city," in *Peasants in cities.* Edited by W. Mangin, 72–84. Boston: Houghton Mifflin.
BROWNING, H., W. FEINDT
1971   "The social and economic context of migration to Monterrey," in *Latin*

American urban research, volume one. Edited by F. Rabinowitz and F. Trueblood, 45–70. Beverly Hills: Sage.

BRYCE-LAPORTE, SIMON
1970   "Urban relocation and family adaptation in Puerto Rico: a case study in urban ethnography," in *Peasants in cities*. Edited by W. Mangin, 85–97. Boston: Houghton Mifflin.

CAMINOS, H., J. U. TURNER, J. A. STEFFIAN
1969   *Urban dwelling environments: an elementary survey of settlements for the study of design determinants*. M.I.T. Report 16. Cambridge, Massachusetts: M.I.T. Press.

CARDOSO, F. H., E. FALETTO
1969   *Dependencia y desarrollo en América Latina*. Mexico: Siglo XXI.

CEVEPOF-CISOR
1973   *El status ocupacional de los jefes de hogares de bajos ingresos*. Serie Investigación y Planificatión de Recursos Humanos. Caracas: CORDI-PLAN.

CHILDERS, VICTOR
n.d.   "Human resource development in Venezuela." Unpublished first draft. (An expansion of the 1967 unpublished doctoral dissertation, "Unemployment in Venezuela." Indiana University, Bloomington.)

CORONADO, JORGE
1955   *Sugestiones para la erradicación del Campamento San Diego (tugurio) en la ciudad de Guatemala*. Guatemala.

CORRADA, RAFAEL
1966   "The housing development program for Ciudad Guayana," in *Housing policy for a developing Latin economy*. Edited by C. Frankenhoff, 108–130. University of Puerto Rico Housing Policy Seminar. Río Piedras.
1969   "The housing program," in *Planning urban growth and regional development*. Edited by L. Rodwin et al., 236–251. Cambridge, Massachusetts: M.I.T. Press.

DAVIS, R. C., N. F. McGINN
1969a   *Build a mill, build a house, build a school: industrialization, urbanization and education in Ciudad Guayana*. Cambridge, Massachusetts: Harvard University Press.
1969b   "Education and regional development," in *Planning urban growth and regional development*. Edited by L. Rodwin et al., 270–285. Cambridge, Massachusetts: M.I.T. Press.

DIETZ, H.
1969   Urban squatter settlements in Peru: a case history and analysis. *Journal of Inter-American Studies* 11:353–370.

DORSELAER, J., A. GREGORY
1962   *La urbanización en América Latina*. Bogotá: Oficina Internacional de Investigaciones Sociales de FERES.

DOWNS, ANTHONY
1969   "Creating a land development strategy for Ciudad Guayana," in *Planning urban growth and regional development*. Edited by L. Rodwin et al., 202–218. Cambridge, Massachusetts: M.I.T. Press.

FLINN, W. L.
1968   The process of migration to a shantytown in Bogotá, Colombia. *Inter-American Economic Affairs* 22:77–88.

FRANKENHOFF, CHARLES, editor
1966   *Housing policy for a developing Latin economy*. University of Puerto Rico Housing Policy Seminar. Río Piedras.

FRIEDMANN, JOHN
1966   *Regional development policy: a case study of Venezuela.* Cambridge, Massachusetts: M.I.T. Press.
GANS, H. J.
1967   *People and plans.* New York: Basic Books.
GARCÍA, MARÍA-PILAR
1971   "Female employment and fertility in one-parent (mother) families in the lower socio-economic class of the metropolitan area of Caracas, Venezuela." Mimeographed paper, Ford Foundation, Bogotá.
GEERTZ, CLIFFORD
1966   *Agricultural involution.* Englewood Cliffs, New Jersey: Prentice-Hall.
GERMANI, GINO
1961   "Inquiry into the social effects of urbanization in a working-class district of Buenos Aires," in *Urbanization in Latin America.* Edited by P. M. Hauser, 206–233. New York: UNESCO.
HARDOY, J. E., R. L. SCHAEDEL
1969   *The urbanization process in America from its origin to the present day.* Buenos Aires.
HAUSER, P. M., *editor*
1961   *Urbanization in Latin America.* New York: UNESCO
HAUSER, P. M., L. F. SCHNORE
1965   *The study of urbanization.* New York: John Wiley and Sons.
Informe anual
1963–1972   *Informe anual.* Caracas: Corporación Venezolano de Guayana (CVG).
Inventario de edificaciones
1967   *Inventario de edificaciones, Ciudad Guayana.* Caracas: Corporación Venezolano de Guayana (CVG).
1969–1971   *Inventario de edificaciones y servicios públicos, Ciudad Guayana.* Caracas: Corporación Venezolano de Guayana (CVG).
KARST, K., M. SCHWARTZ
1968   "The internal norms and sanctions in ten barrios in Caracas." Mimeographed paper. University of California, Los Angeles.
LAUN, JOHN
1973   "Low-cost housing in Colombia, 1942–1972: the rhetoric and reality of reform." Mimeographed paper. University of Wisconsin, Madison.
LESSA, CARLOS
1970   De la constitución actual del capitalismo dependiente (industrialización, marginalización, sociedad opulenta). *Cuadernos de la Sociedad Venezolana de Planificación* 94–95:3–53.
LEWIS, OSCAR
1960   *The children of Sanchez.* New York: Random House.
1966a   *La vida: a Puerto Rican family in the culture of poverty.* New York: Random House.
1966b   The culture of poverty. *Scientific American* 215 (7):19–25.
1968   *A study of slum culture: backgrounds for La Vida.* New York: Random House.
LLERAS-RESTREPO, CARLOS
1955   *De la república a la dictadura.* Bogotá: Argra.
MacDONALD, JOHN S.
1969   "Migration and the population of Ciudad Guayana," in *Planning urban growth and regional migration.* Edited by L. Rodwin et al., 109–125. Cambridge, Massachusetts: M.I.T. Press.

MANGIN, WILLIAM
1963   Urbanization case in Peru. *Architectural Design* 33:366–370.
1967   Latin American squatter settlements: a problem and a solution, *Latin American Research Review* 2 (3):65–98.
1970   *Peasants in cities.* Boston: Houghton Mifflin.
MANGIN, WILLIAM, JOHN TURNER
1968   The barriada movement. *Progressive Architecture* 49 (5):154–162.
MATOS MAR, J.
1961   "Migration and urbanization," in *Urbanization in Latin America.* Edited by P. M. Hauser, 170–190. New York: UNESCO.
1968   *Urbanización y barriadas en América del Sur.* Lima: Instituto de Estudios Peruanos.
MATTELART, A., M. GARRETÓN
1965   *Integración nacional y marginalidad.* Santiago, Chile: Editorial del Pacifico.
Migration survey
1965   *Migration survey.* Caracas: Corporación Venezolano de Guayana (CVG)/Banco Central de Venezuela.
MINISTERIO DE FOMENTO
1950   *Censo de 1950.* Caracas: Oficina Central del Censo.
1965   *Noveno censo general de población, febrero 1961.* Caracas: Oficina Central del Censo.
1970   *Encuesta de hogares.* July. Caracas: Oficina Central del Censo.
MORSE, R. M.
1965   Recent research on Latin American urbanization: a selective survey with commentary. *Latin American Research Review* 1 (1):35–75.
1971   Trends and issues in urban research. *Latin American Research Review* 6 (1):3–52.
OSPINA-PÉREZ, MARIANO
1948   "Le nueva economía colombiana." *XVII Conferencia Agropecuaria de Antioquia.* Medellín.
PATCH, R. W.
1961   *Life in a callejón: a study of urban disorganization.* American Universities Field Staff Reports Service West Coast, South American Series 8 (6). New York.
PEATTIE, LISA
1968   *The view from the barrio.* Ann Arbor: University of Michigan Press.
1969a "Social mobility and economic development," in *Planning urban growth and regional mobility.* Edited by L. Rodwin et al., 400–410. Cambridge, Massachusetts: M.I.T. Press.
1969b "Social issues in housing," in *Shaping an urban future.* Edited by B. J. Freiden and W. Nash, 15–34. Cambridge, Massachusetts: M.I.T. Press.
1969c "Conflicting views of the project: Caracas versus the site," in *Planning urban growth and regional mobility.* Edited by L. Rodwin et al., 453–464. Cambridge, Massachusetts: M.I.T. Press.
1971   "The structural parameters of emerging life styles in Venezuela," in *The culture of poverty: a critique.* Edited by E. B. Leacock, 285–298. New York: Simon and Schuster.
PORTER, WILLIAM
1969   "Changing perspectives on residential area design," in *Planning urban growth and regional mobility.* Edited by L. Rodwin et al., 252–269. Cambridge, Massachusetts: M.I.T. Press.

QUIJANO, ANIBAL
1966   "Notas sobre el concepto de marginalidad social." CEPAL: División de Asuntos sociales. (Mimeographed.)
1968   Dependencia, cambio social y urbanización en América Latina. *Revista Mexicana de Sociología* 30 (3):525–570.
1971   Re-definición de la dependencia y marginalización en América Latina. *Cuadernos de la Sociedad Venezolana de Planificación* 94–95:3–53.

RABINOWITZ, F., F. M. FELICITY
1971   *Latin American urban research*, volume one. Beverly Hills: Sage Publications.

RODWIN, LLOYD *et al.*
1969   *Planning urban growth and regional development.* Cambridge, Massachusetts: M.I.T. Press.

ROGLER, L. H.
1967   Slum neighborhoods in Latin America. *Journal of Inter-American Studies* 9 (4):507–528.

SAFA, HELEN
1964   From shantytown to public housing: a comparison of family structure in the urban neighborhoods in Puerto Rico. *Caribbean Studies* 4:3–12.

SALMEN, LAWRENCE
1966   "Report on Vila Kennedy and Vila Esperança." Brazil: Cooperativa Habitacional, COHAB. (Mimeographed.)
1969   A perspective on the resettlement of squatters in Brazil. *América Latina* 12 (1):73–93.

SANABRIA, TOMÁS
1966   Los ranchos, afflición urbana. *Desarrollo Económico* 3 (1).

SCHULMAN, SAM
1966   Latin American shantytowns. *New York Times Magazine,* January 16.

SILVA, JULIO
1967   "Programa de mejoramiento urbano progresivo." Caracas: Corporación Venezolana de Guayana (CVG). (Mimeographed.)

SILVEIRA, G. P.
1963   Down with shantytowns: Brazilian students lead the way. *Community Development Review* 8:2.

SOBERMAN, RICHARD
1967   *Transport technology for developing regions: a study of road transportation in Venezuela.* Cambridge, Massachusetts: M.I.T. Press.

STINCHCOMBE, ARTHUR
1969   "Social attitudes and planning in The Guayana," in *Planning urban growth and regional development.* Edited by L. Rodwin et al., 411–421. Cambridge, Massachusetts: M.I.T. Press.

TALTON, RAY
1969   *The politics of the barrios of Venezuela.* Berkeley: University of California Press.

TRAVIESO, FERNANDO
1971   ¿Ciudad Guayana: Polo de desarrollo? *Cuadernos de la Sociedad Venezolana de Planificación* 92–93:77–82.

TURNER, JOHN
1963   Dwelling resources in South America. *Architectural Design* 33.
1965   Lima's barriadas and corralones: suburbs versus slums. *Ekistics* 19.
1966a Assentamientos urbanos no regulados. *Cuadernos de la Sociedad Venezolana de Planificación* 36.
1966b "A new view of the housing deficit," in *Housing policy for a developing*

Latin Economy. Edited by Charles Frankenhoff, 35–58. University of
Puerto Rico Housing Policy Seminar. Río Pedras.
1967   Barriers and channels for housing development in modernizing countries. *Journal of the American Institute of Planners* 33 (3):167–181.
1968a Housing priorities, settlement patterns, and urban development in
modernizing countries. *Journal of the American Institute of Planners*
34 (6):354–363.
1968b The squatter settlement: architecture that works. *Architectural Design*
38:355–360.
VEKEMANS, R., R. VENEGAS
1966a Marginalidad y promoción popular. *Mensaje* 15. Santiago de Chile.
1966b *Integración nacional y marginalidad*. Santiago de Chile: DESAL.
VIÑALS, ENRICA
1972   "Consideraciones en torno a Ciudad Guayana." Unpublished doctoral
dissertation, Universidad Central de Venezuela, Caracas.
WAGNER, B., D. McVOY, E. GORDON
1966   *Guanabara housing and urban development*. Agency for International
Development (AID) Housing Report.

Plantation Infrastructure and Labor Mobility in Guyana and Trinidad

BONHAM C. RICHARDSON

Studies of Caribbean migration have concentrated upon interisland movements and out-migration to other parts of the world. These are the most noticeable types of human mobility characteristic of the West Indies. However, in the southern Caribbean there is a more subtle though no less important kind of mobility related directly to plantation settlement patterns. In Guyana (British Guiana until 1966) and Trinidad most rural villagers live in communities originally inhabited by part-time sugar estate workers of the nineteenth century. The rural transportation networks of these two countries are actually remnants of colonial plantation systems. Villagers in Guyana and Trinidad today continue to exhibit a high degree of spatial mobility in commuting to part-time jobs from their residences and back again. Overall similarities in colonial livelihood patterns among the two main ethnic groups in both places suggest that historical-economic determinants are more important than ethnic identity in explaining rural economic behavior in Guyana and Trinidad.

Historical evidence from two periods throws light upon this labor migration. After emancipation, ex-slaves in British Guiana and Trinidad established settlements on the peripheries of plantations. These black freemen commuted short distances to estates for part-time labor. After their indenture periods, Indians also settled near plantations. Though estates had grown larger and technically more complex by this time, they still required periodic inputs of human labor which were provided by the Indian villagers. The roads along which blacks and Indians originally

Fieldwork in Guyana during the summer of 1967 and a one-year period in 1968–1969 was supported by grants and a fellowship from the University of Wisconsin at Madison. Research in Trinidad during the summer of 1971 was made available by awards from the American Philosophical Society, the National Geographic Society and the Society of the Sigma Xi. These research funds are gratefully acknowledged.

settled have now become parts of paved rural infrastructures. Settlement patterns today in Guyana and Trinidad look much as they did throughout the nineteenth century. In neither country have the periplantation villages ever been self-contained "peasant" communities. Ecological problems facing villagers in both places have reinforced the necessity of seeking extra-village sources of income.

Today the populations of both countries are unevenly divided between the same two ethnic groups: (1) blacks and "mixed" descendants of African slaves; and (2) descendants of indentured plantation laborers from India, locally called "East Indians." There are small numbers of whites and Chinese in the cities of both places, and some Amerindians are in southern Guyana though all of these groups taken together would account for only about 5 percent of the total population in either country. East Indians are now about 40 percent of Trinidad's populace of one million, and they are slightly over half of Guyana's 750,000 people. Speaking very generally, one can say that a demographic dichotomy exists between the two groups, blacks dominating the urban areas of Port of Spain and Georgetown, and Indians, especially in Guyana, numerically superior in rural zones. The first free villages in both places, however, were black. Some of their settlements began a pattern which has persisted until today.

THE EVOLUTION OF SETTLEMENT NETWORKS IN GUYANA AND TRINIDAD

Guyana's sea-level coastal plain (see Figure 1), the area in which over 90 percent of the country's populace lives in the 1970's, has been reclaimed from tidal mudflats bordering the Atlantic Ocean. This reclamation was first accomplished by African slaves supervised by planters from the Netherlands and England. Early Dutch trading posts were first established at upriver sites, but by the early eighteenth century Dutch plantations were located along the estuaries of the Essequibo, Demerara, and Berbice rivers. The Dutch colonies of the same names became British early in the nineteenth century. By this time, estates for the production of the tropical staples of cotton, coffee, and sugarcane were being established along the Atlantic littoral. This area is composed of fertile alluvial soil deposited by the equatorial current running from the mouth of the Amazon along the northeastern coast of South America. Necessities for water control led to the distinctive rectangular shape of each of the coastal plantations. In each case a sea defense wall was erected at the foreshore. At the rear of each estate a back-dam was built in order to protect the rear of the plantation from savanna swamp waters. These two water barriers were connected by long irrigation and drainage canals.

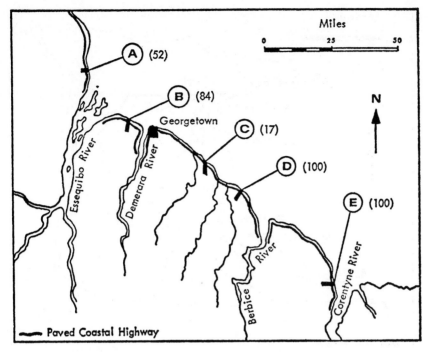

Figure 1. Coastal Guyana, showing study communities and number of villagers interviewed in each

Water was brought from the back of each estate, flowed through auxiliary canals and eventually spilled into the sea. The water movement through the plantation unit was powered by gravity. A large slave population kept water channels cleared of reeds, silt, and other debris which would inhibit the functioning of the plantation canals. The plantation settlement or nucleus, which included the housing units and agricultural processing buildings, was located near the water in every case. Thus, each coastal plantation had a rectangular shape with its settlement close to the ocean. In 1806 a coastal road was laid out linking the many estate nuclei (St. Clair 1947:31–32). This highway had the effect of establishing a settlement network from what had formerly been individual estates fronting the water's edge.

The earliest plantations of Trinidad (see Figure 2) were developed under Spanish rule until the island became British in 1797. The small estate zone was located in the extreme west central portion of the island near Trinidad's best natural port facilities and on the island's most fertile and level land areas. These early cane, cotton, and cacao estates were located on small yet navigable streams which emptied into the Gulf of Paria. Though swampy zones exist along certain coastal areas of the island, plantation owners avoided these areas and did not have to contend

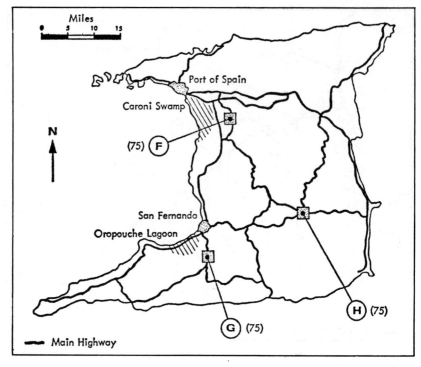

Figure 2. Trinidad, showing study communities and number of villagers interviewed in each

with the problems of water control facing the planters of the Guyana coastline. The few all-weather roads on the island in the late eighteenth century were in the vicinity of coastal estates near Port of Spain and San Fernando (Young Sing 1964:100). The forty-odd years of British rule which preceded slave emancipation in the 1830's saw Trinidad change from a relatively unexploited island to one in which the production of tropical staples by slaves had become greatly intensified. Nevertheless, there were only about 20,000 slaves and their children in Trinidad at emancipation, a mere fraction of the number living in the older British islands of the West Indies.

There is an oversimplified generalization occasionally put forward uncritically by scholars concerning the aftermath of slavery in Guyana and Trinidad (Klass 1961:7; Ehrlich 1971:169). This is that upon serving their periods of "apprenticeship" from 1834 to 1838,[1] newly freed blacks completely abandoned the estates for the freedom of the open coun-

---

[1]   The date of emancipation for the British Caribbean is 1834. In both British Guiana and Trinidad, however, a transitional period of apprenticeship was decreed. Slaves still had to work, but they were clothed, fed, and paid beyond a certain amount of labor. Former slaves were legally freemen in both colonies on August 1, 1838.

tryside. Though complete data are unavailable, there is evidence that in both places groups of ex-slaves settled on the peripheries of plantations. By doing so, former slaves could continue to act as part-time laborers on plantations, thereby deriving cash income, and they could participate in this activity without having to remain within the physical and social confines of the plantations. As slaves in British Guiana and Trinidad, blacks had cultivated their own foodstuffs on plantation grounds and had therefore engaged in a semisubsistence economy combined with the forced labor associated with the cultivation and processing of cash crops. After emancipation in both British colonies a distinctive settlement form developed as an expression of the continuing relationship between the ex-slaves and the plantations.

In Guyana freemen established communal settlements as groups, purchasing abandoned estates in the coastal zone (Farley 1954). These village settlements flanked the coastal highways; newly freed slaves could thus walk back and forth to nearby plantations for part-time work. The ex-slaves had therefore replicated the settlement morphology of the coastal plantation: houses were near the road and farmland was inland. The villagers kept small livestock and grew provision crops on the parts of the village lands closest to the roadside settlements. They did not cultivate the entire rectangle of land owned by the community, often allowing the backlands to become swampy pastures (Farley 1954:97). The overall impact of the livelihoods divided between plantation and village plots was to create a settlement pattern composed of strings of huts and houses extending from the plantation nuclei along the coastal road. The part-time livelihood pattern was also encouraged by the formidable water control requirements associated with maintaining a typical rectangle of coastal land. The black villagers had neither the desire nor the technology to cope with the drainage and irrigation requirements of an entire village unit (Adamson 1972:61). It was simpler to cultivate patches of land close to the foreshore and main highway and to migrate to nearby plantations for day work.

Slave emancipation had roughly similar effects in Trinidad. In many cases black freemen merely settled "over the line" from sugarcane estates onto unoccupied land (Select Committee on West India Colonies 1842:47). As in Guyana, they could thus cultivate their own subsistence crops, yet they could also work for wages on the nearby estates. Hastily passed legislation stipulated minimum acreages for ex-slaves and prohibited squatting on crown lands. These acts were ineffective, however, since plantation owners were reluctant to prosecute the squatters who comprised the only available labor force (Wood 1968:51). Little is known of these periplantation villages themselves though one contemporary historian indicates a settlement morphology similar to that found in coastal Guyana at the same period in history:

Many villages had grown up in a haphazard and unplanned manner. The people had built huts wherever they pleased along the highway; these settlements were . . . like . . . long straggling villages without any centre . . . (Wood 1968:94).

Such a settlement pattern seems entirely reasonable considering the part-time nature of a villager's livelihood, which was divided between estate labor and individual provision farming plots.

CHANGES IN LABOR AND PLANTATION TECHNOLOGY DURING THE LATE NINETEENTH CENTURY

The synergism of slave emancipation, soil exhaustion, competition from both tropical canes and mid-latitude beets, and London's laissez-faire trade practices had dealt the sugar colonies of Barbados, Jamaica, and the Leewards a mortal blow by the 1840's. In order for the West Indian sugar industry to survive, it had to shift to an area which had inherited neither overworked soils nor an infrastructure based upon antiquated means of producing raw sugar. Trinidad's relatively open spaces therefore beck-oned planters from other areas of the Caribbean. British Guiana's fertile coastline was also relatively undeveloped and a source of attraction to those who sought to compete with sugar from other parts of the world.

If the southern Caribbean were to compete successfully for a share of the London sugar market, there would be the necessity not only for fertile lands but also for improved technology to produce raw sugar from each plantation unit far in excess of the earlier West Indian estate. The steam engine had been used to crush canes on the Guiana coastal plain as early as 1805 (Dalton 1855:229). Later in the nineteenth century, vacuum-pan boiling allowed for larger quantities of high-quality sugar to be produced more efficiently in both Trinidad and British Guiana. Multistage rolling mills were installed in British Guiana in 1885 (Beachey 1957:62–63). And all of these innovations, necessitating greater throughput of canes at each mill, meant that each should command a larger area and thus be spaced farther from one another. The canals of the Guiana coast, macadam and gravel roads of Trinidad and, later, tramways in each colony provided more efficient transport for increasingly long distances from fields to mills. The culmination of the nineteenth century's technical and infrastructural improvements in the southern Caribbean's sugar industry was the establishment of the central factory St. Madeleine in southern Trinidad followed by similar centrals and a continuing consoli-dation of the sugar industry under more central control in both colonies (Beachey 1957:84; Adamson 1972:199–213).

After emancipation the existing estates in both Guyana and Trinidad continued to require large amounts of labor. The freed blacks of course provided part-time work from their locations on the fringes of estates. However, the planters disliked the relative independence of ex-slaves who divided their time between village and estate and were therefore regarded as "undependable." Gangs of blacks also bargained for higher wages. Such actions were especially effective at harvest time since ripe canes might rot in the fields if planters were unwilling to pay the workers more. Labor was actively recruited around the Caribbean by agents from Trinidad and British Guiana (Mathieson 1967:44). Planters from each colony grudgingly acknowledged that a worker could earn as much in a few hours in Trinidad or British Guiana as he could in a day on other islands. An independent labor force was, however, less attractive to the planters than were the reliable, more docile indentured laborers from India who first came to British Guiana in 1838 and to Trinidad in 1845.

The indentured plantation workers from India were imported to the West Indies until 1917 (Nath 1950; Weller 1968). Almost 240,000 came to Guiana, 100,000 less to Trinidad, and a few to other West Indian areas. The principal recruiting terminal was Calcutta. Madras was established later as a secondary port of debarkation for migrant workers. Upon arrival in Trinidad or British Guiana, Indians were assigned to estates, usually for five-year periods. Indentured workers were housed in "ranges," long wooden barracks next to the mills and boiling houses. By the late nineteenth century, the plantation's size had greatly enlarged from what it was in the days of slavery, though the relative location of workers to field and factory had remained the same. Indentured workers were awakened early, then walked long distances from barracks to fields in order to cut cane, plow furrows, or clean drainage ditches.

THE ESTABLISHMENT OF AUTONOMOUS INDIAN SETTLEMENTS

Upon completing his indenture period, an Indian could usually choose among reindenture (two five-year indenture periods entitled a worker to repatriation to India at government expense), living as a free worker on the estate, or taking up land of his own provided by the colonial government. The latter option was important during the late nineteenth and early twentieth centuries as a number of Indian settlements were established along the Guiana coast and the sugar belt of western Trinidad.

Indians living in their own communities continued to derive much cash income from their labor on nearby plantations. Estate managers relied upon these laborers for part-time work, especially in field preparation and harvesting, though many stages of raw sugar production had become increasingly mechanized and less demanding of labor. In any case, it appears misleading to interpret the demographic changes of the late nineteenth century in Trinidad as a period in which "former indentured servants did cluster together to form villages" (Ehrlich 1971:169). The villages in both colonies continued to radiate from the cane plantations in linear patterns just as those of black villagers had decades before.[2] The colonies of ex-indentured workers were economic adjuncts of the estates, not self-contained nodes of settlement. For instance, it was reported that Indian colonies in Trinidad did not "thrive" unless they were located near sugar estates (Government of Trinidad and Tobago 1888:42); and in 1911, 74 percent of the Indians in British Guiana engaged in agriculture were considered "agricultural laborers" rather than "independent farmers" though their dwelling places were evenly divided between "estates" and "villages and settlements" (*British Guiana population census* 1911:70–71). By the late nineteenth century, Indian villagers in both colonies were becoming identified with their own village agricultural production, though this activity was usually a kind of semisubsistence activity nibbling at the edges of lands controlled by the large sugarcane plantations.

During the last two decades of the nineteenth century in British Guiana, rice emerged on the coastal plain as a subsistence crop cultivated mainly by Indian villagers (Mandle 1970). The grain was first exported in 1903, and it is now the main crop of Guyana's coastal belt.[3] The low-lying coastal soils are similar to those of Asian deltas in that they support *padi* crops of medium yield without a great deal of human attention to irrigation, drainage, or artificial fertilizers. On the other hand, sugarcane requires better water management, well-drained soils, and marketing expertise for sale of the final product; the cultivation of cane therefore remained under estate auspices where efficient, centralized water systems, maintained by organized gangs of laborers, ensured crops of highest yields. A symbiotic relationship thus developed between the large estates, whose canals and lands were managed under central control, and the nearby "free" villages with poorer water systems and cultivating subsistence rice. The estates required periodic labor, and the villagers, desiring wages over and above the small amounts of income derived from their grain production, supplied it. In some cases, marginal estate land was given over to rice production by estate laborers, and some of the first mechanical *padi* hullers in the colony were located on sugar estates.

It is noteworthy that the earliest areas of "free" Indian villages of

---

[2]   Older residents of villages in both countries have all reported this type of settlement morphology for earliest Indian communities in Guyana and Trinidad.
[3]   There are now approximately 300,000 acres devoted to rice cultivation in Guyana. Sugarcane acreage accounts for about 100,000 acres located mainly near the mouths of the Demerara and Berbice rivers. Guyana's cane land is almost totally controlled by large British-owned companies.

Trinidad were in the areas of the low-lying swamplands of the Caroni Swamp and Oropouche Lagoon (see Figure 2). The best lands of western Trinidad had of course been preempted by plantations, leaving the ex-indentured Indians to cope with the same ecological problems facing their Guianese peers. Indian agriculture in Trinidad at first centered around rice, measurable quantities of *padi* coming from the "Caroni Savanna" as early as 1886 (Government of Trinidad and Tobago 1887:11). Reports from the early twentieth century also indicate recurring flood hazards associated with Indian rice production in the Oropouche Lagoon (Government of Trinidad and Tobago 1903:16). Such hazards reinforced the necessity for part-time work on nearby estates. However, the demand for cane at Trinidadian sugar factories, combined with planters' divided interests between cane and cacao, allowed the emergence of a class of small-scale cane farmers in the late nineteenth century who leased or bought well-drained lands above the coastal swamp zones.

During this period in which Indian villagers in British Guiana and Trinidad were gaining a foothold on the peripheries of plantations, many blacks were drifting into urban areas. The definitive history of this demographic change has yet to be written, though several suggestions may be forwarded to help explain it. The oft-repeated idea that blacks abhorred agricultural work because of plantation memories has probably been overstated. In both places, the bulk of the work on estates was now done by indentured immigrants, forcing rural blacks to seek other means of acquiring incomes. Cheaper Indian labor had thus been substituted for more expensive black labor by the planter class in each colony, and the influx of thousands of indentured laborers had the overall effect of driving plantation wages down.

It has also been suggested that in British Guiana blacks had greater access to education and technical skills which led them away from plantation work (Despres 1969:37–41). Blacks became identified with teaching and manning civil service posts in both colonies, occupational characteristics of this ethnic group which still hold true today in Guyana and Trinidad. In Guyana, the skilled mechanics and boilermen of the plantation factories continued to be mainly black even though fieldwork was done by Indians. The blacks in Trinidad also dominated these more prestigious and better-paying jobs in mills and boiling houses. Since the bulk of skilled mechanics on the island in the early twentieth century were blacks, they provided a convenient labor reservoir for the oil industry, labor for which continues to be dominated by workers of African descent.

Today, in the 1970's, East Indians remain predominant in the rural areas of both countries. The Indian villagers of Guyana are mainly rice producers while rural Indians of Trinidad are often cane farmers. In neither case, however, is the economic activity of the villagers confined to their own village lands.

CONTEMPORARY LIVELIHOOD CHARACTERISTICS AND LABOR MOBILITY IN RURAL AREAS OF GUYANA AND TRINIDAD

Contemporary livelihood data are presented here from eight villages in the two countries, five communities in Guyana and three in Trinidad (Figures 1 and 2).[4] Each of the eight communities is mainly Indian though there are black minorities in each one. Study villages were not selected using statistical sampling methods though each settlement may be considered representative of its district and of the rural areas of the two countries in general. The following discussion of contemporary village economics is based mainly upon personal interviews with 578 heads of households of the eight villages.

The average Guyanese *padi* producer controls about twelve acres of rice land, each acre producing about 1,800 pounds of unhusked rice annually. He earns the equivalent of US$1,300 annually from his *padi* production. Most rice growers cultivate one crop per year, planting in March and harvesting in September or October. Rice inputs are mostly mechanized. Plowing and harrowing is done by tractor while harvesting is usually accomplished with the use of combines. Agricultural machinery is either owned or rented from neighbors or relatives. Two crops of *padi* per year are produced in the communities west of the Demerara river, the area of the coast of highest labor inputs and least mechanization. Yields are always highest in these latter areas for the "big crop" which grows from March to September. In most of the coastal zone, which is east of Georgetown, rice producers grow only one crop annually using labor-saving devices and techniques in rice cultivation thus freeing themselves to participate in other livelihood activities of the coastal region.

In Trinidad, sugarcane is the main village crop. The west central and south central parts of the island, the zones of densest rural settlement, are cane fields interspersed with forest, subsistence crops, and settlement areas. Over 40 percent of 225 randomly selected villagers in the three Trinidad communities controlled cane acreage either through leasing or direct ownership. A typical Trinidad cane producer farms about five acres of cane and earns the equivalent of US$1,350 from this crop each year. Plowing land for cane is done by tractor. The crop is harvested by hand. A single planting of cane provides three to five successive *ratoon* crops so there is less planting overhead than that associated with rice, which involves planting for each crop. Fertilizer and weeding inputs are usual

---

[4] Approximately one month has been spent in each community. Village rice producers were interviewed in Guyana, and the different numbers of interviews in each community reflect relative village sizes. In Trinidad interviews were done on a house-to-house basis, regardless of residents' occupations, along lengths of rural roads.

for each cane crop in rural Trinidad. In neither Trinidad nor Guyana is rural agriculture devoted to only one crop. Guyanese villages always have areas devoted to provisions such as citrus, beans, and root crops. Lower-lying zones of Trinidad cane-farming communities are almost always cultivated in patches of wet rice.

Environmental hazards continue to influence inhabitants of village areas in both countries. The typical rice community of Guyana is poorly suited to the production of a small-scale crop. The large coastal rectangles, originally designed for control by a single owner, are now inhabited by hundreds of *padi* producers. Many individual decisions, each partially dependent upon the levels of the main irrigation and drainage canals, are now made within each village. Poorly maintained master water canals hinder the flow of drainage and irrigation waters, thus accentuating the problems associated with both floods and droughts. In Trinidad the agricultural lands of the Caroni and Oropouche areas are now better drained than they were during their first habitation by ex-indentured Indians. Village farm lands continue to be located on lands peripheral to large estates, however. Small-scale Trinidadian cane farmers have to cope with steeper gradients in their cane fields than do estate owners (Maharaj 1969:130). Also, the rural roads of Trinidad not directly serving estates are invariably poor and are often impassable after heavy rains.

In both countries, there are thus ecological necessities for typical villagers to seek extracommunity sources of livelihood. In rural Guyana, village water systems are usually poorly maintained; a rice producer there would be foolish to devote the majority of his time to rice husbandry only to see his crop seriously damaged by heavy rains at harvest time. In Trinidad, where the best lands are preempted by modern estates, marginal village lands have occasionally impassable roads. Without an active spatial link to a crushing mill, a cane crop is useless. In both places one therefore finds a high degree of livelihood diversification to offset the environmental hazards associated with village farm production.

Over half of the village rice growers from the five Guyanese villages had some sort of wage-paying job (see Table 1). In communities close to existing sugar estates, near the mouths of the Demerara and Berbice rivers, many villagers work as part-time estate laborers. Others act as carpenters, tailors, watchmen, fishermen, shopkeepers, drivers, and public works laborers on roads and canals. The last column of Table 1 puts the "other job" into perspective. Of the 353 *padi* producers interviewed, only sixteen had neither a wage job nor another source of income such as marketing vegetables or livestock. The "other job" is therefore not part-time work at all. To a typical Guyanese rice producer, the extra village job represents an integral part of total livelihood. It represents the economic safety valve which compensates for a potentially

Table 1. Nonrice sources of livelihood among the sample village rice producers in Guyana

Village* (Total interviews)	Rice growers with full-time or part-time wage-paying jobs	Rice growers who grow vegetables for market	Rice growers with cattle	Rice growers depending only on rice for a livelihood
A (52)	8	1	47	3
B (84)	43	31	61	4
C (17)	7	7	10	0
D (100)	72	8	20	4
E (100)	57	12	43	5
Column total (353)	187	59	181	16

* Differences in sample sizes reflect difference in absolute community populations.

poor *padi* crop; it also provides small amounts of cash throughout the year and not only at harvest time.

Similar findings emerged in Trinidad. Of the 225 interviewed households, many were devoid of major elements of agriculture. Sixty-seven households had neither sugarcane nor rice, fifty-seven had neither cane nor vegetables, and forty-one had neither rice nor vegetables. On the other hand, only ten had neither rice nor nonagricultural income, nine neither cane nor nonagricultural income, and eight neither vegetables for market nor nonagricultural income. Clearly, the crucial element of the diversified livelihood type of Trinidad is the extravillage job.

The livelihood diversification in Guyana and Trinidad always involves extra community mobility. Farmers selling vegetables or livestock in neighboring villages may travel only one or two miles. Plantation work occasionally takes a village laborer up to ten miles from his community and back daily. Shorter distances are covered on foot, longer distances by bus, truck, or a local route taxi which carries several passengers. Medium distances are usually traversed by bicycle. Typical commuting distances in Trinidad are shown in Table 2. These data show no well-defined commuting distance threshold for rural Trinidad. The high number of commuters in the eleven to fifteen-mile category for village F, for instance, reflects the distance to Port of Spain. It is remarkable that several villagers travel almost fifty miles one way to work each day. In both Guyana and Trinidad, the contemporary extra community livelihood mobility always takes place along the paved highways which continue to link villages to estates as their mud versions did one hundred years ago.

The contemporary East Indian *padi* cultivator of rural Guyana is therefore similar to his counterpart of the nineteenth century. He supplements village agricultural work with other jobs requiring extra village mobility. The mobility depends upon the coastal highway which is a paved version of the early coastal road. The highway is therefore not only

Table 2. Commuting distances for all non-"village agriculture" workers from the three study communities of rural Trinidad

Distance in Miles	Village F (75 interviews*)	Village G (75 interviews*)	Village H (75 interviews*)	Row total
0–5	47	36	42	125
6–10	14	26	19	59
11–15	36	7	1	44
16–20	1	1	3	5
21–25	0	1	1	2
26–30	0	1	4	5
31–35	0	0	0	0
36–40	1	0	0	1
41–45	0	1	2	3
45–50	1	1	6	8
Column total	100	74	78	252

* Though each interview was conducted with the head of household, often more than one member of the household worked outside his or her village of residence.

a relic landscape feature, but it also continues to act as a directional element for contemporary livelihood activities. Structurally, the settlement network is the same as it was at the time of slave emancipation. Not accidentally, livelihood activities are also much as they were at that time.

The situation in Trinidad is structurally analogous to that in Guyana though there is not a single public highway along the coast. The highly mobile rural populace of Trinidad commutes to work along such main thoroughfares as the Southern Main Road between Port of Spain and San Fernando which is "not really a road at all" but a patchwork of older north–south and east–west plantation roads which were linked up to connect the two largest towns of the island (Lamont 1933:141–142). Trinidad's historically mobile labor force has readily adapted to serve as both part-time workers and daily commuters into Trinidad's urban centers of Port of Spain and San Fernando.

In neither Guyana nor Trinidad has a self-sufficient agrarian-based peasant society been established. Historically, the rural populace of each place has divided its time between village farm plots and plantation work. Though the real extent of plantations in both places has decreased, the highly mobile rural work force continues to divide its time between village agricultural niches and other jobs. The diagnostic settlement form, found in each place, is both a spatial manifestation and a determinant of the propensity for labor mobility on the part of rural Guyanese and Trinidadians. At the time of emancipation estates in both colonies were surrounded by linear settlements of freemen. As the large corporate plantations evolved in the late nineteenth century, similar linear settlements, this time inhabited by Indians, came into being. Ribbons of rural settlement continue to characterize each country. In Guyana this spatial form has been likened to a rural *strassendorf* (Lowenthal 1960:46). In Trinidad it is held partially responsible for a lack of village cohesion and difficulties in realizing rural amenities (Maharaj 1969:118).

CONCLUSIONS

A hypothesized "plantation determinism" helps to explain both histori-cal and contemporary economic behavior among small-scale rural inhabitants of Guyana and Trinidad. The evolving plantation system of the nineteenth and twentieth centuries has etched distinctive similarities into the cultural landscapes of both ex-colonies despite sharp contrasts in their overall environmental characteristics. Infrastructural linkages have provided settlement matrices into which inhabitants have drifted after their plantation experiences. The blacks at the time of emancipation and Indians after indenture have displayed remarkably similar livelihood patterns. These patterns have been directed by the periplantation settle-ment networks, networks which have themselves been formed by the relationships between estates and part-time workers. In explaining rural livelihood behavior, the plantation experience, not ethnic identity, seems to be the independent variable.

Nationwide livelihood differences between the two main ethnic groups in Guyana and Trinidad do of course exist. Blacks are clerks, teachers, and mechanics, and they dominate urban areas while Indians are rural dwellers associated with agrarian activity. This demographic dichotomy developed in the late nineteenth and early twentieth centuries when Indians replaced blacks as plantation workers. The evolving plantation, with its need for a continual supply of cheap labor, merely substituted one ethnic group for another. Members of both ethnic groups, seeking group identity, thus became roughly divided into urban and rural areas. Ethnic identity was important for participants in this period of demographic change, especially when one group was culturally different from the other. But there was little from Africa or India which helped to determine this population pattern. In other words, there is nothing inherently "urban" about descendants of West Africans, and many of the Indians recruited for Caribbean plantation work had artisan and urban back-ground in India (Nath 1950:36; Weller 1968:13).

An extension of this argument is that the well-known animosity be-tween Indians and blacks in the two countries may be partially grounded in the economic rivalry between the two groups in the nineteenth century, rivalry centered around plantation jobs. Black freemen in Trinidad seek-ing higher wages at mid-nineteenth century could not help feeling bitter to see another group taking their places for lower wages. It is reported that in British Guiana in the nineteenth century "the planters always relied on the potential of hostility that was latent between Negro and East Indian" (Adamson 1972:266). And it is probably more than coincidental that the zone west of the Essequibo river was the calmest area of the coastal plain during Guyana's racial violence of the early 1960's. In the Essequibo area there are no estate or mining jobs at stake.

Such a view complements most research done among the Indians of the West Indies, much of which has been biased toward the study of non-economic elements of culture among Caribbean Indians (Schwartz 1964, 1965; Smith and Jayawardena 1958, 1959) and has therefore tended to reinforce the idea that this group is understandable principally on the basis of its ethnic identity (Despres 1969:32–33; Klass 1961). Anthropological predilections have been in devoting efforts toward determining the persistence or dissolution of sociocultural variables from India or of studying Caribbean Indians as part of a "plural society." In contrast, this tracing of the evolution and persistence of plantation-based village settlements and economic activities provides a different filter through which to view the East Indians of the West Indies. Such a view is somewhat similar to those put forth by West Indian economists dealing with the Caribbean as an economic region (Beckford 1972; Best 1968).

The ethnicity variable could be appealed to, of course, in explaining the close areal correlation between rice acreage and concentrations of Indian villages in Guyana. Indeed, early *padi* production in British Guiana was accomplished by indentured estate laborers using methods they had recalled from India. In Trinidad, however, ex-indentured workers from the same areas of India opted for cane farming soon after indenture. All things being equal, cane farming has always been more remunerative than subsistence farming in the British Caribbean partially because plantation crop-biased market outlets have been directed toward serving metropolitan, not local, needs. A more reasonable explanation for the high incidence of rice farming in Guyana is that the ecological constraint associated with water control has never allowed the emergence of a cane-farming peasantry of any size along the coastal plain. Even today small-scale Guyanese cane farming is limited to a few village zones which border contemporary plantations and benefit partially from estate water control systems. Also, it must be remembered that rice was a village staple in each of the three black villages of Guyana analyzed twenty years ago by Raymond Smith (Smith 1956:26–32).

The part-time character of livelihood in both Guyana and Trinidad throws light upon the persistent dilemma associated with finding a convenient typology for rural West Indians (Frucht 1967; Mintz 1953; Norton and Cumper 1966). Spatially, the rural inhabitant of Guyana and Trinidad is indeed neither entirely "peasant" nor totally "proletarian" but some of each. He has always moved, often daily, along the continuum between his community of residence and the rural representatives of metropolitan markets, the plantations. It is this individual mobility, not the exploitation of a single, locationally static niche, which has been the essence of livelihood in much of the rural Caribbean since emancipation. Such mobility blurs contemporary cultural distinctions between urban and rural areas of the West Indies. There is no city-country dichotomy here based upon the stereotyped portrayal of an underdeveloped area characterized by an urban elite surrounded by a countryside of economically traditional peasants.

The mobility exhibited by rural Guyanese and Trinidadians is not "migration" in the sense that it involves a permanent move from point A to point B. The movement described here is reversible. It provides the human linkage between sources of work and areas of residence. It is therefore not adequate to analyze this movement using traditional migration models which emphasize origins influenced by "push factors" and destinations enhanced by "pull factors," the two polar opposites separated by intervening opportunities. The oscillation between village residence and outside work has an inertia of its own in Guyana and Trinidad. This inertia has been embedded in the landscapes of the two areas by plantation systems of two hundred years' duration. Outside change, such as marked alterations of the infrastructural linkages, will be required to alter the system.

There are now first signs of infrastructural change in both countries related to the growing cities of Port of Spain and Georgetown. These changes have begun to alter commuting and occupational patterns of the populace living nearby. A stretch of limited-access highway exists between Port of Spain and San Fernando which is unrelated to plantation needs but has been designed to facilitate transportation between Trinidad's two largest cities (Mulchansingh 1970:44). Indian farmers west of village F have recently substituted vegetables for cane in their fields because they now have a high-speed route into Port of Spain. Good roads also connect Port of Spain and Arima which is on the eastern end of an urbanized corridor extending along the foot of the island's northern range of mountains. Similarly, the attractiveness of Georgetown and coastal road improvements in recent years have inspired commuting "into town" from villages of east coast Demarara which border contemporary sugarcane plantations. A recently planned highway is supposed to extend east from a point south of Georgetown and parallel Guyana's coastal highway (*Barclay's International Review* 1972:56). This highway would perhaps develop its own settlement nodes. Changing infrastructures in both Guyana and Trinidad now and in the future may effectively refocus the attention of rural inhabitants toward the largest cities of the two countries and alter the work migration influenced by old plantation roads

REFERENCES

ADAMSON, ALAN H.
1972 *Sugar without slaves: the political economy of British Guiana, 1838—1904.* New Haven, Connecticut: Yale University Press.
Barclay's International Review
1972 Guyana. *Barclay's International Review* (August):55–56.
BEACHEY, R. W.
1957 *The British West Indies sugar industry in the late nineteenth century.* Oxford: Basil Blackwell.
BECKFORD, GEORGE L.
1972 *Persistent poverty.* New York: Oxford University Press.
BEST, LLOYD A.
1968 A model of pure plantation economy. *Social and Economic Studies* 17:283–326.
British Guiana population census
1911, 1912 *British Guiana population census.* Georgetown.
DALTON, HENRY G.
1855 *The history of British Guiana.* London: Longman, Brown, Green and Longmans.
DESPRES, LEO A.
1969 Differential adaptations and micro-cultural evolution in Guyana. *Southwestern Journal of Anthropology* 25:14–44.
EHRLICH, ALLEN S.
1971 History, ecology and demography in the British Caribbean: an analysis of East Indian ethnicity. *Southwestern Journal of Anthropology* 27:166–180.
FARLEY, RAWLE
1954 The rise of peasantry in British Guiana. *Social and Economic Studies* 2:87–103.
FRUCHT, RICHARD
1967 A Caribbean social type: neither "peasant" nor "proletarian." *Social and Economic Studies* 16:295–300.
GOVERNMENT OF TRINIDAD AND TOBAGO
1887 *Reports of the wardens and assistant wardens for 1886.* Council paper 27. Port of Spain: Government of Trinidad and Tobago.
1888 *Reports of the wardens and assistant wardens for 1888.* Council paper 15. Port of Spain: Government of Trinidad and Tobago.
1903 *Wardens' reports for 1902–1903.* Council paper 114. Port of Spain: Government of Trinidad and Tobago.
KLASS, MORTON
1961 *East Indians in Trinidad.* New York: Columbia University Press.
LAMONT, SIR NORMAN
1933 *Problems of Trinidad.* Port of Spain: Yuille's.
LOWENTHAL, DAVID
1960 Population contrasts in the Guianas. *Geographical Review* 50:41–58.
MAHARAJ, DAYANAND
1969 "Cane farming in the Trinidad sugar industry." Unpublished doctoral dissertation, University of Edinburgh.
MANDLE, JAY R.
1970 Population and economic change: the emergence of the rice industry in Guyana, 1895–1915. *Journal of Economic History* 30:785–801.

406 BONHAM C. RICHARDSON

......

....
MATHIESON, WILLIAM L.
1967 *British slave emancipation, 1838–1849*. New York: Octagon.

MINTZ, SIDNEY W.
1953 The folk-urban continuum and the rural proletarian community. *American Journal of Sociology* 59:136–143.

MULCHANSINGH, VERNON C.
1970 A model approach to the understanding of the transportation network of Trinidad, W.I. *Caribbean Quarterly* 16:23–51.

NATH, DWARKA
1950 *A history of Indians in British Guiana*. London: Thomas Nelson and Sons.

NORTON, A. V., G. E. CUMPER
1966 "Peasant," "plantation," and "urban" communities in rural Jamaica: a test of the validity of the classification. *Social and Economic Studies* 15:338–352.

ST. CLAIR, THOMAS S.
1947 *A soldier's sojourn in British Guiana, 1806–1808*. Edited by Vincent Roth. Georgetown: Daily Chronicle.

SCHWARTZ, BARTON M.
1964 Caste and endogamy in Trinidad. *Southwestern Journal of Anthropology* 20:58–66.
1965 Patterns of East Indian family organization in Trinidad. *Caribbean Studies* 5:23–36.

SELECT COMMITTEE ON WEST INDIA COLONIES
1842 *Report from the Select Committee on West India colonies*. London: Her Majesty's Stationery Office.

SMITH, RAYMOND T.
1956 *The Negro family in British Guiana*. London: Routledge and Kegan Paul.

SMITH, RAYMOND T., CHANDRA JAYAWARDENA
1958 Hindu marriage customs in British Guiana. *Social and Economic Studies* 7:178–194.
1959 Marriage and the family amongst East Indians in British Guiana. *Social and Economic Studies* 8:321–376.

WELLER, JUDITH ANN
1968 *The East Indian indenture in Trinidad*. Río Piedras, Puerto Rico: Institute of Caribbean Studies.

WOOD, DONALD
1968 *Trinidad in transition: the years after slavery*. New York: Oxford University Press.

YOUNG SING. GLORIA E.
1964 "The evolution of the present pattern of agricultural land use in the island of Trinidad in the West Indies." Unpublished doctoral dissertation, Queen's University, Belfast.

Biographical Notes

XAVIER ALBÓ (1934–   ) is Director of the Centro de Investigación y Promoción del Campesinado (CIPCA) in La Paz, Bolivia. His main interests are in socio- and ethnolinguistics of Bolivia, Cochabamba, and Peru, Quechua language and culture, Aymara language and culture, Andean social change and modernization, and contemporary Andean ethnography. His publications include "Dinámica en la estructura intercomunitaria de Jesus de Machaca", *Social constraints on Cochabamba Quecha*, and *El Quecha a su Alcance*.

WILLIAM E. BERTRAND. No biographical data available.

RAE LESSER BLUMBERG received her Ph.D. from Northwestern University in 1970. She taught at the University of Wisconsin, Madison, and is presently Acting Associate Professor of Sociology at the University of California, San Diego. Although she has traveled, conducted research, and lived in many countries (principally in Latin America), her main field experience has been in Venezuela. There, she taught and did sociological research for two years at Andrés Bello University, spent two years as a resident advisor in sociological research for the Ministry of Education, and spent a summer advising in the Ministry of Health and Social Welfare. While at Andrés Bello University, she directed a survey research project on urbanization and development in Ciudad Guayana, Venezuela, and returned there in 1973. Her publications include a book, *Stratification: socio-economic and sexual inequality* (1976), coauthored articles in the *American Journal of Sociology* (on societal complexity and familial complexity), the *American Sociological Review* (on ethnicity and extended familism), and numerous book chapters. Her most recent publications have stemmed from her research on a 1973–1974 Ford Foundation Faculty Fellowship on the role of women in society. Currently, she is working on a book emerging from this fellowship, detailing her theory-testing research (utilizing a 61-society pilot sample) on women's relative economic power as a primary determinant of their status and life options *vis-à-vis* men.

DAVID L. BROWMAN (1941–   ) was born in Montana. He received his B.A. from the University of Montana in 1963 in Math and Physics; and M.A. from the University of Washington in 1966; and a Ph.D. in Anthropology from Harvard in 1970. He is currently teaching anthropology at Washington University, St. Louis. Research interests include general New World prehistory, but particularly Andean archaeology and ethnohistory. Recent articles include "Pastoral nomadism in the Andes" (1974), "Trade patterns in the central highlands of Peru in the first millennium B.C." (1975), and "Demographic correlations of the Wari Conquest of Junín" (1976).

ALEJANDRO CAMINO (1940–   ) was born in Lima, Peru. He received his Licenciatura in Anthropology from Universidad Católica del Perú in 1974. He is currently a Ph.D. candidate at the University of Michigan, Ann Arbor. Since 1972 his fieldwork has been in the Peruvian Andes and Amazonia, and his special interests have been ecological anthropology, ethnobotany, and ethnohistory. He is doing research on continuities between the aboriginal agricultural systems of Amazonia and the high Andes. He is currently the Chairman of the Anthropology section Universidad Católica del Perú.

NINA S. DE FRIEDEMANN (1934–   ) was born in Bogotá, Colombia. She studied at Instituto Colombiano de Antropología, Hunter College, and the University of California. Appointed Permanent International Research Associate at Emory University, Atlanta, she worked in 1967 and 1968 as Research Member in their Center for Research in Social Change. She is Professor in the Department of Anthropology, Universidad Nacional de Colombia. She has written numerous publications on black populations and interethnic relations in Colombia. Her recent publications are: *Minería, descendencia y orfebrería. Litoral Pacífico* (1974); *Indigenismo y aniquilamiento de Indígenas en Colombia* (coauthor) (1975); *Tierra, Tradición y poder en Colombia* (editor) (1976). She has also produced the following films: Güelmambí (1973), Villarrica (1974), and Tierra Es Vida (1974). She is presently Research Associate at Instituto Colombiano de Antropología, Bogotá, Colombia.

JUAN E. FLORES is Professor at Escuela de Ciencias Sociales, Universidad de Oriente, Cumaña, Venezuela. His main interests are fishing communities in western Venezuela, indigenous communities in Peru, Amazonia, and Sierra Central, and rural communities in coastal Peru. His publications include *Compadrazgp, estructura social y grupo de referencia, Comunidad de: 1. Nueva Esperanza, 2. Puca Puquio, 3. Maravilca, 4. Huayao*, and "Patrones de migración Amazónica".

MARÍA-PILAR GARCÍA (1947–   ) received the *Licenciado* degree in Sociology at the Universidad Andrés Bello in Caracas, Venezuela. In 1970, she received an M.A. in Demography at the University of Chicago. Presently she is finishing her Ph.D. dissertation on a sociological model of urban activities for the population of Ciudad Guayana, Venezuela, for that university and working as director of a major research project at the Corporación Venezolana de Guayana. Her areas of interests are urban planning, demography, human ecology, and urban sociology in Latin America. She is author of several articles about the matrifocal family in Latin America.

ESTHER HERMITTE (1921–   ) is Investigadora and Jefe at the Instituto Torcuato di Tella, Centro de Investigaciones Sociales, Buenos Aires, Argentina. Her main areas of interests are economic system, social organization and growth and demographic structure of a community of vicuna weavers, system of beliefs in a contemporary Mayan pueblo, provincial politics of community development, and the present situation of the aborigines of Chaca Province and the politics of their integration. Her publications include "Estructura y crecimiento de una comunidad de tejedores de Ponchos: Belén 1678–1869", "Ponchos, weaving and patron-client relations in northwest Argentina", and *Poder sobrenatural, control social*.

EMILIO MORAN (1946–   ) received his B.A. in Spanish American Literature from Spring Hill College (1968), his M.A. in Brazilian History from the University of Florida (1969), and his Ph.D. in Anthropology (1975) with a dissertation on socioecological adaptation along the Trans-Amazon Highway. He has also received certificates in Economics, Tropical Agriculture, Ecology, and Latin American Studies. His special interests include human adaptation to new environments, the study of agricultural systems with a view to the maximization of production, and the application of energetics to the study of man-environment interactions. His recent publications include: "Energy flow, analysis and *Manihot esculenta* Crantz" (1973); "The adaptive system of the Amazon Cabuclo" (1974); and "Farmers and extractions: men and culture in two Amazon towns" (1975).

JUNE NASH (1927–   ) is Professor of Anthropology and chairs the

Department of Anthropology, City College of the City University of New York. She received her Ph.D.from the University of Chicago. She has done fieldwork in Guatemala and Mexico with the Maya, and in Bolivia with Quechua- and Aymara-speaking Indians. She has written two monographs on the Maya, *Social structure in Amatenango del Valle*, and *In the eyes of the ancestors*, has coedited *Sex and class in Latin America* with Helen Safa, *Ideology and social change* with Juan Corradi, and has recently finished a book on the Bolivian mining community.

WILLIAM L. PARTRIDGE received his Ph.D. in Anthropology (1974). He was a predoctoral Research Fellow of the National Institute of Mental Health and is currently Assistant Professor of Anthropology at the University of Southern California. He is the author of a number of publications, including a book *The hippie ghetto: the natural history of a subculture*. His principal interests include community studies and applied anthropology in the United States and South America; he has done fieldwork in the Caribbean and on the north coast of Colombia.

PEDRO I. PORRAS. No biographical data available.

ALCIDA R. RAMOS. No biographical data available.

BONHAM C. RICHARDSON (1939–   ) received his B.A. (1961) at the University of Arizona and his M.S. (1968) and Ph.D. (1970) in Geography at the University of Wisconsin at Madison. Besides doing fieldwork in Guyana and Trinidad, he worked in Grenada and Carriacou in 1973 on the interrelationships between ecological deterioration and labor migration. He is currently Book Review Editor of *Human Ecology: An Interdisciplinary Journal*.

RONALD A. SCHWARZ (1939–   )received his B.A. in Philosophy from Colgate University, and his Ph.D. from Michigan State University. He completed post-doctoral studies at the Tulane University, School of Public Health and Tropical Medicine. He is currently affiliated with the Department of Behavioral Sciences, The Johns Hopkins University, School of Hygiene and Public Health as well as working as a free-lance consultant on development projects in Latin America and Africa. He also taught at Colgate University, Williams College and Instituto Norte Andino de Ciencias Sociales. He completed twelve years of research and training in Latin America and Africa, concentrating particularly on social organization, social change, aesthetics, and the medical system of the Guambiano Indians of Colombia. His publications include *Spirits, sha-*

mans, and stars (coeditor with David Browman) and *The fabrics of culture* (coeditor with Justine Cordwell). He is currently working on a book on environmental health and development for the American Public Health Association.

SUSAN C. SCRIMSHAW (1945–   ) grew up in Guatemala and has since worked in Bolivia, Barbados, Spanish Harlem, Ecuador, and Colombia. She received her B.A. from Barnard in 1967, an M.A. from Columbia in 1969, and a Ph.D. from Columbia in 1974. She is currently a Research Associate at Columbia University's International Institute for the Study of Human Reproduction, where she also teaches in Columbia's School of Public Health. She is a member of the ICAES Commission on Anthropological and Ethnological Factors in Population and of the Executive Board of the Society for Medical Anthropologists. Her publications have concentrated on anthropology and the delivery of health care, and on factors affecting fertility and the desire for family planning.

HENNING SIVERTS (1928–   ) received his doctorate in 1959 at the University of Oslo and is now Senior Curator at the University of Bergen. In 1953–1954, 1961–1962, and 1964, he did fieldwork in Tzeltal and Trotzil of the Highland Chiapas, Mexico, and in 1970–1971 he worked among the Jívaro (Aguaruna) of the Montaña in North Peru. Other research interests include political systems, ethnicity, ecology and human adaptability in tropical forest regions, and language in society (cognitive systems and ethnographic procedures). Publications on the above topics include "The Aguaruna Jívaro of Peru: a preliminary report" and *Tribal survival in the Alto Marañon: the Aguaruna case*.

PIERRE L. VAN DEN BERGHE (1933–   ) was born in Lumbumbashi, Zaire. He has received his B.A. and M.A. from Stanford University and Ph.D. from Harvard University. Currently, he is Professor of Sociology at the University of Washington, Seattle. His fieldwork and publications are on ethnic relations in South Africa, Kenya, Nigeria, Mexico, Guatemala, Brazil, and Peru.

NORMAN E. WHITTEN, JR. is Professor of Anthropology at the University of Illinois, Urbana. He took his Ph.D. in 1964 at the University of North Carolina, Chapel Hill. Besides fieldwork with the Lowland Quechua of Ecuador, Whitten has worked extensively with black cultures in Nova Scotia, Canada, the southern United States, Colombia, and Ecuador. He is author of two books: *Class, kinship, and power in an Ecuadorian town: the Negroes of San Lorenzo* (1965), and *Black frontiersmen: a South American case* (1973) and senior editor of *Afro-American anthropology*

(1970). He is currently writing a book on Lowland Quechua social structure and cultural adaptation in the face of massive changes in the Amazonian Lowlands.

E. GLYN WILLIAMS. No biographical data available.

Index of Names

Index of Subjects

Abortions, 349, 350
Adaptation, 247–248, 289; to city, 341, 343–346, 353–354
Adultery, Quijo, 29–35
African slaves, 390
Age of marriage, 346
Agrarian reform, 257–258, 272, 279, 307
Agricultural involution, 377
Agriculture, 19, 51, 141, 153, 231, 244; Andean, 139, 141–142, 258; Colombian, 153–156, 158, 298–300, 302; energy flow diagrams, symbols in, 118–120; environment transformed by, 141n, 142–145; Guyana and Trinidad, 393–394, 396–402, 404; Machiguengan, 129–134, 138, 139, 141–144; slash-and-burn, 114, 130, 131, 142, 298. *See also* Manioc
Aguano (Ecuador), 22, 30
Aguardiente, 19, 41, 166, 212, 236
Aguaruna, 216–223
Alama, 228
Alcalá del Rio (Ecuador), 15
Alcohol, 96, 101, 164–166, 170, 211–212
Alcoholism, 30–36
Alguacils, 304, 305
Alliances, Indian, 216, 218–222
Alliance span, 347, 348
Alto Marañon, 222
Alto Napo, 28. *See also* Quijo Indians
Amazonia, 97n, 191; energetics view of manioc cultivation in, 111–123
American way of life, 140
Amethyst, H.M.S., 82
Andean highlands, 251–327; ethnicity and class in, 254–266

Andean migrations, 96–97, 139–149, 144–146, 241
Andes: foothills, 76–77, 84; future of oppressed languages in, 266–288; population problems, 332; rebellion in, 277
Anthropological research, 5, 9–10
Anthropologist, the, and social demography, 331–337
Anthropology, applied, 333–334
Antipa, 219
Anzoátegui (Venezuela), 179
Arahuancan linguistic group, 125
Araucanian Indians, 75, 80, 88, 95, 97–100
Archidona (Ecuador), 15, 18, 20
Archivo Central del Cauca (Colombia), 293, 294
Argentina, 49, 54, 68, 100, 316n. *See also* Belén
Arithmetic, 24–25
Armadillo, 80
Arrows, 134
Assimilation, cultural, 259–260
Avila (Ecuador), 15
Awishiris, 226, 227, 229
Axes, 130n
Ayacucho project, 278n
Aymara language, 255; Catholic publications in, 278n; impoverishment of, 274–275; as oppressed language, 270, 272–276, 280, 282; recovery of, 276–279, 285

Baeza (Ecuador), 15
Bananas, 152–154, 216
Banco Central de Venezuela, 363n, 365n, 378n

Ethnohistory, 7–105, 149–151
Europeans, 95–100, 152–155. *See also*
Colonial period; Spanish conquest
Exploitation: of Bolivian tin miners, 313–
315; of Indians, 4, 207–212, 292–293,
295
Expropriated property, compensation for
improvements to, 361–362, 371–372
Expropriation of Indian lands, 4, 207–210,
242, 244, 292, 295–297

Families to the city, 339–358. *See also*
Rural/urban migration
Family: life, 39; size, 91, 92, 238, 249–353;
structure, 57, 58, 60, 233, 378
Fauna, 78–79, 82
Federal decentralization, 295–296
Federation of Mine Workers Unions
(FSTMB), Bolivia, 315–317, 322–323
Fertility of migrants to city, 339, 346–354;
children ever fathered, by age of men and
alliance years, 351–352; covariance an-
alyses, 352–353; family size and, 349–
353; living children, by age, 350; method-
ology, 340–341, 354–356; pregnancies,
frequency and mean numbers of, 349–
350; by sex, 342
Fiestas, Indian, 208–214
Firearms, 144
Fish: production of, 180–181; trade in,
175–176, 179, 181
Fishing: Canelos Quechua, 232; reed mats
for, 136; technology in Northeastern
Venezuela, change in, 174–182; Upper
Urubamba, 135–136, 145
Food: Catamarca, 51, 67; Colombia, 154;
Machiguengan, 129–137, 144, 145;
Quijo, 18, 40–41; Tehuelche, 78–82, 84,
85
Forced labor, 13, 15
Ford, Bacon and Davis, Inc., 318, 320
Ford Foundation, 339n
Fruit, 79

Garnet, H.M.S., 96
Gathering, 135–137, 145. *See also* Hunting
and gathering cultures
Geese, 79
Genealogical network, Jívaro, 221
Georgetown, 404
Godparents, 43–44
Government, Indian, 293, 299
Granadine Federation, 295
Grasshoppers, catching, 137
Greece under Rome, 270
Guambia (Colombia), 289
Guambiano society, continuity and change

in, 288–307; cabildo system, 293, 299,
303–304; conflicts and prospects in 1973,
305–307; effect of conquest and colonial
institutions, 290–294; from independence
to 1890, 294–299; population growth,
293–294, 298–300, 303–305; social
organization, 294, 299–305; Vereda
system, 303–305
Guanaco (*Lama guanicoe*), 78, 80, 84–
86
Guarani, 268n, 269
Guatemala, 268n
Guayaquil (Ecuador), 354–356; migration
to, 335, 340–358
Guyana: coastal, 390–391; colonial, 390–
397; ethnic groups in, 390, 395–
397, 402–404; livelihood characteristics,
398–406; plantation infrastructure and
labor mobility, 389–406; racial violence,
403

Hallucinogens, 150, 232, 235
Harvard University, 363
Hausipungueros, 227
Headhunters, Jívaro, 215–224
Healers, Quijo, 25–29
Heat sinks, 117
Hemp, 149–150
Highland Indians, Canelos Quechua and,
227. *See also* Andes
Hispanicization, 272, 277–278, 279–280,
283–284, 285n
Hispanic tradition, 4
Home improvements, 361–362, 371–372
Homosexuality, 93
Horses, 79, 80, 95; hunting with, 85–86, 90,
94–95; ritual killing of, 93
Housing: culture of poverty approach
to, 375–376; low income, 369, 370, 372–
373, 377–382; planners' policy, 362,
365–370, 373–374; self-help, 368–
369, 375–376; social cancer approach,
374–375; structural approach, 376–
382
Huambisa, 218–219
Huarani, 226, 227, 229
Hunting, 29, 36–37, 134–135, 144, 232;
and gathering cultures, 75–76, 80–88, 91;
techniques, 85–86, 94–95
Hygiene, absence of, 39–41

Immigration, 153, 156
Improvements, home, 361–362, 371–372
Inca era, 139
Incest, 35; taboo, 89n
INCORA (Colombian National Agrarian
Reform Agency), 153n, 306

Quillabamba mission schools (Peru), 139–140
Quimbayas, gold-working, 3
Quiruba revolt, 221n
Quiteni (Peru), 129

Racial violence, 403
Radio, 279, 285
Reeds, preparing for straw mats, 136
Refuge zones, 245–246, 270, 271
Religious publications in oppressed languages, 276–277, 278n
Reservations, Indian, 292–293, 296–299; abolition of, 295, 300–301, 308
Rhea (*Rhea darwin*), 78–80, 84–86
Rhodesia, 259
Rice, 396–400, 403
Rickets, 101
Role differentiation, 92, 94
Rubber era, 127, 138–139, 227
Runa territories, 229–230, 234, 239
Rural/urban migration, 335, 339–341, 370; covariance analysis, 352–353; family size and fertility, 349–353; fertility and, 339, 346–348, 354; fertility by age and sex, 342, 351–352; methodology, 340–341, 354–356; pregnancies and living children, of migrant and nonmigrant women, by age, 349–350; pregnancies of urban and migrant women, frequency of, 349, 350; reasons for, 341–342

St. Joseph, Order of, 13n
Sáliva Indians, 209n
San Agustin sculptors, 3
San Andres, Universidad Mayor de, 321
San Félix (Venezuela), 363–364, 365
San Jacinto del Pindo, Comuna de, 235–240
San Javier de Pucaurco (Ecuador), 13n
San Jerónimo (Peru), 261–264
San Marcos University (Lima) Plan of Linguistic Support, 277n
Santa Cruz (Argentina), 100
Santa Fé de Bogotá, 150
Santa Rosa (Ecuador), 13n
Santa Rosa (Peru), 126
Santo Domingo, 173
Sanumá pronunciation, 192n
Sanumá society, 191–192; personal names and social classification among, 195–205; social system, 192–194
Sara Yacu-Canelos, 230
Schools, 239; oppressed languages excluded from, 275–276, 278, 285; rural, 207
Screening of anti-social families, 365n
Secoya people, 226, 245
Self-determination, workers', 312

Separation, sexual unions ended by, 347
Serpents, 135
Settlement network, evolution of, in Guyana and Trinidad, 390–394
Sexual unions, 346–349, 378; duration of, by sex, 348
Shamanism, 93
Shamatari villages, 200
Shell Mera, 235–236, 245
Shells, 19, 41
Shrimp fishing, 178
Sierra Nevada foothills, 155
Siona people, 226, 245
Sivioni of Amazonia, 97n
Skunk, 79
Slash-and-burn cultivation, 114, 130, 131, 142, 298
Slavery, 15, 20, 57, 97, 292
Slaves: emancipation of, 389, 392n, 393–394; New Granada, 292; West Indies, 390, 392–393
Slave-trade, 68
Slums: central city, 341, 343, 346, 354, 356; planned, 368, 375
Smallpox, 28, 92
Social cancer approach to urban development, 374–375
Social classification and language, 271
Social classification and naming system in Sanumá society, 192–205; individuation, 200–202; interplay between levels of classification, 202, 203; patronyms, 197–198, 200, 203; personal names, 195–197; sib and lineage names, 192–193, 195, 197–198, 200–203; village settlement names, 199–200
Social demography and the anthropologist, 331–337 .
Social inequality, decline in, 299
Socializing in bars, 370
Social organization in Guambia, 294, 299–302, 304–305
Social scientists, 335
Social stratification in Belén, 57, 59–61, 68, 69
Social structure in Peru, 255
Sociocultural change in Upper Urubamba (Peru), 125–141; factors of, 137–141
Socioecological changes in Upper Urubamba, 141–146
Socioeconomic status of migrants to city, 343–346
Sociolinguistics, 268, 275n
Sociology, 332–333; of dependence approach, 255–257
Socioterritorial organization among Tehuelche, 85–92
Sorcerers, 25–29